International Conference on Digital Transformation and Innovation Management (DTIM2024), and ICT, Society, and Human Beings (ICT2024)

Held at the Multi-Conference on Computer Science and Information Systems (MCCSIS 2024)

Budapest, Hungary
13-15 July 2024

ISBN: 979-8-3313-0303-7

Printed from e-media with permission by:

Curran Associates, Inc.
57 Morehouse Lane
Red Hook, NY 12571

Some format issues inherent in the e-media version may also appear in this print version.

Printed with permission by Curran Associates, Inc. (2024)

For permission requests, please contact International Association for Development of the Information Society (IADIS) at the address below.

International Association for Development of the Information Society (IADIS)
Rua Sao Sebastiao Da Pedreira
No. 100, 30, 1050-209
Lisbon, Portugal

Phone: 351 21 3151373
Fax: 351 21 3151244

secretariat@iadis.org

Additional copies of this publication are available from:

Curran Associates, Inc.
57 Morehouse Lane
Red Hook, NY 12571 USA
Phone: 845-758-0400
Fax: 845-758-2633
Email: curran@proceedings.com
Web: www.proceedings.com

PROCEEDINGS OF THE INTERNATIONAL CONFERENCES ON

DIGITAL TRANSFORMATION AND INNOVATION MANAGEMENT 2024

and

ICT, SOCIETY AND HUMAN BEINGS 2024

Budapest, Hungary
JULY 13 - 15, 2024

Organised by

iadis

international association for development of the information society

As a member of Crossref (a non-profit membership organization for scholarly publishing working with the purpose to make content easy to find, link, cite and assess) each published paper in this book of proceedings will be allocated a DOI (Digital Object Identifier) number for its fast and easy citation and indexation.

Volume Editors:
Pedro Isaías, Paula Miranda and Piet Kommers

Computer Science and Information Systems Series Editors:
Piet Kommers and Pedro Isaías

Associate Editor: Luís Rodrigues

TABLE OF CONTENTS

FULL PAPERS

DIGITAL TRANSFORMATION AND INNOVATION MANAGEMENT

ICT, SOCIETY AND HUMAN BEINGS

SHORT PAPERS

DIGITAL TRANSFORMATION AND INNOVATION MANAGEMENT

FOREWORD

These proceedings contain the papers and posters of the International Conference on Digital Transformation and Innovation Management (DTIM 2024) and of the International Conference on ICT, Society and Human Beings (ICT 2024), which were organised by the International Association for Development of the Information Society, from 13 - 15 July, 2024. These conferences are part of the Multi Conference on Computer Science and Information Systems 2024, 13-15 July, which had a total of 603 submissions.

In the rapidly evolving landscape of technology and business, the International Conference on Digital Transformation and Innovation Management (DTIM 2024) serves as a premier platform for researchers, academicians, and industry practitioners to converge and explore cutting-edge advancements at the intersection of Information Systems and Management Innovation.

This conference aims to foster a collaborative environment that stimulates insightful discussions and paves the way for novel approaches to digital transformation, emphasizing its deep impact on organizational strategies, operations, and global societal progress.

Submissions were accepted under the following 6 main topics:
- Digital Strategy and Leadership:
- Data Analytics and Business Intelligence:
- Emerging Technologies and Disruptive Innovation:
- E-Commerce and Digital Marketing:
- Sustainable Innovation
- Application Areas

The Network period in the evolution of computer technology is very much based on the convergence and integration of three main technologies; computer technology, tele technology and media technology. Telecommunication technology is playing a more and more dominant role in this convergence, especially internet and web technology. Embedded (ubiquitous) computer technology is making the process invisible, and media technologies converge within itself (multimedia and cross media). The convergence process is enforced all the time by smaller, cheaper, and more powerful components.

ICT and its applications are interacting with environments, roles, and processes which can also be modelled by converging circles. The process of social and psychosocial change and ICT from a global perspective is described graphically in the convergence model in figure 1 (Bradley 2006 Routledge) with concepts and their interrelations. Both "convergence" and "interactions" are important features in the model. Read from the left hand side in the model for the titles of some main tracks of the conference:

- Globalisation and ICT: When technology, economy, norms/values and labour market are converging on a global level, what are the hard questions? When the geographical space in the future will be both global and beyond – including virtual reality (VR) what is the state of art in research? (see the list of key words under ´globalisation´)
- Information and Communication Technology (ICT), next cluster of circles to the left in the figure, what applications contribute to desirable goals in the society?

• When Work Environment, Home Environment, and Public Environment are converging and the work and public issues tend to merge into the private sphere of our homes – what main changes in peoples Life Environment occur?.
• If the Professional Role (Work Life), Private Role (Private Life) and Citizen's Role (Public Life) converge forming a Life Role, what are the main social-psychologial changes?
• Four circles representing Virtual Reality (VR) are marked with dotted lines and are surrounding the set of converging circles. These circles reflect our participation in cyberspace on various levels. To the left part in figure we could talk about Virtual Worlds on the global level. Within the concept of ICT, the steps taken by applied Embedded and ubiquitous technology make technology more hidden to the individual and society as a whole.
Virtual Environments are already a common concept. Finally, we could talk about Virtual Human Roles, which could in more extreme forms be another personality that you play e g avatars. The converging circles are forming a Life Role and new life styles are being shaped.
• Effects on humans become more multi faceted and complex. Research focusing upon the individual is crucial i. e. research on how the use of ICT interacts with and impacts identity, social competence, creativity, integrity, trust, dependency etc. A compass rose (card) for "Effects on Humans" (to the right) is used as a metaphor reminding us of the importance to keep the direction towards desirable human and societal goals and qualities at the development and use of ICT.

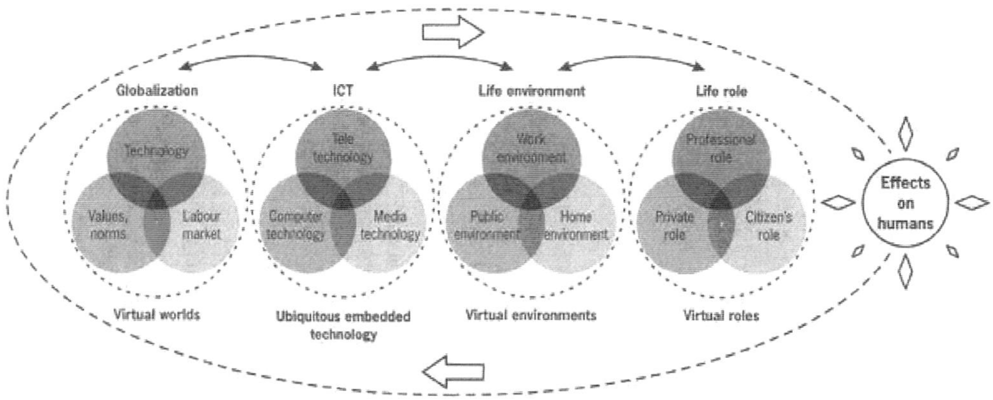

Figure 1. Convergence Model on ICT and Psychosocial Life Environment (Source: Bradley, 2005, 2006)

ICT can provide tools for promoting sustainability (environmental, economic, and social sustainability) but can also be a threat for sustainability. Sustainability as a guiding principle involves system perspective, holism, human aspects, bottom up approach, common good, and equality. A change in focus regarding research and development is taking place. Analysis and design increasingly address both the work process and management connected to the sphere of production life and people's life environment. Analysis and design of ICT and societal systems both at local level and globally become important. What research in the field exists or is needed?

Community research in a broad sense comes to the fore – both physical and virtual communities. There is also a requirement to involve new and additional actors at the deeper and broader integration of ICT in the society (children, elderly, and consumer organisations). Educational programs on Community Informatics and Social Informatics are appearing in many academic institutions. Can a new infrastructure of the society be identified?

The effects of ICT on human beings as well as the interaction between ICT, individuals, and society are all within the focus of this conference. Both analyses of interactions and effects are important. Changes in behaviour, perspectives, values, competencies, human and psychological aspects and feelings are all of interest. Reflections on past, present, and future challenges – especially planning for handling the latter – are encouraged.

Today, computer science and ICT-related disciplines are working more and more together with various behavioural and social sciences including child psychology and developmental psychology. For this reason, the conference pays attention to societal changes, global and more local organisational and institutional changes, changes in values and in lifestyles, as well as individual cognitive effects and changes, motivational and emotional changes. It also appeals to solution-building in terms of desirable goals and actions for reaching a Good Information Society.

In general, all types of research strategies are encouraged, and especially cross-disciplinary and multi-disciplinary studies. Case studies, broader empirical field studies, theoretical analyses, cross-cultural studies, scenarios, ethnographic studies, epistemological analyses may all be presented.

The ICT, Society and Human Beings 2024 conference addresses in detail seven main aspects:
- Globalization and ICT
- Life environment and ICT
- Life role and ICT
- ICT and effects on humans
- Perspectives on ICT
- Desirable goals and ICT
- Actions for reaching the Good Information Society

These conferences received 146 submissions from more than 29 countries. Each submission has been anonymously reviewed by an average of four independent reviewers, to ensure that accepted submissions were of a high standard. Consequently, only 23 full papers were approved which means an acceptance rate of 16%. A few more papers were accepted as short and reflection papers and posters. An extended version of the best papers may be published in the IADIS International Journal on Computer Science and Information Systems (ISSN: 1646-3692), IADIS International Journal on WWW/Internet (ISSN: 1645-7641), and also in other selected journals.

Besides the presentation of full, short and reflection papers and posters, these conferences also included one keynote presentation from an internationally distinguished researcher. We would therefore like to express our gratitude to Professor Helen Crompton, Executive Director of the Research Institute of Digital Innovation in Learning (RIDIL), Old Dominion University, USA, for being our keynote speaker.

This volume has taken shape as a result of the contributions from a number of individuals. We are grateful to all authors who have submitted their papers to enrich the conference proceedings. We wish to thank all members of the organizing committee, delegates, invitees and guests whose contribution and involvement are crucial for the success of the conference.

Last but not least, we hope that everybody enjoyed the presentations, and we invite all participants for next year's edition of these conferences.

Pedro Isaias, Universidade Aberta (Portuguese Open University), Portugal and
The University of New South Wales (UNSW – Sydney), Australia
Paula Miranda, School of Technology, Setubal Polytechnic University, Portugal
DTIM 2024 Program Co-Chairs

Piet Kommers, University of Twente, The Netherlands
ICT 2024 Program Chair

Piet Kommers, University of Twente, The Netherlands
Pedro Isaias, Universidade Aberta (Portuguese Open University), Portugal and
The University of New South Wales (UNSW – Sydney), Australia
MCCSIS 2024 General Conference Co-Chairs

July 2024

PROGRAM COMMITTEE

DIGITAL TRANSFORMATION AND INNOVATION 2024
PROGRAM CO-CHAIRS

Pedro Isaias, Universidade Aberta (Portuguese Open University), Portugal and
The University of New South Wales (UNSW – Sydney), Australia
Paula Miranda, School of Technology, Setubal Polytechnic University, Portugal

ICT, SOCIETY AND HUMAN BEINGS 2024
PROGRAM CHAIR

Piet Kommers, University of Twente, The Netherlands

MCCSIS 2024 GENERAL CONFERENCE CO-CHAIRS

Piet Kommers, University of Twente, The Netherlands
Pedro Isaias, Universidade Aberta (Portuguese Open University), Portugal and
The University of New South Wales (UNSW – Sydney), Australia

DIGITAL TRANSFORMATION AND INNOVATION 2024

COMMITTEE MEMBERS

Aamir Javed, University of Chieti and Pescara, Italy
Abhishek Behl, Management Development Institute, India
Alessandra Costa, University of Messina, Italy
Anastasija Nikiforova, University of Tartu, Estonia
Andrea Appolloni, University of Rome Tor Vergata, Italy
Anis Khedhaouria, Montpellier Business School, France
Antonio Crupi, University of Messina, Italy
Ayham Jaaron, De Montfort University, United Kingdom
Benito Yanez-Araque, University of Castilla-La Mancha, Spain
Caterina De Lucia, University of Foggia, Italy
Chang-Tang Chiang, Chinese Culture University, Taiwan
Cristina Alcaide Muñoz, University of Málaga, Spain
Cristina Mazas, University Eropea del Atlantico, Spain
Debora Di Caprio, University of Trento, Italy
Dinara Davlembayeva, Cardiff University, United Kingdom
Domitilla Magni, Ecampus University, Italy
Elvira Ismagilova, University of Bradford, United Kingdom
Francesco Paolo Appio, Paris School of Business, France
Francisco J. Santos-Arteaga, Universidad Complutense de Madrid, Spain
Giuseppe Basile, University of Foggia, Italy
Giuseppe Lanfranchi, University of Messina, Italy

ICT, SOCIETY AND HUMAN BEINGS 2024

COMMITTEE MEMBERS

Alrence Halibas, RMIT University, Vietnam
Amalia Sabiescu, Loughborough University, England
Ana Isabel Paraguay, Officio e Ambiente, Brazil
Anastasija Nikiforova, University of Tartu, Estonia
Antonio Marturano, University of Rome Tor Vergata, Italy
Bertil P. Marques, Instituto Superior de Engenharia do Porto (ISEP), Portugal
Caroline Parker, Glasgow Caledonian University, United Kingdom
Cristina Martinez Montes, Chalmers University of Technology, Sweden
Eila Jarvenpaa, Aalto University, Finland
Elvis Mazzoni, University of Bologna, Italy
Emil Van Der Poll, University of South Africa, South Africa
Ephias Ruhode, University of the West of Scotland, Scotland
Fabio Cassano, Università Degli Studi di Bari, Italy
Federica Baroni, University of Bergamo, Italy
Florin Popentiu, City University, Romania
Gustavo Mesch, University of Haifa, Israel
Harry Fulgencio, Swinburne University of Technology, Australia
Igor Guerreiro, Universidade Federal do Ceará, Brazil
Istvan Juhos, Institute of Informatics, University of Szeged, Hungary
Izak van Zyl, Cape Peninsula University of Technology (CPUT), South Africa
Jan Kubicek, Technical University of Ostrava, Czech Republic
Jan Meyer (Pr.M), Deputy Director NWU Business School, South Africa
Jorge Franco, Universidade Presbiteriana Mackenzie, Brazil
Kevin Matthe Caramancion, University of Wisconsin–Stout, United States
Kimiz Dalkir, Mcgill University, Canada
Manuela Repetto, University of Turin, Italy
Marco Lazzari, University of Bergamo, Italy
Maritta Pirhonen, University of Jyväskylä, Finland
Matias Dodel, Catholic University of Uruguay, Uruguay
Nestor Garay-Vitoria, Informatika Fakultatea (UPV/EHU), Spain
Nicola Doering, Ilmenau University of Technology, Germany
Nicolas Moreira, Universidade Federal do Ceará, Brazil
Oren Livio, University of Haifa, Israel
Petera Hudson, Massey Univeristy, New Zealand
Przemyslaw Falkowski-Gilski, Gdansk University of Technology, Poland
Robert Pintér , Corvinus University of Budapest, Hungary
Roei Davidson, University of Haifa, Israel
Stamatis Papadakis, University of Crete, Greece
Tarcisio Maciel, Universidade Federal do Ceará, Brazil
Virve Siirak, Tallinn University of Technology, Estonia
Zsolt Demetrovics, Elte Eötvös Loránd University, Hungary

KEYNOTE LECTURE

GENERATIVE AI: AFFORDANCES AND CHALLENGES FOR EDUCATION

Professor Helen Crompton
Executive Director of the Research Institute of Digital Innovation in Learning (RIDIL), Old Dominion University, USA

ABSTRACT

As ChatGPT and other generative AI tools permeate the educational landscape, educators find themselves at a crossroads, reexamining their teaching strategies and assessment methods. This presentation offers a thorough examination of ChatGPT's impact on teaching and learning, highlighting its potential to enhance instructional delivery and the overall learning journey. It underscores the imperative for educators to recognize and tackle the inherent limitations and potential misuses of these tools, promoting a balanced and responsible integration into the educational framework.

Full Papers

LEGAL X-RAY: AN APPROACH TO AUTOMATING INFORMATION EXTRACTION IN PORTUGUESE LEGAL DOCUMENTS

Celso Araujo Fontes
Procuradoria Geral do Estado do Rio de Janeiro
Rua da Carmo 27, Rio de Janeiro, RJ - Brazil

ABSTRACT

This paper describes the creation and implementation of the "Legal X-Ray," an innovative application designed to enhance the drafting process of petitions and official documents within the Attorney General's Office of the State of Rio de Janeiro (PGE-RJ). The application was developed to integrate with PGE Digital, a lawsuit management system, aiming to automate the analysis of initial pleadings and document generation in the context of mass litigation. Employing Named Entity Recognition (NER) and Regular Expression (REGEX) techniques through the SpaCy library, the Legal X-Ray is capable of extracting relevant information from legal documents and converting them into categorized hashtags. These hashtags are then utilized to facilitate and expedite the creation of legal documents, contributing to a significant increase in operational efficiency and reduction in the PGE-RJ's response time. The application has proven to be a valuable tool in processing large volumes of data, allowing legal professionals to focus their efforts on tasks of greater analytical complexity. This case study examines the development and deployment of the Legal X-Ray, discussing its challenges, methods, and the positive outcomes achieved in daily legal practice.

KEYWORDS

Named Entity Recognition, Legal text analysis, Natural Language Processing and Machine Learning

1. INTRODUCTION

The judicial system is often burdened with an overwhelming volume of litigation, particularly in the area of mass litigation where repetitive and standardized processes can lead to inefficiency and delays. In the Attorney General's Office of the State of Rio de Janeiro, (PGE-RJ), the handling of such a vast number of cases necessitates a streamlined approach to document generation, specifically for petitions and official communications. Traditional methods of drafting and reviewing these documents are time-consuming and prone to human error, creating a bottleneck that affects the efficiency of public advocacy.

For instance, in the context of succession law actions, a common practice within the Attorney General's Office involves providing legal opinions as mandated by Brazilian law. Within the templates utilized by the Office for documents related to this matter, placeholders are often used for the name of the "*de cujus*"[1] and their date of death. These critical pieces of information are manually extracted from the lawsuit and replaced each time a new document is generated using the template. In practice, the majority of modifications to these templates involve solely the substitution of these specific data points. This manual process not only consumes valuable time and resources but also increases the likelihood of errors and inconsistencies in the generated documents.

In light of the challenges outlined above, innovative technologies such as Named Entity Recognition (NER) offer promising avenues for addressing the inefficiencies inherent in manual document extraction processes (Saravanan & Sundararaghavan, 2020). NER is a subfield of natural language processing (NLP) that focuses on identifying and categorizing named entities within unstructured text, such as names of individuals, dates, and locations (Li et al., 2016). By leveraging machine learning algorithms, NER systems

[1] Legal term derived from Latin, meaning "of the deceased." In law, it refers to the person who has died, particularly in the context of inheritance or probate matters.

can automatically extract and classify relevant information from legal documents, thereby streamlining the document generation process and reducing the reliance on manual labor.

Previous research has demonstrated the efficacy of NER in various domains, including legal text analysis. For example, Araujo et al. (2018) developed the LeNER-Br dataset specifically for NER in Brazilian legal text, providing a valuable resource for training and evaluating NER models in this context. Additionally, Dozier et al. (2010) showcased the effectiveness of NER systems in identifying legal entities within documents, highlighting the potential for NER to enhance automation in the legal domain.

However, while these previous works have provided valuable insights and resources for NER development in legal text analysis, specific entities unique to the field of public advocacy, such as "*de cujus*" in succession law cases or specific job titles within public service, are often overlooked or not adequately addressed. As a result, existing NER models may not fully meet the requirements of legal professionals within the Attorney General's Office of the State of Rio de Janeiro, where precise identification and extraction of such entities are crucial for document generation and legal opinion formulation.

The aforementioned situations expose significant impediments to the efficiency of legal workflows, underscoring the urgency for a bespoke solution that can navigate the domain-specific complexities of legal documentation. To this end, the creation of Legal X-Ray emerges as a pivotal innovation, meticulously designed to address the unique challenges faced by the Attorney General's Office of the State of Rio de Janeiro. Legal X-Ray is not merely a technological advancement; it is a strategic initiative aimed at revolutionizing the management of legal texts by deploying advanced NER capabilities tailored specifically to the intricacies of public advocacy and succession law. This system is engineered to recognize and accurately extract specialized entities that are of paramount importance to legal practitioners.

The driving force behind Legal X-Ray is the recognition that generic NER models are insufficient for the nuanced demands of legal text processing within the Attorney General's Office. By developing an NER system with a laser focus on the legal lexicon and the specific nomenclature used in the office's documents, Legal X-Ray promises to significantly diminish the time spent on routine tasks, minimize the margin for human error, and thereby accelerate the entire document generation cycle. This bespoke approach ensures that the system is not only adept at identifying common legal entities but also excels in pinpointing the less common yet critically important terms that are unique to the legal environment of public advocacy.

The article begins with an exposition on the corpus utilized in this study, detailing the data sources and preprocessing techniques employed. The methodology section then delves into annotation methodologies, data format conversion, and model training procedures. Following this, the discussion expands to cover the model training process, including experimentation and optimization strategies aimed at enhancing performance. Further, the integration of Legal X-Ray with the PGE Digital system is outlined, elucidating its role in streamlining document generation. Finally, a comprehensive conclusion summarizes the key findings and implications of Legal X-Ray in optimizing legal workflows.

2. CORPUS

2.1 Data Source

The corpus utilized in this study was obtained through web services implementing a standard known as the National Interoperability Model (MNI - *Modelo Nacional de Interoperabilidade*). MNI functions as a protocol designed to streamline the exchange of information pertaining to legal proceedings among various entities within the justice administration and other public institutions. Provided by the National Justice Council (CNJ) as a SOAP schema, MNI offers methods enabling users to submit petitions, retrieve lawsuit metadata and documents, as well as receive summonses and subpoenas (Sewald Jr et al., 2016).

The data were collected via MNI from the following Brazilian courts:

1. Tribunal de Justiça do Estado do Rio de Janeiro (Court of Justice of the State of Rio de Janeiro)
2. Justiça Federal do Rio de Janeiro (Federal Court of Rio de Janeiro)
3. Tribunal Regional do Trabalho da Primeira Região (Regional Labor Court of the First Region)

2.2 Corpus Description

The corpus exclusively consists of complaints filed in the courts of Rio de Janeiro. These 75.289 complaints encompass a variety of legal matters and are representative of the types of cases adjudicated within the region. The complaints are categorized as follows:

Table 1. Total of complaints (initial petitions) per Legal Matter

Legal Matter	Total of complaints
Tax Law	13.567
Administrative Law	9.675
Environmental Law	3.649
Social Security Law	15.830
Public Services Law	4.805
Labor Law	4.056
Succession Law	9.171
Health Law	14.536

2.3 Preprocessing

All documents were converted from PDF to plain text (UTF-8 encoding) format to facilitate text processing and analysis. This conversion process ensured uniformity and compatibility across the corpus.

3. METHODOLOGY

3.1 Annotation

To train a supervised model for the Named Entity Recognition (NER) task, it is essential to prepare a dataset with annotated entities (Nadeau and Sekine, 2007). To fulfill this prerequisite, two annotation approaches were employed within the scope of this work:

3.1.1 Manual Annotation

A portion of the documents, totaling 2.369, was manually annotated using the NER Text Annotator tool available at https://tecoholic.github.io/ner-annotator/. This online tool makes it possible to create tags and use them to mark words or passages of text. The annotated text can be exported to JSON format, which facilitates further processing and analysis. Below is an example of annotated text represented in JSON format, demonstrating the tagging of named entities such as "DE_CUJUS" and "DATA_FALECIMENTO":


```
{
  "classes": [
    "DE_CUJUS",
    "DATA_FALECIMENTO"
  ],
  "annotations": [
    [
      "Faleceu João da Silva em 12/02/2024",
      {
        "entities": [
          [
            8,
            21,
            "DE_CUJUS"
          ],
          [
            25,
            35,
            "DATA_FALECIMENTO"
          ]
        ]
      }
    ]
  ]
}
```


Figure 1. JSON generated by NER Annotator tool

This JSON structure includes a list of classes representing named entity types and annotations containing text passages along with their corresponding tagged entities. The "entities" attribute within each annotation entry is composed of the start position, end position, and the tag assigned to the named entity. This structured format enables easy integration with machine learning models for training and information extraction tasks.

The manual annotation process was conducted by a team of 10 legal residents from the Attorney General's Office of the State of Rio de Janeiro. Each resident brought expertise in various legal domains, ensuring a diverse perspective during the annotation process. Utilizing the NER Text Annotator tool, these residents meticulously labeled named entities within the legal documents. Their collective legal knowledge and professional backgrounds facilitated accurate identification and labeling of entities, enhancing the quality and reliability of the annotated dataset used for model training and analysis.

During the manual annotation process, several measures were implemented to ensure the consistency and reliability of the annotated dataset. A detailed video tutorial was created to instruct annotators on the use of the online annotation tool, covering both technical aspects of the tool and specific guidelines for entity marking. Prior to annotation commencement, annotators participated in a preliminary meeting where the tags to be used were defined and standardized. Each tag was assigned a unique name in uppercase letters and separated by underscores, ensuring consistency in entity marking. Following the completion of annotation for a set of documents, an automated Python script was used to verify if the tags were annotated with the names previously agreed upon. Additionally, any discrepancies or inconsistencies identified were discussed among annotators and corrected as necessary. A legal expert also evaluated the quality of annotations through random sampling, ensuring accuracy and adherence to annotation guidelines. These measures were instrumental in maintaining the quality and reliability of the annotated dataset utilized in the research.

3.1.2 Automatic Annotation

The second approach employed in this study involved automatic annotation using data extracted from the PGE Digital system. Within this system, legal cases are associated with a dataset known as keywords. These keywords consist of a descriptor, representing the keyword itself, along with its corresponding value. By extracting these datasets through SQL queries, Python scripts were then utilized to process the data. The outcome of this process was a JSON format similar to that generated by the manual annotation tool.

3.2 Data Format Conversion and Dataset Splitting

After manual and automatic annotation, the annotated data is typically stored in JSON format, as demonstrated in the example above. However, for efficient training and processing using NLP libraries such as SpaCy, it is necessary to convert this annotated data into a format compatible with the library's requirements. SpaCy, for example, utilizes a binary format called DocBin for training its models.

DocBin is a binary format used by SpaCy to store annotated document data efficiently. It consists of a sequence of serialized documents, where each document is represented as a sequence of tokens along with their annotations. This binary representation allows for fast loading and processing of large datasets during model training and inference. The conversion script is available in https://github.com/explosion/projects/blob/v3/pipelines/ner_demo/scripts/convert.py.

Additionally, during the conversion process from JSON to DocBin, we take the opportunity to partition the dataset into training and development sets. This division is crucial for assessing the performance of the NER model and preventing overfitting. Typically, we allocate 80% of the annotated data to the training set, which is used to train the model, and reserve the remaining 20% for the development set (Kuhn and Johnson, 2013). The development set serves as a validation dataset, allowing us to tune hyperparameters and evaluate the model's performance on unseen data. This approach ensures that the model generalizes well to new documents and achieves robust performance in real-world applications.

4. MODEL TRAINING

4.1 Training Procedure

The model training process was conducted using SpaCy's training pipeline, specifically utilizing the spacy train command-line interface. This approach allows for efficient training of custom NER models using annotated data in the DocBin format, as described in the previous section.

To initiate the training process, several prerequisites are required, including the following:

1. **Annotated Data in DocBin Format**: The annotated dataset, divided into separate files for training and development sets in the DocBin format (*.spacy), serves as the input for training the NER model.
2. **Configuration File (.cfg)**: A configuration file containing important settings for training, such as the language, pipeline components (NER, tagger, etc.), architecture (e.g., transformers), and their respective parameters.

To start the training process, the following command can be used:

```
python -m spacy train config.cfg --output ./output --paths.train ./train.spacy --paths.dev
./dev.spacy
```

This command initiates the training process based on the configurations specified in the configuration file, optimizing the model's parameters to achieve optimal performance on the provided datasets.

4.2 Model Experimentation and Optimization

4.2.1 Transition from CPU to GPU

In the initial version of the Legal X-Ray system, we employed the CPU-oriented architecture of SpaCy, specifically the TOK2VEC model with the Portuguese language model **pt_core_news_lg**. While this configuration demonstrated acceptable precision in some cases within our dataset, overall precision was found to be suboptimal.

To address this issue, we conducted further experiments with different architectures and configurations aimed at improving the model's performance. One significant iteration involved transitioning to a GPU-oriented architecture, leveraging the power of transformers. Specifically, we adopted the **neuralmind/bert-base-portuguese-cased** model (Souza et al., 2020), which is pre-trained on Portuguese text data and fine-tuned for NER tasks.

After implementing the new architecture and model, we conducted a comprehensive evaluation to compare its performance with the previous configuration. The results revealed a notable improvement in precision, with gains ranging from 20% to 40% across various evaluation metrics.

4.2.2 Entity Ruler Integration

Despite the use of transformers, we observed that the precision of certain entities remained low. These entities shared a common characteristic: they were finite standardized numbers or codes that could be represented by regular expressions.

To address this challenge, we leveraged another feature of SpaCy called the Entity Ruler. This component allows for the creation of custom rules based on regular expressions or dictionaries to recognize specific patterns or entities in the text. In the following example, we demonstrate how the Entity Ruler can be utilized to define rules for identifying specific entities based on regular expressions:

```python
import spacy
from spacy.pipeline import EntityRuler

# Load model
nlp = spacy.load("pt_core_news_lg")

# Initialize the EntityRuler
ruler = EntityRuler(nlp)

# Define patterns for specific entities using regular expressions
pattern = {
  "label": "SEI",
  "pattern": [
   {"TEXT":
    {"REGEX": "\\bSEI\\b[\\s*?|A-Z|Nº-.-]*\\d{1,}[^Aa-zZ\\s]*\\s*\\d{1,}[^Aa-zZ\\s]*\\s*\\d{1,}[^Aa-zZ\\s]*\\s*\\d{1,}"}
   }
  ]
 }

# Add pattern to the EntityRuler
ruler.add_patterns([pattern])

# Add EntityRuler to the SpaCy pipeline
nlp.add_pipe(ruler)

# Process the text
text = "O SEI 1234.5678/2023 4 é referente ao processo de número SEI 9876.5432/2022 1."
doc = nlp(text)
```

Figure 2. Entity ruler example

The pattern above is designed to retrieve SEI numbers mentioned specifically within complaints. SEI stands for "Sistema Eletrônico de Informações" (Electronic Information System), a system developed by the Federal Regional Court of the 4th Region (TRF-4) and widely adopted by various public agencies and entities in Brazil for managing electronic processes and documents (Saraiva, 2018).

4.3 Model Evaluation

In SpaCy, precision, a crucial metric for evaluating named entity recognition (NER) models, is calculated as the ratio of correctly predicted entities to the total number of entities predicted by the model. The formula for precision is:

$$Precision = (\text{Number of correctly predicted entities} / \text{Total number of predicted entities}) \times 100\%$$

During evaluation, the model's predicted entities are compared to annotated entities in the test dataset. If a predicted entity exactly matches an annotated entity, it is considered a correct prediction and contributes to the precision score. Precision serves as a vital indicator of the model's ability to precisely identify entities of interest.

The following table showcases the precision (%) scores across various legal domains, offering insights into our model's performance within specific areas of law. By examining these scores, we gain a nuanced understanding of how effectively the model identifies entities within different legal contexts, thereby providing valuable context for its overall evaluation.

Table 2. Precision per Legal Matter

Legal Matter	Precision
Tax Law	**86%**
Administrative Law	**76%**
Environmental Law	**63%**
Social Security Law	**66%**
Public Services Law	**95%**
Labor Law	**59%**
Succession Law	**56%**
Health Law	**43%**

In the specific case of Health law, a significant limitation was encountered with BERT within SpaCy when handling extensive text. This manifested in the extraction output occasionally encompassing entire paragraphs, capturing more than intended and sometimes returning an entire paragraph, particularly in discussions involving medications with dosages. Such occurrences may introduce inaccuracies in entity recognition, especially within the intricate and technical legal documents characteristic of this field. The expansive and diffuse nature of these documents poses a challenge for the model's precise identification and extraction of relevant entities, hampering overall precision. Consequently, future efforts will focus on refining and optimizing the model, as well as exploring alternative libraries like SpaCy-LLM, to overcome these challenges and improve the accuracy of entity recognition in health law-related texts.

5. DATA UTILIZATION IN PGE DIGITAL VIA LEGAL X-RAY

Legal X-Ray's trained models are made available via a RESTful API, allowing seamless integration with the PGE Digital system. Through this API, the client application can submit complaints together with the legal matter of the lawsuit and receive a set of entities and their values as a response.

Upon retrieval, the extracted entities and their associated values are persisted within the PGE Digital system. They are stored as "keywords" linked to each lawsuit, facilitating easy access and retrieval when needed. This ensures that the extracted data remains readily available for use in various document-related tasks.

5.1 Dynamic Utilization via Hashtags

One innovative feature of the PGE Digital system is the dynamic utilization of extracted data through hashtags. These keywords, derived from the extracted entities, can be seamlessly integrated into the system's document editor as hashtags. Users can then incorporate these hashtags directly into their documents, triggering automatic population with the corresponding values during document generation.

This dynamic integration eliminates the need for manual data entry and reduces the risk of errors associated with manual input. Additionally, it empowers users to create accurate and comprehensive legal documents efficiently.

The following figure illustrates the automatic generation of documents in the PGE Digital system using hashtags derived from the extracted data. The left side of the image shows the document editor containing various hashtags, including #pc_decujus (pc stands for "*palavra chave*", keyword in portuguese). The right side shows the document preview with the deceased's name replaced by the hashtag:

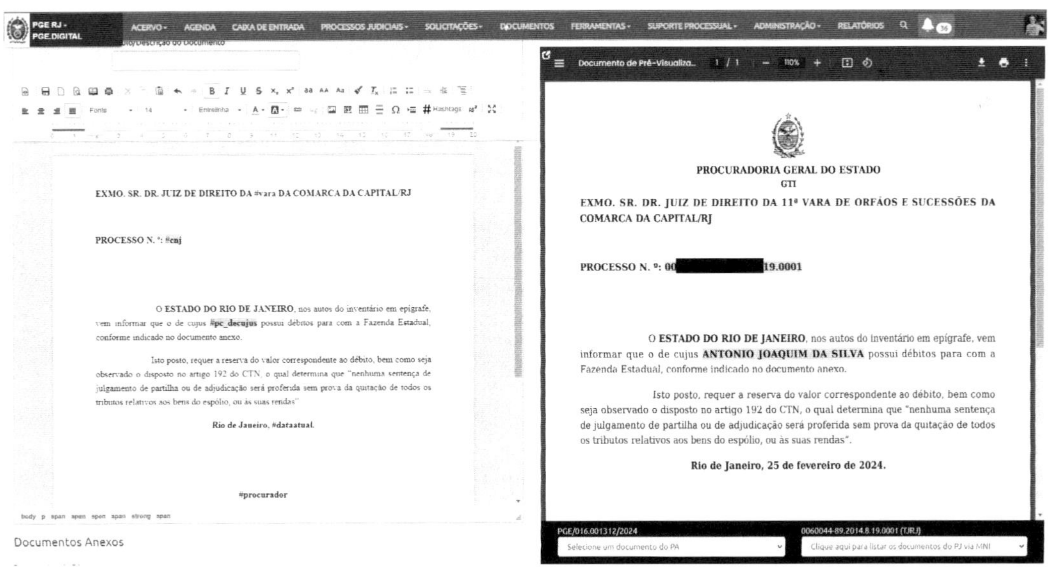

Figure 3. Data extracted via NER available as hashtag

6. CONCLUSION

The implementation of Legal X-Ray signifies a substantial advancement in optimizing legal workflows within the Attorney General's Office of the State of Rio de Janeiro. By addressing specific challenges in processing legal texts, this system demonstrates the feasibility of innovative technologies and underscores the importance of tailored approaches to meet the complex demands of the public sector. The successful integration of Legal X-Ray with the PGE Digital system simplifies the generation of legal documents, enhances accuracy and efficiency, and reduces reliance on error-prone manual processes. Empowering legal professionals with intelligent tools aims to enhance productivity and promote more agile, precise, and accessible public advocacy. Moreover, the utilization of NER technology within the Portuguese language context highlights its crucial role in advancing natural language processing capabilities. NER models trained for Portuguese legal texts significantly improve document processing and analysis, offering tailored solutions that cater to the intricacies of the language and legal terminology. This underscores the importance of further research and development in NLP for diverse linguistic landscapes, ensuring technological advancements benefit users across different languages and cultures.

REFERENCES

Araujo, P.H.L., et al., 2018. LeNER-Br: a dataset for named entity recognition in Brazilian legal text. *Proceedings of the 13th International Conference on Computational Processing of the Portuguese Language (PROPOR 2018)*, Canela, Brazil, pp. 313-323.

Dozier, C. et al., 2010. Named Entity Recognition and Resolution in Legal Text. *Proceedings of the 2010 Conference on Empirical Methods in Natural Language Processing (EMNLP '10)*. Association for Computational Linguistics, Stroudsburg, PA, USA, pp. 273-282.

Kuhn, M. and Johnson, K., 2013. *Applied Predictive Modeling*. Springer, New York, USA.

Li, H. et al, 2016. A survey on error analysis in named entity recognition. *In ACM Computing Surveys (CSUR)*, Vol. 49, No. 5, pp. 1-42.

Nadeau, D. and Sekine, S., 2007. A survey of named entity recognition and classification. *Lingvisticae Investigationes*, Vol. 30, No. 1, pp. 3-26.

Saraiva, A., 2018. A Implementação do SEI - Sistema Eletrônico de Informações, Estudo de Caso. Escola Nacional de Administração Pública (Enap) e Secretaria de Gestão (SEGES/MP). *Coleção: Casos SEGES renovando a gestão pública*. Available at: http://repositorio.enap.gov.br/handle/1/3455 (Accessed: February 23, 2024).

Saravanan, K. et al, 2020. Named entity recognition in information retrieval: A survey. *In International Journal of Information Technology and Computer Science (IJITCS)*, Vol. 12, No. 5, pp. 1-10.

Sewald, E. et al, 2016. Avaliação do modelo nacional de interoperabilidade do Poder Judiciário brasileiro. *Pensar-Revista de Ciências Jurídicas*, Vol. 21, No. 2, pp. 442-483.

Souza, F. et al., 2020. BERTimbau: pretrained BERT models for Brazilian Portuguese. *Proceedings of Intelligent Systems: 9th Brazilian Conference (BRACIS 2020)*. Rio Grande, Brazil, pp. 403-417. Springer International Publishing.

HOP, SKIP, AND … JUMP! DIGITAL BUSINESS TRANSFORMATION AND BEHAVIOUR

Nina Evans
STEM, University of South Australia, Australia

ABSTRACT

Digital Business Transformation (DBT) has become an important topic since the rapid development and diffusion of digital technologies. However, DBT goes beyond technology implementation. To be successful in developing and implementing DBT, organisations must focus on the human side of DBT, especially the behaviours of leaders and employees. This paper reports the findings from a focus group meeting with nine (9) DBT experts, who currently work together as an Enterprise Transformation (ET) team in a large organisation and have each conducted more than one enterprise transformation. The aim of the focus group was to elicit their experience regarding the damaging organisational behaviour and politics displayed by people during an enterprise transformation. Participants spoke about negative organisational behaviours resulting from the disruptive nature of the change and added that the best employees are often the most destructive. The experts also shared possible approaches that will lead to a more successful transformation. Regular change management is not appropriate for an enterprise transformation. Taking all employees on the transformation journey from the outset is not a feasible approach. Instead, the experts suggest that the transformation should start with a small team or department that is isolated from the rest of the business. Once small wins are achieved, the approach can be applied throughout the rest of the business. Enterprise transformation requires a unique 'chaos management' approach that defies the principles of traditional and change management.

KEYWORDS

Digital Business Transformation, Organisational Behaviour, Organisational Politics, Change leadership, Chaos Management

1. INTRODUCTION

Over the past decade, the pace of change in the technology sector has been incredibly rapid; technology is reshaping industries, organisations, and almost every aspect of our lives. Most organisations experience disruption and they must understand the impact that the integration of digital technologies into their business, so-called *digital transformation,* will have on their organisation, the industries in which they participate, and the people they interact with (Lardi, 2023; Ridwansyah et al., 2023). A common misconception is that digital transformation only involves technology. However, technology is only one part of the puzzle that organisations must solve (Vial, 2019). DBT involves a fundamental change of an organisation's culture, operations, and ecosystem, where business is conducted through technology, process, and people (Lardi, 2022; Thomas, 2019). This requires a digital business transformation. Organisations that have been proven successful in developing and implementing their DBT strategies started with people (Lardi, 2023, Matricano et al., 2022). One of the people challenges is how to steer employee behaviours from traditional, top-down technology acceptance and adoption to motivating employees to engage in the digital transformation process voluntarily and actively (Solberg et al., 2020). If organisations ignore the human element, the digital transformation effort is doomed to fail (Alieva & Powell, 2023).

The focus of this paper is on the people aspect and the aim is to investigate the negative organisational behaviours and organisational politics during times of disruptive change and digital transformation of an organisation and to suggest how the organisation may approach the transformation to motivate people to engage and support the leaders of the transformation.

2. LITERATURE REVIEW

2.1 Digital Business Transformation

There is no universally accepted definition of digital transformation, but it can be described from a technology perspective, e.g. as the integration of digital technologies into business processes or developing fully digitised businesses. Several authors have defined digital transformation as the development and adoption of digital technology such as artificial intelligence (AI), big data, Internet of Things (IoT), robotics, and cloud computing (Kane, 2019; Lardi, 2023).

Apart from the technology perspective, some authors view digital transformation from a business perspective, namely a company-wide change that leads to the development of new business models. Digital Transformation is often marketed as a way of converting business processes and everything around them into a digital format – giving bigger cost savings, better and faster results (Ridwansyah et al., 2023). A third perspective of DBT is the people perspective, where some authors refer to DBT as causing changes to the business that require a fundamental reshaping of people's behaviour (Chevallard, 2023; Meske & Junglas, 2021; Moretti, 2020).

2.2 Behavioural Aspects of DBT

Although technology is an enabler and a driver to business innovation, it is not the biggest and most crucial element of digital transformation (Lardi, 2023). Technology is only useful to transform a business if the people who work with it are willing to play an active role in the transformation journey (Benavides et al. 2021; Meske & Junglas, 2021; Prentice, 2022; Scholkmann, 2021). Digital transformation is really about behaviour (Chevallard, 2023; Li et al., 2021; Metallo et al., 2021; Moretti, 2020), i.e., how people deal with change and whether they choose to collaborate (Koor & Associates, 2023). Transformation teams often do not consider the most important element of the final implementation, namely the human factor (Lardi, 2023).

People have a natural tendency to prefer what is well-known and familiar rather than to accept the unknown. DBT will not succeed if people are tied to their old ways; active participation and collaboration require people to be focused on the future direction of the business and to be rewarded for their efforts (Moretti, 2020; Solberg et al., 2020; Stonehouse & Konina, 2019). The typical resistant and negative political DBT behaviours found in literature have been categorised by the author, as indicated in Table 1:

Table 1. Organisational Behaviours During Digital Transformation

Behaviour
Treating colleagues unfairly Attack or blame others; Malicious gossip; Unfair criticism; Spread information that damages their reputation; Exploit weaknesses of others; Workplace bullying; Withhold information; Exclude and isolate colleagues; Deception; Make false allegations; Manipulate others; Block other employees' ideas; Refuse to allow anyone else to undertake a role. **Power play** Use information as a political tool; Control information channels; Maintain alliances with powerful and influential people to create obligations; Use external consultants to support views; Knowledge hiding; Self-promotion; Form factions that commit to winning at any cost. **Sabotaging the DBT** Allow failures to occur; Low interest in the transformation; Spread rumours; Resist learning); Manipulation and sabotage; Block or slow down progress.
Literature
Bloomberg, 2016; Chevallard, 2023; Denning, 2023; Jarrett, 2017; Koor & Associates, 2023; Magnusson et al., 2022; Matricano et al., 2022; McConnell, 2017; Meske & Junglas, 2021; Metallo et al., 2021; Mete & Eyel, 2020; Prentice, 2022; Roberts, 2022; Sainger, G. 2018; Scholkmann, 2021; Solberg et al., 2020; Tiefenbeck, 2017; Tiersky, 2022; Trittin-Ulbrich et al., 2021; Visser, 2022; Wade & Obwegeser, 2019; Weber et al., 2022; Zicar, 2023

3. METHODOLOGY

A focus group is a special type of group interview that is structured and organised to gather detailed valuable opinions, experiences, and knowledge from selected participants about a particular topic. Due to the exploratory nature of this research, we conducted a focus group session to gather data about i) the behaviours observed during the digital transformation they are currently leading as an ET team, ii) the impact of the behaviour on the transformation and iii) ways to support the transformation. The focus group approach was chosen, as it allowed participants to share their experience and build on one another's views and comments. The data collected from the focus group therefore reveal more information than one-to-one interviews, which enables the researcher to understand the issues in greater depth. The researcher acted as a facilitator and used questioning and summarising techniques to stimulate discussions, seek clarification, and prompt participants to share actual experiences. During the research attention was paid to the confidentiality of sensitive corporate and personal information. Given that the names of individuals and organisations remain unidentified, the participants were forthcoming with examples. The session lasted 90 minutes, was audio-recorded, and transcribed for analysis. Topic and analytic coding guided the effort to draw insights from the data. The goal was to let practice inform theory and vice versa. The focus group included nine DBT experts:

Table 2. Focus group participants

Participant	Relevant experience	Number of DBTs	Industry and types of organisations (Large, Medium, or Small	Leadership experience (years)
P1	40 years in IT, Business Analyst (BA), developer, CIO, COO, Enterprise Digital Transformation expert, Enterprise Architect	5	Financial, Government, Defense, Health, Mining (L, M, S)	35
P2	30 years in IT, project manager, developer, BA	2	Financial, Government, Manufacturing, Health, Mining (L, M, S)	25
P3	30 years in IT project manager, developer, HR, BA	2	Financial, Government, Manufacturing, Health, Mining (L, M, S)	25
P4	Data specialist, AI, BA	1	Financial, Gaming and Hospitality (L)	10
P5	BA, SME (Super/insurance)	2	Financial (L)	-
P6	BA	2	Financial (L)	-
P7	Financial industry expert, BA, PM	1	Financial (L)	-
P8	BA, Data Scientist	2	Financial (L)	-
P9	40 years in IT, BA, database expert	2	Financial, Government, Mining, Health (L, M, S)	35+

4. FINDINGS

4.1 Resistance to Digital Transformation

The focus group participants indicated that behaviours change during the digital transformation:

You may have great leaders and employees on board, they're productive, they're working with you. Then you introduce digital transformation, and those very best people suddenly turn on you. (P1)

The strongest employees display the most resistance to change, as they are invested in their jobs and therefore willing to fight to maintain the status quo:

> *If someone is at the top of their game [..], they're kicking goals and meeting targets, they are going to fight very hard if someone comes in and says all of that's now in the bin because we're going to put in a new platform. The more a mother loves her cubs the harder she fights for them.* (P1)

The experts refer to their implementation of a digital platform, i.e. the software and technology used to streamline business operations and IT systems. Although the platform serves as the organisation's backbone for operations and customer engagement, executives do not recognise the success of the ET team:

> *Even executives that are getting pay raises and bonuses, based on what we're doing now, refuse to recognise that it's the digital platform that led to the success. We have found that success translates to silence. There are no flowers, no congratulations, no cake for us.* (P3)

4.2 Observed DBT Behaviours

The ET team encountered various negative behaviours during business transformation that are in line with those found in the literature (Table 3).

Table 3. DBT behaviours

Behaviour	**Supporting quotes**
Treating colleagues unfairly	
Nasty behaviour	*People go from being nice people to being mean to ugly.* (P1)
Disrespect the ET team	*They don't acknowledge the skills that the ET team bring and depth of our knowledge.* (P2)
Act in an exclusionary way	*They recognise only themselves and don't celebrate our success.* (P3)
Success equals silence	*The more successful we are, the worse the cultural issues we face. I pulled off what was nothing short of a miracle and they said that's how we planned it, why would we celebrate it?* (P4)
Treat ET as outsiders, 'us and them'	*We're sitting on the wrong side of the fence* (P7)
Start positively and then they start to complain	*They complain because that is how they are rewarded and recognised. After 12 months they have their own list of 12 things they don't like about you.* (P6)
Power play	
Resist because they feel powerful in their current role	*They can say they have 600 people reporting to them, whereas in the new world they don't have a role.* (P3)
Passive aggressive	*I'm trying to be helpful; I appear to be helpful; I say I'm helpful; but in reality, I'm not helpful.* (P1)
Block progress	*They don't cooperate because they are either scared and under-skilled, or scared and skilled.* (P4)
Merely comply with regulations	*The way the data is handled meets the criteria of the regulator, not of the organisation or common sense.* (P4)
Not willing to self-serve	*This is because they think we are there to do it for them.* (P9)
Sabotaging the DBT	
Sabotage by taking a long time to respond or ignoring requests	*They just ignore you.* (P5)
Don't want the ET team to succeed	*They need you to fail to let you know 'see I told you this enterprise transformation rubbish won't work'.* (P3)
Gatekeeping	*They overcomplicate things and point you in 20 different directions.* (P6)
Anchored to their original position	*This is my department, it's perfect what you're criticizing.* (P1)
Can't see their future in the organisation	*They think they're going to fail, or they are just comfortable where they are.* (P3)
Siloed thinking versus enterprise thinking	*I only live in my silo, and I only do what was good for my silo.* (P1)
Regard the ET team as temporary and their other leaders as long-term people	*They feel disloyal to their manager when they talk to the ET team.* (P2)

4.3 DBT Requires 'Outside-In' Thinking

The participants indicated that DBT is different from anything the company has experienced before. It requires 'outside-in thinking'.' This means that the transformation starts with a vision of the destination: the new digital platform, the new processes, new job roles and titles, new ways of leadership, etc. This approach is different from continuous process improvement. P1 commented that "if you try to do digital transformation using 'inside-out' thinking, or continuous process improvement, you will fail". It is difficult for people to accept that their old way of working is not relevant anymore:

> *It's like saying to 'horse and cart operators' that now we need 'drone operators. We don't want to know about your processes, your delivery routes, how you take and fulfill orders, provide a service. How you do that today is not significant at all in the future. We're going to define a new world and figure out how to run it in a way that you haven't even thought of. We're not going to ask your permission or even get you involved. You're going to run the old world until we switch it off. For good people, for staff that are really bought in and switched on, this is a very hard message.* (P1)

4.4 Change Management is not a Suitable Approach for DBT

The approach taken to transform the organisation influences the resulting behaviours. In times of change, organisations usually revert to familiar change management approaches, which P1 refers to as 'horse and cart type leadership' to get people on board:

> *They set up incentives, communication forums, HR is involved, Marketing is involved, there's bonuses and incentives to help people understand and get them on board. This is traditional change management where you're going from the old situation to the new situation. In doing that you can predict how employees will behave. Good employees will get on board and your average employees will be middle of the road. Employees will usually go along.*

However, the experts indicated that the observed destructive behaviours manifest because leaders try to apply traditional leadership approaches, old-fashioned change management, continuous process improvement:

> *A digital transformation is a hop, skip and.. a jump. A hop and a skip equate continuous process improvement. Digital transformation needs a jump. All the leadership styles and change management principles that work for a hop and a skip have the opposite effect in a jump. (P1)*

4.5 What is Required for Successful Transformation?

4.5.1 Start Small

The experts suggest that the first part of a transformation should be done on a part of the business that is not core business or that is not performing particularly well. A section of the employees is then invited to apply for the different roles required to create this digital part of the business, to the point where people can see the value. Then the others can start moving across; one cannot take everyone on the journey from the start:

> *We say we're leaving you a hundred percent alone, we're starting a new little piece over here, just this part of the business. Please just ignore it, carry on, you're doing a phenomenally good job. We'll get to you at some of the later date. So, people don't feel threatened. They don't think it's their flagship. They don't feel that they need to even be involved in this, and so we can get the platform up and start kicking goals. For example, we had a 200% turnaround in a $0 area that the company didn't care about at all. Suddenly everybody's fighting to own it because it's now a very profitable part of the business.* (P1)

Transformation requires a jump into the future, which means leaving everything behind. Some people are not prepared to do that. They believe they are an expert at the old, and they like the old. They choose to stay with the current way of doing things and run the risk of not having a job 5 or 6 years down the track. Others take the jump, they jump, they go hop, skip,.. jump.

4.5.2 Leadership Commitment

Referring to past experience, P1 commented:

> *I'm now looking back and I've learnt that the transformation depends on the style and strength of leadership of each organisation.*

A supportive message from the executive leader about the role of the ET team is important:

> *The [leader]said [P1] will join the company for a few years, she'll be disruptive and then she'll go away. I'm putting the fox in the henhouse and then we'll go back to being chickens, we'll settle back down. And people thought, okay, how do we make the fox go away faster? He should rather have said we're going to do something fundamentally different that's going to disrupt your world and it will stay disrupted, because the model will be 100% different. He did not say that, probably because a key KPI of a CEO is to keep employees happy. He is measured on feedback from employees, and that's wrong.* (P1)

Managers should change their way of thinking and credit the new way of working (P4). P8 commented that one manager 'effectively congratulated his team on surviving ET'. Leaders should give people room to experiment, learn and fail (P7). A change management approach is causing digital transformation to fail. People's jobs, their future, their pay, their bonus, their SLAs depend on them not joining the enterprise transformation, not taking the journey (P2). Organisations should therefore not keep incentivising and rewarding people for their current job. They should be rewarded for supporting the transformation:

> *As soon as someone sees the new world, they cannot unsee it; they can no longer stay in the old world.* (P1)

The experts emphasised that they are not saying that change management is bad, but that it is simply the wrong technique for digital transformation. Instead of change management, organisations need 'chaos management', i.e. a catalyst for change and innovation in organisations.

5. DISCUSSION AND CONCLUSIONS

Digital transformation is different from anything a company has experienced before. Companies that start a digital transformation with a focus on technology are often disappointed; their investments and efforts don't have the intended impact (Kane, 2019). Organisations and leaders that understand what facilitates employee engagement will be more successful with their DBT (Solberg et al., 2020; Matricano et al., 2023; Tiefenbeck, 2017). Change and innovation is often greeted with fear or mistrust (Benavides et al., 2021; Prentice, 2022), which results in negative political behaviours that maximise self-interest and conflict with the goals and interests of others. Understanding the change in employee attitudes and the way in which DBT is managed is an important field of research (Matricano, 2023; Stonehouse & Konina, 2019).

A successful transformation requires 'outside-in thinking'. The focus group participants explained that the ET team do not want to understand what the current processes or systems look like or what people are currently doing. They're starting with the new and working back to see what must be changed in the old (P1). The research participants aim to move employees' mindset from *You don't understand, we've been doing it this way for years and we cannot do it differently* towards *What must we do to transform, what are the risks, and can we live with them?* The research participants posit that DBT is not just a 'hop and a skip', but it requires a jump into the future, which means leaving everything behind.

The most effective way to get people's support for the transformation is by starting small with an area of the business that has a low turnover and is not a flagship area. Then, build the platform out slowly in iterative releases, showing success, until eventually most of the company has been transformed. Some of the good employees can be asked to transition across and manage the new environment. It takes a strong leader to manage a company that focuses on today and tomorrow at the same time whilst keeping these parts separate and then motivate enough people to transition across to the new ways of working (P1). Literature refers to this ability as organisational ambidexterity (O'Reilly & Tushman, 2013).

Leadership alignment and employee buy-in and commitment plays a critical role in the transformation journey (Lardi, 2023; Stonehouse & Konina, 2019). Leaders must assess their own fundamental beliefs about the changes, i.e., their 'digital mindset' (Solberg et al., 2020) and carefully consider the explicit and implicit messages they convey to employees (Larjovuori et al., 2018). To enable this, Kotter (2014) and Reynolds (2018) posit that 'change leadership' is required, which is significantly different from change management as it does not aim to contain and manage the effects of change, but is consciously disruptive, constantly challenging the status quo and looking for innovation opportunities. The research participants refer to such a change leadership approach as 'chaos management'.

From the research, the following propositions are formulated:

Proposition 1: DBT is different, it requires outside-in thinking', working back from the future vision to the present.

Proposition 2: The best way to transform is to start with a small part of the business and show success.

Proposition 3: DBT requires strong leadership and a strong message of support by senior executives.

Proposition 4: Change management approaches are unsuitable for DBT; it requires change leadership or chaos management. It requires a hop, skip.. and jump.

In summary, all companies, leaders, and employees can learn to thrive in a digital transformation if they approach it in the right way. As Solberg et al. (2020) laments: 'If only digital transformation had been named more completely ... if only it had been branded the digital transformation of people!'

This paper is limited in its generalisability, as only one focus group session was conducted. However, we believe that the data captures the perspectives of an experienced team of experts who have each been responsible for various enterprise transformations. For future research, we suggest exploration of the propositions and the emotional aspects of DBT.

ACKNOWLEDGEMENT

The author sincerely thanks the participants in the focus group for their time and valuable contributions.

REFERENCES

Alieva J. & Powell D.J., 2023. The significance of employee behaviours and soft management practices to avoid digital waste during a digital transformation. International Journal of Lean Six Sigma, Vol. 14, No. 1, pp 1-32.

Benavides C. & Arias J. & Burgos D., 2021. Behavior Analysis of Digital Transformation in Latin American and Colombian Universities, Based on a General Identification of Variables. 10.1007/978-981-16-3941-8_8

Bloomberg J., 2016. How To Sabotage Your Digital Initiative Forbes, https://www.forbes.com/sites/jasonbloomberg/2016/12/27/how-to-sabotage-your-digital-initiative/?sh=2a4a31a75ddb

Chevallard F., 2023. A Behavioral Guide to Digital Transformation. Neurofied, https://sloanreview.mit.edu/article/neutralize-internal-politics-in-digital-initiatives/

Denning S., 2023. Recognizing and outmaneuvering the resistance to digital transformation. Strategy & Leadership, Vol. 51, No. 2, pp 10-16.

Jarrett M., 2017. The 4 Types of Organizational Politics. Harvard Business Review, https://hbr.org/2017/04/the-4-types-of-organizational-politics

Kane G., 2019. The Technology Fallacy. Research-Technology Management, Vol. 62, No. 6, pp 44- 49. DOI: 10.1080/08956308.2019.1661079

Koor & Associates, 2023. Transformation success depends upon human behaviour change, pp 1-2. https:// koorandassociates.files.wordpress.com/2021/05/transformation-success-depends-upon-human-behaviour-change.pdf

Kotter, J. P., 2014. Accelerate: Building Strategic Agility for a Faster-Moving World. Harvard Business Review Press.

Lardi K., 2023. *The Human Side of Digital Business Transformation*. Wiley, Sussex, UK, pp 1-301.

Larjovuori R., Bordi L. & Heikkilä-Tammi K., 2018. Leadership in the digital business transformation. *Proceedings of the 22nd International Academic Mindtrek Conference,* New York, pp 212-221.

Magnusson J., Elliot V. & Hagberg J., 2022. Digital transformation: why companies resist what they need for sustained performance. Journal of Business Strategy, Vol. 43, No. 5, pp 316-322.

Matricano D., Castaldi L. & Sorrentino M., 2022. The behavior of managers handling digital business transformations: theoretical issues and preliminary evidence from firms in the manufacturing industry. International Journal of Entrepreneurial Behavior & Research, Vol. 28 No. 5, pp 1292-1309.

McConnell J., 2017. Neutralize Internal Politics in Digital Initiatives. MIT Sloan Management Review, https://sloanreview.mit.edu/article/neutralize-internal-politics-in-digital-initiatives/

Meske C. & Junglas, I., 2021. Investigating the elicitation of employees' support towards digital workplace transformation. Behaviour & Information Technology, Vol. 40, No.11, pp 1120-1136.

Metallo C., Ferrara M., Lazazzara A. & Za, S., 2021. *Digital Transformation and Human Behavior: Innovation for People and Organisations*. Lecture Notes in Information Systems and Organisation, Springer, Vol. 37.

Mete I. & Eyel C.S., 2020. Investigating User Resistance of Employees Working at Technology Companies in Istanbul towards Digital Transformation. *Proceedings of International Journal of Information Science and Management*, Vol. 19, No. 2, pp 93-106.

Moretti L.T., 2020. Digital transformation is about human behaviour and culture, https://digileaders.com/digital-transformation-is-about-human-behaviour-and-culture/

O'Reilly III, C. A., & Tushman, M. L., 2013. Organizational ambidexterity: Past, present, and future. Academy of Management Perspectives, 27(4), 324-338.

Prentice S. 2022. *The Future of Workplace Fear: How Human Reflex Stands in the Way of Digital Transformation.* Springer, USA.

Reynolds P., 2018. Effective change leadership critical for successful digital transformation. Hydrocarbon Processing, https://www.arcweb.com/blog/effective-change-leadership-critical-successful-digital-transformation

Ridwansyah A., Lantu D.C. & Anggoro Y., 2023. Leadership dimensions and behaviors in business schools' forced digital transformation. *International Journal of Research in Business & Social Science*, Vol. 12, No. 3, pp 159-170.

Roberts D., 2022. How tech leaders can better navigate organizational politics. Feature Dec 14, 2022, https://www.cio.com/article/416180/how-tech-leaders-can-better-navigate-organizational-politics.html

Sainger G., 2018. Leadership in Digital Age: A Study on the Role of Leader in this Era of Digital Transformation. International Journal on Leadership, Vol. 6, No. 1, http://www.publishingindia.com

Scholkmann A.B. Resistance to (Digital) Change: Individual, Systemic and Learning-Related Perspectives. In D. Ifenthaler et al. (eds.), Digital Transformation of Learning Organizations, pp 219 – 236.

Solberg E., Traavik L.E.M & Wong S.I., 2020. Digital Mindsets: Recognizing and Leveraging Individual Beliefs for Digital Transformation. California Management Review, Vol. 62, No. 4, pp 105 –124.

Stonehouse G.H. & Konina N.Y., 2019. Management Challenges in the Age of Digital Disruption. Advances in Economics, Business and Management Research, Vol. 119.

Thomas J., 2019. Inside the Institutions: Culture and Communication from Digital Transformations to Automation. Cultural Studies Review, Vol. 25, No. 2, pp 89-95. http:// dx.doi.org/10.5130/csr. v25i2.6882

Tiefenbeck V., 2017. Bring behaviour into the digital transformation. Nature Energy, Vol. 2, pp 1-3.

Tiersky H. How to Sabotage a Digital Transformation. DX Weekly, https://www.linkedin.com/pulse/how-sabotage-digital-transformation-howard-tiersky-1e/

Trittin-Ulbrich H., Scherer, A. G., Munro, I., & Whelan, G., 2021. Exploring the dark and unexpected sides of digitalization: Toward a critical agenda. Organization, Vol. 28, No. 1, pp 8-25.

Visser J., 2022. Four Factors that Sabotage Digital Transformation. Architecture & Governance Magazine, https://www.architectureandgovernance.com/applications-technology/four-factors-that-sabotage-digital-transformation/

Wade M. & Obwegeser, N., 2019. How to Choose the Right Digital Leader for Your Company. MIT Sloan Management Review, https://mitsmr.com/2HtLYTg

Weber E., Büttgen, M. & Bartsch, S., 2022. How to take employees on the digital transformation journey: An experimental study on complementary leadership behaviors in managing organizational change. Journal of Business Research, Vol. 143, pp 225–238.

EXPLORING EMERGING BUSINESS MODELS FOR ELECTRIFIED MACHINERY

Saeid Heshmatisafa and Marko Seppänen
Unit of Information and Knowledge Management, Faculty of Management and Business, Tampere University, Finland

ABSTRACT

The heavy machinery industry is transitioning towards electric mobile working machines in response to increasing pressure to decarbonize. Despite recent technological advancements in electric vehicles, mainstream adoption remains challenging. The economic sustainability of these machines depends not only on technological development but also on the implementation of innovative business models. This study analyzed 684 documents from the LexisNexis Academic database, focusing on the mining industry, through thematic content analysis. The results revealed seven sustainable business model archetypes and 22 specific business models, including Deliver functionality, rather than ownership, Sustainable Intelligence, Skill sharing, Sustainable Energy Transition, Create value from 'waste', Carbon Stewardship, and Eco-Commercial Synergy. By bridging the gap between technological innovation and economic feasibility, these initiatives aim to facilitate the widespread adoption of electric machinery in the mining industry and beyond.

KEYWORDS

Sustainable Value Creation, Sustainable Business Model, Green Companies, Electrified Machinery, Decarbonization

1. INTRODUCTION

The world's energy sources are changing. Recent geopolitical developments and the demand for decarbonization require significant changes across all industries to devise net-zero pledges. The commitment to achieve carbon neutrality by the year 2050 makes electrification a critical enabler to reaching net-zero emissions (e.g., Williams et al., 2021). In this regard, the heavy machinery industry is entering a new era with electric mobile working machines (e-MWMs). These machines aim to reduce scope 1 and scope 2 emissions.

"Mobile working machines" refers wheeled or tracked machines that are targeted at specific tasks in off-road conditions. Unlike stationary industrial machines with fixed operational procedures, mobile working machines are subject to various demands, including forestry (e.g., forwarders and harvesters), construction and mining (e.g., loaders, dumpers, and excavators), and cargo handling (e.g., forklifts and mobile cranes). As these industries are the world's largest carbon emitters - the mining sector alone accounts for 4 to 7 percent of global greenhouse gas emissions – decarbonizing these machines will significantly impact international decarbonization efforts.

Despite recent technological advancements of electric machineries, electrification faces challenges in penetrating mainstream markets. A major obstacle is prevailing business practices that heavily rely on fossil fuels (Jacobsson, 2004). In the case of e-MWMs, what matters most is recognizing that the economic sustainability of electric vehicles depends on their business models (Dunbar et al., 2020; Kley et al., 2011). Therefore, the research question is formulated as follows: *What are the emerging sustainable business model innovations enabled by the electrification of machinery in the mining industry?* We focus on MWMs in the mining industry as they have idiosyncratic characteristics in complex industrial products. These characteristics include incumbents seeking to leverage their capital-intensive investments and exploit recent technological innovations, but a strong culture around MWMs, resistant to change, challenges the transition (Luthra et al., 2011).

2. PREVIOUS WORKS

2.1 Evolution of Electric Vehicles and Prospects

Recent improvements in lithium-ion batteries have enhanced energy density, charging times, and efficiency, making them suitable for heavy-duty applications in mining (Feng et al., 2022). Additionally, geopolitical factors and climate change have incited national and international programs to support vehicle electrification. For instance, European policy measures aim to halve the number of fossil-fueled vehicles by 2030 (Amanatidis, 2020). Mining industry is highly regulated, placing it at the forefront of heavy-duty sectors experiencing this revolution (Hristova, 2024). According to a study by Paraszczak et al. (2014), replacing diesel-powered machinery with electric alternatives can reduce air pollutants by up to 64% in underground mining operations. This reduction not only helps mining companies meet stringent environmental regulations but also contributes to global efforts to combat climate change. For instance, the new threshold limit value–time-weighted average limits for NO2 (0.5 ppm) and diesel particulate matter (DPM) (0.05 mg/m^3 of elemental carbon) pose compliance challenges for diesel machines, even those equipped with Euro VI compliant engines, making e-MWMs the most feasible option to comply (Gyamfi et al., 2022). Additionally, the European European Commission's 'Fit for 55' package includes the new Carbon Border Adjustment Mechanism, which will tax diesel machinery starting in 2027 to incentivize cleaner fuel use (European Commission, 2023).

The economic benefits of e-MWMs are also noteworthy. While the initial investment in electric machinery is higher than that for diesel-powered equipment, the long-term operational costs are significantly lower. e-MWMs have fewer moving parts, resulting in lower maintenance costs and longer lifespans (Nieto et al., 2020). They do not emit CO2, DPM, and produce significantly less heat, thus reducing ventilation needs and operational expenses (Gyamfi et al., 2022). Furthermore, the cost of electricity is often lower and more stable than diesel fuel, resulting in substantial savings over the equipment's lifetime (Paraszczak et al., 2014).

Several mining companies have begun to adopt e-MWMs. For instance, the Borden Gold Mine in Ontario, Canada, the world's first all-electric underground mine where all machines are battery electric vehicles (BEVs), significantly reducted emissions and operational costs (Gyamfi et al., 2022). Similarly, inspired by the success of the Diavik Diamond Mine, the Raglan nickel mine in northern Quebec, Canada, constructed a 6 MW wind farm paired with a 3 MW multi-storage system in 2015 to meet 10 percent of its power requirements. This renewable energy system saves 4.4 million liters of diesel fuel annually, reduces carbon emissions by 12,000 tonnes, and eliminates the equivalent emissions of 2,700 vehicles from the roads (Kalantari et al., 2021).

2.2 Sustainable Business Model Innovation

Business Model Innovation (BMI) refers to a new way to create and capture value by designing a novel business model (BM) or reconfiguring an existing one (Geissdoerfer et al., 2018). Innovation for sustainability aims to create positive social or environmental impact. Sustainable business model innovation (SBMI), a type of sustainable innovation, seeks beyond generating economic benefits and calls considering other types of benefits (i.e., ecological, and social) to balance the competing and complementary interests of all involved stakeholders (Evans et al., 2017; Schaltegger et al., 2016). Business sustainability should therefore ensure economic viability while also contributing to societal and environmental sustainability. Studies show that BMI can be crucial in promoting sustainability, unlike the limitations of relying solely on technological innovation (Girotra & Netessine, 2013). In addition, while technological innovation is industry specific, BMI can be applied across various sectors, allowing companies to adopt models from other fields.

Academic literature offers various methods and tools to facilitate innovation for sustainable transitions (Pieroni et al., 2019; Rosa et al., 2019). Archetypes are one the tools focusing on grouping different mechanisms or solutions to create or modify BMs for specific purposes like a circular economy or sustainability (Bocken et al., 2014). These archetypes span perspectives from product technology to company-centric viewpoints. From a product technology perspective, SBMIs aim to minimize resource usage through efficiency, promote resource reuse via closed-loop production, or use renewable resources (Lüdeke-Freund et al., 2018).

From a functional perspective, they replace ownership with services to deliver functionalities, ensure supply chain sustainability, or promote sustainable consumption (Bocken et al., 2014). Functionality delivery meets customer needs through sharing options and usage-based pricing (Bocken et al., 2014; Clinton & Whisnant,

2019). Stewardship ensures ethical sourcing (Bocken et al., 2014; Wells, 2015), while sufficiency aims to alter consumption patterns and promote long-life products (Clinton & Whisnant, 2019).

From a company perspective, SBM patterns include scaling solutions, inclusive value creation, and repurposing for societal and environmental benefits (Bocken et al., 2014; Lüdeke-Freund et al., 2018). Scaling solutions propagate sustainable value through open innovation or franchising models (Bocken et al., 2014; Clinton & Whisnant, 2019). Inclusive value creation mitigates unsustainable impacts through shared or collaborative consumption (Bocken et al., 2014; Palmié et al., 2021). Repurposing prioritizes environmental and social benefits using models like cooperative ownership and net-positive initiatives (Bocken et al., 2014; Clinton & Whisnant, 2019; Lüdeke-Freund et al., 2018). These classifications often overlap, and inconsistent terminology hinders communication among researchers and practitioners. Further, there has been insufficient focus on decarbonization and ecological SBMIs. A decarbonization lens support national and international initiatives and unlocks new avenues for business value creation.

3. METHODOLOGICAL APPROACH

To identify emerging BMs enabled by the electrification of MWMs, we conducted a content analysis based on news articles. News articles reflect expert narratives on prominent insights into industry changes, offering contextual meanings for two reasons:.1) Scientific journals predominantly focus on analytical descriptions of established BMs, often omitting emerging ones, and.2) news articles offer narrative descriptions that capture the dynamic and evolving nature of these BMs, highlighting new opportunities arising from the sustainable transition within the landscape of MWMs.

We selected the mining industry due to its idiosyncratic and complex industrial characteristics. This sector is characterized by incumbents leveraging their capital-intensive investments in plants, patents, and tools, with a focus on efficiency and the utilization of accumulated manufacturing knowledge (Sánchez & Hartlieb, 2020). The mining industry is undergoing a significant transformation towards digitalization and sustainability, resulting in the emergence of new ecosystems and BMs (Heshmatisafa & Seppänen, 2023, 2024). Apart from identifying emerging BMs, we also include established ones, as it is necessary to understand conventional BMs within the sector. Hence, theoretical sampling was deemed appropriate to ensure the inclusion of the most important SBMIs (Research approach is depicted in Figure 1).

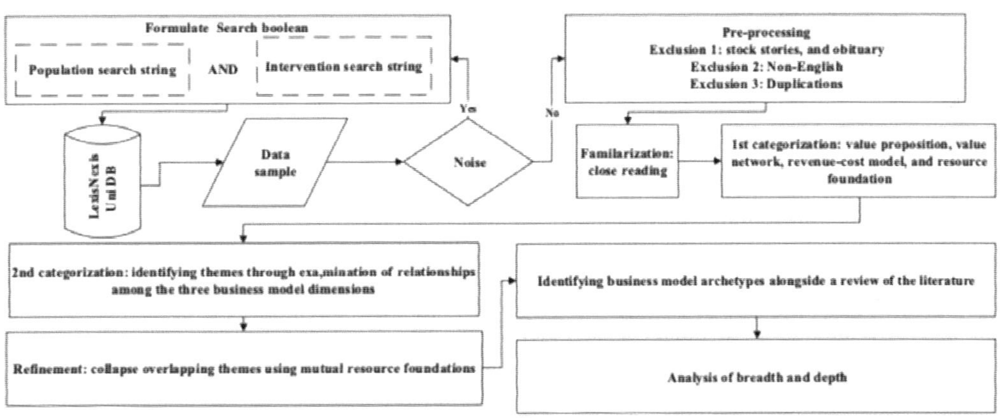

Figure 1. Graphical representation of the research design

To systematically collect and review gray literature, we followed the PRISMA-S statement checklist by Rethlefsen et al. (2021). This approach consists of four main steps: 1) information sources 2) search strategies 3) peer review and 4) managing record. Aiming to derive a comprehensive set of BMs and archetypes, we used LexisNexis Uni news database (over 15,000 sources) to collect a large dataset of relevant articles. An initial search string was aligned with the study's scope, structured within the established 'population' and 'intervention' framework described by Kitchenham et al. (2011). We used the case "industry" (i.e., mining industry) as the unit of population and the phenomena in question (i.e., sustainable business model) as the unit of intervention.

The initial formulated search string was then used in a pilot search to identify noise and irrelevant articles. Subsequently, a random sample of 50 search results was extracted to provide an overview of noise in the dataset. Afterwards, a primary screening was conducted using keyword frequency analysis to identify terms contributing to noise within the sample. For example, the term "mining industry" is used in both the contexts of mineral mining and extraction and text mining and extraction. Hence, each block of the search string was refined by incorporating exclusion or inclusion criteria, such as adding 'not Text mining' in this instance. This iterative refinement process continued until data saturation was reached, ensuring no new relevant information emerged and an adequate dataset size was obtained. Table 1 demonstrates the final two blocks of keywords used in combination with Boolean operators ('AND' and 'OR') to encompass multiple facets of e-MWMs and SBMIs, yielding results that contained keywords related to both concepts.

Table 1. Boolean search query blocks used in the search settings

Block	Keywords
Electric mobility working machine industry	industry("Electric Mobility" AND "Electric Vehicles" AND "Sustainable Transportation" AND "Mine & Mining")
Sustainable business model	("decarboni*ation" OR "sustainable value" OR "sustainable practice" OR "business model" OR "business model" OR "green model" OR "circular economy" OR "sustainable development" OR "sustainable orientation") AND not Text mining AND not Lithium

The final two blocks of keywords resulted in 1000 articles, in which stock stories, and obituary documents were excluded. The results were further filtered to include only English business news, and duplicates were removed. his process yielded a preliminary collection of 684 documents with 54,528 words. The Number of articles per source type were: 234 independent reports, 157 journalistic articles, 120 company reports, 30 academic paper, and 153 government reports.

Given the multidisciplinary nature of the retrieved documents, thorough filtering, analysis, and synthesis were essential. We employed a five-step qualitative analysis procedure for content analysis as outlined by Thomas (2006): 1) preparation of raw files, 2) close reading of the text, 3) creation of categories, 4) overlapping of coding and uncoded text, and 5) continuous revision and refinement of the category system.

Initially, we imported the filtered dataset into the qualitative data analysis software, Atlas.ti, for organization and coding. We then immersed ourselves in the data reading and digesting to understand "what is going on" through reflexivity and open-mindedness. After familiarizing ourselves with the dataset, we utilized a semi-structured coding scheme to analyze the data. This involved a sequential approach: starting with a deductive method based on existing literature, followed by an inductive method to derive themes directly from the data. This approach complemented our research question by integrating BM phenomenology into the deductive content analysis process, while also allowing themes to emerge organically through inductive coding.

Using the deductive approach, BMs enabled by the e-MWMs in the mining sector were examined. Relevant statements were coded into categories representing key components of the BM: value proposition, value network, and revenue-cost model. This granularity facilitated the comparability of different BMs. During the coding process, statements demonstrating a causal relationship to value creation and value capture characteristics were highlighted and coded. In addition, we highlighted and coded statements related to resource foundations, such as digital technologies.

The inductive approach derived themes from the data. Relationships among the three BM dimensions (i.e., value proposition, value network, and revenue-cost model) were examined to identify themes. These themes were then refined by collapsing overlapping and ambiguous relationships into higher-level themes using resource foundations. This iterative process, conducted alongside a review of the literature, helped derive criteria for identifying BM archetypes. Ultimately, the themes were assigned to different archetypes, allowing for the identification and comparison of six distinct archetypes. Table 2 provides examples of the final codes and themes based on the text content. All archetypes and their interactions were then consolidated into a matrix to construct the evolution of individual BMs and their narrative descriptions (see Table 3 in the next section).

Table 2. Example of final codes and themes based on the text content

Quote from the textual content	Code	Theme
"Bellevue believes that there could be a potential market for net-zero emissions gold which could increase demand for gold produced at Bellevue and potentially attract a premium."	Certified net-zero emission products	Eco-Commercial Synergy
"ZERO Automotive is a cleantech mobility company founded in 2018 which creates a sustainable future by decarbonizing environments through custom battery electric Light Vehicle (bELV) conversions of internal combustion engine vehicles (ICEV)."	Remanufacturing and conversion	Resource Valorization and Transformation
"Global engineering group Sandvik has signed a memorandum of understanding (MOU) with Northern College, a post-secondary apprenticeship and industry training provider, to work collaboratively to develop a Northern College Battery Electric Vehicle (BEV) Technician program."	Platform as a service	Skill sharing
"Epiroc, which uses power packs made up of Northvolt AB, said the initial cost of buying a battery-powered vehicle would be about double that of a conventional one. While that is offset by lower fuel and energy costs, the initial expense could be prohibitive. In an attempt to increase sales, Epiroc will rent batteries for its new line of vehicles, which would cause the initial cost to be only slightly higher than an equivalent diesel machine."	Battery as a services	Integrated Product-Service Ecosystem

4. KEY INSIGHTS

Widespread adaptation of e-MWMs depends on the development of new innovative BMs. This involves rethinking partnerships to foster new collaborative BMs. Using thematic content analysis, we identified seven SBMI archetypes and 22 BMs within mining e-MWMs industry. The overview of the archetypes and their contrast with each other in terms of the configuration of their value propositions, value networks, and revenue–cost models are presented at Table 3. In the following we introduce each archetype.

4.1 Deliver Functionality Rather than Ownership

This archetype has been widely debated, particularly regarding the need to understand changes in consumption patterns by reducing the initial purchasing costs and the need for product ownership (Bocken et al., 2014; Clinton & Whisnant, 2019). e-MWMs are capital-intensive (two to two-and-a-half times the price of a comparable diesel machine), and reducing upfront costs increases commercialization and customer willingness to pay. This concept is based on Product-Service Systems and Servitization, shifting from offering a manufactured product (i.e., product-oriented) to a combination of products and services such as Battery as a Service, and various leasing and renting solutions (Tukker, 2015).

The value proposition includes diversified offerings that provide complementary solutions to customers to improve their experience. These may include removing the responsibility of equipment ownership and shifting costs from a capital expenditure to operating expense, potentially offering tax deductions. Most OEMs, namely Caterpillar and Volvo, are developing such BMs in-house or in collaboration with external parties such as financial solution providers and rental companies. However, adopting servitization models requires considerable changes, such as redesigning for durability, reparability, and upgradability. Since customers use these solutions as needed, so they should be guaranteed to be available and function properly.

These BMs generate revenue through various schemes, such as delivering functionality (i.e., result-oriented) on a pay-per-use basis or delivering use (i.e., use-oriented) via rent or leasing. These models are based on establishing trust and long-term relationships with customers, creating a lock-in mechanism, being data-intensive, and offering opportunities for innovation. Data obtained through various channels, such as application programming interfaces (APIs), is an important non-monetary revenue stream, particularly in the form of industry insights such as customer needs, changes in customer behavior, and market vibrancy.

Table 3. The overview of business model archetypes enabled by electric mobile working machines

Description	Business models	Value proposition	Value network	Revenue-cost model
		Deliver functionality, rather than ownership		
Adjacent business models that complement the core business by creating synergy while expanding into new solutions and ecosystems	• Battery as a services • Machine as a service	• Access to Functionality without Ownership • Flexible Usage Options • Enhanced Product Reliability • Tax Deductions and Variable Costs	• Dependent on financial Partners • Data Partners • Mostly outsourced to external ecosystem	• Diversified revenue model (renting, various leasing options, Pay-Per-Use) • Service Fees • Data Monetization
		Sustainable intelligence		
Focusing on maximizing productivity, enhancing resource efficiency, and minimizing waste through digital technologies combined with data analytics.	• Software as a service • Data-Driven Services • Digital twin as a service	• Cost Reduction (e.g., energy, water, material) • Improve productivity • End-to-end operational visibility • Improve environmental sustainability	• Dependent on external knowledge and technology provider • Platform approach, functions as a gatekeeper	• Diversified revenue model (freemium, premium, subscription, pay per use) • License for software • Data are considered a non-monetary revenue stream but play a relatively minor role
		Skill sharing		
Facilitating the exchange of knowledge and expertise to enhance collective skills, promote collaboration, and drive mutual growth and development	• Platform as a service • Subscription Training Pass • Bundle training • Pay-Per-Class Training	• Community support • Aspiring technicians • Improve • Improve reputation • Environmental and social sustainability	• Dependent on external distribution networks • Mostly outsourced to external ecosystem	• Diversified revenue model (subscription, pay per use, bundle license)
		Sustainable energy transition		
Facilitating the shift from traditional energy sources to renewable and low-carbon alternatives	• Energy as a service • Power Purchase Agreements • Renewable Integration • Battery Energy Storage Systems	• Reduce energy cost • Improve reputation • Environmental sustainability	• Dependent on external knowledge and technology provider • Mostly outsourced to external ecosystem	• Diversified revenue model (fixed rate, progressive purchasing, pay per use, Net metering, dynamic pricing) • Data monetization
		Create value from 'waste'		
Enhancing the value of resources through innovative processes and technologies, converting waste or impending waste into valuable products and/or services	• Remanufacturing and conversion • Circular economy • Reuse and second life	• Environmental sustainability • Energy cost saving • Regulatory Compliance • Corporate Social Responsibility	• Dependent on external knowledge and technology • Outsourced to external ecosystem	• Licensing • Energy sales • Data monetization • Service frees • Product sales
		Carbon stewardship		
Focuses on strategies to manage, mitigate, and remediate environmental emissions, aiming to "helping nature to repair itself"	• Carbon capture and utilization • Carbon sequestering • Carbon offset • Carbon credit	• Economic Incentives • Environmental Sustainability • Market Differentiation • Long-term Resilience	• Dependent on external stakeholders • Outsourced to external ecosystem	• Project-Based Pricing • Bundled Pricing • Tiered Pricing • Value-Based Pricing • Cost-Plus Pricing
		Eco-Commercial Synergy		
Integrating ecological sustainability with commercial viability to attract financial capital to support sustainable solutions	• Government-Supported Commercialization • Certified net-zero emission products • Green bond framework • ESG/impact investment	• Environmental Sustainability • Financial Incentives • Market Differentiation • Increase commercialization • Take accountability for sustainable investment • Improve reputation • Quantifying investment social and environmental sustainability	• Dependent on external stakeholders • Mostly outsourced to external ecosystem	• Premium pricing • Government funds and subsidies • Impact investment and green bond returns • Carbon credits

4.2 Sustainable Intelligence

Here, BMs focus on maximizing productivity, enhancing resource efficiency, and minimizing waste using digital technologies combined with data analytics. Companies leverage machine-to-machine and machine-to-cloud connectivity to offer services such as automation and maintenance recommendations. They provide the basic set-up for digital initiatives in e-MWMs and develop smart solutions in collaboration with the OEMs, who in turn pass them on to the customer. These services aim to improve material handling, identify critical areas, ensure site and operator protection, and reduce energy and resource. Consequently, the value propositions encompass a wide range of services, emphasizing sustainable management practices and advisory services. For example, by utilizing digital technologies like the Internet of Things (IoT) and APIs, along with advanced analytics, companies can augment realities and optimize automated processes in mining operations. OEMs such as Sandvik and Epiroc collaborate with technology firms like Rockwell and ABB to integrate electric machinery with IoT devices. This integration result in solutions that enhance process efficiencies, cost control, and worker health and safety. These solutions may include complementary add-ons or stand-alone services that create new revenue streams.

Such solutions are offered through various revenue models, including "Free/Freemium/Premium" subscriptions, modular pricing, and software licensing. Additionally, the integration of electric machines with IoT devices not only improves operational efficiencies but also generates valuable customer data. Monetizing this data presents a potential new revenue stream, although it is not yet widely recognized.

4.3 Skill Sharing

Another set of firms has adopted the skill share archetype to address workforce skills and compliance tracking challenges. Due to the novelty of these machines, there is a lack of standards for battery types, charging stations, and connections. Additionally, e-WMWs have fewer mechanical components and more electrical components than diesel-powered machines, requiring a different skill set for servicing and maintaining e-fleets.

To address this need, companies such as MyPass and Northern College, through a Memorandum of Understanding (MOU), collaborated with OEMs and mining companies to train a new generation of service technicians. These training programs are delivered through various methods, including on-site training, online courses, and digital platforms, ensuring accessibility and flexibility for different learning preferences. The identified BMs include Platform as a Service (PaaS), subscription-based Training Passes, bundled training packages, and pay-per-class options.

The most prominent BM is Paas, which connects workers, employers, and training providers on a single platform. This integrated approach facilitates seamless skill-sharing and continuous learning, critical for keeping up with regulatory and technological advancements in the industry. Firms in this archetype believe that sharing skills and educating the workforce not only generates income but addresses skill gaps and enhance workforce competency. Moreover, it enhances the reputation of all involved parties by showcasing their commitment to innovation and sustainable practices. The revenue models are similarly diversified, encompassing subscription fees, pay-per-use options, and bundled licenses.

4.4 Sustainable Energy Transition

Sustainable Energy Transition involves providing renewable energy services, such as solar and wind-generated electricity. This archetype stems from the increasing development of electrified machines, which raises concerns about electricity demand and the energy sources necessary for decarbonization. The rising demand presents opportunities across all three scopes of emissions within the electrification value chain, including green energy, energy storage, and charging infrastructure, supporting the transformative shift in the mining sector. Consequently, numerous companies are transitioning into providers of sustainable energy solutions.

For example, Shell has transformed from a traditional oil and gas company into an energy transition company. Shell offers onsite renewable energy solutions and battery storage to address intermittent issues, along with micro-grids for distributed energy management. These solutions aim to reduce energy costs by utilizing various energy sources, such as solar, wind, hydrogen, or biofuels, while creating positive environmental and social impacts. This shift improves the company's reputation and addresses skill shortages. Several mines have already started large-scale initiatives to fully renewable electricity: Rio Tinto's

Gudai-Darri mine will have 65% of its total electricity consumption supplied by a combination of solar farms and battery storage; Boliden has already set up a pantograph-charged hybrid at Aitik; and Newmont Goldcorp has established the world's first fully electric mine at Borden (Kalantari et al., 2021).

BMs within this archetype include Energy as a Service, Power Purchase Agreements, Renewable Integration, and Energy Storage Systems. These models generate diverse revenue streams, such as fixed rates, progressive purchasing, pay-per-use, net metering, and dynamic pricing. Additionally, data monetization, even in non-monetary forms, is a central component of these BMs.

4.5 Carbon Stewardship

Companies in this archetype aims to provide comprehensive strategies for managing and mitigating environmental emissions and damages through a combination of carbon capture, utilization, sequestration, credit, and offset mechanisms. Emerging companies like Vedanta are developing solutions to capture CO2 emissions from industrial processes or power plants. These captured emissions can be repurposed to produce chemicals, fuels (a.k.a., the synthetic fuel pathway), or building materials. They also are developing novel services to transform mine waste into valuable resources through carbon sequestering. This process involves long-term capture and storage of byproducts such temperature, pressure, and carbon emissions to prevent their release into the atmosphere. For example, BHP is investing in carbon capture and storage projects to sequester CO2 from their mining operations in deep geological formations.

Additionally, companies can offset emissions by investing in environmental projects that reduce or sequester carbon. In the mining sector, companies like Vale have invested in reforestation projects to redemiate their carbon footprint. As carbon credits become scarce, companies are proactively acquiring additional credits, can be traded in carbon markets, providing an economic incentive to adopt sustainable practices. For instance, Anglo American engages in carbon credit markets to balance their operational emissions.

The value propositions include economic incentives, environmental sustainability, market differentiation, and long-term resilience. Engaging with government programs, investors, stakeholders, and certification bodies creates a strong value network that supports these initiatives. The revenue models for these business initiatives are diverse and innovative. Project-based and bundled pricing allows companies to offer comprehensive carbon management solutions tailored to specific client needs. Tiered pricing provides different Additionally, cost-plus pricing ensures transparency by adding a standard profit margin to the costs of carbon management projects.

4.6 Eco-Commercial Synergy

The final archetype bridge sustainability and profitability through four key BM initiatives that facilitates the large-scale development of sustainable solutions. Government programs and investors play a crucial role by providing the necessary financial resources to accelerate the commercialization of e-MWMs, advance clean technologies, create jobs, and reduce greenhouse gas emissions. Companies are also designing their own BMs to enter the low-carbon economy, such as offering certified net-zero emissions products at premium prices. For instance, Bellevue offers stakeholders the opportunity to purchase certified net-zero emissions gold. Additionally, companies like Epiroc have designed green bond frameworks and ESG impact investments to take accountability, allowing investors to finance sustainable investments that promote climate-resilient growth and the transition to a zero-waste and low-carbon environment. These BMs also enable investors to quantify their assets' impact.

The value propositions focus on enabling participatory activities in the expanding opportunities within sustainable businesses. Engaging with government programs, investors, stakeholders, and certification bodies forms a robust support network. Revenue models include premium pricing for certified net-zero emissions products, securing government funds, and attracting environmentally conscious investments. Additionally, companies generate revenue by selling carbon credits associated with net-zero emissions products.

5. CONCLUSION

This paper attempted to reveal the emerging SBMIs in the mining industry, driven by electrification and decarbonization. The economic sustainability of electric machineries depends on their BMs (Dunbar et al., 2020; Kley et al., 2011). We contribute to expanding the body of knowledge of SBMI by identifying seven BM archetypes and 22 BM initiatives, showing how diverse stakeholders in the value network can construct a novel business practice by engaging with decarbonization efforts and gaining positive contributions regarding economic, social, and environmental impacts. The adoption of electrification depends on the local power-generation mix, highlighting the importance of renewable-generation capacity. Electrification needs to be seen as an opportunity to improve energy efficiency and reduce emissions, rather than simply replacing conventional equipment. In addition to saving the world, decarbonization can also be good for business.

Our results extend SBMI archetypes (Bocken et al., 2014) to the mining industry. The underlying research identifies which sustainability strategies and BMs are employed for sustainability and decarbonization across the value network of the mining industry. The expectation is that these archetypes can assist entrepreneurs in analyzing sustainable strategies broadly and in designing specific BM characteristics. Novel and young companies, often seen as initiators of sustainability transitions (Schaltegger et al., 2016), can particularly benefit from this research.

Depending on a company's current BM, firms can use the identified models to sense opportunities for exploration or to redesign and reconfigure their existing BMs for exploitation, thereby overcoming inertia to change.For instance, a mining company can use the Eco-Commercial Synergy archetype to innovate its BM, transitioning towards more sustainability-oriented value creation. This transition also ensures financial sustainability through the production of certified net-zero emission products, achieved by decarbonizing all three scopes of emissions.

Our research solely focused on exploring emerging SBMIs within the mining industry, specifically targeting e-MWMs. Although we argue that innovative BMs can be tailored and leveraged across various sectors, we acknowledge that developing new BMs should be iterative and ongoing, with significant potential for exploring radical innovations to transform the industry and enhance its image (Bocken et al., 2014). Naturally, after identifying novel BMs, the next step is evaluating, testing, and validating them in large settings. Future studies could look at the BM adaptation process of realized BMs. In addition, it is expected that large language models can be trained using Table 3 along with similar studies (Bocken et al., 2014; Lüdeke-Freund et al., 2018) to automate identification of BMs with weak signals and industry profile of BM portfolio.

REFERENCES

Amanatidis, G. (2020). European policies on climate and energy towards 2020, 2030 and 2050.

Bocken, N. M. P., Short, S. W., Rana, P., & Evans, S. (2014). A literature and practice review to develop sustainable business model archetypes. Journal of Cleaner Production, 65, 42–56. https://doi.org/10.1016/j.jclepro.2013.11.039

Clinton, L., & Whisnant, R. (2019). Business Model Innovations for Sustainability. In G. G. Lenssen & N. C. Smith (Eds.), Managing Sustainable Business: An Executive Education Case and Textbook (pp. 463–503). Springer Netherlands. https://doi.org/10.1007/978-94-024-1144-7_22

Dunbar, W. S., Fraser, J., Reynolds, A., & Kunz, N. C. (2020). Mining needs new business models. The Extractive Industries and Society, 7(2), 263–266. https://doi.org/10.1016/j.exis.2019.07.007

European Commission. (2023). Carbon Border Adjustment Mechanism—European Commission. https://taxation-customs.ec.europa.eu/carbon-border-adjustment-mechanism_en

Evans, S., Vladimirova, D., Holgado, M., Van Fossen, K., Yang, M., Silva, E. A., & Barlow, C. Y. (2017). Business Model Innovation for Sustainability: Towards a Unified Perspective for Creation of Sustainable Business Models. Business Strategy and the Environment, 26(5), 597–608. https://doi.org/10.1002/bse.1939

Feng, Y., Liu, Q., Li, Y., Yang, J., & Dong, Z. (2022). Energy efficiency and CO2 emission comparison of alternative powertrain solutions for mining haul truck using integrated design and control optimization. Journal of Cleaner Production, 370, 133568. https://doi.org/10.1016/j.jclepro.2022.133568

Geissdoerfer, M., Vladimirova, D., & Evans, S. (2018). Sustainable business model innovation: A review. Journal of Cleaner Production, 198, 401–416. https://doi.org/10.1016/j.jclepro.2018.06.240

Girotra, K., & Netessine, S. (2013). OM forum—Business model innovation for sustainability. Manufacturing & Service Operations Management, 15(4), 537–544.

Gyamfi, S., Halim, A., & Martikainen, A. (2022). Development of Strategies to Reduce Ventilation and Heating Costs in a Swedish Sublevel Caving Mine—A Unique Case of LKAB's Konsuln Mine. Mining, Metallurgy & Exploration, 39(2), 221–238. https://doi.org/10.1007/s42461-021-00483-y

Heshmatisafa, S., & Seppänen, M. (2023). Business model diversification through Product-Service Systems: Demand-relatedness perspective. Proceedings of XXXIV ISPIM Innovation Conference.

Heshmatisafa, S., & Seppänen, M. (2024). Exploring the Dynamics of Business Model Portfolio: Unveiling Strategic restructuring. 2024 Portland International Conference on Management of Engineering and Technology (PICMET).

Hristova, T. (2024). Tracking mining company electric vehicles for sustainable development optimization using Distributed Ledger Technologies. Journal of Sustainable Mining, 23(3), 299–314. https://doi.org/10.46873/2300-3960.1425

Jacobsson, S. (2004). Transforming the energy sector: The evolution of technological systems in renewable energy technology. Industrial and Corporate Change, 13(5), 815–849. https://doi.org/10.1093/icc/dth032

Kalantari, H., Sasmito, A. P., & Ghoreishi-Madiseh, S. A. (2021). An overview of directions for decarbonization of energy systems in cold climate remote mines. Renewable and Sustainable Energy Reviews, 152, 111711. https://doi.org/10.1016/j.rser.2021.111711

Kitchenham, B. A., Budgen, D., & Pearl Brereton, O. (2011). Using mapping studies as the basis for further research – A participant-observer case study. Information and Software Technology, 53(6), 638–651. https://doi.org/10.1016/j.infsof.2010.12.011

Kley, F., Lerch, C., & Dallinger, D. (2011). New business models for electric cars—A holistic approach. Energy Policy, 39(6), 3392–3403. https://doi.org/10.1016/j.enpol.2011.03.036

Lüdeke-Freund, F., Carroux, S., Joyce, A., Massa, L., & Breuer, H. (2018). The sustainable business model pattern taxonomy—45 patterns to support sustainability-oriented business model innovation. Sustainable Production and Consumption, 15, 145–162. https://doi.org/10.1016/j.spc.2018.06.004

Luthra, S., Kumar, V., Kumar, S., & Haleem, A. (2011). Barriers to implement green supply chain management in automobile industry using interpretive structural modeling technique: An Indian perspective. Journal of Industrial Engineering and Management, 4(2), 231–257. https://doi.org/10.3926/jiem.2011.v4n2.p231-257

Nieto, A., Schatz, R. S., & Dogruoz, C. (2020). Performance analysis of electric and diesel equipment for battery replacement of tethered LHD vehicles in underground mining. Mining Technology, 129(1), 22–29.

Palmié, M., Boehm, J., Friedrich, J., Parida, V., Wincent, J., Kahlert, J., Gassmann, O., & Sjödin, D. (2021). Startups versus incumbents in 'green' industry transformations: A comparative study of business model archetypes in the electrical power sector. Industrial Marketing Management, 96, 35–49. https://doi.org/10.1016/j.indmarman.2021.04.003

Paraszczak, J., Svedlund, E., Fytas, K., & Laflamme, M. (2014). Electrification of Loaders and Trucks – A Step Towards More Sustainable Underground Mining. Renewable Energy and Power Quality Journal, 81–86. https://doi.org/10.24084/repqj12.240

Pieroni, M. P. P., McAloone, T. C., & Pigosso, D. C. A. (2019). Business model innovation for circular economy and sustainability: A review of approaches. Journal of Cleaner Production, 215, 198–216.

Rethlefsen, M. L., Kirtley, S., Waffenschmidt, S., Ayala, A. P., Moher, D., Page, M. J., Koffel, J. B., PRISMA-S Group, Blunt, H., Brigham, T., Chang, S., Clark, J., Conway, A., Couban, R., De Kock, S., Farrah, K., Fehrmann, P., Foster, M., Fowler, S. A., … Young, S. (2021). PRISMA-S: An extension to the PRISMA Statement for Reporting Literature Searches in Systematic Reviews. Systematic Reviews, 10(1), 39. https://doi.org/10.1186/s13643-020-01542-z

Rosa, P., Sassanelli, C., & Terzi, S. (2019). Towards Circular Business Models: A systematic literature review on classification frameworks and archetypes. Journal of Cleaner Production, 236, 117696. https://doi.org/10.1016/j.jclepro.2019.117696

Sánchez, F., & Hartlieb, P. (2020). Innovation in the Mining Industry: Technological Trends and a Case Study of the Challenges of Disruptive Innovation. Mining, Metallurgy & Exploration, 37(5), 1385–1399. https://doi.org/10.1007/s42461-020-00262-1

Schaltegger, S., Lüdeke-Freund, F., & Hansen, E. G. (2016). Business models for sustainability: A co-evolutionary analysis of sustainable entrepreneurship, innovation, and transformation. Organization & Environment, 29(3), 264–289.

Thomas, D. R. (2006). A General Inductive Approach for Analyzing Qualitative Evaluation Data. American Journal of Evaluation, 27(2), 237–246. https://doi.org/10.1177/1098214005283748

Tukker, A. (2015). Product services for a resource-efficient and circular economy – a review. Journal of Cleaner Production, 97, 76–91. https://doi.org/10.1016/j.jclepro.2013.11.049

Wells, P. (2015). Economies of Scale Versus Small Is Beautiful: A Business Model Approach Based on Architecture, Principles and Components in the Beer Industry. Organization & Environment, 29(1), 36–52. https://doi.org/10.1177/1086026615590882

Williams, J. H., Jones, R. A., Haley, B., Kwok, G., Hargreaves, J., Farbes, J., & Torn, M. S. (2021). Carbon-Neutral Pathways for the United States. AGU Advances, 2(1), e2020AV000284. https://doi.org/10.1029/2020AV000284

DEVELOPING A MUSICIAN'S DIGITAL IDENTITY AS A CO-CREATOR OF THE DIGITAL ECOSYSTEM

Jelena Duras Gled and Ljerka Luic
University North
Trg dr. Zarka Dolinara 1, Koprivnica, Croatia

ABSTRACT

A musician develops digital identity within the digital ecosystem across various music platforms, generating unique music content and engaging in communication with the audience. In this process, the musician plays the role of a co-creator of the digital ecosystem, becoming established as an artist, communicating with the audience, and distributing music. The digital ecosystem undergoes significant structural changes due to the continuous development of new digital communication tools for creative music production, promotion, and distribution, placing independent musician in the demanding position of mastering multidisciplinary skills that go beyond music production, including understanding of information and communication technology and the importance of public relations in the digital environment. The aim of this research is to explore the challenges that independent musicians face in developing their digital identity in relation to their understanding of information and communication technology and the management of public relations within the digital ecosystem. The research applies a qualitative methodology through autoethnography research based on personal experiences of developing digital identity of an independent musician entrepreneur through the process of releasing a digital album during the 2021-2023 period. Six key information and communication challenges that musician encounters in developing digital identity are identified, and corresponding public relations activities are proposed. Considering that the current research is insufficiently dedicated to the challenges faced by independent musicians who enthusiastically work on their music careers in the digital environment, this study contributes to the development of musician's digital identity as a co-creator of the digital ecosystem as well as to further research in the field of media and communication.

KEYWORDS

Digital Identity, Musician, Digital Ecosystem, Digital Public Relations, Creativity

1. INTRODUCTION

The development of a musician's digital identity is closely linked to the advancement of technology, which has brought revolutionary changes within the music industry, providing independent musicians with unrestricted access to their audience. In the pre-internet era, musicians had limited influence in creating their music albums since record labels acted as intermediaries in the recording process and discographers were responsible for promotion, focusing mostly on radio broadcasting and sales. The advent of the internet has transformed the role of the musician in relation to the music production, distribution, and consumption (Kiresci, 2021). Due to the significant development of digital technology, musicians can now proactively engage with their target audience (Selva-Ruiz & Fénix-Pina, 2021) and directly distribute their music (Morris, 2020). Most of the music industry today is represented by independent musicians or so-called musicians- entrepreneurs who do not have contracts with major record labels but rather, through their own engagement on digital platforms, manage to showcase their music and find their own audience (Blanning, 2008). They operate in a digital ecosystem undergoing significant structural changes, including the use of new digital communication tools for creative music production, promotion, and distribution (Baker, 2018). The emergence of digital platforms also presents significant challenges for independent musicians who need to perform multiple roles within rapidly growing digital system and a saturated music market. To build an attractive digital identity and reach a target audience within the digital environment, independent musician needs to master multidisciplinary skills that go beyond creativity, music performance, or production, toward understanding of information and communication technology as well as the importance of public relations in the digital environment. In this process, musicians become an integral part of the digital ecosystem in which they develop their digital identity. The purpose of this research is to explore the importance of developing a musician's digital identity as a co-creator of the digital ecosystem and the role of public relations in this process. The aim of the research encompasses the challenges musicians face while developing their digital identity in relation to their understanding of information and communication technology and digital public relations management.

In line with the purpose and objectives of the research, the following research questions are posed:

RQ1: What are the information and communication challenges that musicians encounter in the development of their digital identity?

RQ2: Which public relations activities in the digital environment contribute to the formation of a musician's digital identity?

2. LITERATURE REVIEW

The development of independent musician shapes the way the music industry operates, following radical changes in the late 1990s with the introduction of P2P (peer-to-peer) music sharing through Napster, allowing free music downloads, and transitioning to digital MP3 recordings (Owsinski, 2014). Digital technology has enabled musicians to promote their own music, engage in direct sales, and communicate with their audience (Stewart, 2018), contributing to development of musician entrepreneur and a new music business model (Tronvoll, 2019). With the advancement of digital technologies, new values are created through digital ecosystems varying in type and size, while sharing the need for a community of participants within which products and services are developed based on the platform's resources (Valdez-de-Leon, 2019). Virtual communities emerge within the digital ecosystem where individuals establish a digital presence through virtual interaction, emphasizing the importance of developing and creating new identities in the digital environment that reflect real identities (Zimmerman & Woolf, 2014). Therefore, the development of a musician's digital identity signifies the transformation of a human identity into digital data and should be observed through digital identity systems as sources of data (Masiero, 2023), given that the portrayal of a digital identity that reflects a real identity is dominated by a view of its systems (Masiero & Arvidsson, 2021). This process of presenting oneself in a virtual community, in this case, a musician, is built through the user's relationship with the digital system, by creating user profile as an identity for the system to process activity and present active identity to the public (Ertzcheid, 2016). Therefore, a digital identity also includes activities that define the user through specific written, audio, or video content that the user publishes on various platforms, which the system defines through numerical variables in relation to the number of followers or friends (Ertzcheid, 2016). The result of user activities within the system that arise during the construction of a digital identity determines the creation of a digital reputation that can be partially controlled through a series of strategies and recommendations (Ertzcheid, 2016).

Technological development has enabled musicians to create, launch, and distribute their own music without the need for a record label, which has significantly influenced the independent sector development, which now represents 32.5% of the music industry (Tronvoll 2019; Houghton, 2020). However, it also resulted in market oversaturation where a musician acts as an entrepreneur trying to achieve a successful music career within a digital environment placing emphasis on development of digital identity, while still focusing on traditional values of having good songs, quality recordings, brand development, and promotion, only with a significant difference in approach (Miller, 2019). Independent musicians operate within a changing digital ecosystem where new digital communication channels are being developed enabling successful promotion (Armit & Oliver, 2019). In this process they are faced with the challenging task of shifting from music creation processes to entrepreneurial activities that require mastering of new information and communication skills (Caves, 2000). New forms of interaction with end-users emerge within new communication environment (Kwilinski et al., 2019), as well as new opportunities for innovative processes applicable in the creative industry (Peris-Ortiz et al., 2019). Musicians can now have an open connection toward audience as all types of barriers are removed, including geographic distances (Morris, 2020). The internet offers several advantages over traditional media in terms of increased visibility for musicians, their official websites through search engine optimization (SEO), real-time stakeholder interaction, obtaining valuable data about the target audience, and measuring the effectiveness of public relations (Amodu, 2019). Musicians now use digital technology in the very process of music creation to foster creativity (Kucic, Luic, 2023) mostly within their home studios (Kalliris, 2019). They then launch their music through online global distributors such as CD Baby or TuneCore and promote it on various platforms (Giones, 2017). Development of platforms, accelerated by the development of mobile media (Zhang & Negus, 2021), affects market oversaturation, changing the needs of the audience, which can now choose from the pool of many musicians. The fact that there is a growing number of smaller record labels and musicians' entrepreneurs in the music industry, sharing the common goal of finding their own audience (Hesmondhalgh and Meier, 2018) presents a significant market opportunity for independent public relations practitioners in the digital environment (Tankosic, 2016; Hyatt, 2012).

However, current research primarily focuses on the impact that music industry has on record labels, audience, and media (Coelho & Mendes, 2019; Tronvoll, 2019), while there has been insufficient research on the impact of digital technology on independent musicians. Some research reflects on the need for musicians to adopt a new way of thinking in the process of developing music careers (Blanning, 2008) and the importance of financial planning (Morrow, 2018). Still, research is limited when it comes to the information and communication challenges that musicians face in developing their digital identities. Furthermore, the field of public relations, especially within the music industry, has undergone significant changes due to the development of new media. The importance of high-quality public relations has increased, but it's noted that public relations practices in the digital environment are not well-researched. Practitioners often use techniques developed for traditional media, focusing on various online channels for information dissemination to the public and gathering feedback, including email marketing, websites, press releases, and blogs (Grunig, 2009).

3. METHODOLOGY

The research applies autoethnographic investigation as a qualitative research method based on personal experience. Within the multidisciplinary domain, using the first co-author's own experience as a musician and public relations practitioner, it examines the information and communication challenges faced by musician, while developing digital identity on the example of a digital album release during the 2021-2023 period, and analysing digital public relations activities that contribute to quality digital identity creation as a response to specific challenges. The study utilizes desk methods of analysing notes during complex decision-making processes and work tasks, aiming to describe and systematically analyse personal experience in releasing a digital album and development of digital identity, as well as possible public relations activities in the digital environment. This research employs autoethnographic methodology to identify key challenges faced by musicians who release their music in the digital environment and integrates these findings into a multidisciplinary discussion, with a focus on public relations.

The practice-based approach places the first co-author in the role of a participant observer and a public relations practitioner. The observer allows for a deeper level of study (Barrett & Bolt, 2010), while the technique of comparative analysis theory enables the integration of a comprehensive literature review from various disciplines, in contrast to methodologies based on a single discipline (Murphy, 2020). This multidisciplinary study represents an innovative approach in the context of the digital environment, where autoethnography is used to portray the challenges and guide discussions, also serving as a valuable framework for self-reflection and further improvement in the field of music industry and public relations (Duras Gled et al., 2023). By researching key challenges from a practice-based perspective, one becomes both the driver and the result of the research process (Murphy, 2020). This approach to research and writing seeks to describe and systematically analyse personal experience to understand the cultural experience (Anderton et al., 2012). Therefore, multidisciplinary approach could offer new insights into challenges within the music industry (Anderton et al., 2012; Burnard, 2020) and provide strategic insights into new activities used in music public relations, contributing to the development of this profession in the digital environment.

3.1 Methodological Limitations

Autoethnographic research is subject to the usual constraints associated with qualitative research, such as the researcher's personal involvement, thus the results are context-specific and cannot be generalized (Adams et al., 2014). However, the results provide new data and insights into the relatively underexplored experiential perspective of independent musicians and public relations experts in the digital environment.

4. RESULTS

The analysis of the release of the digital album by a Croatian musician during the 2021-2023 period enabled the mapping of 6 key challenges, as presented in Table 1:

Table 1. Key information and communication challenges in the development of the musician's digital identity

1.	Digital literacy	Creating quality content for various platforms, websites, and social media profiles requires knowledge and skills in using various communication tools.
2.	Digital network management	Album promotion on digital networks, including communication with the audience and new posts, requires good communication strategy to maintain a digital presence.
3.	Promotional campaign	Releasing a digital album requires studying promotional possibilities through various social networks within specified algorithms, which has proven to be quite challenging.
4.	Audience engagement	Increased audience interest requires frequent communication, responding to individual comments and inquiries, as well as emails related to performances, album sales, and more.
5.	Media relations	To establish a good relationship with the media requires communication skills and a promotional approach in presenting the digital album in an attractive way.
6.	Virtual concerts	Quality album promotion during virtual concerts requires good technical equipment and an expert support in maintaining the quality of broadcasts and audience communication.

Table 2 lists the digital public relations activities that were used during the release of the album and have contributed to development of musician's digital identity, serving as possible responses to the previously identified and categorized challenges:

Table 2. Public Relations Activities in the Digital Environment

1.	Target audience analysis	Before the album release, research was conducted by creating test profiles on social media to determine the appropriate communication approach toward the target audience.
2.	Communication channels	The research analysed certain primary platforms of communication with the target audience, defining Facebook and YouTube channel for further activities.
3.	Promotional activity strategy	Promotional activities such as releasing singles, music videos, and audience communication encourage content sharing, direct advertising, and networking.
4.	Creative content	Creative content published during communication with the audience is related to the theme of the digital album with the aim of attracting a new audience.
5.	Generating interest	Video clips from the album were used to depict stories and anecdotes from attractive locations. The public was engaged through rewards with significant media interest.
6.	Live communication	The audience interacted with the performer during virtual concerts. Interaction occurred through comments to the extent that it did not disrupt the context of the performance.

5. DISCUSSION

The obtained results of the research have led to the mapping of six key information and communication challenges musicians face within the digital ecosystem and for each of these challenges, specific digital public relations activities, contributing to building the musician's digital identity, have been proposed.

The first challenge of musician's digital literacy requires knowledge of using various communication tools. Research has confirmed that a lack of communication skills poses a challenge to the career of an independent musician (Throsby et al., 2023), and that observing communication methods prior to joining a specific social network is a good strategy for connecting with the target audience, becoming familiarized with communication tools and the use of platform advantages (Barry, 2013). Public relations activities focus on the target audience to determine primary social networks and reach more audience through album promotion and communication. Creating quality profiles on social media platforms has been crucial in building a successful music career, along with utilizing the platform's tools for content monitoring and posts (Wiebe, 2015).

The second challenge involves managing digital platforms and requires a sound communication strategy on social media. Research has shown that social media significantly influence musicians' development as it facilitates audience engagement and music promotion, crucial for networking and reputation building (Stafford, 2010). The primary communication networks Facebook and YouTube channel were determined as part of public relations activities. These platforms proved to be successful in attracting the target audience and were used for the promotion of the digital album. In the presentation of the digital album videos, Youtube proved to be a better way of presenting the songs because the option of subscribing enabled the audience to follow the news and announcements of music singles. Previous research has also confirmed that YouTube is the most popular video sharing platform for musicians due to its wide range of features (Mulligan, 2018). Direct communication with the target audience was mostly taking place on Facebook, which also coincides with research proving that Facebook has a strong impact on changing the approach of the music industry and the promotion of musicians (Stafford, 2010).

Creating a promotional campaign for the digital album represents the third challenge, requiring specific information and communication skills and mastering algorithms of various social networks. As part of the promotion the first single was released with great success, followed by audience networking. Through Tune Core, the digital album was made available on Spotify, Deezer, Apple Music and YouTube Music streaming platforms, as one of the first digital albums on the Croatian market. Having in mind that Deezer entered Croatian market in 2013, while the rest of the platforms became available in 2020 (HDS, 2020). Although the promotion mainly took place on Facebook, users were also directed to the official web page where, in addition to the digital version of the album, music enthusiasts could order the copy of the physical CD edition. Research has confirmed that algorithms and digital public relations in music are the new music industry gatekeepers because they affect the visibility and success of musicians (Frenneaux, 2023; Morgan, 2019). PR activities encompass advertising, content sharing, networking, and the engagement of communication experts to develop effective promotion and distribution strategies (Swedberg, 2006; Barry, 2013). Over thousand e-mail addresses were generated within first month of promotion, which were later used for direct advertising to control music promotion while engaging audience.

Maintaining audience relations represents the fourth challenge which consumes a significant amount of time. Research has confirmed that it is important to keep the audience interested in their creativity as they become quickly saturated with content (Maksimow, 2016) and that two-way interaction between musicians and the audience is recommended because from such communication it is possible to develop a long-term sustainable career (Bennett, 2016). The focus has been on attracting truly loyal fans who are willing to attend concerts, therefore consistency in publishing of quality content has been essential. With the new era of communication, the audience has developed a refined taste, having a large music pool to choose from (Wiebe, 2015), and requiring constant interaction with the musician (Barry, 2013). As part of the creative process the focus was on recording informal content, for instance, using motivational lyrics of songs from the album along with attractive video content from the nature. The use of different rewards on social networks is also considered useful and can increase the attention of the audience (Barry, 2013; Wiebe, 2015).

One of the challenges of presenting a new album is the relationship with the media. Regardless of the media convergence, traditional media still play a significant role (Meier, 2017; Armit & Oliver, 2019). For instance, media interest increased because the album was available in both digital and physical formats and had achieved silver status in Croatia within one year of sales. This achievement gave a professional recognition to the album quality, providing credibility and assurance to the audience. Television broadcasts of music videos gave an additional promotional value, affecting increase in number of views on YouTube channel.

Promoting the album through virtual concerts represents the sixth challenge, as the latest trend in the music industry that boomed during the COVID-19 pandemic and is still growing (Vandenberg et al., 2021). Live concerts were taking place on social platforms, particularly on Facebook and YouTube Live (Breese et al., 2020). Virtual concerts rely on quality production and technology incorporating virtual reality and live streaming (Lee et al., 2020). Live communication through virtual concerts plays an increasingly important role in the development of new communication approaches and enhances the audience's experience, as an integral part of the music industry's development and an upgrade to concerts in a real environment (Breese et al., 2020).

The research proved that the new digital public relations methods within music industry are focused on increasing the engagement of the audience as part of the promotion process (Gamble et al., 2019). It is inevitable that within digital ecosystem fans participate in communication, placing artists in a demanding role of being constantly accessible (Baym, 2018). The dynamics of the digital ecosystem plays an increasingly important role in the further development of the musician's digital identity, which could have a profound impact on the musician in the pursuit of their audience, while maintaining balance between active content production and artistic focus. Therefore, it is important to build a healthy digital identity for musicians, which requires a multidisciplinary approach in collaboration with a public relations expert in the digital environment.

6. CONCLUSION

The analysis of the study has revealed digital literacy, digital network management, promotional campaign, audience engagement, media relations and virtual concerts as the key information and communication challenges, thus providing an answer to the first research question of defining the information and communication challenges that musicians encounter in the development of their digital identity. Additionally, the specific public relations activities were provided as possible responses to these challenges through target audience analysis, communication channels, promotional activity strategy, creative content, generating interest and live communication, as an answer to the second research question of defining public relations activities taking place in the digital environment and contributing to the development of the musician's digital identity. The results are context-specific therefore future research should focus on generalizing the findings of this study to include the broader range of musicians, as well as to analyse the long-term effects of the proposed public relations tactics on musician's career. The development of the digital identity of independent musician has proven to be crucial in the musician's career development, relying on overcoming information and communication challenges closely linked to public relations activities in the digital environment, thus confirming the purpose of the study itself. Since previous research insufficiently addresses the challenges faced by independent musicians who enthusiastically develop their music careers in the digital environment, this study contributes to the development of the musician's digital identity as a co-creator of the digital ecosystem. The mapped challenges and correlating public relations are being supported by a theoretical multidisciplinary ground, aiming to improve a more effective approach to development of the musician's digital identity while exploring contemporary perspectives in the field of digital public relations.

ACKNOWLEDGEMENT

The publication of this paper was made possible through the University North funds, intended to support the scientific research project "d-learning: Digital Competences for Innovation Culture", to which these authors express their gratitude.

REFERENCES

Adams, T.E., Holman, S.J. & Ellis, E. (2014). *Autoethnography*, Oxford, Oxford University Press, 2014.

Amodu, L., Oladokun, O., Nelson, O., Babatunde, A. & Evaristus, A. (2019). Potentials of Internet of Things for effective public relations activities: Are professionals ready?, *Cogent Business & Management*, Vol. 6. No.1, https://doi.org/10.1080/23311975.2019.1683951

Anderton, C., Dubber, A. & James, M. (2012). *Understanding the Music Industries*, SAGE Publications, Los Angeles.

Armit, B. & Oliver, P. G. (2019). Crowdfunding and the DIY artist: the effects of web 2.0 on DIY music communities. University of West London repository. https://doi.org/10.2139/ssrn.3297206

Baker, B. (2018). *Internet Promotion & Online Social Media: Guerrilla Music Marketing Series*, Vol. 2, Spotlight Publications, USA.

Barrett, E. & Bolt, B. (2010). *Practice as research: approaches to creative arts enquiry,* I. B. Tauris, London.

Barry, M. (2013). *The New Rules of Music Marketing*, 1st edition, Princeton Creative Marketing. LLC, New York.

Baym, N. K. (2018). *Playing to the crowd: Musicians, audiences, and the intimate work of connection*. New York University Press.

Blanning, T. C. (2008). *The triumph of music: The rise of composers, musicians and their art*, Harvard University Press, Cambridge, MA.

Bennett, L. (2016). *The Cambridge Companion to the Singer-Songwriter*, Cambridge University Press.

Breese, JL., Fox, MA., Vaidyanathan, G. (2020). Live music performances and the internet of things. *ISS* 21(3):179–188. https:// doi. org/ 10. 48009/3_ iis_ 2020_ 179- 188

Burnard, P. (2012). *Musical Creativities in Practice*, OUP Oxford, Oxford.

Caves, R. (2000). *Creative industries: Contracts between art and commerce*, Harvard University Press, Cambridge, MA.

Coelho, M. P. & Mendes, J. Z. (2019). Digital music and the 'death of the long tail, Journal of Business Research, Vol. 101, pp. 454-460. hppts://www.doi.org/10.1016/j.jbusres.2019.01.015

Duras Gled, J., Bagaric., Z., Strucic, E. (2023). In-service education of music therapist aiming to help the vulnerable groups supported by auto-ethnographic research, EDULEARN23, *Proceedings 2023*, pp. 6412-6420. Doi: 10.21125/edulearn.2023.1704

Ertzcheid, O. (2016). *What is Digital Identity? Issues, Tools, Methodologies*. Marseille, France: OpenEdition Press.

Frenneaux R. (2023). The rise of independent artists and the paradox of democratisation in the digital age: Challenges faced by music artists in the new music industry, *SAGE*, Vol. 1, No. 2, pp. 125–137. https://doi.org/10.1177/27538702231174200

Gamble, J. R., McAdam, R., & Brennan, M. (2019). How user-centric innovation is affecting stakeholder marketing strategies: Exploratory findings from the music industry. *European Management Review*, 16(4), pp. 1175–1193.

Giones, F., Brem, A. (2017). Digital Technology Entrepreneurship: A Definition and Research Agenda. *Technology Innovation Management Review*, Vol. 7, pp. 44–51. https://doi.org/10.22215/TIMREVIEW/1076

Grunig, J.E. (2009). Paradigms of global public relations in an age of digitalisation. *Prism*, Vol. 6, No. 2, pp. 1-19.

Hesmondhalgh, D. & Meier, L. (2018). What the digitalisation of music tells us about capitalism, culture and the power of the information technology sector. *Information, Communication & Society*, Vol. 21, No.11, pp. 1555-1570. https://doi.org/10.1080/1369118X.2017.1340498

Houghton, B. (2020). DIY musicians earned $873 Million from recorded music last year, as industry grew 11.4%. Hypebot. Online available from: https://www.hypebot.com/hypebot/2020/03/diy-musicians-earned-873m-from-recorded-music-last-year-as-industry-grew-11-4.html (Accessed: 17.12.2023).

HDS, Hrvatsko društvo skladatelja (2020). Available from https://www.zamp.hr/clanak/pregled/2354/konacno-spotify-od-danas-dostupan-i-u-hrvatskoj (Accessed: 18.12.2023).

Hyatt, A. (2012). *Cyber PR for musicians: Tools, tricks, & tactics for building your social media house*. New York. Huntercat Press.

Kalliris, G., Dimoulas, C.A. & Matsiola, M. (2019). *Media management, sound editing and mixing*. In Foundations in Sound Design for Linear Media; Routledge: Abingdon-on-Thames, UK.

Kiresci, A. (2021). The Impact of Innovative Technologies on Small Players in The Recorded Music Sector: A Chronological Overivew, *Creative Industries Journal*, Vol. 16, No. 1, pp. 96-111. https://doi.org/10.1080/17510694.2021.1939545

Kucic, M., Luic L. (2023). Tailorscore: Application of innovative teaching and artificial intelligence to encourage creativity, EDULEARN23, *Proceedings 2023*, 7390-7397, doi: 10.21125/iceri.2023.1836

Kwilinski, A., Dalevska, N., Kravchenko, S., Hroznyi, I. & Kovalenko, O. (2019). Formation of the entrepreneurship model of e-business in the context of the introduction of information and communication technologies. *J. Entrep. Educ.* Vol. 22, pp. 1–7.

Lee D., Baker, W., Haywood, N. (2020), Coronavirus, the cultural catalyst. Hypotheses. Dostupno na https:// wim. hypot heses. org/ 1302. (Accessed 07.12.2023.)

Masiero, S. (2023). Digital identity as platform-mediated surveillance. Big Data and Society. *Sage*. DOI: 10.1177/20539517221135176

Masiero, S. & Arvidsson, V. (2021). Degenerative outcomes of digital identity platforms for development. *Information Systems Journal,* Vol. 31, No. 6, pp. 903–928. https://doi.org/10.1111/isj.12351

Meier, L. M. (2017). *Popular music as promotion: Music and branding in the digital age*, John Wiley & Sons, Hoboken.

Miller, L. (2019). Same Heart. New Beat: How Record Labels Amplify Talent in the Modern Music Marketplace. http://musonomics.org/new-report-illustrates-how-modern-record-labels-remade-themselves-in-the-streaming-era/ (Accessed 28.11.2023.)

Morgan, BA. (2019). Revenue, access, and engagement via the in-house curated Spotify Playlist in Australia. *Popular Communication*, Vol. 18, No.1, pp. 32–47. https://doi.org/10.1080/15405702.2019.1649678

Morris, J. W. (2020). Music Platforms and the Optimization of Culture. *Social Media + Society*, Vol. 6, No. 3. https://doi.org/10.1177/2056305120940690

Morrow, G. (2018). *Artist Management: Agility in the Creative and Cultural Industries*, Routledge, New York and London.

Mulligan, M. (2018). State of the YouTube Music Economy 2.0. *MiDIA Research*. https://www.midiaresearch.com/blog/state-of-the-youtube-music-economy-2-0-a-turning-point-for-all-parties (Accessed 14.12.2023.).

Murphy, S. (2020). Music marketing in the digital music industries – An autoethnographic exploration of opportunities and challenges for independent musicians, *International Journal of Music Business Research*, Vol. 9, no. 1. https://musikwirtschaftsforschung.files.wordpress.com/2020/04/volume-9-no-1-april-2020-murphy_end.pdf (Accessed 13.12.2023.).

Owsinski, B. (2014). *Music 4.0: A Survival Guide for Making Music in the Internet Age*. Milwaukee: Hal Leonard Books.

Peris-Ortiz, M., Gomez, J. A. & Lopez-Sieben, M. (2019). *Cultural and creative industries: A Path to Entrepreneurship and Innovation*; Peris-Ortiz, M., Mayer Cabrera-Flores, R., Serrano Santoyo, A., (Eds.); Springer: Washington, USA

Selva-Ruiz, D. & Fénix-Pina, D. (2021). Soundtrack music videos: The use of music videos as a tool for promoting films. *Communication & Society*, Vol. 34, No. 3, pp. 47-60. https://www.doi.org/10.15581/003.34.3.47-60

Stafford, S.A. (2010). Music in the digital age: The emergence of digital music and its repercussions on the music industry. *The Elon Journal of Undergraduate Research in Communications*. Vol. 1, No. 2, pp. 112-120

Stewart, S. (2018). The development of the artist-fan engagement model. *International Journal of Music Business Research*, Vol. 7, No. 2, pp. 52-82. https://doi.org/10.25101/19.34

Swedberg, R. (2006). *Principles of Economic Sociology*; Princeton University Press: Princeton, NJ, USA.

Tankosic, M., Ivetic, P. & Vucurevic, V. (2016). Features of interactive public relations: Using web 2.0 to establish a t wo-way communication with the consumers. *Int. Journal of Economic and Management Systems*, Vol. 1, pp. 290–295.

Throsby, D., Zednik, A. & Council, A. (2023). Do you really expect to get paid?: An economic study of professional artists in Australia, Australia Council for the Arts. Available from: https://creative.gov.au/advocacy-and-research/do-you-really-expect-to-get-paid/ (Accessed 13.12.2023).

Tronvoll, B. (2019). Digital enabled experience – the listening experience in music streaming. *International Journal of Music Business Research*, Vol. 8, No. 1, pp. 6-38.

Valdez-de-Leon, O. (2019). How to Develop a Digital Ecosystem: a Practical Framework. *Technology Innovation Management Review*, Vol. 9, No. 8, pp. 43-54. http://doi.org/10.22215/timreview/1260

Vandenberg, F., Berghman, M. Schaap, J. (2021). The 'lonely raver': music livestreams during COVID-19 as a hotline to collective consciousness? *Eur Soc* 23:S141–S152. https:// doi. org/ 10. 1080/ 14616 696.2020.18182 71

Wiebe, D. A. (2015). *The New Music Industry – Adapting, Growing, and Thriving in The Information Age*, CreateSpace Independent Publishing Platform, Scotts Valley, California.

Zimmerman, J. M., & Woolf, J. L. (2014). Building a Digital Identity in the Sciences. *PLOS Biology*, 12(4), e1001849. https://doi.org/10.32388/G85LX9

Zhang, Q. & Negus, K.(2021). Stages, platforms, streams: The economies and industries of live music after digitalization. *Popular Music and Society*, Vol. 44, No. 5, pp. 539-557.https://www.doi.org/10.1080/03007766.2021.1921909

THE ROLE OF DIGITAL TECHNOLOGIES AND STAKEHOLDERS IN PROMOTING BIODIVERSITY

Mauro Capestro and Stefano Denicolai
Department of Economics and Management, University of Pavia
Via San Felice al Monastero 5, 27100, Pavia, Italy

ABSTRACT

Biodiversity loss presents a serious risk for business and society. Companies can use digital technologies to offer innovative services that aim at protecting and promoting biodiversity, Moreover, a key role is also played by stakeholders, from business partners to clients and individuals, that can support the actions of a company in pursuing biodiversity goals. However, biodiversity can be seen also as a lever to improve innovation. Indeed, biodiversity can promote the innovation of business models to reach client needs as well as the social perception of this topic, affecting their role and actions in the society. In this context, culture about biodiversity represents a key factor that should be promoted to support actions. In this sense, policy-makers could play a key role. Through a multiple case studies approach, the study tries to assess the role of biodiversity taking into consideration digital technologies, stakeholders' involvement, business model and social innovation. The results of analysis (desk analysis and interviews) of three case studies considered, emphasize the relevance of both stakeholders and digital technologies for biodiversity practices and of biodiversity for business and social innovation. In addition, results highlight the key role of culture in tackling biodiversity loss.

KEYWORDS

Digital Technologies, Biodiversity, Stakeholder Theory, Business Model Innovation, Social Innovation

1. INTRODUCTION

In the field of environmental sustainability an important issue is concerning the prevention and promotion of biodiversity (Jones and Solomon 2013), meant as "the variety of life, including variation among species and functional traits" (Cardinale et al., 2012, p. 60). In the field of business, organizations are introducing new frameworks and tools to reduce the impacts of their activities on climate change, air, soil, water quality, and more recently to protect biodiversity (Reale et al., 2019). Biodiversity loss poses serious risks to business operations, threatening resource availability, supply chains, and ecosystem services, here meant as the benefits that human populations and organizations derive—directly or indirectly—from proper ecosystem functioning (Costanza et al., 1997; Whiteman et al., 2013). These risks are recognized at a global level, but further research is needed to understand business perceptions and actions regarding biodiversity in local contexts (Reade et al., 2015; Winn and Pogutz, 2013).

Contributing to this topic, a growing number of scholars and practitioners are recently looking at managing biodiversity issues by considering the role played by both digital technologies (Broccardo et al., 2023; Pichlak and Szromek, 2021) and stakeholders (Bronzetti et al., 2023) respect the activation of sustainable business solutions that could positively affect biodiversity practices. Specifically, for biodiversity practices, scholars refer to the activities that can help to tackle the loss of biodiversity (Salmi et al., 2023). Boiral and Heras-Saizarbitoria (2017) proposed a framework that differentiates biodiversity practices into: (i) *internal practices* that are implemented by the firm itself; and (ii) *external practices* implemented in association or collaboration with various stakeholders.

Despite the relevance of biodiversity issues, there is a lack of research that investigates how it relates with business. The purpose pf the study is to identify new theoretical patterns (Sabherwal and King, 1991) about how biodiversity is dealt with by companies and how it can be related to innovation. We attempt to reach our research goals by selecting "information-rich" cases (Patton, 2015), summarizing varied or extensive raw data, establishing relationships between findings and research objectives and developing a theoretical framework based upon "the underlying structure of experiences or processes that are evident in the text data" (Thomas, 2006, p. 238).

2. BODY OF PAPER

2.1 Theoretical Background

In the recent years, there has been a growing attention on how new digital technologies included in the Industry 4.0 paradigm – from big data to Internet of Things (IoT) and artificial intelligence (AI) solutions – are supporting firms and other organizations in the optimization of business processes included environmental sustainability concerns (Piccarozzi et al., 2022, 2023). Recent studies assessed the impacts of Industry 4.0 and foud a positive effect (Yadav et al., 2020) within firms oriented towards a sustainable development (Stock et al., 2018). On one side, digital technologies can serve as solutions also for facing biodiversity issues in different ways, as they can be used to offer innovative regenerative solutions in agriculture (Cumming et al., 2020), but also to tackle biodiversity loss playing a complementary role alongside existing technology, or supporting other innovation processes (Ziegler et al., 2022). In this context, ecological knowledge is important in motivating operational activities to tackle biodiversity issues. Specifically, ecological knowledge is vital in influencing biodiversity culture and shaping learning about biodiversity in the social context. Stakeholders are integrated into this learning process (Smith et al., 2020) as they can be played a key role in terms of opportunities for value co-creation (Boiral and Heras-Saizarbitoria, 2017). According to stakeholder theory, companies and organizations must consider the interests and expectations of their various stakeholders, defined as "any identifiable group or individual who can affect the achievement of an organization's objectives, or who is affected by the achievement of an organization's objectives" (Freeman and Reed 1983, p. 91). Some studies have highlighted the importance of stakeholders' involvement in managing complex environmental issues and promoting proactive environmental strategies (e.g., Buysse and Verbeke 2003; Cragg and Greenbaum 2002).

On the other side, reaching biodiversity goals could have effect on both business innovation processes as well as on social innovation, which refers to the individuals' response to the view that economic activity has expanded with little or no regard for sustainable yields or the fragile balances in nature (Lettice and Parekh, 2010). In the management literature, it has been found that different forms of diversity, such as gender, culture, education, background and cognitive (Mitchell, 2008; Østergaard et al., 2011), as well as the diversity of cooperation and relationships among companies and stakeholders (Vence and Trigo, 2009) have positive effects on innovation processes. Diversity is considered a driver of innovation (Hewlett et al., 2013). In this context, companies have started to innovate their business models to include environmental, social, and economic considerations (Feger and Mermet, 2022). These sustainable business models are designed to integrate sustainability into companies to create financial, ecological and social values, to adapt the firm to the changing external environment. Moreover, literature suggests that that it is necessary to develop tools that allow to provide an adequate response to the needs of creating and delivering sustainable products, systems, or services (Rafael et al., 2022).

Despite the relevance of biodiversity for business and society, there is a lack of studies that explore how biodiversity is managed and how it can affect innovation. In particular, there is the need of a deeper understating of how digital technologies and stakeholders improve business biodiversity practices and if biodiversity supports business and social innovation. Specifically, through our study we aim at answering to the main following research questions:

RQ1: *What is the role of digital technologies in biodiversity practices?*
RQ2: *How do firms/organizations involve stakeholders in biodiversity practices?*
RQ3: *How does biodiversity affect both business and social innovation?*

2.2 Methodology

Because of the exploratory nature of our research, we adopted a bottom-up inductive approach (e.g. Gioia et al., 2013; Thomas, 2006) "wherein theories are formulated by drawing general inferences from particulars or cases of empirical data" (McAbee et al., 2017, p. 278). In doing so, the qualitative method through a multiple case study approach (Yin, 2014) using multiple material sources from in-depth interviews to secondary company's data extracted online (companies' websites and companies' LinkedIn webpages), is the more suitable for a deeper first understanding of the phenomenon (XXX). This is a preliminary version of the research that aims at analyzing data coming from different companies of different industries that consider biodiversity goals into their business strategy. Currently we have collected data about three different companies, detailed in Table 1 that can allow us to have some preliminary insights related to our research goals.

Table 1. Case studies

COMPANY	FOUNDED	SIZE	INDUSTRY/ACTIVITY	INTERVIEWED
Company 1	2017	Medium-sized	Technology/Technology provider; Consulting and education services	Marketing manager
Company 2	2019	Medium-sized	Food/Food delivery services; Education services	Co-founder
Company 3	2018	Medium-sized	Consulting/Innovation and technology business consulting services; Training services	Marketing manager and Agronomist

Source: Authors' elaboration

Company 1 is a medium-sized leading nature-tech company aiming at favoring biodiversity through technology. The company's goal is to create Europe's largest ecological corridor, consisting of interconnected biodiversity oases, to restore 40% of global biodiversity. The honeybee is a key bioindicator that company assesses by collecting and interpreting data through innovative proprietary systems to monitor the health of bees, pollinators and their connection to ecosystems. Biodiversity is an integral part of the business.

Company 2 is a medium-sized digital company mainly focused on (healthy) food production (recipes) and delivery. It's main goal bases on the idea that delivering the "right quantity" of ingredients for the different dishes and recipes an individual chooses to eat can totally eliminate food waste and, consequently, having a positive impact on nature. Indeed, the company's desire is to have a positive sustainable impact on the entire ecosystem to sustain nature and protect biodiversity, which is important to offer several ingredients for its own customers.

Company 3 is a medium-sized tech-company that offers several consulting services for businesses and other organizations with the aims of transforming territories and industrial districts into sustainable places where safeguarding the environment by saving resources, combating climate change and valuing biodiversity. In this case, biodiversity is strategically relevant for company's business.

We performed two steps of analysis: a first desk analysis of companies' website and LinkedIn web page, and a following content analysis of the interviews done. We interviewed marketing managers and co-founder (with marketing competences) because of our interest in the market perspective of the phenomenon. The interviews were conducted between December 2023 and March 2024, and aimed at investigating the firms' activities (practices) adopted to prevent or promote biodiversity and the effect these practices. As consequence, the desk and content analysis focused on emphasizing evidences and concepts that stress the connection, from one side, between digital technologies, stakeholders and biodiversity and, from the other side, between biodiversity and innovation.

2.3 Results

2.3.1 Case Studies

The evaluation of the three companies started from the desk analysis of company website and LinkedIn page to assess what they do, in terms of activities, and how biodiversity is part of the business. A summary of the main results is reported in Table 2.

Table 2. Main results of desk analysis

COMPANY	PRODUCTS/SERVICES	DIGITAL TECHNOLOGIES
Company 1	Monitoring; Regeneration; Education; Innovative service for citizens: adopting a beehive / tree / bee	IoT, Sensors, App
Company 2	Food production (recipes) and delivery for individuals and organizations; Personalized nutrition	Digital platform, App
Company 3	Nature-based solutions; Local and industrial resource efficiency solutions services; Biodiversity monitoring and innovative regeneration services; Open Innovation and Venture Capital	Sensors, Satellite images

Source: Authors' elaboration

The first business idea was the development of a technology for beeves monitoring because they perceived a great risk. Then, the activity enlarged involving more services with the aim of bridging nature with technology. In this sense, company developed IoT, sensors and analysis tools (machine learning algorithms) and started to offer the opportunity to experience regenerative activities that preserve and promote biodiversity. The business of Company 1 bases on 3 main pillars (services): (1) the monitoring through technologies of the nature habitat health (data on pollinators, bees, flora, etc.); (2) regeneration of low-biodiversity lands, providing nectariferous species of trees and plants, selected according to the specific characteristics of the land; and (3) education programs to raise awareness of biodiversity issues among businesses and communities. Moreover, Company 1 provides additional services, such as education. In this regard, through LinkedIn, it publishes news and information as well as webinars about biodiversity. On company's website there is a blog and a podcast supported by various business partners to spread the culture of biodiversity. In addition, it offers an educational program for secondary school students, to integrate biodiversity into the official program. Finally, Company 1 offers to the citizens, the possibility to "adopt" a beehive (monitored through the app) managed by beekeeper that periodically send the honey produced by the "adopted" bees. In addition, there is also the opportunity to "adopt" a solitary bee house, and a nectariferous tree. For these two kind of activities Company involves different stakeholders, such as beekeepers, land owners, research centers and universities, and other business partners, as well as citizens in pursuing biodiversity practices.

Company 2 is a digital company offering a new way of sustainable grocery shopping (health food). The kits are provided in compostable containers of portioned, ready-to-cook ingredients that allow to have zero food waste at a sustainable cost. It offers a large variety of ingredients to assure the possibility of cocking several different recipes for several different cultures (people). In doing so, Company 2 creates synergies with host territory, involving various stakeholders (producers, bistros, restaurants, pick-up points, etc.) with the intention of enhancing and protecting biodiversity, as element of the same delicate ecosystem to be protected. The ecosystem consists of: a digital portal; a production/distribution center; a network of companies that cultivate, breed and produce raw materials and semi-finished products in the national territory; the users of the service. The main goal is to optimize resources and reduce waste, generating a real change to protect "People, Work and the Planet". In addition, to support clients, Company 2 has partnered with nutrition experts (biologist nutritionists) who will provide to clients a personalized diet plan designed on client needs. A highly personalized service, new to the market, flexible and tailor-made that favors collaborations with different several actors of food industry. Through their services, mainly focused on protect environment (short-chain/zero-kilometer products for less environmental impact; plastic-free, fully compostable containers; weighed and portioned ingredients to reduce food waste), Company 2 reduces food waste that with positive effects on environmental sustainability and on the prevention of biodiversity loss. Moreover, Company 2 is also active on promoting, also thoruhg the involvement of other actors (partners, universities, etc.) the culture of sustainability and biodiversity mainly through the LinkedIn page, by publishing posts on these topics.

Company 3 is a tech-company that provides to its clients consulting nature-based solutions, including its own technologies, to improve environmental sustainability reducing the use of natural resources. This is done to address major critical environmental issues and provide resilience to the Planet of the Future. Company 3 develops and aggregates technologies, solutions, innovations and skills to transform the industrial supply chain and territories into resources for people and the environment, in order to combat the scarcity of natural resources by limiting their extraction and promoting the reuse of those already present, promote the regeneration of biodiversity and counter climate change, creating a true circular symbiosis between people, economy, business and the environment. Company 3 activity starts with the analysis of an actor's needs and try to involve all the main client' stakeholders into the project. In this case, it aims at creating a superior value for sustainability and biodiversity goals. Company 3, as the other two ones, uses the LinkedIn page (with the participation of different others actors) to promote the culture of sustainability and biodiversity through the publishing of information and events on the topics.

2.3.2 Interviews

In addition to the desk analysis of companies' website and LinkedIn pages, we analyzed the interviews done with managers and a co-founder of the three companies considered in this study. First of all, for all three companies, even if in different ways, biodiversity has a central role for the business.

"*We started our business with the aim of monitoring beehives to prevent the death bees, but immediately we perceived the key value of biodiversity and focused this new perspective.*" (Company 1)

"*Biodiversity protection and promotion is a key aspect for our business goals and activity, because it allows to assure a large variety of ingredients to satisfy all types of diets for different types of ethnicities.*" (Company 2)

"*When we interact with our clients we highlight the relevance that Nature Based Solutions for resource efficiency have in terms of biodiversity and how it is important for the development of society. In this way, clients become aware to our solutions.*" (Company 3)

As far as digital technologies are concerned, the three companies use them for different purposes. In particular, Company 1 uses IoT and sensors for monitoring beehives (initially) and biodiversity of lands (later). When started the "beehive adoption" project, they developed an app for this purpose. Thus Company 1 uses different technologies to for biodiversity goals. Company 2 is a digital company that offers its own services throng a digital platform. In this case, technology (platform and app) is used to foster its own activity and philosophy (health nutrition and food waste reduction), thus biodiversity is a result and in the same time an added value for the business as it allows to deliver different ingredients for different (cultural) diets. Finally, for Company 3, technologies support the Nature Based Solutions they offer, and biodiversity loss prevention is a goal of the business activities.

"*To provide our services we need technology and data to precisely meet need of beekeepers as well as of individuals that adopt a beehive...Technology is for us necessary to assure biodiversity.*" (Company 1)

"*In promoting our Nature Based Solutions, we consider technologies necessary to reach efficient sustainable results. Moreover, technologies allow us to monitor biodiversity and act immediately.*" (Company 3)

In addition to the relevance that technologies have for the business of the three companies considered, an element of analysis regarded the role of the different stakeholders. For all three companies, the involvement of stakeholders is extremally important for the achievement of sustainable and biodiversity goals.

"*In addition to the beekeepers, land owners and citizens directly involved in the business, we collaborate with different research, universities and other institutions as well as with other partners.*" (Company 1)

"*In our business we need of the involvement of other organizations and of clients. They should be culturally prepared to the concepts of zero food waste to save resources useful for sustainability and biodiversity goals.*" (Company 2)

"*Biodiversity needs of stakeholders involvement. This is a cultural innovation first of all. We try to imprint this concept to other companies highlighting the value of nature for businesses and society.*" (Company 3)

Finally, though interviews we aimed at assessing the relationship between biodiversity and innovation. For Company 1, biodiversity allowed to innovate the business model. Indeed, from a technology for beekeepers moved on a technology that allows to involve individuals in adopting beehives, initially, and then trees and bees. Company 2 considers biodiversity essential to offer different food products (ingredients and diets) and services (personalized nutrition). Company 3 uses biodiversity to innovate the clients' business processes and models.

"*Initially, our business model idea was to sell this device to beekeepers. Then, we noticed that people were interested protecting bees and prevent biodiversity loss, so we basically innovated our business model by offering through an app the opportunity to remotely adopt and monitoring hives. In this case, culture is important. Understanding the relevance of biodiversity affects the social approach to the topic.*" (Company 1)

"Biodiversity protection allow us to offer different ingredients for different people needs. In this way we can innovate our business also promoting personalized nutrition." (Company 2)

"In our solutions, from a circular economy viewpoint, we offer to the clients the opportunity to innovate the business models by considering the re-use of their waste in other business activities." (Company 3)

The results of desk and content analyses of the three companies here considered allowed us to depict a possible conceptual framework (Figure 1) that summarize how the different variables relate among them, highlighting the double face of biodiversity promotion or loss prevention, as output of innovative services and a driver for innovation.

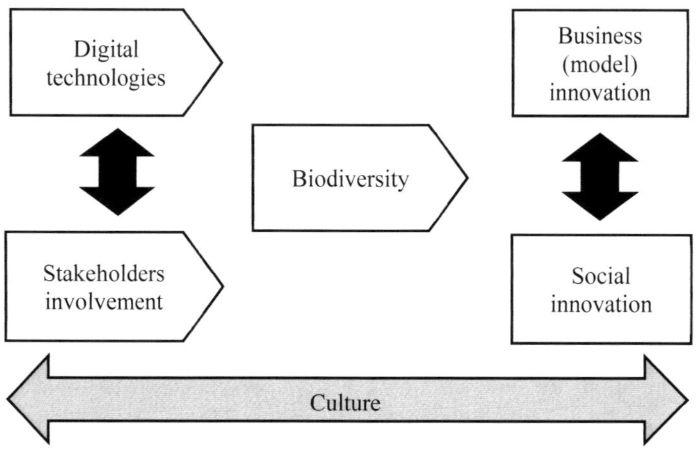

Source: Authors' elaboration.

Figure 1. Theoretical framework proposed

3. CONCLUSION

The research aims at assessing how biodiversity goals could be included into the business activities and how it relates to innovation from a business perspective and a connection with the social perspective. Based on a multiple case studies approach, this preliminary version of the study highlights the relevance of digital technologies and stakeholders' involvement for the achievement of biodiversity goals, and that the latter can be a driver for business and social innovation. Moreover, the study provides further knowledge in describing how policy-makers can support biodiversity acting on the promotion of a culture about biodiversity relevance.

Although this is only a preliminary step of the study, it has different theoretical and practical implications. Theoretically, the study advances literature about the use of digital technologies for sustainable goals by highlighting their relevance, combined with the involvement of stakeholders, in a sort of open innovation strategy (Rafael et al, 2022) to foster biodiversity protection and promotion. Secondly, the study enriches the literature about diversity and innovation relationships (Hewlett et al., 2013) by showing that also biodiversity can be a driver of innovation for business and society as it allows to innovate business processes and model and to foster the social engagement into biodiversity practices. All factors are relevant but culture assumes a key role, Indeed, thirdly, these preliminary findings shows that culture is a central element to reach sustainable goals both in the business and social domains.

Practically, companies should consider the use of digital technologies (various kind of technologies for various kind of activities and purposes) as well as the involvement of (different) stakeholders as the main factors to reach positive results in terms of biodiversity protection and promotion. Digital technologies allow to favor the development of an efficient ecosystem of services (preventing, monitoring but also promoting) needed for biodiversity (Pimm et al., 2015). The involvement of stakeholders leads to an integrated strategy that accelerates the process of transition towards sustainable businesses that favor biodiversity (Leclère et al., 2020). Moreover, by reaching biodiversity goals, companies have to consider the opportunity to innovate their own business model to reach new individuals' needs. In this way, companies can favor the spread of ecological knowledge, which is very important in influencing business and social perceptions and actions regarding biodiversity.

Finally, the results of analysis highlighted the relevance of culture for this kind of topics. Culture is a cross-sectional factor that affects all the different linkages among the variables analyzed. In this sense, policy-makers should contribute to improve the social context, not only through rules and regulations, but also through communication and promotion policies for organizations and citizens to favor learning about biodiversity. Social learning describes the process through which new ecological knowledge translates into business (Siebenhüner and Arnold, 2007) and social actions (Siebenhüner et al., 2016) regarding biodiversity.

The study has some limitations that could be thought as hints for the future research. Firstly, the study is based only on the analysis of three companies. More case studies of different industries will improve the understanding of the phenomenon. Moreover, the study bases on a qualitative exploratory analysis. A more comprehensive research considering a quantitative analysis and other variables in addition to those reported in Figure 1, such as culture, could be improve the understanding of relationships among the different variables.

REFERENCES

Boiral O. and Heras-Saizarbitoria I. 2017. Managing Biodiversity Through Stakeholder Involvement: Why, Who, and for What Initiatives?. *In Journal of Business Ethics*, Vol. 140, No. 3, pp. 403-421.

Broccardo L. et al, 2023. How Digitalization Supports a Sustainable Business Model: A Literature Review. *In Technological Forecasting and Social Change*, Vol. 187, DOI: 10.1016/j.techfore.2022.122146.

Bronzetti G. et al, 2021. Disclosure of Innovation on Sustainability Report. *In European Journal of Innovation Management*, Vol. 26, No. 3, pp. 885-907.

Buysse K. and Verbeke A. 2003. Proactive Environmental Strategies: A Stakeholder Management Perspective. *In Strategic Management Journal*, Vol. 24, No. 5, pp. 453-470.

Cardinale B. J. et al, 2012. Biodiversity Loss and Its Impact on Humanity. *In Nature*, Vol. 486, pp. 59– 67.

Costanza R. et al, 1997. The Value of the World's Ecosystem Services and Natural Capital. *In Nature*, Vol. 387, pp. 253-260.

Cragg W. and Greenbaum A. 2002. Reasoning about Responsibilities: Mining Company Managers on What Stakeholders Are Owed. *In Journal of Business Ethics*, Vol. 39, No. 3, pp. 319-335.

Cumming D. et al, 2020. The Unintended Consequences of Biotechnology Innovation Adoption. *In Industry & Innovation*, Vol. 27, No. 10, pp. 1089–1109.

Feger C. and Mermet L. 2022. New Business Models for Biodiversity and Ecosystem Management Services: An Action Research with a Large Environmental Sector Company. *In Organization & Environment*, Vol. 35, No. 2, pp. 252–281.

Freeman R.E. and Reed D.L. 1983. Stockholders and Stakeholders: A New Perspective on Corporate Governance. *In California Management Review*, Vol. 25, No 3, pp. 88-106.

Hewlett S.A. et al, 2013. How Diversity Can Drive Innovation. *In Harvard Business Review*, Vol. 91, No. 12, pp. 30.

Jones M.J. and Solomon J. F. 2013. Problematising Accounting for Biodiversity. *In Accounting, Auditing & Accountability Journal*, Vol. 26, No. 5, pp. 668-687.

Leclère D. et al, 2020. Bending the Curve of Terrestrial Biodiversity Needs an Integrated Strategy. *In Nature*, Vol. 585, pp. 551-574.

Lettice F. et al, 2010. The Social Innovation Process: Themes, Challenges and Implications for Practice. *In International Journal of Technology Management*, Vol. 51, No. 1, pp. 139–158.

Mcabee S.T. et al, 2017. Inductive Reasoning: The Promise of Big Data. *In Human Resource Management Review*, Vol. 27, No. 2, pp. 277-290.

Mitchell R. 2008. Knowledge Creation in Groups with Diverse Composition. *In Academy of Management Proceedings*, Vol. 8, No. 1, pp. 1–6.

Østergaard C.R. et al, 2011. Does a Different View Create Something New? The Effect of Employee Diversity on Innovation. *In Research Policy*, Vol. 40, No. 3, pp. 500–509.

Piccarozzi M. et al, 2023. Industry 4.0 Technologies as a Lever for Sustainability in the Communication of Large Companies to Stakeholders. *In European Journal of Innovation Management*. DOI: 10.1108/EJIM-11-2022-0641.

Piccarozzi M. et al, 2022. Is This a New Story of the 'Two Giants'? A Systematic Literature Review of the Relationship Between Industry 4.0, Sustainability and Its Pillars. *In Technological Forecasting and Social Change*, Vol. 177, pp. 1-25.

Pichlak M. and Szromek A.R. 2021. Eco-Innovation, Sustainability and Business Model Innovation by Open Innovation Dynamics. *In Journal of Open Innovation: Technology, Market, and Complexity*, Vol. 7, No. 2. doi: 10.3390/joitmc7020149.

Pimm S. et al, 2015. Emerging Technologies to Conserve Biodiversity. *In Trends in Ecology Evolution*, Vol. 30, pp. 685-696.

Rafael, S. et al, 2022. Bio-Centered Interaction Design: A New Paradigm for Human-System Interaction. *Proceedings of International Conference on Human-Computer Interaction*. Cham, Springer International Publishing, pp. 69-79.

Reade C. et al, 2015. Invisible Compromises: Global Business, Local Ecosystems, and the Commercial Bumble Bee Trade. *In Organization & Environment*, Vol. 28, pp. 436-457.

Reale R. et al, 2019. Biodiversity Conservation Actions as a Tool to Improve the Management of Sustainable Corporations and Their Needs Ecosystem Services. *In Journal of Cleaner Production*, Vol. 219, pp. 1-10.

Sabherwal R. and King W.R. 1991. Towards a Theory of Strategic Use of Information Resources: An Inductive Approach. *In Information and Management*, Vol. 20, No. 3, pp. 191-212.

Salmi, A. et al, 2023. Biodiversity Management: A Supply Chain Practice view. *In Journal of Purchasing & Supply Management*, Vol. 29. DOI: 10.1016/j.pursup.2023.100865.

Siebenhüner B. and Arnold M. 2007. Organizational Learning to Manage Sustainable Development. *In Business Strategy and the Environment*, Vol. 16, pp. 339-353.

Siebenhüner B. et al, 2016. Social Learning Research in Ecological Economics: A Survey. *In Environmental Science & Policy*, Vol. 55, pp. 116-126.

Smith T. et al, 2020. Social Underpinnings of Ecological Knowledge: Business Perceptions of Biodiversity as Social Learning. *In Organization & Environment*, Vol. 33, No 2, pp. 175–194.

Stock T. et al, 2018. Industry 4.0 as Enabler for a Sustainable Development: A Qualitative Assessment of Its Ecological and Social Potential. *In Process Safety and Environmental Protection*, Vol. 118, pp. 254-267.

Thomas D.R. 2006. A General Inductive Approach for Analyzing Qualitative Evaluation Data. *In American Journal of Evaluation*, Vol. 27, No. 2, pp. 237-246.

Vence X. and Trigo A. 2009. Diversity of Innovation Patterns in Services. *In The Service Industries Journal*, Vol. 29, No. 12, pp. 1635-1657.

Whiteman G. et al, 2013. Planetary Boundaries: Ecological Foundations for Corporate Sustainability. *In Journal of Management Studies*, Vol. 50, pp. 307-336.

Winn M.I. and Pogutz S. 2013. Business, Ecosystems, and Biodiversity: New Horizons for Management Research. *In Organization & Environment*, Vol. 26, pp. 203-229.

Yadav, G. et a, 2020. A Framework to Achieve Sustainability in Manufacturing Organisations of Developing Economies Using Industry 4.0 Technologies' Enablers. *In Computers in Industry*, Vol. 122, pp. 1-13.

Yin R.K. 2014. *Case study research: Design and methods, 5th ed.*, Sage, Los Angeles, CA.

Ziegler R. et al, 2022. Social Innovation for Biodiversity: A Literature Review and Research Challenges. *In Ecological Economics*, Vol. 193, DOI: 10.1016/j.ecolecon.2021.107336.

IMPLEMENTATION OF INSTRUCTIONAL DESIGN FOR SELF-PACED LEARNING

Kurt Englmeier
Schmalkalden University of Applied Science, Faculty of Computer Science
Blechhammer, 98574 Schmalkalden, Germany

ABSTRACT

This paper addresses self-paced learning within digital courses, focusing on instructional design paradigms to cater to the needs of individual learners. Through content structuring and leveraging large language models (LLMs), digital learning platforms can provide learners with a clear understanding of the subject matter while enabling flexible learning. However, challenges arise in measuring and managing learners' study efforts and cognitive loads effectively. Strategies such as setting minimum reading times, recommending study breaks, and assigning individual Learning Complexity Indices (LCIs) help optimize the learning experience. The paper also explores the role of metacognition in self-regulated learning, emphasizing learners' responsibility in managing their learning processes. Despite advancements in digital learning environments, challenges persist in supporting learners with diverse backgrounds and abilities, especially in chat-based learning settings. Examples from the prototypical implementation of a learning platform demonstrate how personalized learning experiences can be enhanced through data-driven insights and tailored recommendations.

KEYWORDS

Self-Paced Learning, Instructional Design, Digital Courses, Metacognition, Cognitive Load, Personalized Learning

1. INTRODUCTION

Self-paced learning is a very comfortable and flexible way of learning. It allows them to learn whenever they want and wherever they want and enables them to adapt learning to their individual pace. Autonomously learning with a book lends itself to provide a first image of the content scope and the learning setting suitable for self-paced learning, though digital environments can and must support the learner's knowledge acquisition in many more ways.

The overall goal shall be the learners' sustainable adoption of knowledge. There is no single design paradigm for digital learning environments supporting self-paced learning. There manyfold ways to address sustainable knowledge acquisition in such a setting. They all depend on the characteristics of the target audience. In any case, there are some aspects beside the learnability of the content itself, common in all approaches for self-paced learning. Learners require support in planning and managing their journey through the learning content. Just because learners learn, does automatically mean that they know how to learn. Ideally, the knowledge to be learned shall be stored in the long-term memory to be recalled again and again over a long period (Forsberg, 2021). For instance, students tend to cram for their exam. They learn the content required for the exam in the shortest possible time. However, it is well known that this knowledge is prone to oblivion within few days after the exam. This learning behavior of students is just an example why it is necessary that digital learning environments must support learners in managing their journey to acquire sustainable knowledge.

The next important aspect is the structure of the knowledge addressed by the digital course. Beginners, or those new to a topic, often lack a clear understanding of the breadth and structure of the subject matter. Structured digital environments can guide these learners through their educational journey by clearly delineating the knowledge into interrelated parts. This helps learners integrate new information with their existing knowledge, fostering a deeper understanding and retention.

Chat-based learning environments offer a unique approach to self-paced learning. While chatbots have proven to be effective tools for interactive learning, engaging students in conversation and providing mostly accurate responses, their efficacy largely depends on the learners' ability to pose relevant questions and steer the dialogue effectively. Successful interaction with a chatbot generally presupposes a foundational knowledge of the subject matter. Without this, learners may struggle to ask appropriate questions and guide the dialogue to meet their learning needs and interests. Furthermore, unlike more comprehensive digital learning platforms, chatbots often lack the visual cues that help clarify the knowledge structure of the digital learning material.

Structured digital learning environments, on the other hand, provide a clear picture of the scope and structure of the knowledge to be learned. They can clearly indicate the effort learners should dedicate to studying the subject matter at any stage of their learning journey. However, they also require thoughtful implementation of support structures to help learners effectively manage their educational journey and achieve sustainable mastery of the subject matter.

This paper presents design and implementation of self-paced learning in structured digital learning environments. The courses offered in this format address learners that have no or only very little previous knowledge of the course subject. These learners usually require intensive guidance along their journey through the learning content. The Schmalkalden University currently offers three courses using the digital learning format described here. They are part of its international course program and have an audience of about 250 students in the third year of their Bachelor program. The paper and the design presented here, therefore, reflect also their experiences and the university's lessons learnt with this learning format.

Furthermore, the paper describes the role of large language models (LLMs) in enhancing these learning platforms. The incorporation of LLMs is seen as a transformative element that can provide personalized assistance and enriched interactive experiences, thereby augmenting the learning process. By integrating advanced technological tools such as LLMs, the learning format presented here aims to revolutionize traditional paradigms of educational delivery and support, offering scalable, adaptable, and learner-centered educational environments.

2. SUPPORTING THE LEARNERS' METACOGNITION – RELATED WORK

The efficacy of learning depends not only on learners' confidence in their learning abilities but also on their capacity to develop and manage effective learning strategies and activities. Pivotal in this context is the learners' metacognition (Flavell, 1977), the cognitive control they exert over their learning endeavors and their outcomes. Learners establish goals and tailor their learning processes to suit their individual needs and progress. However, empirical evidence indicates that learners often misjudge their abilities, either underestimating or overestimating them (Azevedo, 2004).

Learners have to assume responsibility for their learning journey, particularly in developing their own metacognitive self-regulation strategies (SRL) (Lajoie, 2008). These strategies empower learners to manage their cognitive processes, monitor their learning efforts, and regulate their thinking to enhance learning outcomes. Metacognition enables learners to set realistic and achievable goals, monitor progress, and employ diverse techniques to comprehend and retain learning materials. Proficient SRL skills facilitate ambitious metacognitive self-regulation strategies, crucial for successful completion of digital courses (Kizilcec, 2017).

While self-paced learning offers learners tremendous flexibility in managing their learning processes, it also places greater responsibility on them for managing their learning progress, simply because the freedom to learn at one's convenience may not automatically translate into a successful learning journey. Early experiences with self-paced digital courses at our university revealed significant disparities in students' metacognitive abilities, often resulting in inappropriate learning strategies such as cramming for exams.

The primary goal for learners should be to establish new knowledge within their long-term memory, thereby achieving truly sustainable knowledge. Long-term memory serves as the repository for enduring knowledge (Anderson, 2020), while working memory is generally utilized for short-term objectives like reasoning or problem-solving (Baddeley, 1992). Although working memory can store information temporarily, the crucial process is the "transfer" of information from working to long-term memory, essential for generating sustainable knowledge. Experts stand out not merely due to their ability to hold information in working memory, but by their capacity to retrieve information from long-term memory independently of their working memory's capacity (Brown N. C., 2024).

The successful acquisition of sustainable knowledge, however, emerges not only from the learners' ability to assume self-responsibility for their learning journey (Winne, 2015) (Zimmerman, 2015) (Rheinberg, 2000). In self-paced learning, the learners have to actively manage their learning processes without external guidance, from a personal tutor for instance. Without such support, the degree of ownership directly impacts learners' success rates (Douglas, 2007). Weak SRL skills often impede learners' ability to assume sufficient ownership to complete a course successfully.

To support and enhance learners' SRL strategies, various interventions and approaches have been proposed (Lau, 2022). These may include methods for setting realistic goals, fostering effective self-monitoring habits, managing study time efficiently, and employing cognitive and metacognitive strategies for improved comprehension and retention.

3. INSTRUCTIONAL DESIGN FOR SUSTAINABLE LEARNING

Effectively implementing strategies to support self-paced and sustainable learning demands meticulous attention to several key elements. These include instructional design, interaction design, and pedagogical support mechanisms. Crucial features such as collaborative opportunities with peers, and immediate feedback from tutors or chatbots, must be integrated to facilitate effective learning experiences.

In this paper we concentrate on the first implementation of the instructional design for our digital courses. Our main focus here is on courses providing factual and conceptual knowledge including principles, methods and theories that govern a fundamental and wide-spread knowledge of the subject addressed. Examples of such subjects are foundations of (agile) project management, blockchain technology, data security and privacy, and import regulations.

3.1 Fostering Individual Mental Models of the Course Content

The design paradigm of the structured learning environment outlined here prioritizes simplicity to reduce extraneous cognitive load (Brown N. C., 2024). Navigating the course content and using the learning controls must be as straightforward as possible. Therefore, the courses are structured traditionally with chapters and subchapters. Learning controls, which typically conclude subchapters, consist of three to twelve questions depending on the subchapter's scope. The amount of information provided on each page is kept minimal. The basic design of text and quiz pages, as well as navigation options, remains consistent across courses. Furthermore, the use of gaming elements is limited, despite their potential to boost learner motivation. This design principle focuses the intrinsic cognitive load on its most important objective: integrating pieces or chunks of information to form knowledge of a higher-level top (Brown N. C., 2024).

Each page and subchapter are meticulously titled, with content organized into manageable chunks. These titles are generated through sophisticated text summarization techniques enabled by large language models. This semantic representation allows learners to easily retrieve specific course content at any stage of their learning journey. Our platform features an AI-driven search function that enables learners to state free-text queries and locate the most relevant pages or content chunks within the course.

The initial structuring of the course content (as shown in figure 1), reflected in the titles, serves as a guiding framework for learners, providing them with an overview of the course subject and its intricacies. For novice learners, focusing on these titles provides a good starting point to grasp the surface details of the content. However, as learners delve deeper into the course and begin to navigate the content using their own terminology, they gradually develop a more nuanced understanding (figure 5). This iterative process not only helps learners construct individual mental models of the content but also cultivates the ability to form abstract representations, mirroring the perspective of subject matter experts. The formation of an individual abstract representation of the course content is essential for the learners' sustainable adoption and organization of the course knowledge.

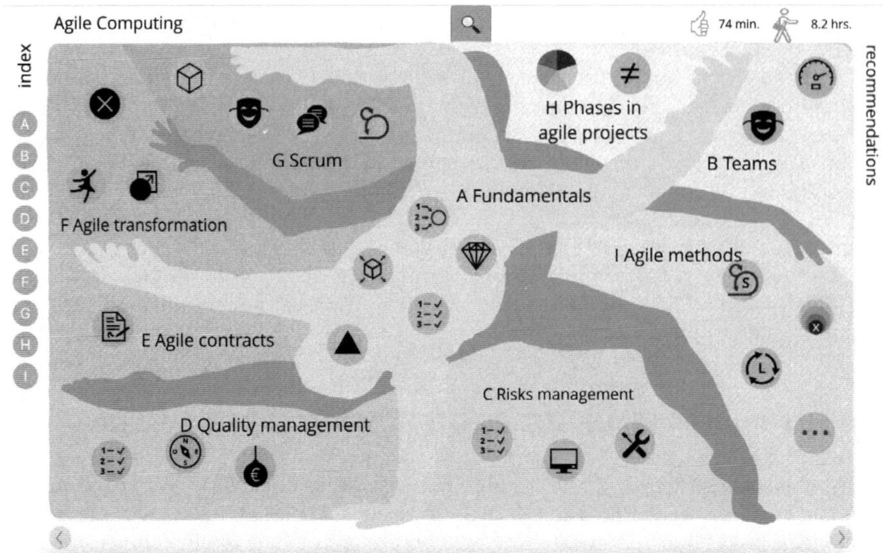

Figure 1. Overview of the course "Agile Project Management" and its structuring into chapters. In the upper right corner, the system indicates the learning effort (time) already completed by the learner and the remaining studying time

3.2 Supporting the Learners' Time Management

Measuring the effort required to learn a certain material can be complex, as it often involves multiple factors. Effort in learning is not solely determined by various parameters (Broadbent, 2015). The most basic elements are the time spent on a text or quiz query and the results achieved in learn controls. By recording these values for every learner of the course we can obtain a series of important parameters indicating the performance of the learners and the (intrinsic) cognitive load of the different sections of the course:

- Average studying time of a page, subchapter, chapter, or quiz (across all learners)
- Average studying time of each learner
- Average points achieved in the learn controls (quizzes)

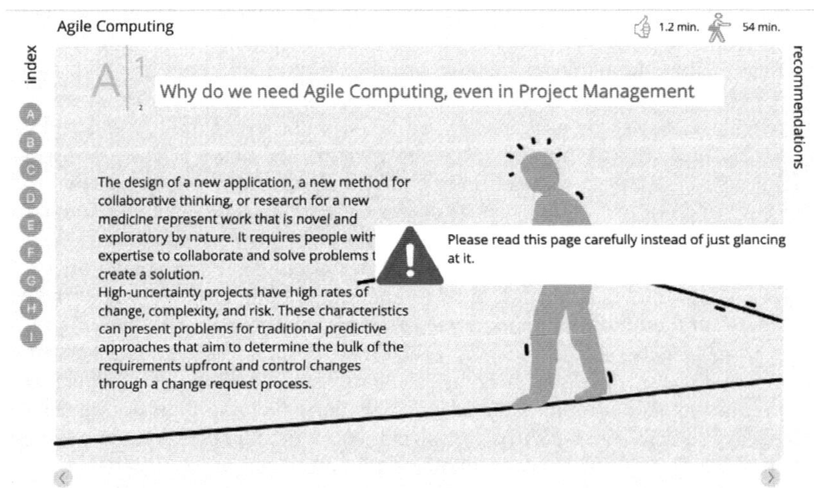

Figure 2. When accessing a page for the first time, learners are required to spend a minimum amount of time reading the text before they can proceed to the next page. While navigating through a chapter, the system displays the total time spent and the remaining time required for the chapter in the upper right corner

Initial study duration benchmarks are established by the course instructor. For instance, we assume that the average reading speed for academic texts defaults to 100 words per minute. This value serves as the minimum reading duration indicated to learners. Upon initial engagement with a page, the system ensures comprehensive reading by restricting navigation until the minimum reading duration elapses (see figure 2). Subsequently, learners enjoy unrestricted navigation across all pages they have previously visited and carefully read. The recommended reading time also accounts for breaks between study sessions, as optimal learning occurs when new knowledge is allowed to settle over brief intervals (Dempster, 1988). The minimum break time in our course aligns with the duration required to study the respective subchapter.

Furthermore, there's a recommended maximum study time per day or week. At the start of each session, the system informs the learners of the recommended learning term and alerts them if the minimum study time required exceeds the maximum study time. Alongside this notification, the system informs the learners about their achievements (figure 4b) and recommends the next step on the learning journey, typically suggesting a return to the point where they previously left off (figure 4a). However, the system also considers the natural process of forgetting and may recommend revisiting text sections based on elapsed time since initial study. For quizzes, recommendations are tailored based on performance levels. If quiz results indicate weak performance, the system may suggest retaking the quiz after a shorter interval than for excellent results.

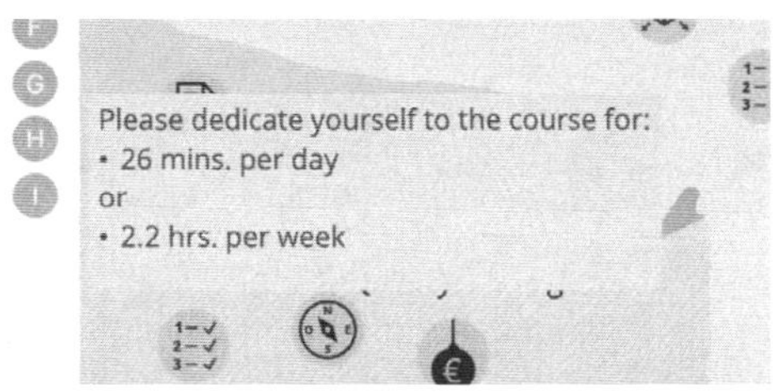

Figure 3. At the beginning of each session the learners are informed on the effort they should dedicate to studying the remaining learning material of the entire course

Course sections require varying study effort, with complexity and difficulty influencing learner effort significantly. To reflect this, we assign an individual Learning Complexity Index (LCI) to each course section (Sweller, 2019). Initially, it's the tutor's responsibility to assess the depth, technicality, and conceptual difficulty of each section, with an index of 1.0 representing average complexity. Observing learner study behavior allows us to refine the LCI, adjusting it to accurately reflect the effort required by learners.

Recognizing that each learner's journey is unique, the indicator model must be sensitive to individual learner characteristics. By calculating the individual Learning Effort Index (iLEI) for each learner, we can personalize the remaining time required to study new chapters or complete remaining sections. The iLEI also applied when individualized learning calendars (see figure 4a) are generated.

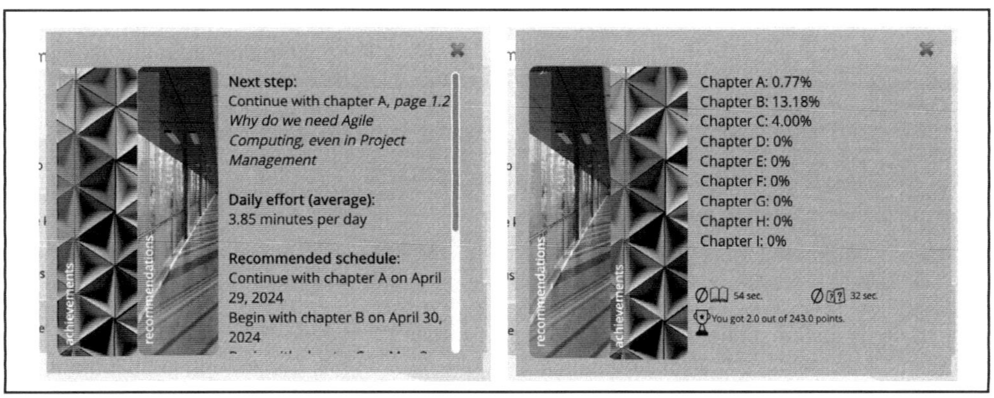

Figure 4. (a) The learners get recommendations for the next steps in their learner journey and the learning effort. (b) They get an overview on their achievements indicating the learning material completed, their average time for reading texts and answering questions, and their results in the learn controls

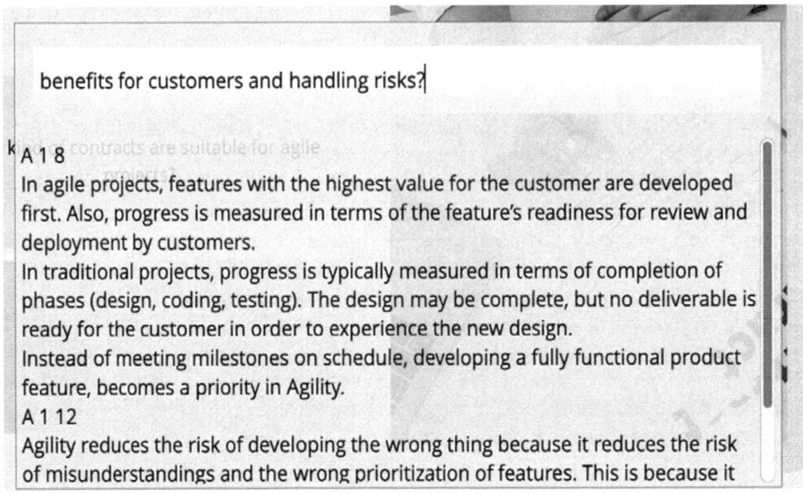

Figure 5. The learners have the possibility to retrieve selected sections from the course at any point along their learner journey. Without leaving the actual page, they can ask the system to provide them with the course content most suitable to their search query. The matching algorithm in the background uses large language models to identify the content sections that match the user query

4. CONCLUSIONS

Digital learning platforms are increasingly emphasizing self-paced or self-directed learning, sometimes with the support of chatbots. This paper has focused on instructional design for self-paced learning, ensuring that learners maintain a clear and comprehensive focus on the content throughout their learning journey. For learners unfamiliar with the course subject, close guidance is provided, indicating both scope and the expected time commitment to successfully complete the digital learning material.

Efforts to measure the required study effort for specific material typically rely on parameters such as reading time and performance in learning assessments. By leveraging these observations, digital learning environments can develop tailored recommendations to guide learners effectively. However, benchmarks for study effort vary individually, necessitating the adaptation of recommendations to suit each learner's unique needs and interests.

Using and evaluating the digital course format for self-paced learning is crucial for understanding the cognitive load experienced by learners. These results provide insights for improving course layout, enhancing interaction features, and refining recommendations to better align with individual learner profiles. Analyzing the time learners spend on specific text pages or quiz questions, for instance, can help identify course sections that may be difficult to understand and need improvement. Furthermore, the immediate with the learners of these courses revealed and will reveal even more hints on possibilities for improvements. They indicated, for instance, that they would like to see more possibilities for individual adaptations, i.e. course content arrangements, responding to their quiz results. The system could, for instance, propose certain course section for repeated or further reading depending on the result in the quizzes. All in all, they request further dynamic and situation-specific composition of content that can only be achieved by applying AI-based text analysis features.

This responsiveness to individual strengths, weaknesses, and constraints ensures sustained learner engagement and motivation, as the learning journey is tailored to their specific requirements. Looking ahead, the next challenge in our project is to deepen our understanding of learner performance and integrate more tailored recommendation features into the system's interaction, further enhancing the personalized learning experience.

ACKNOWLEDGEMENT

Research as outlined here is part of the eduplex_api project under the research framework INVITE of the Federal Institute for Vocational Education and Training (BIBB) funded by the German Federal Ministry of Education and Research.

REFERENCES

Anderson, J. (2020). *Cognitive Psychology and Its Implications*. Worth Publishers, London, UK.

Azevedo, R. and Cromley, J.G., 2004. Does training on self-regulated learning facilitate students' learning with hypermedia? Vol. 96. *Journal of Educational Psychology*. Vol. 96, No. 3, pp 523-535.

Baddeley, A., (1992). Working memory. *Science*. Vol. 255, No. 5044, pp 556-559.

Broadbent, J. and Poon, L.P. (2015). Self-regulated learning strategies & academic achievement in online higher education learning environments: A systematic review. *The internet and higher education*. Vol. 27, pp 1-13.

Brown, N.C.C. et al., (2024). 10 Things Software Developers Should Learn about Learning. *Communications of the ACM*. Vol. 67, No. 1, pp 78-87.

Dempster, F., (1988). The spacing effect: A case study in the failure to apply the results of psychological research. *American Psychologist*. Vol. 43, No. 8, pp 627-634.

Douglas, I. and Alemanne, N., (2007). Measuring student participation and effort. *Proceedings of the IADIS International Conference on Cognition and Exploratory Learning in Digital Age*. Algarve, Portugal. Pp 299-302.

Flavell, J. H., (1977). *Cognitive development*. Prentice-Hall, Englewood Cliffs, USA.

Forsberg, A. et al., (2021). Chapter One - The role of working memory in long-term learning: Implications for childhood development. *Psychology of Learning and Motivation*. Academic Press, Cambridge, USA. Pp 1-45.

Kizilcec, R.F. et al., (2017). Self-regulated learning strategies predict learner behavior and goal attainment in Massive Open Online Courses. *Computers & Education*. Vol. 104, pp 18-33.

Lajoie, S. P., (2008). Metacognition, Self-Regulation, and Self-regulated Learning: A Rose by any other Name? *Educational Psychology Review*. Vol. 20, pp 469-475.

Lau, K. and Jong, M.S.Y., (2022). Acceptance of and self-regulatory practices in online learning and their effects on the participation of Hong Kong secondary school students in online learning. *Education and Information Technologies*. Vol. 28, pp 8715–8732.

Rheinberg, F. et al., (2000). Motivation and Self-Regulated Learning. *Advances in Psychology*. Vol. 131, pp 81-108.

Sweller, J. et al., (2019). Cognitive architecture and instructional design: 20 years later. *Educational Psychology Review*. Vol. 31, No. 2, pp 261–292.

Winne, P., (2015). Self-Regulated Learning. *International Encyclopedia of the Social & Behavioral Sciences*. Pp 535–540.

Zimmerman, B., (2015). Self-Regulated Learning: Theories, Measures, and Outcomes. *International Encyclopedia of the Social & Behavioral Sciences*. Pp 541-546.

METAVERSE TECHNOLOGY IN HIGHER EDUCATION: A CONCEPTUAL MODEL

Mutaz M. Al-Debei[1], Omar Hujran[2] and Hazar Y. Hmoud[1]
[1]*Department of Management Information Systems, Business School, The University of Jordan, Amman, Jordan*
[2]*College of Business and Economics, United Arab Emirates University, Al Ain, United Arab Emirates*

ABSTRACT

Metaverse applications would soon be as prevalent as TikTok, Instagram, and Facebook. Recently, metaverse applications have begun to emerge in numerous fields, including higher education. As technology advances and provides new 3D immersive and fictional worlds, HEI is keen to learn how to meet these new opportunities. They are truly interested in understanding the aspects that would facilitate the successful adoption of metaverse technology by Gen Z students, who represent the current student generation. Nonetheless, there is a scarcity of research that provides useful insights into the salient factors that influence students' intentions and behaviors towards the usage of metaverse technology in higher education (Hi-Eduverse). Thus, this research aims at developing a consolidative conceptual model that combines a decomposed version of the TPB and PIIT. This model will then be used as part of an ongoing research project to examine Jordanian Gen Z university students' intentions to adopt metaverse technology and their positive Word-of-Mouth (WoM) behavior.

KEYWORDS

Metaverse, HEI, Educational Technology, TPB, PIIT, Personal Innovativeness

1. INTRODUCTION

The development of metaverse technology has sparked a great deal of interest and discussion in various sectors over the years, mostly surrounding its applications in higher education (Akour et al., 2022; Al-Adwan and Al-Debei, 2023). A highly dynamic and creative metaverse-based platform is available to Higher Educational Institutions (HEIs), which is often described as a single 3D immersive room in which the physical and virtual worlds are mingled (Dhawan, 2020). All the learners could involve with various ways of interaction inside the Metaverse where they could manipulate avatars through alternatively connectivity/measurement devices like motion sensors and peripherals (Al-Adwan & Al-Debei, 2023). Indeed, there are numerous opportunities to implement transformative developments in educational settings by incorporating metaverse technology (Dhawan, 2020; Dwivedi et al., 2022). This implies changing traditional educational patterns with a paradigm that focuses on personalized, embodied, interactive, collaborative and experiential learning.

Notwithstanding the increasing enthusiasm surrounding the implementation of metaverse technology in higher education, there is a significant lack of study on the factors that influence students' intentions and actions towards adopting metaverse technology in higher education settings, which will be referred to as Hi-Eduverse, perhaps due to the infancy of these implementations (Dwivedi et al., 2022; Al-Adwan and Al-Debei, 2023). Although numerous studies have examined the use of technology in different educational environments, there is a noticeable absence of targeted research on the factors that impact the intentions and actions of students in the metaverse context. The current body of research frequently lacks a thorough comprehension of the cognitive, social, and personal factors that influence students' choices to embrace metaverse technology in higher education. This study is one of the initial investigations on the intentions of students to adopt the metaverse within higher education institutions, to the best knowledge of the authors.

Therefore, the current study aims to fill this research gap by developing an integrative research model to thoroughly examine the factors that drive the adoption of metaverse technology and the consequent positive word-of-mouth behaviors demonstrated by students. Indeed, it is essential to address this gap in order to advance our knowledge in this context given that the decisive success of Hi-Eduverse initiatives depends on the students. It also pertinent to policymakers and higher education institutions who aim to strategically incorporate metaverse technology into the educational experience of the current generation of students.

To accomplish the goals and objectives of this study, we are integrating a decomposed form of the Theory of Planned Behavior (TPB) along with the Personal Innovativeness in the domain of Information Technology (PIIT). The standard theory of planned behavior is useful for the analyses of people's intentions and behaviors that are shaped by their attitudes toward the behavior, their sense of control over it, and the perceptions of important others (Ajzen, 1991). Nevertheless, we specifically in this study decomposed the "subjective norm" part of the theory to examine how both peers and superiors impact students' intentions to use the Hi-Eduverse environment. Not only that, but we also expanded the theory to include the Personal Innovativeness in the domain of IT (PIIT) to get a clearer picture of what motivates Gen Z students to adopt Hi-Eduverse and talk positively about it to others. By doing so, we trust that this approach is practical to comprehensively examine the various behavioral factors that would influence Gen Z students' decisions toward Metaverse technology and within the context of higher education.

2. THEORETICAL BACKGROUND

2.1 Theory of Planned Behavior (TPB)

The Theory of Planned Behavior (TPB) is a well-known psychological theory that is considered valuable in understanding and justifying people's decisions and actions (Ajzen, 1985; 1991). The TPB is useful in explaining and predicting people's behaviors by considering their intentions and the factors that shape those intentions. In fact, the TPB is an extension of the Theory of Reasoned Action (TRA). TPB builds on TRA by adding the notion of perceived behavioral control which refers to how much control a person feels they have over their actions.

In TPB, three main constructs influence a person's intention to act and behave in a specific way: this involves their perceptions toward the behavior (attitude), they pressure they feel towards performing the behavior (subjective norm), and their perception of the level of control they have over the behavior (perceived behavioral control). Attitude is the extent to which a person has a positive opinion towards the behavior. The subjective norm is around friends, family, instructors, or colleagues, and how they feel about the behavior. Perceived behavioral control is defined as users' perceptions of how difficult or easy it will be to engage in the behavior in question.

TPB has been established to be a strong model as well as been utilized in many fields; however, some scholars argue that it fails to provide an adequate understanding of how and why individuals act in a certain manner (Al-Debei et al., 2013). The author of the theory, namely Ajzen, was confident enough that TPB could be enhanced further with the incorporation of other pertinent constructs. Consequently, prior studies have revealed that enhancing the TPB with appropriate and contextual variables enhances the theory's ability to predict and explain user behavior (see Taylor & Todd, 1995; Brown & Venkatesh, 2005; Al-Debei et al., 2013; Leong et al., 2023). Consequently, this study extends the TPB construct through including Perceived Innovativeness in the domain of IT (PIIT) to have a better measure of prediction accuracy of Hi-Eduverse adoption by Gen Z students.

Furthermore, and within the context of subjective norms, we have explored the roles of both peers and superiors in shaping the intentions of Gen Z students to participate in the Hi-Eduverse environment. We believe that this decomposition of the subjective norms construct would provide a detailed understanding and analysis on the effectiveness of each of the type of social pressures in deriving Gen Z to use the Hi-Eduverse and spread a positive WoM about this emerging learning platform.

2.2 Personal Innovativeness in IT (PIIT)

As identified, the Theory of Planned Behavior has been expanded in this study by including Perceived Innovativeness in IT. In accordance with Agarwal and Prasad (1998), PIIT is an individual's tendency to adopt and consider new and emerging technology. The majority of innovative individuals are much more mature in terms of their level of digital literacy as well as their level of technical skills. They hence will always perceive any new technology, for instance, the Metaverse, to be easier to use and less threatening. They are usually motivated to learn and explore new technologies and try those that have just emerged (Fan et al., 2020; Al-Adwan and Al-Debei, 2023).

Hence, incorporating PIIT in the research model makes our study more insightful, useful, and effective in taking a look at how well prepared the Gen Z students are to embark onto the Hi-Eduverse. We postulate that PIIT may be best suited to Gen Z who are totally 'tech-savvy' and comfortable with digital interaction and emerging technologies. Inclusion of PIIT makes the research model more tailored to meet Gen Z's level of familiarity with technology since it takes into account the individual's innovativeness. Indeed, this addition to TPB assists us in understanding the characteristics that might make an individual adopt new technology. On the basis of PIIT, it is actually based on psychological traits like the willingness to try new technologies, openness to technological advances and comfort using technology that determines what makes Gen Z students committed to Hi-Eduverse and spread positive word-of-mouth about it.

3. HYPOTHESES DEVELOPMENT

The primary objective of this study is to investigate the factors that influence Gen Z learners' adoption of Hi-Eduverse and their intentions to share positive word-of-mouth (PWoM) about this new learning platform. To achieve this, we are using a contextualized and decomposed version of the Theory of Planned Behavior (TPB). The study model, which illustrates these determinants along with the consequences, is presented in Figure 1.

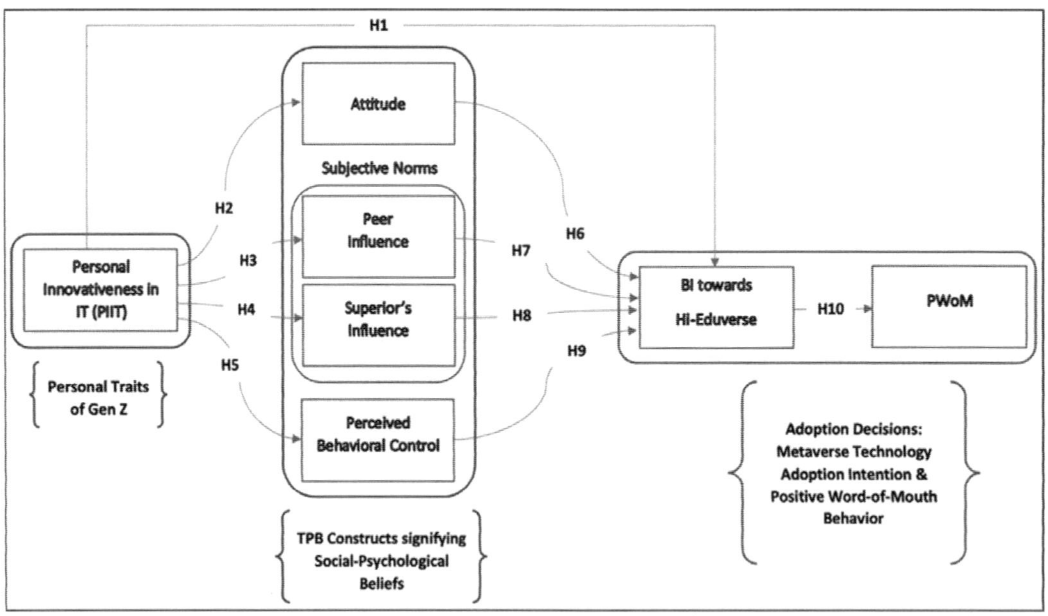

Figure 1. Research Model

3.1 Personal Innovativeness

Agarwal and Prasad (1998) define personal innovativeness as an attribute and predictor, signifying an individual's inclination to explore relatively novel information technologies. The notion of innovativeness has been thoroughly examined as a determinant that impacts the adoption of innovations (Aldahdouh et al., 2020). It is also frequently believed that individual inventiveness is a crucial element in fostering positive attitudes towards the use of new technologies (Chahal and Rani, 2022). In addition, personal innovativeness is also found as a vital enabler of various educational technology the adoption intention (Al-Adwan and Al Debei, 2023; Maisha and Shetu, 2023; Chahal and Rani, 2022). Moreover, Scholars agree that self-efficacy critically affects perceived behavioral control (Hung et al., 2021). With mounting consensus validating the connection between personal innovativeness and self-efficacy (Chahal and Rani, 2022; Bubou and Job, 2022), scant yet indicative evidence supports the transformative potential of personal innovativeness on perceived behavioral control. Therefore, despite limited research, this study presumes personal innovativeness holds a prominent position in modelling perceived behavioral control, serving as a decisive element in steering individuals' command over their own conduct. Furthermore, although there is very limited research exploring the link between personal innovativeness and subjective norms, this study argues that when highly innovative individuals combine their conviction in a technology's advantages with positive subjective norms, they create a powerful force driving technology adoption. Hence, the following hypotheses are proposed:

H1. Personal innovativeness positively influences student's behavioral intention towards Hi-Eduverse

H2. Personal innovativeness positively influences student's attitude towards Hi-Eduverse

H3. Personal innovativeness positively influences peer influence

H4. Personal innovativeness positively influences superior's influence

H5. Personal innovativeness positively influences perceived behavioral control

3.2 Attitude

Attitude is defined by Fishbein and Ajzen (1975) as the extent to which an individual holds a positive or negative evaluation regarding the performance of a specific behavior is referred to as their attitude toward that behaviour. These beliefs exert a tangible influence on the phases of the adoption process among individuals (Al Breiki et al., 2023). In particular, an individual who holds a more favorable perception of that behavior would exhibit a greater degree of intention to engage in that behavior. Consequently, attitude is considered a crucial determinant in urging behavioral intention (Chu and Chin, 2016). Thus, we posit:

H6. Attitude positively influences student's behavioural intention towards Hi-Eduverse

3.3 Perceived Behavioral Control

PBC is just the perceived ease or difficulty to perform a specific behaviour as evaluated in a subjective approach by an individual. The TPB sums up that an individual has beliefs concerning control linked with their perceptions that can hinder or facilitate performing particular behaviour. Research conducted pertaining to PBC revealed that perceived behavioural control was significantly related to the intention to use and accept technology. Previously conducted studies on educational technology are in support of this relationship (Wang, 2023; Wu, 2023; Lung-Guang, 2019). It is thus hypothesized that:

H7. Perceived behavioural control positively influences student's behavioural intention towards Hi-Eduverse

3.4 Subjective Norms

Social pressure to perform or abstain from a particular behaviour is referred to as subjective norms; this includes the influence of significant others (Fishbein and Ajzen, 1975). Individuals are influenced by a complex network of subjective normative beliefs, which reflect their perception of the expectations held by significant people in their lives (Al Breiki et al., 2023). Prior studies on educational technology adoption have shown the substantial effect of subjective norms on behavioural intention (Mashroofa et al., 2023; Songkram et al., 2023). Hence, we hypothesize:

H8. Peer influence positively impacts student's behavioral intention towards Hi-Eduverse

H9. Superior's influence positively impacts student's behavioral intention towards Hi-Eduverse

3.5 Behavioral Intention

Scholarly investigations emphasize the significance of behavioral intention in elucidating the adoption of learning-based technologies (Al-Adwan and Al-Debei, 2023). Behavioral intention itself is shaped by three fundamental components outlined in TPB. Of these, attitude assumes a particularly crucial position in explaining the emergence of positive word-of-mouth (PWoM). An individual holding a positive outlook towards a product or service is more inclined to communicate favorably about it, translating their enthusiasm into tangible words and phrases directed at others (Haverila et al., 2023). Accordingly, we posit:

H10. Student's behavioral intention towards Hi-Eduverse positively impacts positive word of mouth

4. CONCLUSIONS

There is a limited research that examines the determinants of metaverse adoption for academic purposes. This study sheds light on the key factors that may impact the intentions of Jordanian Gen Z higher education students to employ metaverse technology, more specifically the Hi-Eduverse framework, as well as their word-of-mouth behaviours in this regard. A conceptual research model has been developed in the current study as part of a larger research project. As a future work, an extensive empirical survey research will be carried out in Jordan to empirically validate the proposed model.

Of particular significance, however, are the theoretical implications of our work when viewed against the unique characteristics and tendencies of Generation Z students. As true natives to the technology, Generation Z members offer some very unique perspectives and behaviours within the realm of educational technology. This research, therefore, contributes to the knowledge base not only by emphasizing the Gen Z student but also by extending the TPB with the extremely relevant PIIT for Gen Z students. With the distinctive personality traits and inclinations of Gen Z, theoretical models need to be reframed to also capture the complexities introduced by the structures of authority, autonomy, and social influence during this very technology-savvy generation. With these findings therefore, theorists will be informed on the foundational frameworks that will reflect on unique characteristics of these Gen Z students. Theories will be up to date and applied in a field where educational technology is transformative and continuously evolving.

REFERENCES

Agarwal R., Prasad J. (1998). A conceptual and operational definition of personal innovativeness in the domain of information technology. *Inform. Syst. Res.* 9 204–215. https://doi.org/10.1287/isre.9.2.204

Ajzen, I. (1985). From intentions to actions: A theory of planned behavior. In *Action control: From cognition to behavior* (pp. 11-39). Berlin, Heidelberg: Springer Berlin Heidelberg.

Ajzen, I. (1991). The theory of planned behavior. *Organizational behavior and human decision processes*, *50*(2), 179-211.

Ajzen, I. (2020). The theory of planned behavior: Frequently asked questions. *Human Behavior and Emerging Technologies*, *2*(4), 314–324. https://publons.com/publon/10.1002/hbe2.195

Akour, I. A., Al-Maroof, R. S., Alfaisal, R., & Salloum, S. A. (2022). A conceptual framework for determining metaverse adoption in higher institutions of gulf area: An empirical study using hybrid SEM-ANN approach. *Computers and Education: Artificial Intelligence*, *3*, 100052.

Al-Adwan, A.S., Al-Debei, M.M. (2023). The determinants of Gen Z's metaverse adoption decisions in higher education: Integrating UTAUT2 with personal innovativeness in IT. Education and Information Technology. https://doi.org/10.1007/s10639-023-12080-1

Al Breiki, M., Al Abri, A., Al Moosawi, A. M., & Alburaiki, A. (2023). Investigating science teachers' intention to adopt virtual reality through the integration of diffusion of innovation theory and theory of planned behaviour: the moderating role of perceived skills readiness. *Education and information technologies*, *28*(5), 6165-6187.

Aldahdouh, T. Z., Nokelainen, P., & Korhonen, V. (2020). Technology and social media usage in higher education: The influence of individual innovativeness. *Sage Open*, *10*(1), 2158244019899441. https://doi.org/10.1177/2158244019899441

Al-Debei, M. M., Al-Lozi, E., & Papazafeiropoulou, A. (2013). Why people keep coming back to Facebook: Explaining and predicting continuance participation from an extended theory of planned behaviour perspective. *Decision support systems*, *55*(1), 43-54.

Brown, S. A., & Venkatesh, V. (2005). Model of adoption of technology in households: A baseline model test and extension incorporating household life cycle. *MIS quarterly*, 399-426.

Bubou, G. M., & Job, G. C. (2022). Individual innovativeness, self-efficacy and e-learning readiness of students of Yenagoa study centre, National Open University of Nigeria. *Journal of Research in Innovative Teaching & Learning*, *15*(1), 2–22. https://doi.org/10.1108/JRIT-12-2019-0079

Chahal, J., & Rani, N. (2022). Exploring the acceptance for e-learning among higher education students in India: combining technology acceptance model with external variables. *Journal of Computing in Higher Education*, *34*(3), 844-867. https://doi.org/10.1007/s12528-022-09327-0

Chu, T. H., & Chen, Y. Y. (2016). With good we become good: Understanding e-learning adoption by theory of planned behavior and group influences. *Computers & Education*, *92*, 37-52. https://doi.org/10.1016/j.compedu.2015.09.013

Dhawan, S. (2020). Online learning: A panacea in the time of COVID-19 crisis. *Journal of educational technology systems, 49*(1), 5–22. https://doi.org/10.1177/0047239520934018

Dwivedi, Y. K., Hughes, L., Baabdullah, A. M., Ribeiro-Navarrete, S., Giannakis, M., Al-Debei, M. M., et al. (2022). Metaverse beyond the hype: Multidisciplinary perspectives on emerging challenges, opportunities, and agenda for research, practice and policy. *International Journal of Information Management, 66*, 102542. https://doi.org/10.1016/j.ijinfomgt.2022.102542

Haverila, M., Currie, R., Haverila, K. C., McLaughlin, C., & Twyford, J. C. (2023). The impact of word-of-mouth (WOM) on attitudes, behavioural intentions, and actual usage of non-pharmaceutical interventions (NPIs) among early and late adopters. *International Journal of Pharmaceutical and Healthcare Marketing*. https://doi.org/10.1108/IJPHM-01-2022-0009

Hung, S. W., Chang, C. W., & Ma, Y. C. (2021). A new reality: Exploring continuance intention to use mobile augmented reality for entertainment purposes. *Technology in Society*, *67*, 101757. https://doi.org/10.1016/j.techsoc.2021.101757

Fan, W., Liu, J., Zhu, S., & Pardalos, P. M. (2020). Investigating the impacting factors for the healthcare professionals to adopt artificial intelligence-based medical diagnosis support system (AIMDSS). *Annals of Operations Research, 294*(1), 567–592. https://doi.org/10.1007/s10479-018-2818-y

Fishbein, M., & Ajzen, I. (1975). *Belief, attitude, intention and behavior: An introduction to theory and research*. Reading, MA: Addison-Wesley.

Leong, L. Y., Hew, T. S., Ooi, K. B., Metri, B., & Dwivedi, Y. K. (2023). Extending the theory of planned behavior in the social commerce context: A meta-analytic SEM (MASEM) approach. *Information Systems Frontiers*, *25*(5), 1847-1879.

Lung-Guang, N. (2019). Decision-making determinants of students participating in MOOCs: Merging the theory of planned behavior and self-regulated learning model. *Computers & Education*, *134*, 50-62. https://doi.org/10.1016/j.compedu.2019.02.004

Maisha, K., & Shetu, S. N. (2023). Influencing factors of e-learning adoption amongst students in a developing country: the post-pandemic scenario in Bangladesh. *Future Business Journal*, *9*(1), 37. https://doi.org/10.1186/s43093-023-00214-3

Mashroofa, M. M., Haleem, A., Nawaz, N., & Saldeen, M. A. (2023). E-learning adoption for sustainable higher education. *Heliyon*. *9*(6), e17505. https://doi.org/10.1016/j.heliyon.2023.e17505

Songkram, N., Chootongchai, S., Osuwan, H., Chuppunnarat, Y., & Songkram, N. (2023). Students' adoption towards behavioral intention of digital learning platform. *Education and Information Technologies*, 1-23. 28,11655–11677. https://doi.org/10.1007/s10639-023-11637-4

Taylor, S., & Todd, P. A. (1995). Understanding information technology usage: A test of competing models. *Information systems research*, *6*(2), 144-176.

Wang, K. (2023). The Perception and Behavioral Intention Toward MOOCs: Undergraduates in China. *The International Review of Research in Open and Distributed Learning*, *24*(1), 22-46. https://doi.org/10.19173/irrodl.v24i1.6677

Wu, T. (2023). An Integrated Model to Assess EFL Learners' Online Learning Behaviour. *International Journal of Technology-Enhanced Education (IJTEE)*, *2*(1), 1-17.

DIGITAL TRANSFORMATION IN HIGHER EDUCATION: A ROADMAP

Anusuyah Subbarao and Nasreen Khan
Faculty of Management, Multimedia University, Cyberjaya, 63100, Selangor, Malaysia

ABSTRACT

Mobile technology has become an integral part of modern education, offering new avenues for learning and engagement. As today's students, including the tech-savvy Generation Z (Gen Z), increasingly turn to mobile learning applications for educational purposes, it becomes imperative to understand the critical success factors that shape their adoption and utilization. This research investigates the key determinants influencing students' use of mobile learning applications. It also considers the impact of these factors on students' engagement and academic performance. By examining these factors through a systematic literature review and semi-structured interview methodology, we seek to uncover insights into the nuances of mobile learning applications adoption in diverse educational settings. This research presents the roadmap to formulate an academic mobile learning application designed to engage and motivate students to use it regularly. This research contributes to the ongoing dialogue on integrating mobile technology in education by providing actionable recommendations for educators, institutions, and app developers. It underscores the importance of designing mobile learning applications that align with students' preferences and needs, emphasizing the significance of user-centric approaches in educational technology. Moreover, the study offers insights into the potential of mobile learning applications to foster engagement, enhance collaboration, and facilitate personalized learning.

KEYWORDS

Digital Transformation, Higher Education, Mobile Learning Applications, Academic Performance, Gen Z

1. INTRODUCTION

We are currently in the midst of the Fourth Industrial Revolution, but there remains uncertainty regarding the readiness of universities to embrace this revolution and the preparedness of educational leaders to fully harness the potential of Industry 4.0 for the benefit of higher education's stakeholders. Digital transformation (DT) is intricately linked to this fourth industrial revolution, where digital technologies are shaping the future of our society. As Kaputa et al (2022) pointed out, there is a pressing need for a comprehensive understanding of how digital technologies can enhance the student experience. According to Rampelt et al. (2019), DT has a pervasive influence on all activities within Higher Education Institutions (HEIs), permeating every facet, including processes, locations, formats, and objectives related to teaching, learning, research, and work in the higher education sector.

In recent times, there has been a growing emphasis on digital transformation (DT), a phenomenon that has captured the attention of both researchers and practitioners. However, our current grasp of this subject remains incomplete. A multitude of mobile learning applications have been specifically designed and developed to facilitate and enhance teaching and learning. Notably, these apps incorporate features such as ubiquity, collaboration, and social interaction, rendering them intriguing tools to employ (Oyelere et al. 2018). Furthermore, these applications provide convenient access to learning resources. This technological advancement has transformed the conventional closed classroom environment into an open and enriched learning space, offering educators and students a suite of enhanced teaching and learning tools to elevate their educational experiences.

The integration of mobile learning applications into education has witnessed a significant paradigm shift in recent years. The proliferation of smartphones and tablets, combined with the demands for flexibility and accessibility in education has led to the widespread adoption of mobile learning applications as tools for enhancing the learning experience (Haleem et al., 2022). This trend is particularly pronounced among today's student population, including Gen Z learners, who have grown up in an era characterized by digital ubiquity (Yalcin-incik & Incik, 2022). Mobile learning applications in education offer a multitude of opportunities to transform traditional learning methodologies which makes educational resources and interactive materials readily available to students anytime, anywhere. However, the successful utilization of these apps depends on various critical factors that can significantly influence their adoption, effectiveness, and impact on students' learning experiences (Demir & Akpinar, 2018). Understanding these critical success factors is vital for educators, institutions, and app developers seeking to harness the full potential of mobile technology in education. By addressing these factors, educators can create a more engaging and tailored learning environment, institutions can optimize resource allocation, and developers can design apps that align with students' needs and preferences.

This research aims to delve into the critical success factors that influence students' use of mobile learning applications in education. By examining these factors comprehensively, we seek to provide valuable insights into the key determinants of app adoption, usage patterns, and the impact on students' learning outcomes. Furthermore, this research seeks to contribute to the broader discourse on the integration of mobile technology in education, shedding light on best practices and strategies for creating effective mobile learning experiences.

Together with this, this paper will present the related work, methodology, validity in qualitative research, initial results, and finally the conclusion.

2. RELATED WORK

This section discusses the key factors influencing students' adoption of mobile learning applications, the impact of mobile learning on Gen Z student engagement and academic performance, and design principles for engaging and motivating students through mobile learning applications.

2.1 Key Factors Influencing Students' Adoption of Mobile Learning Applications

The adoption and utilization of mobile learning applications by students are influenced by several key factors. Technical aspects, such as device connectivity, cross-platform compatibility, sufficient memory, and reliable network coverage, are crucial in determining the acceptance of these apps (Alghazi et al., 2021; Wai et al., 2018). The seamless performance and intuitive interface design of these apps can improve their uptake, while performance glitches can hinder it (Almaiah & Alismaiel, 2019). The integration of apps into course activities and aligning them with learning goals is more effective than using them as supplemental add-ons (Pechenkina et al., 2017). Education-specific apps outperform multipurpose ones, and instruction tailored for mobile learning is more effective in enabling meaningful education than repurposed traditional content (Elaish et al., 2019). Individual motivation factors, such as game-like features, can also contribute to engagement by leveraging enjoyment, challenge, and curiosity (Ciampa, 2014; Moorthy et al., 2019). Positive habits reinforced by mobile learning can encourage ongoing app use. This will cause students to appreciate the autonomy and flexibility offered by it. Academically, apps that demonstrate objective gains in achievement and grades are more likely to be accepted (Jou et al., 2016; Pechenkina et al., 2017). Overall, the factors of technical stability, instructional design, motivation triggers, measurable learning gains, and habit formation play a massive role in shaping sustained educational app use.

2.2 Impact of Mobile Learning on Gen Z Student Engagement and Academic Performance

Mobile learning applications have become an integral part of daily life for Gen Z students. Preliminary research suggests that mobile learning applications have the potential to positively impact both engagement and achievement. Customized apps, which leverage game-like features to promote curiosity, enjoyment, and motivation, have been found to outperform traditional classroom settings in terms of engagement (Ciampa, 2014). By enabling student control over learning while providing convenient access, mobile learning applications can promote active learning (Moorthy et al., 2019) and foster habitual use (Gallegos et al., 2019).

Engineering-focused apps, in particular, have been shown to improve test scores compared to conventional teaching methods (Jou et al., 2016). Sustained use of gamified mobile learning applications has also been correlated with higher grades in humanities and social sciences (Pechenkina et al., 2017). Apps can support peer interaction, resource access, and vocabulary gains, all of which contribute to academic success. Research shows that the effectiveness of mobile learning applications is due to their differentiated scaffolding, personalized pathways, interactive modules, immediate feedback, and multidimensional skill-building capabilities, which sets them apart from traditional learning methods (Elaish et al., 2019). However, it should be noted that disconnected supplemental apps have a limited impact on student engagement and performance unless they are thoughtfully integrated into the educational process (Willacy & Calder, 2017). In summary, early research suggests that mobile learning applications, when purposefully designed and deployed, can enhance Gen Z student engagement and performance when compared to conventional methods.

2.3 Design Principles for Engaging and Motivating Students through Mobile Learning Applications

Concerning the design principles for mobile learning apps, research has highlighted several key strategies for enhancing student engagement. Incorporating gamification elements such as rewards, levels, challenges, leaderboards, badges, and points can be highly effective in capitalizing on positive student orientations to gameplay (Ciampa, 2014). This approach fosters a stimulating sense of progress and repeat use. Supporting learner autonomy through personalization, flexible pacing, and custom content paths also promotes engagement (Moorthy et al., 2019). Providing adaptive on-demand help to scaffold independence enhances engagement further. Simplicity in navigation and information design tends to reduce barriers to adoption (Almaiah & Alismaiel, 2019). Interactive multimedia exceeds static approaches and can facilitate learning through different representations. Pedagogically, aligning activities and resources to targeted learning goals reinforces the purpose and validates sustained app use by demonstrating academic gains (Pechenkina et al., 2017). Socially, built-in features for collaboration, annotation, discussion, sharing, and peer assistance will satisfy intrinsic motivations (Gallegos et al., 2019). Ultimately, these evidence-based design principles can increase students' voluntary engagement with mobile learning apps by promoting interactivity, feedback, personal agency, variety, social connectivity, and clarity of learning purpose.

3. METHODOLOGY

The formulation of a mobile learning application to increase students' performance in higher education is the initial idea of our research. Our main objective is to share the complete roadmap to receive feedback on our model formulation. Figure 1 illustrates the entire steps of the model formulation.

This paper will adopt qualitative research where the phenomenological approach will be implemented. Phenomenology research explores how various individual's experiences manifest themselves. To give a thorough description of the student's real-world experiences with mobile learning applications in higher education, this method would demonstrate how things appear to them through their experiences. Figure 2 illustrates the research flowchart. Thus, to achieve the first research question which is to investigate the critical success factors that influence students' use of mobile learning applications, the Systematic Literature Review (SLR) method is used. Initial findings from the SLR are discussed in Section 4 with a list of critical factors that influence mobile learning applications' adoption among students from higher education.

Next, to answer the second research question, a semi-structured interview method will be used to determine whether learning through mobile learning applications affects Gen Z students' levels of engagement in learning and improves academic performance. The study's targeted sample consists of students from higher education institutions in Klang Valley, Malaysia. Respondents will be selected via purposive sampling. Face-to-face interviews will be used as the mode of interaction. The interview instrument will be sent for content validation by an expert. Then a cognitive interview will be carried out before the actual interviews. Each interviewer will be given a unique Identification Number (ID). Then data transcription from the interview will take place using Microsoft Word. Once the data is transcribed, the data transcription will be given to two different raters to identify the themes. Thematic Analysis will be adopted to analyze the interview data (Subbarao & Mahrin, 2018).

The researcher will use Cohen's Kappa approach (Creswell and Báez, 2020) to assess the reliability of the coding and themes found using the thematic analysis. The values of Cohen Kappa range from 0.00 – 1.00 with a value of >0.90 = 'Almost Perfect Agreement', > 0.80 – 0.90 = 'Strong Agreement', 0.60 – 0.79 = 'Moderate Agreement', 0.40 – 0.59 = "Weak Agreement", 0.21 – 0.39 = 'Minimal Agreement', <0.21 = 'No Agreement' (McHugh, 2012; Creswell & Báez, 2020).

To conduct the reliability assessment, the data transcriptions will be given to two different raters. The raters will be chosen randomly and will be asked to identify several codes. Only one specific question will be selected for this purpose.

Finally, based on the findings gathered from the SLR (Research Question 1) and the interview (Research Question 2), the third research question will be answered. To develop a mobile learning application that will be designed to engage and motivate students to use it regularly, system requirements need to be determined. Once the mobile learning application is developed, it will be given to the students for testing. Focus groups will be held for application usage validation. Based on the feedback given, the mobile learning application will be modified.

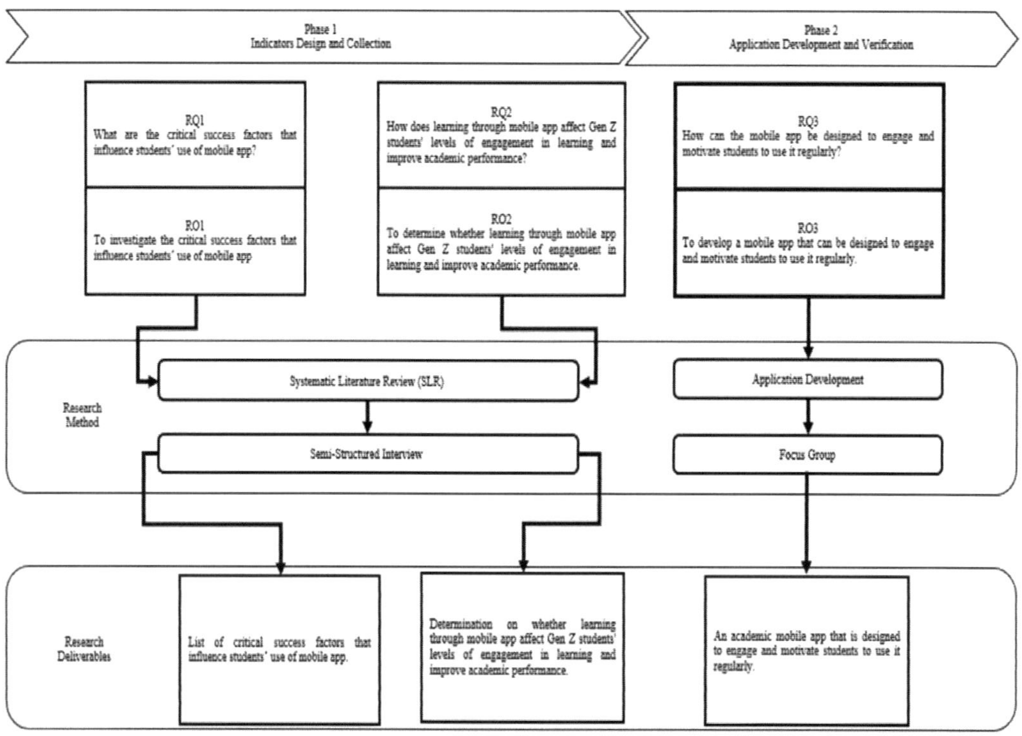

Figure 1. Research Overview

4. VALIDITY IN QUALITATIVE RESEARCH

To enhance the reliability of the findings from this qualitative study, three distinct strategies will be employed: triangulation, member checking, and maintaining an audit trail (Creswell & Báez, 2020; Carcary, 2020).

Triangulation, a validity procedure that reinforces evidence from multiple sources to corroborate emergent themes (Creswell & Báez, 2020), will be achieved by collecting data from multiple methods, including a SLR, and semi-structured interviews. This approach aimed to confirm the triangulation and strengthen the findings.

Member checking involves seeking participants' feedback on the researcher's interpretations to ensure the credibility of the findings (Creswell & Báez, 2020). This will be implemented by inviting respondents to reconfirm the accuracy of the identified themes, indicators, and model.

Furthermore, an audit trail, a strategy designed to enhance the rigor and transparency of qualitative research (Carcary, 2020), will be maintained. The researcher meticulously will document the research problem, SLR protocol, framework construction process, sample selection criteria, and timestamps for key milestones, including the commencement of interviews, compilation of results, and interpretation of findings.

5. INITIAL RESULTS

According to Moya & Camacho (2021), critical success factors that have the highest impact on mobile learning adoption among students are leadership, perceived usefulness and ease of use, teacher attitude and competence, pedagogical affordances, integration with curriculum and instruction, professional development and support, student acceptance and engagement, infrastructure, and technical support. The author mentioned that effective leadership within educational institutions, including school leaders and education inspectors, is crucial for driving the adoption and implementation of mobile learning initiatives.

Moreover, if individuals perceive mobile learning as useful and easy to use, they are more likely to adopt it. Positive attitudes and sufficient competence in using mobile learning can encourage its adoption in educational settings. The ability of mobile learning to support collaborative learning, inquiry-based learning, and personalized learning can influence its adoption. When mobile learning is aligned with the curriculum goals and instructional strategies, it becomes more relevant and meaningful for educators and students.

In addition to that, providing adequate professional development and support for teachers in using mobile learning can positively impact its adoption. When students perceive mobile learning as beneficial and engaging, they are more likely to embrace it and actively participate in learning activities. The availability of reliable infrastructure and technical support is essential for the successful adoption of mobile learning.

According to Althunibat et al. (2021), the factors that influence the actual use of mobile learning applications include self-motivation, self-efficacy, content quality, usability, technology mindset, facilitating conditions, usefulness and benefits, organizational support, system quality, and instructor characteristics. These factors collectively contribute to the decision and motivation to use mobile learning applications.

6. CONCLUSION

To conclude, the goal of this paper is to formulate “An academic mobile learning application that is designed to engage and motivate students to use it regularly.”. This research demonstrates the methodical process of formulating the model with the activities and our initial findings of the Systematic Literature Review process. The next step of this study will be conducting interviews to determine whether learning through mobile learning applications affects Gen Z students' levels of engagement in learning and improves academic performance.

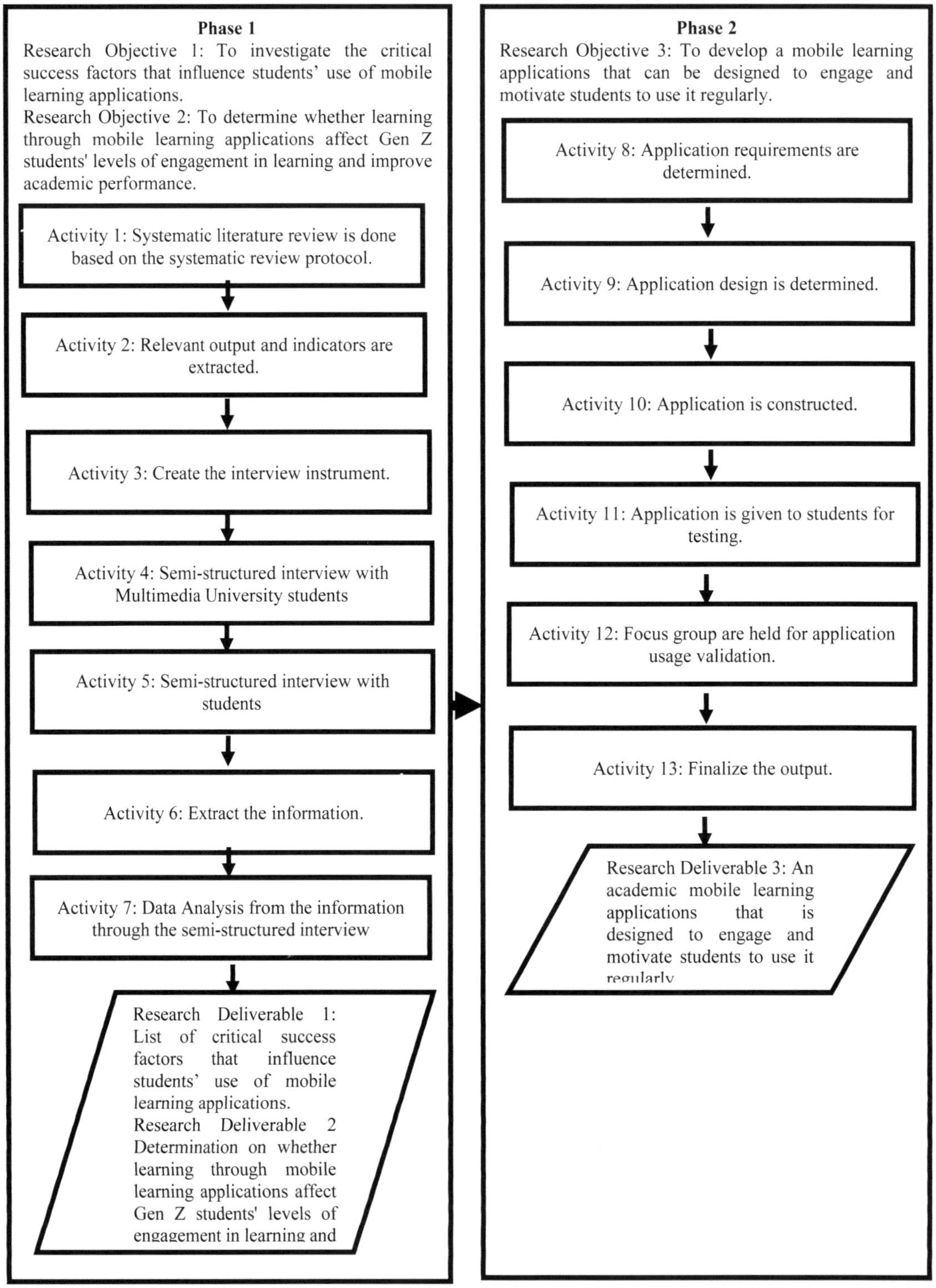

Figure 2. Research Flowchart

ACKNOWLEDGEMENT

This research is funded under MMU-UI (Universitas Indonesia) titled, "Digital Transformation in Higher Education: Do we need mobile learning applications as Campus Support Services for I Generations?" with Project ID MMUI/240009 under Multimedia University.

REFERENCES

Alghazi, S. S., Kamsin, A., Almaiah, M. A., Wong, S. Y., & Shuib, L. (2021). For sustainable application of mobile learning: An extended utaut model to examine the effect of technical factors on the usage of mobile devices as a learning tool. *Sustainability (Switzerland),* 13(4). https://doi.org/10.3390/su13041856

Almaiah, M. A., & Alismaiel, O. A. (2019). Examination of factors influencing the use of mobile learning system: An empirical study. *Education and Information Technologies*, 24(1). https://doi.org/10.1007/s10639-018-9810-7

Althunibat, A., Almaiah, M. A., & Altarawneh, F. (2021). Examining the factors influencing the mobile learning applications usage in higher education during the COVID-19 pandemic. Electronics, 10(21), 2676. https://doi.org/10.3390/electronics10212676

Carcary, M. (2020). The research audit trail: Methodological guidance for application in practice. Electronic Journal of Business Research Methods, 18(2), pp166-177.

Ciampa, K. (2014). Learning in a mobile age: An investigation of student motivation. *Journal of Computer Assisted Learning*, 30(1). https://doi.org/10.1111/jcal.12036

Creswell, J. W., & Báez, J. C. (2020). 30 essential skills for the qualitative researcher. Sage Publications.

Demir, K., and Akpinar, E. (2018). The effect of mobile learning applications on students' academic achievement and attitudes toward mobile learning. *Malaysian Online Journal of Educational Technology*, 6(2): 48-59, http://dx.doi.org/10.17220/mojet.2018.02.004

Elaish, M. M., Ghani, N. A., Shuib, L., & Al-Haiqi, A. (2019). Development of a Mobile Game Application to Boost Students' Motivation in Learning English Vocabulary. *IEEE Access*, 7. https://doi.org/10.1109/ACCESS.2019.2891504

Gallegos, C., Gehrke, P., & Nakashima, H. (2019). Can Mobile Devices Be Used as an Active Learning Strategy? Student Perceptions of Mobile Device Use in a Nursing Course. *Nurse Educator*, 44(5). https://doi.org/10.1097/NNE.0000000000000613

Haleem, A.; Javaid, M.; Qadri, M. A. and Suman, R. (2022). Understanding the role of digital technologies in education: A review, Sustainable Operations and Computers, 3, (275-285), ISSN 2666-4127, https://doi.org/10.1016/j.susoc.2022.05.004

Jou, M., Lin, Y. T., & Tsai, H. C. (2016). Mobile learning applications for motivation to learning: an engineering case. *Interactive Learning Environments*, 24(8). https://doi.org/10.1080/10494820.2015.1075136

Kaputa, V., Loučanová, E., Tejerina-Gaite, F.A. (2022). Digital Transformation in Higher Education Institutions as a Driver of Social Oriented Innovations. In: Păunescu, C., Lepik, KL., Spencer, N. (eds) Social Innovation in Higher Education. Innovation, Technology, and Knowledge Management. *Springer*, Cham. https://doi.org/10.1007/978-3-030-84044-0_4

McHugh M. L. (2012). Interrater reliability: the kappa statistic. Biochemia Medica, 22(3), 276–282.

Moorthy, K., Yee, T. T., T'ing, L. C., & Kumaran, V. V. (2019). Habit and hedonic motivation are the strongest influences in mobile learning behaviours among higher education students in Malaysia. *Australasian Journal of Educational Technology*, 35(4). https://doi.org/10.14742/ajet.4432

Moya, S., & Camacho, M. (2021). Identifying the key success factors for the adoption of mobile learning. Education and Information Technologies, 26, 3917-3945. https://doi.org/10.1007/s10639-021-10447-w

Pechenkina, E., Laurence, D., Oates, G., Eldridge, D., & Hunter, D. (2017). Using a gamified mobile learning applications to increase student engagement, retention and academic achievement. *International Journal of Educational Technology in Higher Education*, 14(1). https://doi.org/10.1186/s41239-017-0069-7

Rampelt, F., Orr, D., & Knoth, A. (2019). Bologna digital 2020 white paper on digitalisation in the European higher education area. Research Document. *Hochschul forum*. Accessed from https://hochschulforumdigitalisierung.de/de/news/white-paper-bologna-digital-2020.

Subbarao, A., & Mahrin, M. N. R. (2018). Identification of Coordination Strategies and Indicators for Global Software Development Projects: Interview Outcome. In *New Trends in Intelligent Software Methodologies, Tools and Techniques* (pp. 545-558). IOS Press.

Wai, I. S. H., Ng, S. S. Y., Chiu, D. K. W., Ho, K. K. W., & Lo, P. (2018). Exploring undergraduate students' usage pattern of mobile learning applications for education. *Journal of Librarianship and Information Science*, 50(1). https://doi.org/10.1177/0961000616662699

Willacy, H., & Calder, N. (2017). Making mathematics learning more engaging for students in health schools through the use of apps. Education Sciences, 7(2). https://doi.org/10.3390/educsci7020048

Yalçın-İncik, E., & İncik, T. (2022). Generation Z students' views on technology in education: What they want what they get. *Malaysian Online Journal of Educational Technology*, 10(2), 109-124. http://dx.doi.org/10.52380/mojet.2022.10.2.275

EXPLORING CYBERSECURITY MINDSETS: A COMPARATIVE ANALYSIS OF AGE, LEADERSHIP, WORK EXPERIENCE AND EXPERTISE

Gregor Eibl and Olga Litvyak
University of Continuing Education Krems, Dr.-Karl-Dorrek-Straße 30, 3500 Krems, Austria

ABSTRACT

The frequency of cybersecurity threats is on the rise, underscoring the need for individuals and organisations to adopt proactive measures to safeguard their sensitive information. The primary research question of the study focuses on the significance of human factors in the perception of cybersecurity. This study employed a cross-sectional survey design to examine the perceptions of cybersecurity among a diverse cohort of participants to comprehensively understand the nuances of cybersecurity mindset among information security professionals and non-experts. The target population included individuals with varying levels of expertise in cybersecurity, including both professional and non-professionals in Austria. Data were collected via an online survey and analysed for group differences. The results indicated that there were generally consistent opinions across demographic groups regarding cybersecurity threats. However, significant differences were observed in certain areas, particularly related to work experience, age, and professional roles. The highest levels of concern regarding intentional cybersecurity threat acts were reported by those with no work experience (M = 5.14) and those with over 10 years of experience (M = 5.08), while those with 4-10 years reported lower levels of concern (M = 4.21). Age differences significantly affected risk perceptions regarding educational institutions, with older groups showing higher levels of concern. The perception of risk regarding the potential for harm to life and limb exhibited significant variation with age. The youngest cohort (19-29 years) and the oldest (over 48 years) exhibited the highest levels of concern (M = 5.45 and 5.25, respectively). The originality of the paper and its contribution lies in the analysis of these different human factors at the same time on a novel dataset. The findings highlight the necessity of tailoring cybersecurity awareness and training strategies to account for the diverse backgrounds of individuals within an organisation.

KEYWORDS

Cybersecurity, Experts, Perceptions, Professionals, Group Comparison

1. INTRODUCTION

The prevalence of cybersecurity threats is on the rise, underscoring the need for individuals and organisations to adopt proactive measures to safeguard their sensitive information. The 2023 ENISA Threat Landscape report (European Union Agency for Cybersecurity 2023) reveals a persistent surge in cyberattacks globally, with Europe experiencing a similar increase. The report also anticipates an uptick in the number of observable cyber incidents in the future. A study by Eling and Wirfs (2019) examined 1,579 instances of cyber incidents and identified human error as the primary source of such incidents. The mean cost of cyber risk per occurrence was found to be 43.49 million US dollars, which was considerably higher than the median loss of 1.53 million US dollars. This suggests that the most extreme forms of cyber risk can result in substantial financial losses.

The most significant threats are those directed at critical infrastructure, which includes the structures and functions that are vital to the functioning of society. Attacks against these critical infrastructure have increased in number and complexity, and have become more targeted as a result of the involvement of more professional attackers (Lehto, 2022) .

Social engineering activities that exploit a human error or human behaviour have grown significantly in 2023 and have been further enhanced by the use of Artificial Intelligence, according to the ENISA report (European Union Agency for Cybersecurity 2023). As observed by Nobles (2018), human factors have been largely overlooked in the field of information security. The increasing frequency of cyberattacks, data breaches, and ransomware attacks is, however, often attributed to errors committed by humans, with estimates suggesting that 95% of all cyber incidents are caused by human error. The cybersecurity threats that originate from human errors could be mitigated by adopting a 'human-as-solution' mindset, as proposed by Zimmermann and Renaud (2019). This approach views the human actor as a contributor to the success of maintaining and enhancing cybersecurity. It emphasises collaboration, communication, respect for expertise, and learning from positive outcomes to enhance cybersecurity.

The mindset may be influenced by previous experiences with cybersecurity and the distinction between cybersecurity professionals and regular employees in an organisation, which is the focus of this paper. The primary research question of this paper is to investigate the significance of human factors in the perception of cybersecurity. Previous research has indicated that the demographic profile of employees and students differs significantly in their perception of cybersecurity (Mittal & Ilavarasan, 2019). Given that the majority of cyber-attacks are attributable to human error, research should prioritize human-centric interventions (Bishop et al., 2020). However, contrary to expectations, another study found that age, gender and education did not relate to any cyber-security behaviours. Thus, the findings on the influence of human factors on cybersecurity behaviour in existing scholarship remain inconclusive. Nobles and McAndrew (2023) therefore advocate for a more intensive focus on scholarly research at the nexus of cybersecurity and human factors, with the aim of developing effective defence mechanisms that take into account the human element and policies that consider both human and technological aspects. Jeong (2019) called for a more comprehensive understanding of human factors in cybersecurity, suggesting the consolidation of attributes, interdisciplinary approaches, and qualitative research. Kostyuk and Wayne (2019) attested the lack of strong empirical evidence regarding how individuals assess the risk from cyber operations and how this impacts their personal online behaviour or shapes their support for various cybersecurity policies. Bridging this gap, this study provides a comprehensive analysis of how different human factors influence cybersecurity threat perceptions. By understanding possible group differences, organizations can develop more effective cybersecurity strategies and better protect their IT systems and data from cyber threats.

The remainder of the paper is structured as follows. Section 2 presents the background to this work, including cybersecurity mindsets, cybersecurity threats, elementary threats, critical infrastructure, and damage from cyberattacks. Section 3 presents the details of the research approach used in this paper. Section 4 analyses group differences in cybersecurity perceptions, along with some exploratory interpretations of the data collected. Section 5 contrasts the findings with the related findings from the literature and interprets the results. Section 6 provides a conclusion and some recommendations for industry and research.

2. THEORETICAL BACKGROUND

New ideas frequently necessitate technical solutions, particularly when contemplating the involvement of users with advanced technical expertise (Schweitzer et al., 2014), where numerous involved actors must comprehend the significance of cybersecurity. Saulaiman et al. (2023) and Lloyd (2020) both illustrate how cybersecurity measures can enhance organisational resilience, process maturity, and product quality, resulting in augmented innovation and growth. The awareness of cybersecurity policies among employees is associated with an increase in their competence in managing cybersecurity tasks and a positive influence on their cybersecurity compliance behaviour (Li et al., 2019). Furthermore, security training and education are positively associated with a reduction in the number of cybersecurity incidents in organisations from a quantitative perspective (Kweon et al., 2019). These findings highlight the importance of cybersecurity for the management of organisations.

Cybersecurity needs to be considered as a socio-technical challenge (Hills, 2015), as the human factor can be seen as both a threat and a countermeasure. The literature has repeatedly addressed cybersecurity mindsets, mostly trying to understand cybersecurity behaviour habits (Brase et al., 2017; Hong & Furnell, 2021). Research has empirically examined the relationships between demographic factors—such as age, work experience, and qualifications—and individual cybersecurity-threatening behaviours, including leaving printouts unattended, password complexity, and clicking on links from unknown sources (Mittal & Ilavarasan, 2019). Additionally, investigations into generational differences have highlighted distinct online behaviours between people entering the workforce and older generations (Cummings & Connolly, 2017). Others have examined the effect of exposure to cyber-attacks on support for governmental regulation, suggesting that such exposure is associated with increased support for different types of regulatory policy (Snider et al., 2021).

Zwilling et al. (2022) focus in their study on the relationship between cyber security awareness, knowledge and behaviour with protection tools showing that higher cyber knowledge is connected to the level of cyber awareness.

In contrast to these studies, focusing on individual awareness of cybersecurity in general, our research aims to reveal differences between cybersecurity specialists and non-experts in assessment of threats, risk factors, vulnerable critical infrastructure sectors, together with their potential severity, and finally the damage these risks cause. In addition to asking our participants whether their profession falls within the field of cybersecurity, we also considered further factors such as general work experience, age, and leadership role. Given inconclusive or even lacking findings of the previous research on the influence of these diverse factors on cybersecurity perceptions, the study poses an explorative research question: *RQ: How do age, work experience, leadership roles, and cybersecurity specialisation affect perceptions of cybersecurity threats?*

3. METHOD

This study employed a cross-sectional survey design to investigate the perceptions of cybersecurity among a diverse cohort of participants. The survey instrument was designed to gather both quantitative and qualitative data to comprehensively understand the cybersecurity mindsets among information security professionals and non-experts in Austria.

The target population for this study included individuals with varying levels of expertise in cybersecurity, encompassing both professionals and non-experts. Participants were recruited among students enrolled in cybersecurity and data analytics courses at select educational institutions. This ensured representation from individuals undergoing formal education in cybersecurity-related fields, thus usually having a high level of computer skills. Additionally, the survey was disseminated to recognized cybersecurity experts identified through professional networks. This facilitated the inclusion of participants with extensive practical experience and expertise in the field.

Prior to the main survey administration, a pretest with the scientific staff from two universities was conducted to evaluate the reliability and validity of the survey instrument. Feedback from the pretest participants was used to refine the survey questions and ensure clarity in the formulation of questions.

The survey was administered online using the SurveyMonkey tool. Participants were provided with clear instructions regarding the purpose of the study, voluntary participation, and confidentiality assurances. The survey remained open for responses between November 15, 2023, and March 14, 2024, allowing participants of both courses to complete the questionnaire.

Data collection involved the systematic collection of responses from survey participants. The survey instrument comprised a combination of closed-ended and open-ended questions, covering various aspects of cybersecurity perceptions, including attitudes, beliefs, and behaviours. Participant responses were anonymized to ensure confidentiality and privacy.

The threats list used in our survey relies on the threat landscape report by ENISA (European Union Agency for Cybersecurity, 2022). The eight most important threats identified by ENISA for the reporting period were: ransomware, malware, social engineering threats, internet threats against availability, denial of service threats against availability, threats against data for unauthorized access, disinformation – misinformation and supply chain attacks.

The most relevant risk factors examined are derived from the IT-Grundschutz-Kompendium (Bundesamt für Sicherheit in der Informationstechnik, 2022) listing 47 elementary threats, which are categorized by A-SIT (A-SIT, 2021) into five groups: human error, technical error, deliberate acts, organizational shortcomings, force majeure.

Critical infrastructure includes both private and public facilities which, if they were to fail or be severely damaged, or if other dramatic consequences were to be expected, would endanger the supply of the population and internal security (Wewer, 2023). Many nations have developed a national strategy for the protection of critical infrastructure, which defines the sectors that are regarded critical. Expended on the list found in (BMI, 2011), we refer to sectors such as energy (electricity, mineral oil, gas), information technology and telecommunications, transport and traffic, health, water, food and beverages, finance and insurance, government and administration, and media and culture. Although security is implicitly included within the government and administration sector, it merits explicit mention. In addition, the inclusion of the education and science sector as a critical infrastructure is under debate for future iterations and is currently being evaluated in a pilot study (Bundesamt für Bevölkerungsschutz und Katastrophenhilfe, 2021). Both sectors security and education and science are included in the final list of critical infrastructure sectors.

As there is a lack of frameworks for understanding the harms that organizations face from cyber-attacks, the taxonomy developed by Agrafiotis et al. (2018) was used as a basis, which identified five themes: physical or digital harm, economic harm, psychological harm, reputational harm, and social and societal harm. Process delay was added in place of reputational and social harm, which we believe will have an impact on reputational and social harm but is more concrete than the terms it replaces.

The final count of valid responses ranged from 97 to 100, varying by question, the exact sample size for each analysis is provided in the Results section. For the analysis, the data was further categorized by age groups (19-28, 29-38, 39-48, older than 48), work experience (less than a year, 1-3 years, 4-10 years, more than 10 years, no experience), and roles (leadership vs. non-leadership, specialists vs. non-specialists). Responses were rated on a six-point Likert scale, ranging from 1 (not at all agree) to 6 (totally agree). Quantitative data analysis was conducted using the R statistical software. First, descriptive statistics were employed to summarize demographic information and survey responses, providing an initial exploration of the data for further analysis and the choice of the analytical tools. Since the descriptive analysis revealed a non-normal distribution of the data, inferential statistical analysis relied on non-parametric tests for means comparison to examine group differences in cybersecurity perceptions.

4. RESULTS

The study sought to uncover perceptions of cybersecurity threats and the potential impacts of cyberattacks, using a sample of cybersecurity professionals and non-experts. It contrasted attitudes towards threats across groups with diverse cybersecurity-related professional expertise, age, work experience, and leadership roles. The analysis demonstrated a generally consistent outlook across different groups regarding cybersecurity threats. While perceptions of cybersecurity threats were broadly aligned as confirmed by statistically non-significant findings on group differences, the results reveal statistically significant differences in certain aspects, more often associated with factors such as age and work experience, than professional expertise in cybersecurity. These findings suggest that more often than not there is a common baseline in perceptions of cybersecurity threats, though specific human factors not limited to professional expertise in cybersecurity influence the nuances of these perceptions.

In exploring cybersecurity threats, significant variance emerged in perception of threats to supply chains according to work experience (N=100). Specifically, individuals with 4-10 years of experience perceived this threat at a lower level ($M = 3.5$), as opposed to the highly experienced individuals ($M = 4.88$) and almost 1 point below the overall mean threat perception across all groups ($M = 4.48$). The results of Kruskall-Wallis test between the groups found significant differences in perceptions across experience levels ($\chi 2(4) = 10.622$, $p = 0.03116$). This finding suggests that mid-career professionals might underestimate or be less aware of supply chain vulnerabilities compared to their less experienced or more veteran counterparts.

Concerning risk factors, the results on age and leadership show significant influence on perceptions of some risk factors. Older participants (over 48) exhibited a heightened concern for force majeure events such as natural disasters ($M = 4.33$), in contrast to the 39-48 age group ($M = 2.50$). The results of Kruskall-Wallis test (N=100) revealed statistical significance of the differences in perception of force majeure events between the age group ($\chi 2(3) = 16.431$, $p = 0.0009253$). When it comes to organizational deficiencies (e.g., unclear responsibilities, savings, lengthy processes), non-leaders felt this factor less of a threat ($M = 4.49$) compared to participants in leadership roles ($M = 5.17$), with this difference confirmed through Mann-Whitney-U statistical testing ($W = 475.5$, $p = 0.01488$, N=100).

Differences in the perception of intentional acts such as cyber-crime and acts of revenge were also pronounced across groups differing in their work experience (N=100). Notably, those with no work experience ($M = 5.14$) and those with more than ten years of experience ($M = 5.08$) expressed the greatest concern. Mid-career professionals with 4-10 years of experience reported lower concern ($M = 4.21$). The Kruskal-Wallis test confirmed that these differences between the groups are statistically significant ($\chi 2(4) = 10.539$, p-value = 0.03226), highlighting the acute awareness of cyber threats at the entry and advanced stages of professional careers, but less so among mid-career professionals.

The analysis further revealed the impact of human factors on perceptions of critical infrastructure vulnerability. Work experience significantly affected perceptions of cyber risks for the food and nutrition sector (N=98), illustrating a heightened sensitivity to threats among more experienced individuals (M = 4.09), as compared to the other groups, confirmed by significant results of the Kruskal-Wallis test ($\chi2$ (4) = 18.29, p = 0.001083). In the groups of respondents without any work experience the perception of this risk was at the lowest level (M = 2.86). In transportation and traffic sectors, specialists (M = 4.05, N=100), perceived less cybersecurity threat to the sector than non-specialists (M = 4.55), revealing the influence of specialized knowledge on risk assessment in this infrastructure segments with significant results of Mann-Whitney-U test (W = 1468.5, p = 0.03336).

Age disparities further contribute to the perception of risks to science and education sector and physical safety from cyber-attacks. Older age groups were more concerned about the security of science and education sector (M = 4.58) with significant differences among the groups (N=99) revealed by the Kruskal-Wallis test ($\chi2(3)$ = 8.3422, p = 0.03944). The youngest (M = 5.45) and the oldest participants (M= 5.25) were the most perceptive to danger to life and limb, with significant differences observed across age groups (N=98) as revealed by the Kruskal-Wallis test ($\chi2(3)$ = 9.0832, p = 0.02821).

In conclusion, the results reveal that age, experience, and leadership are often more important in shaping perceptions of cybersecurity threats and responses than whether one is a cybersecurity specialist or not. Thus, consideration of diverse human factors is instrumental in tailoring cybersecurity policies within organisations and training programs that effectively address the specific needs and vulnerabilities of different groups. This nuanced understanding of cybersecurity mindsets is essential for enhancing cybersecurity awareness and resilience for employees of diverse age, cybersecurity expertise, work experiences, and leadership responsibilities.

5. DISCUSSION

The results of our study revealed generally similar uniform mindsets across groups of diverse age, work experience, cybersecurity-related expertise, and leadership level. However, some human factors emerged crucial in perceptions of particular cybersecurity threats, risks, and consequences of cyberattacks. Thus, the findings of the study extend the existing literature on the role of human factors and variations in cybersecurity awareness and behaviour. Notably, the study highlights the need of combining both expertise and demographic factors to fully understand the nuances of the cybersecurity mindset.

However, some findings were unexpected and deserve further discussion. Contrary to our expectations, cybersecurity perceptions rarely differ between experts and non-experts and other human factors are often more important. For example, the significantly lower perception of threats among mid-career professionals (4-10 years of work experience) is surprising, given their likely exposure to cybersecurity issues and consequences of cyberattacks. This may suggest a potential for continuous education in this field within organisations. Additionally, the concern for cybersecurity in the transportation and nutrition sectors among cybersecurity specialists and highly experienced professionals highlights the importance of knowledge and cybersecurity awareness campaigns and trainings.

Contrary to the findings of Mittal and Ilavarasan (2019), the results of the study revealed the heightened sensitivity to cyber threats and risks among those with substantial work experience. The differences between the studies may stem from more fine-grained identification of work experience within the study, as compared to Mittal and Ilavarasan (2019). Given diverse regional samples between this study and Mittal and Ilavarasan (2019), who mostly rely on the data collected in India and Bangladesh, this difference might also reflect regional diversity in cybersecurity mindset.

The study raises new questions about the effectiveness of current cybersecurity education practices and cybersecurity awareness across different career stages. It suggests that continuous training tailored to career stage and industry might be more effective than one-size-fits-all approaches. Implementing continuous, role-adjusted training could mitigate complacency in mid-career professionals and enhance the overall cybersecurity awareness within organisations. Investment into cybersecurity awareness trainings could limit potentially costly consequences of cyberattacks. Future research could explore the impact of targeted cybersecurity interventions on cybersecurity threat perception and mitigation practices across groups of different age, leadership and expertise.

While the study provides valuable insights into the perceptions of cybersecurity threats and risks, its generalisability is constrained by several factors. First, the geographic focus on Austria may limit the applicability of the findings to other regions, where cultural, economic, and regulatory differences could alter the perception and handling of cybersecurity threats. The specific context of Austria might not mirror those of other countries or regions. Comparison of the results with existing research from other regions further revealed the need for comparative research, as mindsets might be influenced by regional policies and practices in the field of cybersecurity and cybersecurity education in addition to human factors explored within the study.

Second, the composition of the sample, which includes experts in cybersecurity and students of cybersecurity and data analytics, is both a strength and on the same time introduces a limitation. While this group is highly relevant for understanding cybersecurity mindsets, it may not reflect the broader awareness and behaviour patterns within workforce or population. Experts and students in these fields are likely to have a heightened awareness and baseline understanding of cyberthreats compared to the general population, what might explain the results of generally similar mindsets revealed in comparisons between the groups. Though some studies (Green & Smith, 2016; Naiakshina et al., 2019) show that even software developers lack necessary cybersecurity threat awareness. Future studies should further consider longitudinal designs to track changes in perceptions and behaviours over time.

These limitations suggest that while the findings are indicative of trends among cybersecurity specialists and non-professionals in Austria, their applicability for other groups or regions requires caution. Future studies could enhance generalisability of these results by incorporating a more diverse geographic and demographic sample, including participants from various professional backgrounds and countries to compare how diverse human and demographic factors impact cybersecurity threat perceptions. This broader approach would help validate the current study's findings and provide a more comprehensive understanding of cybersecurity mindsets.

6. CONCLUSION

In conclusion, this study has provided valuable insights into the perceptions of cyber-threats, particularly highlighting the influence of experience on the broader understanding of threats rather than individual cybersecurity behaviours. The data, enriched by contributions from respondents within the cybersecurity education sector, underscores the complexity of cybersecurity awareness and its multifaceted nature. However, the research is not without its limitations; its focus on Austria and the sampling method that primarily targeted student groups may affect the generalizability of the findings.

The novelty of the study lies in its comprehensive analysis of the influence of diverse factors shaping cybersecurity threats perceptions from technical expertise (being cybersecurity specialist or not) to non-technical factors such as age, experience, and leadership. The novel quantitative dataset used in the study included an extensive array of questions, enabling an in-depth exploration of perceptions across a wide range of cybersecurity threats. By combining the technical expertise with various human factors, the study opens new avenues for understanding the multifaceted nature of cybersecurity mindsets.

The main theoretical implication of our findings is the recognition that cybersecurity threat perception and, as a result, awareness, is deeply influenced by a combination of factors with age and work experience playing a major role. The models of cybersecurity behaviour need to integrate these dimensions more explicitly and address existing vulnerabilities among specific groups.

To facilitate future research into the mental mindsets of cybersecurity, it is recommended that a more diverse approach be considered, including age, work experience, leadership roles and cybersecurity expertise. This would enable a more comprehensive understanding of the varying perceptions. From a practical standpoint, organisations aiming to enhance their cybersecurity maturity must acknowledge the human element and prevailing mindsets. From a managerial perspective, the results imply that organizations should tailor their cybersecurity training and policies to account for the diverse backgrounds and experiences of their employees. This tailored approach can lead to more effective engagement and implementation of cybersecurity measures. This study provides a foundation for future academic inquiry and the development of more effective organisational strategies in cybersecurity.

ACKNOWLEDGEMENT

This work was done within the project: SHIFT- 'Sichere Simulationstechnologien für cyber-physische Systeme' No. 893367). SHIFT is a project within the FORTE program partly funded by the Österreichische Forschungsförderungsgesellschaft mbH (FFG), Vienna, financed by the Austrian Bundesministerium für Finanzen. We acknowledge the use of ChatGPT and Deepl Write to identify improvements in the writing style.

REFERENCES

Agrafiotis, I., Nurse, J. R. C., Goldsmith, M., Creese, S., & Upton, D. (2018). A taxonomy of cyber-harms: Defining the impacts of cyber-attacks and understanding how they propagate. *Journal of Cybersecurity*, *4*(1). https://doi.org/10.1093/cybsec/tyy006

A-SIT. (2021). *IT-Grundschutz-Kompendium*. https://www.onlinesicherheit.gv.at/Themen/Experteninformation/Handbuecher/IT-Grundschutz-Kompendium.html

Bishop, L. M., Morgan, P. L., Asquith, P. M., Raywood-Burke, G., Wedgbury, A., & Jones, K. (2020). Examining Human Individual Differences in Cyber Security and Possible Implications for Human-Machine Interface Design. In A. Moallem (Ed.), *HCI for Cybersecurity, Privacy and Trust* (Vol. 12210, pp. 51–66). Springer International Publishing. https://doi.org/10.1007/978-3-030-50309-3_4

BMI, B. (2011). Schutz Kritischer Infrastrukturen: Risiko und Krisenmanagement. *Leitfaden Für Behörden Und Unternehmen. Bonn: Bundesministerium Des Inneren Und Bundesamt Für Bevölkerungsschutz Und Katastrophenhilfe*.

Brase, G. L., Vasserman, E. Y., & Hsu, W. (2017). Do different mental models influence cybersecurity behavior? Evaluations via statistical reasoning performance. *Frontiers in Psychology*, *8*, 306785.

Bundesamt für Bevölkerungsschutz und Katastrophenhilfe. (2021). *Ist das Bildungswesen eine Kritische Infrastruktur?* https://crisis-prevention.de/katastrophenschutz/ist-das-bildungswesen-eine-kritische-infrastruktur.html

Bundesamt für Sicherheit in der Informationstechnik (Ed.). (2022). *IT-Grundschutz-Kompendium*. Bundesanzeiger-Verl.

Cummings, J., & Connolly, A. J. (2017). *Impacts of Generational Work Experience on Users' Perceptions of Information Security*.

Eling, M., & Wirfs, J. (2019). What are the actual costs of cyber risk events? *European Journal of Operational Research*, *272*(3), 1109–1119. https://doi.org/10.1016/j.ejor.2018.07.021

European Union Agency for Cybersecurity. (2022). *ENISA threat landscape 2022: July 2021 to July 2022*. Publications Office. https://data.europa.eu/doi/10.2824/764318

European Union Agency for Cybersecurity. (2023). *ENISA threat landscape 2023: July 2022 to June 2023*. Publications Office. https://data.europa.eu/doi/10.2824/782573

Green, M., & Smith, M. (2016). Developers are not the enemy!: The need for usable security apis. *IEEE Security & Privacy*, *14*(5), 40–46.

Hills, M. (2015). Beyond simple human threats to cybersecurity: The need for strong proactive measures and resilient responses to cyber risk. *Cyber Security Review*, *2015*, 1–5.

Hong, Y., & Furnell, S. (2021). Understanding cybersecurity behavioral habits: Insights from situational support. *Journal of Information Security and Applications*, *57*, 102710.

Jeong, J., Mihelcic, J., Oliver, G., & Rudolph, C. (2019). Towards an Improved Understanding of Human Factors in Cybersecurity. *2019 IEEE 5th International Conference on Collaboration and Internet Computing (CIC)*, 338–345. https://doi.org/10.1109/CIC48465.2019.00047

Kostyuk, N., & Wayne, C. (2019). *Communicating Cybersecurity: Citizen Risk Perception of Cyber Threats*.

Kweon, E.-H., Lee, H., Chai, S., & Yoo, K. (2019). The Utility of Information Security Training and Education on Cybersecurity Incidents: An empirical evidence. *Information Systems Frontiers*, *23*, 361–373. https://doi.org/10.1007/s10796-019-09977-z

Lehto, M. (2022). Cyber-Attacks Against Critical Infrastructure. In M. Lehto & P. Neittaanmäki (Eds.), *Cyber Security* (Vol. 56, pp. 3–42). Springer International Publishing. https://doi.org/10.1007/978-3-030-91293-2_1

Li, L., He, W., Xu, L. D., Ash, I. K., Anwar, M., & Yuan, X. (2019). Investigating the impact of cybersecurity policy awareness on employees' cybersecurity behavior. *Int. J. Inf. Manag.*, *45*, 13–24. https://doi.org/10.1016/j.ijinfomgt.2018.10.017

Lloyd, G. (2020). The business benefits of cyber security for SMEs. *Computer Fraud & Security*, *2020*(2), 14–17. https://doi.org/10.1016/S1361-3723(20)30019-1

Mittal, S., & Ilavarasan, P. V. (2019). Demographic Factors in Cyber Security: An Empirical Study. In I. O. Pappas, P. Mikalef, Y. K. Dwivedi, L. Jaccheri, J. Krogstie, & M. Mäntymäki (Eds.), *Digital Transformation for a Sustainable Society in the 21st Century* (Vol. 11701, pp. 667–676). Springer International Publishing. https://doi.org/10.1007/978-3-030-29374-1_54

Naiakshina, A., Danilova, A., Gerlitz, E., Von Zezschwitz, E., & Smith, M. (2019). 'If you want, I can store the encrypted password': A Password-Storage Field Study with Freelance Developers. *Proceedings of the 2019 CHI Conference on Human Factors in Computing Systems*, 1–12. https://doi.org/10.1145/3290605.3300370

Nobles, C. (2018). Botching Human Factors in Cybersecurity in Business Organizations. *HOLISTICA – Journal of Business and Public Administration*, *9*(3), 71–88. https://doi.org/10.2478/hjbpa-2018-0024

Nobles, C., & Mcandrew, I. (2023). The Intersectionality of Offensive Cybersecurity and Human Factors: A Position Paper. *Scientific Bulletin*, *28*(2), 215–233. https://doi.org/10.2478/bsaft-2023-0022

Saulaiman, M. N.-E., Kozlovszky, M., & Csilling, Á. (2023). Side Benefits of Cybersecurity Measures an Empirical Study. *2023 IEEE 21st Jubilee International Symposium on Intelligent Systems and Informatics (SISY)*, 000581–000588. https://doi.org/10.1109/SISY60376.2023.10417952

Schweitzer, F., Gassmann, O., & Rau, C. (2014). Lessons from ideation: Where does user involvement lead us? *Creativity and Innovation Management*, *23*(2), 155–167. https://doi.org/10.1111/caim.12058

Snider, K. L. G., Shandler, R., Zandani, S., & Canetti, D. (2021). Cyberattacks, cyber threats, and attitudes toward cybersecurity policies. *Journal of Cybersecurity*, *7*(1), tyab019. https://doi.org/10.1093/cybsec/tyab019

Wewer, G. (2023). Kritische Infrastrukturen (KRITIS). In T. Klenk, F. Nullmeier, & G. Wewer (Eds.), *Handbuch Digitalisierung in Staat und Verwaltung* (pp. 1–11). Springer Fachmedien Wiesbaden. https://doi.org/10.1007/978-3-658-23669-4_106-1

Zimmermann, V., & Renaud, K. (2019). Moving from a 'human-as-problem" to a 'human-as-solution" cybersecurity mindset. *International Journal of Human-Computer Studies*, *131*, 169–187. https://doi.org/10.1016/j.ijhcs.2019.05.005

Zwilling, M., Klien, G., Lesjak, D., Wiechetek, Ł., Cetin, F., & Basim, H. N. (2022). Cyber Security Awareness, Knowledge and Behavior: A Comparative Study. *Journal of Computer Information Systems*, *62*(1), 82–97. https://doi.org/10.1080/08874417.2020.1712269

DATA CLEANING IN BIG DATA: A SYSTEMATIC LITERATURE REVIEW

Cláudio Iwata, Napoleão Galegale, Márcia Ito, Marilía Azevedo, Marcelo Duduchi and Carlos Arima
CEETEPS – Centro Estadual de Educação Tecnológica Paula Souza, Brazil

ABSTRACT

This paper aims to conduct a systematic analysis of the literature on existing data cleaning methods in Big Data. It is a constantly evolving research area due to the growing importance of using large volumes of data in artificial intelligence and the significant heterogeneity of data. The systematic review used the Parsifal online platform and was based on the PRISMA-P protocol. The selection of articles was carried out through the Scopus, Web of Science, and CAPES databases with keywords selected in accordance with the research objectives. A total of 69 articles were analyzed. The analysis revealed an active and constantly evolving field of research with a wide variety of techniques used, including machine learning, data mining, natural language processing, and other advanced techniques. The review also highlighted the diversity of publication formats and the extensive dissemination and discussion of research on data cleaning in Big Data at conferences and academic events. This study is expected to serve as a starting point for researchers interested in the topic, providing perspectives and guiding future investigations in the field of data cleaning in Big Data.

KEYWORDS

Data Cleaning, Big Data, Technical Approach

1. INTRODUCTION

Big Data is a heterogeneous concept encompassing different types and volumes of digital information and specific analytical tools depending on the industrial context (Manyika et al. 2011). The definition of big data is based on the ability of companies to capture, manage, and process large amounts of data that could not be handled by conventional computers within an acceptable time frame. Big data is characterized by its novelty since the technologies and architectures used to handle large volumes of data have not yet been fully incorporated into commercial systems and management software (Chen et al. 2012). It is important to highlight the role of information security policies in processing large volumes of data (Galegale et al. 2017) and risk analysis on how to adequately protect this data (Souza et al. 2020). Big data analysis brings interesting insights to different knowledge domains and industries, such as sales forecasting methods (Martins et al. 2022, 2023), doctor-patient relationship analysis methods (Ito et al. 2017) and studies that seek the development of solutions aimed at children's learning in the health area (Ito et al., 2013), among others

Data refers to any set of observations or measurements that can be analyzed to generate insights or support decision-making. Data can be structured or unstructured, and its quality is crucial for obtaining accurate and reliable insights. To ensure data quality, it is necessary to perform data preparation activities such as cleaning, transforming, and integrating data. Data quality is a critical factor for the success of data-driven decision-making, as inaccurate or incomplete data can lead to incorrect or misleading insights for decision-making (Wamba et al. 2017). Therefore, it is essential for organizations to adopt rigorous data management practices to ensure data quality.

Data cleaning is a fundamental process in preparing data for analysis, involving the identification and correction of errors, inconsistencies, and anomalies in the data (Y.-Y. Zhang et al. 2021). Data cleaning is a critical step in any data mining project, as dirty data can lead to inaccurate results and erroneous conclusions. The goal of data cleaning is to ensure that the data is correct, complete, and consistent so that it can be used with confidence in analyses and decision-making (Hellerstein 2008). Data cleaning can involve several steps, such as removing missing values, correcting typos, standardizing formats, and detecting and removing outliers (Zhang et al. 2021).

Thus, data cleaning is a critical step in the Big Data analysis process and must be performed with care and attention to detail. It can be done manually or through automated algorithms, depending on the size and complexity of the data. Additionally, it can be an iterative process, as identifying errors can lead to new discoveries and the need to collect more data (Manyika et al. 2011).

The volume and complexity of data is one of the main challenges in data cleaning with Big Data. Traditional methods may not be scalable or efficient enough to handle large and complex datasets. Additionally, the heterogeneity and variability of data sources can pose significant challenges, as different data sources may have different formats, structures, and levels of quality. Another challenge is the need for real-time or near-real-time data cleaning, especially in applications that rely on streaming data. This requires fast and efficient algorithms that can detect and repair anomalies in real-time, minimizing the impact on overall system performance. Addressing these challenges requires the development of new methods and techniques, as well as the integration of data cleaning into the overall data management and analysis pipeline (Y.-Y. Zhang et al. 2021).

This study aims to identify the main data cleaning techniques used in Big Data, evaluate their effectiveness, and explore their applicability in different industrial sectors. The study also seeks to synthesize and validate previous studies through the categorization of articles and the exploration of the relationships between Big Data and the practice of data cleaning.

2. RESEARCH METHODOLOGY

To consolidate evidence and deepen the understanding of the implementation of data cleaning practices in Big Data environments, a Systematic Literature Review (SLR) was conducted with the aim of identifying the main sources, authors, techniques, and industrial sectors addressed by the articles exploring this topic. The conduct of this systematic review aimed to evaluate the scientific production related to data cleaning in Big Data contexts. Specific metrics were employed for the analysis and selection of articles, covering aspects such as production, dissemination, impact, and interrelationships between academic works.

The SLR is a meticulous, clear, comprehensive, and replicable process aimed at identifying, evaluating, and comprehensively summarizing the complete works produced by academic and professional researchers (Gallardo-Gallardo 2016). The SLR must be comprehensive and independent, following a clear and explicit methodology to describe the procedures used. It is essential that the review covers all relevant material and be replicable by other researchers who wish to adopt the same approach in reviewing the topic in question (Okoli 2019).

The online platform Parsifal - Performing a Systematic Literature Review (https://parsif.al/) was adopted for conducting the SLR. The platform enables the selection of pertinent articles directly from the Web of Science, Scopus, and CAPES databases. The choice of these databases was based on their wide coverage of academic publications and frequent content updates. No specific time restriction was established during the search period, except for the exclusion of the year 2023, the current year of the research, as the annual publication analysis could be hampered by incomplete data. The keywords were selected in accordance with the research objectives and the questions sought to be addressed. In this context, the research adopted the following keywords: “data cleaning” AND “big data" AND (technique OR process OR method).

The systematic review was based on the PRISMA-P protocol (Moher et al. 2015), which consists of four stages: identification, screening, eligibility, and documents selected for critical analysis.

The design of the inclusion and exclusion criteria for articles to be considered for analysis is an important step to be executed after the collection of articles by search engines.

Inclusion criteria were considered as follows: (i) articles that comment on technology evaluation; (ii) articles that comment on data cleaning; and (iii) articles that respond to the research questions.

Exclusion criteria were considered as follows: (i) articles that are not in English; (ii) articles that do not meet our research criteria; and (iii) articles that are not primary studies.

After applying the criteria, a total set of 1073 potential academic works were identified in the Scopus, Web of Science, and Capes databases. Of this total, 27.56% had duplications between the databases, with 27.34% coming from the Web of Science, 36.54% from the Scopus, and 8.56% from the CAPES. Subsequently, 132 duplicated works were removed, 23 articles published in 2023 were excluded, and 4 articles without date information were invalidated, resulting in a total of 914 academic works for analysis.

Through the analysis of titles and abstracts, it was found that some works did not have a direct relationship with the topic in question or did not configure as case studies. Given this finding, 727 works were not selected as they did not contribute to the research objective.

Subsequently, 103 publications were excluded due to free access restriction, redirection to pages without a download link, or excessive delay in the download process. Subsequently, the remaining 84 articles were distributed among the authors for full-text reading. At this stage, 6 articles that consisted of systematic literature reviews and 7 articles that were not clearly related to Big Data were identified and eliminated.

Figure 1 illustrates the flowchart based on the PRISMA-P protocol, containing step by step the screening process in which, from 1073 articles, the result of 69 selected was obtained

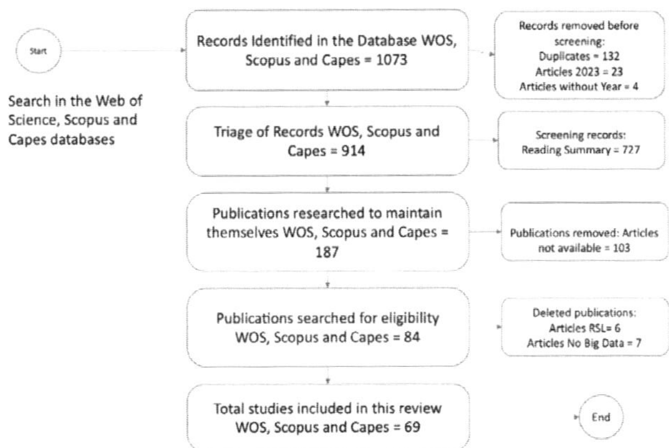

Figure 1. Flowchart based on the PRISMA-P protocol

3. RESULTS AND DISCUSSION

Table 1 presents a synthesis of the results of data cleaning practices in Big Data from the 69 selected articles. The analysis of each article (author) sought to identify when declared:

- The technical approach used: refers to the strategies and methodologies employed for data cleaning (benchmark, framework, method, etc.);
- The specific technique: refers to the specific techniques used for deduplication, handling missing values, error correction, and normalization, among others (algorithms, neural networks, machine learning, etc.);
- Type of industry: refers to the specific data treatment requirements of each segment (health, finance, construction, manufacturing, transport, etc.); and
- Database used: refers to the origin and volume of the data used in the data cleaning process.

Table 1. Analysis of Articles

Author (Article)	Approach	Technique	Industry	Database
(Jäger et al. 2021)	Benchmark	Benchmark with 69 heterogeneous datasets	General	General
(Liu et al. 2020)	Framework	Local Outlier Factor and Random Forest algorithms	Electrical	Electrical
(Du et al. 2017)	Framework	Conditionally combined functional dependency	General	Health/NBA
(Jin et al. 2018)	Model	Graphs, CNN Models, and "Tensorflow" Framework	General	Celebrities
(Oni et al. 2019)	Method	Evaluation of 4 data cleaning tools	General	Climate
(X. Yang et al. 2018)	Method	GPS trajectories using movement consistency	General	GPS
(Shen et al. 2021)	Method	Data cleaning algorithm for PMUs	Electrical	Electrical
(Zhou et al. 2021)	Framework	Algorithms, frameworks, and Big Data tools	Health	Health
(J. Wang et al. 2014)	Framework	Sample-and-Clean Framework	General	Citation Index

Author (Article)	Approach	Technique	Industry	Database
(Feric et al. 2021)	Framework	Django web framework for data harmonization	Biomedical	Biomedical
(Mok et al. 2017)	Framework	Reynolds Decomposition	Finance	Finance
(Abu Ahmad & Wang 2018)	Model	MAWRG and MAWR-ER algorithm	General	Bibliographic
(Dong et al. 2018)	Framework	Support for the PROTECT/Porto Rico project	General	Health
(Elouataoui et al. 2022)	Model	Real-time machine learning	General	None
(Rahul et al. 2020)	Benchmark	Various Big Data cleaning techniques	General	None
(Mavrogiorgos et al. 2022)	Method	Natural Language Processing (NLP)	General	Health
(Kenda & Mladenić 2018)	Method	Kalman Filter3	General	Water Sensors
(De et al. 2014)	Framework	Probabilistic models and rewriting techniques	General	None
(Ribeiro et al. 2022)	Framework	BDC package (new tool)	Biological	Biodiversity
(Fayyad et al. 2017)	Benchmark	Data management tools	General	None
(T. Wang et al. 2020)	Method	Experimental research	Manufacturing	Networks
(Prakash et al. 2019)	Benchmark	Data preprocessing techniques	General	None
(Tang 2015)	Model	RDF data quality	General	RDF Data
(Tian et al. 2017)	Framework	Bleach (data cleaning system)	General	None
(Yang et al. 2019)	Framework	Deep recurrent neural networks	Construction	Energy
(Staegemann et al. 2021)	Method	Deep recurrent neural networks	Construction	Energy
(Farid et al. 2016)	Framework	CLAMS (data cleaning system)	General	None
(Nugroho et al. 2021)	Benchmark	Algorithms for missing data prediction	General	None
(P.-I. D. Lin et al. 2022)	Model	Growthcleanr algorithm	Health	Health
(Shende et al. 2022)	Framework	CleanTS (R package)	General	None
(F. Li et al. 2021)	Framework	5S data management methodology	Manufacturing	None
(W. Zhang & Tan 2019)	Benchmark	Supervised machine learning	General	None
(Yousef 2015)	Framework	Duplicate record detection	General	None
(Z. Chen et al. 2019)	Framework	Scalable and customizable fuzzy join	General	None
(Y.-Y. Zhang et al. 2021)	Framework	Clustering for data quality	Construction	Energy
(Xu et al. 2015)	Benchmark	Various data cleaning techniques and methods	General	None
(Bramantoro 2018)	Method	Performance measures in duplicate removal	General	None
(Martinez-Mosquera et al. 2017)	Benchmark	Fellegi-Sunter theory for data cleaning	General	None
(Y. Lin et al. 2019)	Method	Scalable index-based algorithm	General	None
(Kim et al. 2019)	Model	SALT-C algorithm	Health	Health
(Chiang et al. 2021)	Method	Deep data cleaning	Health	Health
(S. Zhang et al. 2022)	Model	Bayesian Networks-based algorithm	General	None
(Sainju et al. 2021)	Benchmark	Algorithms for handling incomplete data	General	None
(Sheoran & Parmar 2022)	Framework	GeoWebCln (geospatial metadata cleaning)	General	Geospatial
(Xu Chu et al. 2013)	Framework	Heterogeneous rules in conflict hypergraph	General	None
(Xie & Cheng 2020)	Model	Imbalanced data cleaning algorithm	General	None
(Ding et al. 2018)	Framework	Improve3C (data quality framework)	General	None
(Koehler et al. 2021)	Method	Data preparation process automation	General	None
(Wenfei Fan et al. 2013)	Method	Heuristic consistency inference algorithms	General	None
(G. Chen et al. 2017)	Framework	Filtering for metric space search acceleration	General	None
(Maccio et al. 2014)	Method	Distributed data cleaning behavior	General	None
(Hossen et al. 2018)	Method	Random Forest and Linear SVM algorithms	General	None
(Huang et al. 2018)	Framework	PACAS (privacy-aware data cleaning framework)	General	None
(B. Li et al. 2021)	Method	BERT-based clustering algorithms	General	Competitions
(Drakopoulos & Megalooikonomou 2016)	Method	Conjugate gradient and finite difference matrix	Biomedical	Cardiology
(Roy et al. 2022)	Method	Hybrid detection algorithm and fuzzy filter	Multimedia	M-IOT
(Wu et al. 2018)	Method	Data mining	General	None
(Lyu 2021)	Method	Data cleaning for data quality improvement	Transportation	None
(Van Keulen et al. 2018)	Method	Random variable remapping	General	None
(Adolfo et al. 2021)	Method	Artificial Neural Networks (ANNs)	General	Physiological
(Rollo et al. 2022)	Framework	FFIDCAD model application	Traffic	Traffic
(A. Zhang et al. 2016)	Method	Algorithms and heuristic methods for cleaning	General	GPS
(H. Yang et al. 2019)	Method	Customization of cleaning rules and algorithms	General	None
(Shimizu et al. 2019)	Method	Visualization-based data cleaning	General	Scientific
(O'Shea et al. 2020)	Model	Model-Driven Development (MDD)	General	None
(Ilyas & Chu 2015)	Method	Clustering rules and machine learning	General	None
(Cao et al. 2017)	Model	Bradley-Terry model-based algorithm	General	None
(Ganibardi & Ali 2018)	Method	Algorithms evaluated by a confusion matrix	General	Web Records
(Li et al. 2019)	Framework	Attribute correlation under blocking	General	None

The technical approach used in the articles was grouped by similarity with decreasing frequency as follows: (i) Method: 36 – 52%; (ii) Framework: 24 – 35%; and (iii) Benchmark: 9 – 13%.

Regarding the specific techniques cited in the articles, it was initially expected that traditional data cleaning methods would be the most used. However, the review revealed a wide variety of techniques, including approaches based on machine learning, data mining, natural language processing, and other advanced techniques.

Regarding the type of industry referenced, about 74% of the articles do not specify any particular industry. The remaining articles have a small highlight for health, manufacturing, and construction.

Databases were used or specified for about half of the articles. There is a small highlight for health data.

This review has some limitations that should be acknowledged. First, the exclusion of non-English articles might have resulted in the omission of relevant studies conducted in other languages. Second, the reliance on certain databases (Scopus, Web of Science, CAPES) may have introduced a selection bias, potentially overlooking significant works indexed in other databases. Additionally, the exclusion of articles published in 2023 due to incomplete data could have excluded recent developments in the field. Future research should consider these limitations and aim to include a broader range of sources to mitigate these biases.

To further illustrate the applicability of data cleaning techniques in different industrial sectors, we include specific examples:

- Healthcare: Techniques like real-time machine learning (Elouataoui et al., 2022) and deep data cleaning (Chiang et al., 2021) have been applied to improve the diagnostic validity and mortality assessment in healthcare settings.
- Finance: The Reynolds Decomposition approach (Mok et al., 2017) has been used to clean security price data, improving the accuracy of financial models.
- Manufacturing: Methods such as the 5S data management methodology (F. Li et al., 2021) have been utilized to enhance data quality in manufacturing processes, leading to more efficient production workflows.
- Transportation: Data cleaning for data quality improvement (Lyu, 2021) has been applied in transportation systems to enhance pedestrian detection algorithms, contributing to safer and more efficient transit systems.

4. CONCLUSIONS

The SLR on data cleaning in Big Data revealed the growing importance of this research field, highlighting approaches and techniques used to handle large volumes of data in Big Data. The methodology adopted in this study, based on the Parsifal online platform and a specific protocol, Prisma-P, allowed for a comprehensive and independent approach following a clear and explicit methodology to describe the procedures used.

The review evidenced the use of a wide variety of advanced techniques based on artificial intelligence, including machine learning, data mining, natural language processing, among others. This diversity of techniques reflects the complexity and heterogeneity of data in Big Data environments, as well as the need for innovative approaches to deal with these challenges.

The use of a method was the main approach adopted in the articles, to the detriment of the framework and benchmark. There were no highlights for the type of industry and data source in data cleaning.

It is observed that data cleaning in Big Data is a multifaceted process that requires a well-planned technical approach, effective specific techniques, and an understanding of the peculiarities of the database used. Effective data cleaning ensures that data is reliable and useful, providing a solid foundation for accurate analyses and informed decision-making.

This study is expected to serve as a starting point for researchers interested in the topic, providing perspectives and guiding future investigations in the field of data cleaning in Big Data. Future research should focus on developing new data cleaning techniques that can handle real-time data processing and integrating these techniques into the broader data management and analysis pipeline to enhance the reliability and usability of Big Data.

REFERENCES

Abu Ahmad, H., & Wang, H. (2018). An effective weighted rule-based method for entity resolution, 36(3), 593–612.

Adolfo, C. M. S., Chizari, H., Win, T. Y., & Al-Majeed, S. (2021). Sample Reduction for Physiological Data Analysis Using Principal Component Analysis in Artificial Neural Network. Applied Sciences, 11(17), 8240.

Bramantoro, A. (2018). Data Cleaning Service for Data Warehouse: An Experimental Comparative Study on Local Data. TELKOMNIKA (Telecommunication Computing Electronics and Control), 16(2), 834.

Cao, B., Chen, L., & Lie, H. (2017). Vast Amounts of Video Data Clean Algorithm Base on Bradley-Terry Model: 2016 7th International Conference on Education, Management, Computer and Medicine (EMCM 2016), Shenyang, China.

Chen, Chiang, & Storey. (2012). BI and Analytics: From Big Data to Big Impact. MIS Quarterly, 36(4), 1165.

Chen, G., Yang, K., Chen, L., Gao, Y., Zheng, B., & Chen, C. (2017). Metric Similarity Joins Using MapReduce. IEEE Transactions on Knowledge and Data Engineering, 29(3), 656–669. Chen, Z., Wang, Y., Narasayya, V., & Chaudhuri, S. (2019). Customizable and scalable fuzzy join for big data. Proceedings of the VLDB Endowment, 12(12), 2117.

Chiang, H.-Y., Liang, L.-Y., Lin, C.-C., Chen, Y.-J., Wu, M.-Y., Chen, S.-H., Wu, P.-H., Kuo, C.-C., & Chi, C.-Y. (2021). Electronic Medical Record-Based Deep Data Cleaning and Phenotyping Improve the Diagnostic Validity and Mortality Assessment of Infective Endocarditis: Medical Big Data Initiative of CMUH. BioMedicine, 11(3), 59–67.

De, S., Hu, Y., Chen, Y., & Kambhampati, S. (2014). BayesWipe: A multimodal system for data cleaning and consistent query answering on structured bigdata. 2014 IEEE International Conference on Big Data (Big Data), 15–24.

Ding, X., Wang, H., Su, J., Li, J., & Gao, H. (2018). Improve3C: Data Cleaning on Consistency and Completeness with Currency. ArXiv, abs/1808.00024.

Dong, S., Feric, Z., Yu, L., Kaeli, D., Meeker, J., Padilla, I. Y., Cordero, J., Vega, C. V., Rosario, Z., & Alshawabkeh, A. (2018). An Efficient Data Management Framework for PROTECT. 2018 IEEE Int. Conf. on Big Data, 5316–5318.

Drakopoulos, G., & Megalooikonomou, V. (2016). Regularizing large biosignals with finite differences. 2016 7th International Conference on Information, Intelligence, Systems & Applications (IISA), 1–6. Du, Y.-F., Shen, dr, Nie, T.-Z., Kou, Y., & Yu, G. (2017). A cleaning method for consistency and currency in related data. 40, 92–106.

Elouataoui, W., Alaoui, I. E., Mendili, S. E., & Gahi, Y. (2022). An End-to-End Big Data Deduplication Framework based on Online Continuous Learning. International Journal of Advanced Computer Science and Applications, 13(9).

Farid, M., Roatis, A., Ilyas, I. F., Hoffmann, H.-F., & Chu, X. (2016). CLAMS: Bringing Quality to Data Lakes. Proceedings of the 2016 International Conference on Management of Data, 2089–2092.

Fayyad, U. M., Candel, A., Ariño De La Rubia, E., Pafka, S., Chong, A., & Lee, J.-Y. (2017). Benchmarks and Process Management in Data Science: Will We Ever Get Over the Mess? Proceedings of the 23rd ACM SIGKDD International Conference on Knowledge Discovery and Data Mining, 31–32.

Feric, Z., Agostini, N. B., Beene, D., Signes-Pastor, A. J., Halchenko, Y., Watkins, D., MacKenzie, D., Karagas, M. R., Manjourides, J., Alshawabkeh, A. N., & Kaeli, D. R. (2021). A Secure and Reusable Software Architecture for Supporting Online Data Harmonization. 2021 IEEE International Conference on Big Data (Big Data), 2801–2812.

Galegale, N. V., Fontes, E.L.G. & Galegale, B. P. (2017). Uma contribuição para a segurança da informação: um estudo de casos múltiplos com organizações brasileiras. Perspectivas em Ciência da Informação, v.22, n.3, (pp.75-97).

Gallardo-Gallardo, E. (2016). Systematic Literature Reviews. Unpublished.

Ganibardi, A., & Ali, C. A. (2018). Web Usage Data Cleaning: A Rule-Based Approach for Weblog Data Cleaning. Em C. Ordonez & L. Bellatreche (Orgs.), Big Data Analytics and Knowledge Discovery (Vol. 11031, p. 193–203).

Hellerstein, J. M. (2008). Quantitative Data Cleaning for Large Databases.

Hossen, J., Jesmeen H, M. Z., & Sayeed, S. (2018). Modifying Cleaning Method in Big Data Analytics Process using Random Forest Classifier. 2018 7th International Conference on Computer and Communication Engineering, 208–213.

Huang, Y., Milani, M., & Chiang, F. (2018). PACAS 2018 IEEE International Conference on Big Data, 1023–1030.

Ilyas, I. F., & Chu, X. (2015). Trends in Cleaning Relational Data: Consistency and Deduplication. Foundations and Trends® in Databases, 5(4), 281–393.

Ito, C., Marinho Filho, A., Ito, M, Azevedo, M.M. & Almeida, M. A. (2013). Preliminary evaluation of a serious game for the dissemination and public awareness on preschool children's oral health. In: MEDINFO 2013. IOS Press. p. 1034.

Ito M., Appel A. P., de Santana V. F., Moyano L. G. (2017) Analysis of the Existence of Patient Care Team Using Social Network Methods in Physician Communities from Healthcare Insurance Companies. Stud Health Technol Inform. 245.

Jäger, S., Allhorn, A., & Bießmann, F. (2021). A Benchmark for Data Imputation Methods. Frontiers in BD, 4, 693674.

Jin, C., Jin, R., Chen, K., & Dou, Y. (2018). A Community Detection Approach to Cleaning Extremely Large Face Database. Computational Intelligence and Neuroscience, 2018.

Kenda, K., & Mladenić, D. (2018). Autonomous Sensor Data Cleaning in Stream Mining Setting, 9(2), 69–79.

Kim, M., Shin, S.-Y., Kang, M., Yi, B.-K., & Chang, D. K. (2019). Developing a Standardization Algorithm for Categorical Laboratory Tests for Clinical Big Data Research: Retrospective Study. JMIR Medical Informatics, 7(3), e14083.

Koehler, M., Abel, E., Bogatu, A., Civili, C., Mazilu, L., Konstantinou, N., Fernandes, A. A. A., Keane, J., Libkin, L., & Paton, N. W. (2021). Incorporating Data Context to Cost-Effectively Automate End-to-End Data Wrangling, 169–186.

Li, B., Wang, J., & Liu, X. (2021). Parallel Cleaning Algorithm for Similar Duplicate Chinese Data Based on BERT. Scientific Programming, 2021, 1–11.

Li, Dai, & Wang. (2019). When Considering More Elements: Attrib. Correlation in Unsupervised Data Cleaning, 11(4).

Li, F., Li, X., Yang, Y., Xu, Y., & Zhang, Y. (2021). Collaborative Production Task Decomposition and Allocation among Multiple Manufacturing Enterprises in a Big Data Environment. Symmetry, 13(12), 2268.

Lin, P.-I. D., Rifas-Shiman, S. L., Aris, I. M., Daley, M. F., Janicke, D. M., Heerman, W. J., Chudnov, D. L., Freedman, D. S., & Block, J. P. (2022). Cleaning of anthropometric data from electronic health recs using automated alg, 5(4).

Lin, Y., Wang, H., Li, J., & Gao, H. (2019). Data source selection for inf. Int. in big data era. Inf. Sciences, 479, 197–213.

Liu, J., Cao, Y., Li, Y., Guo, Y., & Deng, W. (2020). A big data cleaning method based on improved CLOF and Random Forest for distribution network. CSEE Journal of Power and Energy Systems.

Lyu, Z. (2021). Research on Subway Pedestrian Detection Algorithm Based on Big Data Cleaning Technology. Wireless Communications and Mobile Computing, 2021, 1–10.

Maccio, V. J., Chiang, F., & Down, D. G. (2014). Models for Distributed, Large Scale Data Cleaning. Em W.-C. Peng, H. Wang, J. Bailey, V. S. Tseng, T. B. Ho, Z.-H. Zhou, & A. L. P. Chen, Trends and Apps in Knowledge Discovery p380.

Manyika, J., Chui, M., Brown, B., Bughin, J., Dobbs, R., Roxburgh, C., & Byers, A. H. (2011). Big data: The next frontier for innovation, competition, and productivity (p. 156).

Martinez-Mosquera, D., Luján-Mora, S., López, G., & Santos, L. (2017). Data Cleaning Technique for Security Logs Based on Fellegi-Sunter Theory. Em S. Wrycza & J. Maślankowski, Inf. Sys: Research, Dev, App, Ed. (Vol. 300, p. 3–12).

Martins, E. & Galegale, N. (2022). Retail sales forecasting information systems: comparison between traditional methods and machine learning algorithms. In Proceedings of the 2022 International Conf. Information Systems (pp. 30-38).

Martins, E. & Galegale, N.V. (2023). Machine learning: A bibliometric analysis. Int. Journal of Innovation, 11(3), 1-37.

Mavrogiorgos, K., Mavrogiorgou, A., Kiourtis, A., Zafeiropoulos, N., Kleftakis, S., & Kyriazis, D. (2022). Automated Rule-Based Data Cleaning Using NLP. 2022 32nd Conference of Open Innovations Association (FRUCT), 162–168.

Moher, D. et al. (2015). Preferred reporting items for systematic review and meta-analysis protocols (PRISMA-P) 2015 statement. Systematic Reviews, v. 4, n. 1, p. 1.

Mok, R. V., Mok, W. Y., & Cheung, K. Y. (2017). A Security Price Data Cleaning Technique: Reynold's Decomposition Approach. Em J. A. Lossio-Ventura & H. Alatrista-Salas (Orgs.), Inf. Man. and Big Data (Vol. 656, p. 108–119).

Nugroho, H., Utama, N. P., & Surendro, K. (2021). Class center-based firefly algorithm for handling missing data. Journal of Big Data, 8(1), 37. Okoli, C., Duarte, T. por:David W. A., & Mattar, R. T. E. introdução:João. (2019). Guia Para Realizar uma Revisão Sistemática de Literatura. EaD em Foco, 9(1).

Oni, S., Chen, Z., Hoban, S., & Jademi, O. (2019). A Comparative Study of Data Cleaning Tools. Int. J. DW. Min., 15-65.

O'Shea, E., Khan, R., Breathnach, C., & Margaria, T. (2020). Towards Automatic Data Cleansing and Classification of Valid Historical Data An Incremental Approach Based on MDD. 2020 IEEE Int. Conf. on Big Data, 1914–1923.

Prakash, A., Navya, N., & Natarajan, J. (2019). Big Data Preprocessing for Modern World: Opportunities and Challenges. Em J. Hemanth, X. Fernando, P. Lafata, & Z. Baig, Int. Conf. on Int Data Com Tech. (ICICI) 2018 (V26, p. 335–343).

Rahul, K., Banyal, R. K., & Goswami, P. (2020). Analysis and processing aspects of data in big data applications. Journal of Discrete Mathematical Sciences and Cryptography, 23(2), 385–393.

Ribeiro, B. R., Velazco, S. J. E., Guidoni-Martins, K., Tessarolo, G., Jardim, L., Bachman, S. P., & Loyola, R. (2022). bdc: A toolkit for standardizing, integrating and cleaning biodiversity data. Methods in Ecology, 13(7), 1421–1428.

Rollo, F., Bachechi, C., & Po, L. (2022). Semi Real-time Data Cleaning of Spatially Correlated Data in Traffic Sensor Networks: Proceedings of the 18th International Conference on Web Information Systems and Technologies, 83–94.

Roy, A., Bandopadhaya, S., Chandra, S., & Suhag, A. (2022). Removal of impulse noise for multimedia-IoT applications at gateway level. Multimedia Tools and Applications, 81(24), 34463–34480.

Sainju, A. M., He, W., Jiang, Z., Yan, D., & Chen, H. (2021). Flood Inundation Mapping with Limited Observations Based on Physics-Aware Topography Constraint. Frontiers in Big Data, 4, 707951.

Shen, L., He, X., Liu, M., Qin, R., Guo, C., Meng, X., & Duan, R. (2021). A Flexible Ensemble Algorithm for Big Data Cleaning of PMUs. Frontiers in Energy Research, 9, 695057.

Shende, M. K., Feijóo-Lorenzo, A. E., & Bokde, N. D. (2022). cleanTS: Automated (AutoML) tool to clean univariate time series at microscales. Neurocomputing, 500, 155–176.

Sheoran, S. K., & Parmar, V. (2022). GeoWebCln: An Intensive Cleaning Architecture for Geospatial Metadata, 41-62.

Shimizu, T., Omori, H., & Yoshikawa, M. (2019). Toward a view-based data cleaning architecture. ArXiv, abs/1910.11040.

Staegemann, D., Volk, M., Saxena, A., Pohl, M., Nahhas, A., Häusler, R., Abdallah, M., Bosse, S., Jamous, N., & Turowski, K. (2021). Challenges in Data Acquisition and Management in Big Data Environments: Proceedings of the 6th International Conference on Internet of Things, Big Data and Security, 193–204.

Tang, N. (2015). Big RDF data cleaning. 2015 31st IEEE International Conference on Data Engineering, 77–79.

Tian, Y., Michiardi, P., & Vukolic, M. (2017). Bleach: A Distributed Stream Data Cleaning System. 2017 IEEE International Congress on Big Data (BigData Congress), 113–120.

Van Keulen, M., Kaminski, B. L., Matheja, C., & Katoen, J.-P. (2018). Rule-Based Conditioning of Probabilistic Data. Em D. Ciucci, G. Pasi, & B. Vantaggi (Orgs.), Scalable Uncertainty Management (Vol. 11142, p. 290–305).

Wamba, S. F., Gunasekaran, A., Akter, S., Ren, S. J., Dubey, R., & Childe, S. J. (2017). Big data analytics and firm performance: Effects of dynamic capabilities. Journal of Business Research, 70, 356–365.

Wang, J., Krishnan, S., Franklin, M. J., Goldberg, K., Kraska, T., & Milo, T. (2014). A sample-and-clean framework for fast and accurate query processing on dirty data. Proceedings of the 2014 ACM SIGMOD Int Conf. 469–480.

Wang, T., Ke, H., Zheng, X., Wang, K., Sangaiah, A. K., & Liu, A. (2020). Big Data Cleaning Based on Mobile Edge Computing in Industrial Sensor-Cloud. IEEE Transactions on Industrial Informatics, 16(2), 1321–1329.

Wenfei Fan, Geerts, F., Nan Tang, & Wenyuan Yu. (2013). Inferring data currency and consistency for conflict resolution. 2013 IEEE 29th International Conference on Data Engineering (ICDE), 470–481.

Wu, L., Li, W., Wang, C., Yang, Y., An, Z., & Zhang, N. (2018). Research on Acquisition of Clean Governance Evaluation Techniques for Big Data. Proceedings of the 2017 4th International Conference on Machinery, Materials and Computer (MACMC 2017). 2017 4th International Conference on Machinery, Materials and Computer 2017, Xi'an, China.

Xie, W., & Cheng, X. (2020). Imbalanced big data classification based on virtual reality in cloud computing. Multimedia Tools and Applications, 79(23–24), 16403–16420. Xu Chu, Ilyas, I. F., & Papotti, P. (2013). Holistic data cleaning: Putting violations into context. 2013 IEEE 29th International Conference on Data Engineering (ICDE), 458–469.

Xu, S., Lu, B., Baldea, M., Edgar, T. F., Wojsznis, W., Blevins, T., & Nixon, M. (2015). Data cleaning in the process industries. Reviews in Chemical Engineering, 31(5).

Yang, H., Liu, W., Wang, X., Liu, H., Yu, B., & Zhou, H. (2019). The Design and Implementation of a Cleaning System Prototype. IOP Conference Series: Earth and Environmental Science, 252, 032218.

Yang, Tan, Santamouris, & Lee. (2019). Building Energy Consumption Raw Data Forecasting Using Data Cleaning and Deep Recurrent Neural Networks. Buildings, 9(9), 204.

Yang, X., Tang, L., Zhang, X., & Li, Q. (2018). A Data Cleaning Method for Big Trace Data Using Movement Consistency. Sensors (Basel, Switzerland), 18. https://api.semanticscholar.org/CorpusID:4717373

Yousef, A. H. (2015). Cross Language Duplicate Record Detection in Big Data. Em A. E. Hassanien, A. T. Azar, V. Snasael, J. Kacprzyk, & J. H. Abawajy, Big Data in Complex Sys (V9, p.171). Zhang, A., Song, S., & Wang, J. (2016). Sequential Data Cleaning: A Statistical Approach. Proceedings of the 2016 Int. Conf. on Mgt of Data, 909–924.

Zhang, S., Wang, Y., & Lv, Q. (2022). Exploring AI in Data Cleaning Based on Bayesian Networks. Adv. MM, 2022, 11.

Zhang, W., & Tan, X. (2019). Combining Outlier Detection and Reconstruction Error Minimization for Label Noise Reduction. 2019 IEEE International Conference on Big Data and Smart Computing (BigComp), 1–4.

Zhang, Y.-Y., Hu, Z.-Z., Lin, J.-R., & Zhang, J.-P. (2021). Data Cleaning for Prediction and its Evaluation of Building Energy Consumption. 38th International Symposium on Automation and Robotics in Construction, Dubai, UAE.

Zhou, S., Zhang, R., Chen, D., & Zhu, X. (2021). A novel framework for bringing smart big data to proactive decision making in healthcare. Health Informatics Journal, 27(2), 146045822110246.

INTELLECTUAL CAPITAL AND KNOWLEDGE MANAGEMENT: ARE THERE ANY RELEVANT DIFFERENCES?

Óscar Teixeira Ramada[1], Amaro Fernando da Fonseca Correia[2],
António José Dumont Vilares Teixeira de Melo[3] and Sílvio Roberto Stéfani[4]
[1]*Instituto Superior de Ciências Educativas do Douro, ISCE Douro, Penafiel, Portugal*
[2]*Atlântico Business School, Gaia, Portugal*
[3]*Universidade da Maia, Maia, Portugal*
[4]*University of the Midwest UNICENTRO, Brazil*

ABSTRACT

The main goal of this paper is to find out if there are distinct differences between the topics of intellectual capital and knowledge management. Given the scarcity of research focusing on them, only one case was obtained, encompassing the 2, within the scope of a sports company. It is concluded that there are differences, despite the topics being intangible in nature. Some insights can be highlighted. Knowledge-based businesses create value. The relationship established between them is bidirectional. Even though they are autonomous, they have a complementary relationship with each other. Its result can culminate in both the creation and destruction of value, for all or some stakeholders. The strategies that are at the base can be located at either an optimal or sub-optimal level. Explanations for verifying this can be found in the codification of intellectual capital and in the institutional (asymmetry of information and knowledge) and agency (incentive to define strategies that are more favorable to managers and less to other stakeholders) theories.

KEYWORDS

Intellectual Capital, Knowledge Management, Sport Organizations

1. INTRODUCTION

Andriessen (2004) defines intellectual capital "as a set of skills or qualifications that allows someone to do something". It's a generic definition. More broadly, it covers property rights, brands, image rights, etc., and other assets of an intangible nature. Thus, according to this author, knowledge will be the component that, included in intellectual capital, is the one from which the other figures derive. Whoever holds intellectual capital holds knowledge, but whoever holds this does not necessarily hold that.

Reinhardt et al. (2001), in turn, define intellectual capital, according to specific criteria, such as (market value/book value), as well as others such as the sum of human capital with structural capital (only 2) and human capital plus organizational capital more customer capital (3). As calculation measures, financial ones (Tobin's ratio, Value Added Intellectual, ...) and non-financial ones (market share, number of employees, ...) stand out. According to Abeysekera (2021), he recognizes the 2 topics as being distinct, although, in essence, they are interconnected with each other. In effect, this author establishes relationships between knowledge management and intellectual capital. The first, being created, stored and setting the background, through its management, is an object of use. The second, based on your measurement and report, creates value.

Marr et al. (2003), have another opinion. Indeed, for them, intellectual capital is the driving factor of innovation and competitive advantages, but knowledge management, at the same time, is recognized as constituting the crucial activity to obtain the growth and sustainability of intellectual capital in organizations. Therefore, its management is in close relationship with knowledge management processes, which means that its use guarantees the acquisition and growth of intellectual capital. On the other hand, it also appears that the creation of knowledge and intellectual capital are also associated with the epistemological points of view of individuals. Such, according to Marr et al. (2003), this is so, because "epistemology" consists of the study of knowledge. However, this concept had a definition with Plato and other later philosophers and, therefore, there are different "epistemologies", differing between individuals, which implies divergent concepts of the process of creating knowledge. Fundamentally, these authors define 3 classes of the concept of "epistemology": "autopoetics" (when there is an individual interpretation of knowledge), "cognitivists" (when knowledge is transferred) and "connectivists" (when knowledge is the property of a team). In terms of the most important conclusions, it is mentioned by these authors that the thrust of the research that covers the 2 topics mentioned, lies in the correct understanding of the epistemological characteristics, in order to choose a successful approach to knowledge management within of intellectual capital.

Understanding the different types of value creation involves understanding the requirements, demanded and possessed, by the different groups involved.

As argued by these 2 authors and, contrary to what one might mistakenly think, these 2 types of intangible assets have connections, not to be confused with each other, although of the same nature: intangible.

The source for collecting the most representative paper on this topic was Google Scholar. The concern was that it was recent, the years 2021 and 2020, to give an idea, although very brief, of the Literature Review, as possible.

Therefore, the "research question" was asked: *are there differences between intellectual capital and knowledge management? If so, which are the most relevant?*

2. LITERATURE REVIEW

Abeysekera (2021), is an author who carries out research (from the past to the future), focused on intellectual capital and knowledge management, with the goal of creating value. In this sense, a selection of papers is made that introduce relevant concepts and applications, essential for research in this field. Essentially, the research demonstrated that, even though these 2 concepts are separate, they are interconnected and complement each other.

In effect, companies, due to the difficulties of measurement in accounting, do not show the value of knowledge in their Financial Statements. It is for this reason that, researching this hidden value, constitutes a strong motivator for researchers to know its measurement, its report, as well as its contribution to the creation of value. There are 5 topics covered by the author in this framework:

First topic, "intellectual capital measurement and reporting". In fact, some ideas can be highlighted. One is that accounting cancels out assets such as intellectual capital, leading to undervaluation of companies, causing them to invest less in R&D. Another is that there are few techniques to deal with this accounting obstacle. The Balanced Scorecard (BSC), the Economic Value Added (EVA), are not suitable for compensating for the shortcomings revealed. Economics factors can also be mentioned, as the fundamentals of knowledge-based activity sectors, denote some changes: they can follow the law of increasing or decreasing returns, simultaneously. Finally, government policies must provide the right environment for companies to be competitive and successful in the face of rapidly changing economies.

Second topic, "knowledge and knowledge management". In this regard, 5 sub-topics can be referenced. The definition of knowledge is not only scarce but also subject to criticism for being incomplete. The organization of knowledge and learning has different meanings for different people. The theory of companies, based on resources, states that these increase competitive advantages, but to do so, they must have more inimitable and more sustainable resources. The framework for managing knowledge, so that it does not depreciate (lose its value), is important for companies to be able to take advantage of its benefits. Finally, there are several definitions of knowledge management, although none are consensually accepted, because the way it is used by people is different: as an object (a resource) or as a process (a qualification).

Third topic, "knowledge capture". In this, 4 aspects are related to technology and 1 to the processes through which knowledge is obtained. Regarding the first aspect, "expert systems", states the author, constitute a very important tool in the proliferation of expertise throughout the workspace. In the second, "databases", are also an essential but neglected knowledge tool that allows access to a huge volume of data. In the third, "web-based applications", most of them comply with databases, allowing the use of HTLM type documents, and allowing companies to convert programs written in other languages into Java. With regard to the fourth, "interactive online decisions support systems", it is clear that they allow us to overcome weaknesses in data, based on text, via verbal access to experts. The fifth, "knowledge-capture processes", basically states that it uses a bottom-up approach, that is, it means that companies cannot see which activities create value if they do not have balanced structured and unstructured processes. each other. Companies must, therefore, know which processes facilitate knowledge and create sustained competitive advantages that, at the same time, limit the ability of competitors to create knowledge.

Fourth topic, "knowledge transfer". It has 2 sub-topics. One, relating to "role information", and which refers to R&D activities, including the technologies that generate them. If the uncertainty in a given activity is greater, the information needed to carry it out will also have to be greater. Another, relating to "information strategy", in which it highlights the need for there to be, to some degree, human intervention. Therefore, workers must learn to communicate face-to-face before planning to take full advantage of electronic communications.

Fifth topic, "knowledge leverage". There are 3 sub-topics here. What refers to "knowledge types", that is, the knowledge held by people, can be explicit (that which is available in the conscious mind, and can be examined in documents, procedures, and computer programs) and implicit (that which is not in the conscious of having it, and that it is embedded in technology and management practices). The latter must be assimilated by companies, in such a way that it is translated into the former. In addition to the types, Abeysekera (2021) states that knowledge takes place at 4 levels ("knowledge levels"): implicit-to-implicit, implicit-to-explicit, explicit-to-implicit and explicit-to-explicit. They all exist in companies, and it is clear that they are given different possibilities for achieving "knowledge leverage" goals. The last sub-topic, called "knowledge leverage strategies", consists of 2 knowledge sharing strategies within companies – personalization and codification. Your choice is related to the type of customers, business, hired workers and activity sectors. Generally, companies need these 2 strategies simultaneously.

The most notable conclusions listed by the author are that the literature refers to the existence of 2 types of intellectual capital: internal capital (embedded in company structures) and external capital (what is embedded in its staff). The same is essential for creating value in companies. But, however, it is hidden within them. Knowledge requires management for its use, in processes and objects, to then be translated into the production of goods and-or services. This allows companies to create value, be more efficient, more rigorous and secure in the returns received. The use of their own data, added to those of partners, allows companies to create value in the future.

Three types of implications are also highlighted by the author: theoretical, regulatory and practical. In theoretical terms, it is worth highlighting, according to the author, the fact that this research facilitates research questions, such as serving as a foundation for the various phases of knowledge management, and analyzing the 2 dimensions of knowledge: implicit or explicit and the degree of sharing (individual, group and close to open). In regulatory terms, it makes it possible to provide insights to political decision-makers to build activities in order to participate in the digital economy, in addition to motivating companies to digitalize processes and objects in the production of goods and/or services. For these to be produced, increased attention is needed on cybersecurity and information, communication and technologies. Finally, in practices, the author states that the approach to knowledge management can change, due to the context in which the new economy operates, since it has become digital. This fact increased demand and made knowledge management and intellectual capital inseparable. In this economy, companies resort to business intelligence that is built from database management systems and resource planning systems.

Garcia-Perez et al. (2020), carry out research that reviews and presents theoretical perspectives relating knowledge management to intellectual capital in organizations that are based on knowledge, more specifically, those whose core business is professional sport.

According to the authors, business models based on knowledge are those that generate the most competitive advantages, meaning companies need to manage knowledge for these and, ultimately, the creation of value. Both knowledge management and intellectual capital are interrelated in a bidirectional way. The authors state that the existence of this relationship can both create and destroy value, which is one of the reasons why knowledge management strategies may be at a sub-optimal level. One of the causes may lie in the fact that optimal strategies create value for all stakeholders and sub-optimal ones create value only for one party and destroy it for another. One of the explanations for this lies in the codification of intellectual capital (corporate reporting). Some literature consulted by the authors highlights that this coding plays a key role in understanding the efficiency of the organizations' intellectual capital and their capabilities. This coding allows you to store knowledge, communicate and share information. They also note a lack of structuring of information, which leads to difficulties in evaluating organizations and comparing them. The bidirectional relationship between the 2 topics mentioned is sometimes the basis for wrong decision-making by managers.

The case of sports organizations (companies) is an example of knowledge-based companies. In the recent past, according to the authors, their knowledge has increased, based on strategic management, which means that it is possible to deepen the bidirectional study between knowledge management and intellectual capital. Sports organizations depend on resources of an intangible nature, which allow them to create value (while also being an indicator of the organizations' market value) via processes that are based on the knowledge of recognized experts. According to Garcia-Perez et al. (2020), sports organizations create events that allow them to transform their tacit knowledge into intellectual assets in the form of consumer experiences and sports goals. As the events are not regular, according to the authors, they require complex management and networks that have the ability to encompass a broad expertise, in addition to technical knowledge, of specific sports, which includes equipment, promotions, locations, programs and merchandising. Each sporting organization, the authors emphasize, is based on knowledge, operating in a highly competitive environment, in which success is measured according to 2 criteria: achieved sporting goals (which are the results obtained in competitions) and sporting success (financial results).

Therefore, although there is difficulty in generalizing, with regard to its knowledge management strategies, knowledge-based resources are rooted in the components of intellectual capital (human, structural and relational capital), which constitute the core of policies and management tools. Thus, the aforementioned authors argue that it is necessary to understand the determinants of knowledge management and intellectual capital, related to each other to understand the processes of value creation/destruction and, at the same time, the codifications carried out in sports organizations, having such resulting in improvements in operations and the growth of the economy, which has knowledge as its main pillar. As a result, stakeholders can build and maintain competitive advantages in the value chains of sports organizations.

With regard to the research design, the authors applied the systematic literature review method (scientific and transparent process that is replicable, minimizing hypothetical bias), with the aim of carrying out an analysis and identifying future research avenues.

This review method consisted of several phases:

1. Firstly, a pilot study was carried out, in which research chains were defined, used in Scopus (journal papers database). These chains were the result of the combination of management and accounting keywords, which were related to knowledge management and intellectual capital. The authors intended to obtain titles, abstracts and keywords from various authors. In total, 604 papers were selected;
2. In the second, they analyzed papers obtained In the second, they analyzed papers obtained in the first phase, with a view to identifying suitable samples for the review. It was found that there was a great heterogeneity of papers, on knowledge management and intellectual capital, with regard to sports organizations. Thus, software was used to perform content analysis of the words in the 604 selected papers;
3. In the third, software was also used, so that, from the 345 papers (out of 604), those with a frequency related to intellectual capital greater than 70 and related to knowledge management greater than 20 were selected. Via this inclusion and exclusion criterion, the authors ended up taking 46 papers as the final number, for the purposes of research to be drawn up in 3 typologies – studies relating to the understanding of intellectual capital (and accounting) in a sporting context; studies that contribute to understanding the characteristics of sports organizations; and economic studies that were only considered if they contained relevant implications for management purposes. Analyzing the abstracts, of the remaining 259, the authors added 4 more papers, which totaled 50, respecting the same criteria. The analysis of the 50 papers allowed the addition of 16 more, which made the total sample 66 papers;
4. In the fourth, the authors used another software, with the aim of building co-occurrence networks of terms collected in the 66 titles of the papers and abstracts;
5. On Thursday, they systematized and compared the 66 selected papers, from the point of view of empirical evidence, with the themes of knowledge management strategies, for the creation of value from intellectual capital and its respective codification.

Another particularity addressed by the authors in their research was related to the creation/destruction of value in sports organizations and the impacts of this, on the bidirectional relationship between knowledge management and intellectual capital.

In this way, they resort to 3 specific aspects:

- Discussion of the virtuous cycle of value creation resulting from knowledge management strategies;
- Analysis of models of sports organizations, insofar as they constitute the base point of influence of knowledge management strategies, with regard to investments in intellectual capital;
- Finally, they examine the dysfunctionalities of knowledge management, with regard to investments in intellectual capital (multiple theoretical framework – agency and institutional theory), in order to obtain

insights regarding sub-optimal knowledge management strategies and the related implications with the destruction of value.

Regarding the discussion of the value creation cycle and its strategies, all 3 components of intellectual capital represent information and create knowledge shared by professional sports organizations. The relationships between the 3 components constitute a source of knowledge that allows value to be created in organizations. These apply knowledge management strategies to develop the 3 components of intellectual capital and generate more intangible assets and thus trigger the virtuous circle of value creation. An example of which is the transformation of stored knowledge into the human capital component in sports performance. The development of strategies in this field allows the flow of knowledge (from players to coaches) to be boosted. According to the authors, there are 2 types of knowledge: explicit (knowledge in detail of instructions of a technical nature) and implicit (knowledge of general principles of sports dynamics). Another type of implementation of knowledge management strategies is gaming strategies, as they explore the storage of the intellectual capital component, which is the structural capital, of players' performance. This influences the success of sports and creates value for relational capital in 2 ways – in sports organizations by being part of popular culture and in entertainment (satisfying the passion of fans), in addition to companies being focused on profit. Athletes, in their performance, create value in 2 ways: generating, directly and indirectly, revenue.

In the first case, expressed in cash prizes, when participating in international competitions while, in the second, it is expressed in the price of tickets paid by fans and in other commercial rights arising from mass media advertising. Revenues have a positive impact on income and the contribution to dividends distributed by investors, in addition to making it possible to comply with budgetary requirements imposed by regulatory authorities. This ensures the national interest in the financial stability of sports organizations. On the other hand, as the authors state, the aforementioned relational capital (one of the 3 components of intellectual capital) is based on the athletes' performance (from an emotional and financial point of view), inducing a potentially virtuous cycle of value creation.

Regarding the analysis of models of sports organizations, and their relevance in the context of knowledge management (related to investments in intellectual capital), Garcia-Perez et al. (2020), state that they are characterized by the existence of a trade-off between sporting and business objectives. Knowledge management strategies make use of intellectual capital and develop it to maximize the objectives of sports organizations (profit, in particular). In this context, optimal decisions create value (for stakeholders), while suboptimal decisions only create value for those who have interests that are in line with the organizations' objectives and destroy value for everyone else.

Finally, the authors address the dysfunctionalities of knowledge management, obtaining insights related to the suboptimal strategies of that management and the respective implications associated with the destruction of value. Empirical evidence supports the assumption that most knowledge management strategies regarding intellectual capital are suboptimal and can trigger value destruction mechanisms. Thus, to explain these suboptimal strategies, as well as their dysfunctionalities regarding investment in intellectual capital, we have institutional and agency theories.

Institutional theory states that suboptimal knowledge management strategies and the repercussions on value destruction are due to the institutional complexity of sports organizations.

Regarding agency theory, it states that managers have advantages, in the domain of information, in relation to stakeholders and, therefore, can define knowledge management strategies that enable them to work in their favor (to the detriment of stakeholders). These divergences of interests, which oppose managers, fans and even those in the mass media, can lead to managers adopting strategies on investment in intellectual capital, which satisfy the interests of multiple stakeholders. For the authors, these strategies are suboptimal because they create value for some stakeholders and not for others. Regulators can act to evaluate sports organizations according to financial objectives but not according to management decisions. Thus, managers can exploit this information asymmetry.

Regarding the effects of the codification of intellectual capital on knowledge management strategies, these can facilitate accounting and reporting practices, facilitating the storage of knowledge. However, some limitations arise: the lack of structured coding of intellectual capital can have effects on the transparency of the information disclosed, which can lead to managers being prevented from following optimal knowledge management strategies. This could result in suboptimal strategies and activate forms of value destruction.

Thus, we have 2 strands of approach that are developed by the authors: accounting practices and disclosure of intellectual capital and the effects of coding intellectual capital on the transparency of financial reports.

Thus, with regard to the first, the authors state that the literature consulted addresses the codification of knowledge storage as human capital, in particular, in accounting and disclosure practices, related to player management. The acquisition of players has been recognized as an intangible asset, posing challenges regarding its evaluation. This recognition depends on managers' decisions about the type of acquisitions. Essentially, the literature identifies 3 types of acquisitions: "contracts with free players", "development of young players" and "transaction of players in the transfer market". Instead of other assets decreasing in value, players increase in value over time. As this is not recognized in the Balance Sheet, problems arise in revealing the fair value. These are the biggest difficulties facing sports organizations.

Regarding the second, the disclosure of financial information must be transparent and reliable regarding the stored knowledge, supporting optimal knowledge management strategies. However, the codification of intellectual capital sometimes undermines the transparency of financial information, not making it optimal (negatively affecting knowledge management strategies). Codification creates impairments in financial reports, which may be the basis for misrepresentation of provisions, by not recording all impairment losses.

In general, with regard to the general discussion of the paper, the authors emphasize that it allowed us to understand a bidirectional relationship between knowledge management and intellectual capital, in the context of value creation. Two relevant themes were identified: value creation strategies for intellectual capital and its codification. Which made it possible to explain the aforementioned bidirectional relationship. Sports organizations exploit the components of intellectual capital to create additional intangible assets. Knowledge management strategies about intellectual capital can either create (for all stakeholders) or destroy value (for some stakeholders). Institutional and agency theories help to explain these effects a little better.

As main conclusions, Garcia-Perez et al. (2020), note that the relationship between knowledge management and intellectual capital, in general and, in sports organizations, specifically, is under-researched. The process of creation and destruction of value, and the codification of intellectual capital are also in this handicap. With regard to the theoretical and practical contributions of the paper, it is worth highlighting the enrichment of the literature relating to knowledge management and intellectual capital and the bidirectional relationship between these 2 topics. As well as in the processes of value creation and destruction.

As future research avenues, the authors refer to the extent to which management, policies, procedures and performance management systems can mitigate suboptimal knowledge management strategies, in relation to investments in intellectual capital. Ethonographic and interpretative studies, such as interviews and surveys, are equally necessary.

3. CONCLUSIONS

This paper's main objective is to research whether, between intellectual capital and knowledge management, there are differences and, if so, whether they are relevant. In fact, the question arises since they are assets of the same nature: intangible. But, more than that, it took place in an eminently practical approach, that is, in a sports services company. The extension given, only one paper from the year 2020 was considered.

Some insights can be highlighted:

- Due to the difficulties in measuring the value created by companies, they do not disclose the same in their Reports;
- Due to this fact, its existence constitutes a motivation for research;
- Business models based on knowledge are those that create the most value. Therefore, it is extremely important to manage it;
- However, there are few definitions of knowledge and they are all incomplete;
- For knowledge to be used internally in companies, management is necessary in processes and objects;
- The most recent literature review (until 2021), addresses 5 topics, relating to knowledge management and intellectual capital: "intellectual capital measurement and reporting", "knowledge and knowledge management", "knowledge capture", "knowledge transfer" and "knowledge leverage";
- The relationship established between knowledge management and intellectual capital is bidirectional in nature;
- The result of this relationship is not certain: it can either create or destroy value (for all stakeholders or just for some);

- It is imperative to know what are the determinants that underlie the management of knowledge and intellectual capital to understand the creation/destruction of value and the aforementioned underlying processes;
- Knowledge and intellectual capital management strategies, which can both create and destroy value, may be at a sub-optimal level;
- An explanation for this reality lies in the way intellectual capital is codified;
- It is through codification that knowledge is stored, transmitted and shared;
- If this knowledge is unstructured, one of the consequences is that it will be difficult or impossible to evaluate and/or compare companies (organizations);
- However, in a more systematic way, to explain suboptimal strategies, and their dysfunctionalities regarding investment in intellectual capital, Garcia-Perez et al (2020), invoke 2 theories: institutional theory and agency theory;
- Institutional theory explains the existence of suboptimal strategies based on the complexity of organizations (sports, in this case);
- Agency theory, in turn, explains that, as managers have advantages in knowledge and information (asymmetry) in relation to stakeholders, they have an incentive to define knowledge management strategies that are (more) favorable to them, to the detriment of other stakeholders.

Regarding the research question, *are there any differences between intellectual capital and knowledge management? If so, which are the most relevant?*

The answer is "yes". In fact, within the scope of a company belonging to the sports sector, these 2 types of assets, intangible, are of the same nature, but with different characteristics. Intellectual capital is broader and more comprehensive, while knowledge management has underlying knowledge, itself, subordinate to its management, which is different depending on the organizations in question and the strategic goals defined to be pursued by them.

As main limitations, it is clearly pointed out, 2: scarce research that focuses on these topics, related to each other, and the fact that a specific case (case study) does not allow generalizations, which would make it possible to draw other conclusions.

Within the scope of the contributions, it can be inferred that the intangible nature of the 2 topics is more difficult to address and, therefore, develop scientific knowledge.

In the implications, it is highlighted the fact that the 2 topics are eminently dynamic and, the case in question, was limited to a merely static approach. As long as the framework is this, these 2 topics will see little scientific evolution.

Finally, as future avenues of research, it will be pertinent to extend it to other cases, from the same and different activity sectors and, above all, from technological sectors, where knowledge management and intellectual capital are highlighted as the most important pillars.

REFERENCES

Abeysekera, I. (2021). *Intellectual Capital and Knowledge Management Research Towards Value Creation. From The Past to the Future*, *Journal of Risk and Financial Management*, Volume 14, Issue 238, pp. 1-18.

Andriessen, D. (2004). *Making Sense of Intellectual Capital – Designing a Method for the Valuation of Intangibles*, Elsevier, Butterworth-Heinemann.

Garcia-Perez, A.; Occhipinti; Z.; Ghio, A.; Verona, R. (2020). "*Knowledge Management and Intellectual Capital in Knowledge-Based Organizations: A Review and Theoretical Perspectives*", *Journal of Knowledge Management*, July.

Marr, B.; Gupta, O.; Pike, S.; Roos, G. (2003). *Intellectual Capital And Knowledge Management Effectiveness*, *Management Decision*, Emerald, Volume 41, Number 8, pp. 771-781.

Reinhardt, R.; Bornemann, M.; Pawlowsky, P.; Schneider, U. (2001). *Intellectual Capital and Knowledge Management*, in H. Dierkes, J. Child J., I. Nonaka (Hrsg): Handbook of Organization Learning, pp. 775-793.

IMPACT OF BUSINESS-INTELLIGENCE ON IMPROVING THE ACTIVITIES OF AN NGO SUPPORTING RURAL FARMERS IN LUBUMBASHI

Yann Munganga, Israël Kayamba, Thierry Ilunga, Cedrick Vumisa and Efrem Mbaki
Researchers at Institut Supérieur d'Informatique, Programmation et Analyse (ISIPA), Kinshasa, Democratic Republic of Congo

ABSTRACT

Today, agriculture and information technology work hand in hand to improve farming practices. In fact, among several advantages of using information technologies in agriculture are the introduction of precision farming, the utilization and representation of meteorological data, the management and improvement of agricultural resources, the automation of agricultural equipment, supply chain management, and the adoption of agricultural information systems. The increasing integration of New Information and Communication Technologies (NICT) into agriculture has revolutionized the way farmers manage their businesses. The abundance of data generated in the process, often referred to as agricultural 'Big Data', offers immense opportunities to improve the efficiency, sustainability and profitability of farms. In this context, Business Intelligence (BI) becomes crucial for analyzing and making the most of this massive data. It enables farmers and agricultural businesses to make informed decisions based on accurate, real-time information. Thus, our study focused on the critical function that business intelligence (BI) plays in providing insightful guidance and tools for thoughtful decision-making in an environment of diverse and multifaceted agricultural digital data. After defining the fundamental concepts of BI and presenting some theoretical considerations, we illustrated these concepts using predefined reports and the decision-making process based on data from an organization supporting agricultural producers in Lubumbashi. Finally, we present some useful indicators and show how these numerical values influence decision-making in the operation of the above-mentioned Non-Governmental Organization (NGO).

KEYWORDS

Business-Intelligence, Decision-Making Process, Digital Data, Digital Agriculture, Dashboard, Key Performance Indicator, Crops, IT Tools

1. INTRODUCTION

Information technologies are increasingly present in agriculture. For many players, digital farming is seen as the final stage in the industrialization of agriculture, but also as the most effective way of achieving the ecological transition, particularly in industrialized societies. Although it is often presented as the "solution" to all the problems caused by the industrialization of agriculture, it is based on the industrial logic that has prevailed in industrialized countries for the last century and a half (Chen L. & Kim Y.J., 2017; Collectif, 2022). Indeed, in the modern world, it is rare to find a farmer who does not mention Information Technology (IT) tools in one of his activities. In rural areas, very few farmers work in isolation. They often form associations or are accompanied by NGOs. Generally, IT tools are used to measure their yields, with the aim of helping them to do better by changing practices, techniques, fertilizers or seeds. The Congo has an abundance of arable land, but most of its food needs are met by imports. Two entrepreneurs, Kersten Pucks and Aziz Khabirpour, have combined their company, GoCongo, with George Forrest's ranching business, Grelka. The result is a giant agri-food company. There are also a number of NGOs helping farmers in the Democratic Republic of Congo (DRC), providing them with technical, financial and logistical support to improve their farming practices, access markets and strengthen their resilience in the face of challenges such as climate change and food insecurity. These include Oxfam DRC, an international development organization working in the DRC to support rural communities in a range of areas, including sustainable agriculture, food security and natural resource management. Also, World Vision DRC, a humanitarian organization that implements agricultural development programs in the DRC, including initiatives to build farmers' capacity, promote sustainable farming techniques and improve access to markets. However, the content of this article echoes the activities of NGO CARE DRC which an international anti-poverty organization working in the DRC to support small farmers by providing them with training, tools and funding to improve their productivity and resilience. NGOs gather information on farming operations, including areas farmed, yields and farming methods, via internet platforms and apps. It is feasible to monitor farmers' advancement over time and pinpoint regions in need of extra assistance thanks to this data. In all cases, digital technology is now traversing the entire production chain, from farm to fork, with contributions at both agricultural production and distribution levels, gradually leading to a reconfiguration of food systems. The resulting data and information are immaterial, enabling fluid exchanges between the various stages of the value chain while supporting the flow of products and information between the different players. By providing valuable information for informed decision-making and by correctly structuring the relationships between these data, Business Intelligence (BI) plays a crucial role in the agricultural sector. Therefore, the main objective of this study is to model data provided by an organization that collaborates with rural producers in the city of Lubumbashi in the Democratic Republic of Congo (DRC) to calculate some key performance indicators. In other words, the main objective of this study is to explore the possibilities offered by business intelligence to improve the yields of rural farmers in the city of Lubumbashi, in collaboration with an international NGO. For a thorough understanding, we have structured our analysis into seven distinct sections, except for the introduction and conclusion. The first section will be devoted to a literature review, where we will examine in detail existing work demonstrating the crucial role of business intelligence (BI) in agriculture. In the second section, we will clearly present the objectives of our study, highlighting our specific intention to harness BI to increase agricultural yields for rural farmers in Lubumbashi. The third section will describe in detail the methodology we used to conduct this research, including data collection and analysis methods. In the fourth section, we will provide a brief description of the BI technologies we employed in this study, highlighting their relevance and applicability to our research objective. The fifth section will be devoted to the IT development conducted, detailing the steps and processes involved in creating and implementing our BI system for rural farmers in Lubumbashi. The sixth section will present the results obtained through our study, providing an in-depth analysis of the effects of using BI on agricultural yields in the Lubumbashi region. Finally, in the seventh and last section, we will discuss the commercial relevance of our work, highlighting the potential benefits for international NGO and other agricultural actors working in the region. This organized structure aims to provide a coherent and comprehensive overview of our study, facilitating a thorough understanding of our methodology, findings and their potential impact on agriculture in the city of Lubumbashi.

2. LITERATURE REVIEW

The use of business intelligence in agriculture dates back several decades but has expanded significantly in recent years with the advent of advanced digital technologies. The publication (Gebbers, R et al., 2010) perfectly illustrates this evolution by highlighting the growing importance of agricultural precision in global food security and the crucial importance of BI in this evolution. This study examines the potential benefits of using advanced technologies such as Geographic Information Systems (GIS), sensors and drones to improve crop management, optimize yields and reduce costs. Since then, this research has continued unabated, as the (Islam et al, 2021) study shows. Indeed, decision-making computers now have a significant potential to improve agricultural practices by giving farmers access to invaluable information that helps them make informed decisions. Stated differently, business-intelligence (BI) computing offers a wide range of potentially useful applications to raise agricultural productivity, sustainability, and profitability. To avoid being exhaustive, we will list a few studies in this part that show how the intelligent use of data and information technologies can change agricultural practices and improve global food security. Without going into too much detail, we will list a few studies that support the contribution of decision-making computing in agriculture. To begin with, the books (Liu et al., 2017; Liu et al., 2021) describe how BI enables farmers to analyze historical data on crops, soils, climate and other factors to optimize agricultural yields. For example, farmers can anticipate weather conditions and adjust their farming practices accordingly using predictive analytics techniques. In addition, the authors of (Cai et al., 2018) show that farmers can use BI to effectively monitor and manage natural resources such as water and soil. Mapping and monitoring changes in land use and environmental conditions can be carried out using geographic information systems (GIS) and remote sensing technologies. In another study (Gebbers et al., 2018), BI helps farmers find inefficiencies and optimize their farming processes by analyzing data on crop performance, input prices and production costs. For example, analysis of yield data can help maximize yields while reducing costs by optimizing irrigation and fertilization levels. Similarly, in (Koldehofe et al., 2017; Sugiura et al., 2019), the authors show that BI plays an important role in the development of precision agriculture by enabling farmers to adapt their farming practices according to spatial and temporary variations in soil, water and climate. Technologies such as drones and sensors collect data in real time to help make decisions about managing agricultural plants. Lastly, the authors of (Martinez et al., 2016) show how BI supports farmers in making strategic decisions by offering customizable dashboards and insights on agriculture commodity pricing, market trends, and possible hazards. For instance, by using data-driven market analysis, farmers can identify new business prospects and schedule their planting operations appropriately. To put it briefly, there are many possible uses for business information that could raise agricultural production, sustainability, and profitability. The aforementioned research demonstrate how farming practices can be altered and global food security can be increased through the wise use of data and information technologies. In this way, we validate that BI may enhance agricultural practices by giving farmers relevant data to support their decision-making. Moreover, it might contribute to increased profitability, sustainability, and productivity in agriculture. Therefore, building on this research, our studies concentrate on how an NGO assists rural farmers in examining how data and information technology might be wisely used to alter farming techniques and enhance food security for the Congolese people.

3. OBJECTIVES

The aim of our research is to support the NGO in monitoring its interventions, which carry out various interventions to support farmers, such as training, supply of seeds and fertilizers, and technical assistance. We used BI to assess the Impact of training and measure the follow-up of resource distribution ((Raut, R. D. et al., 2021; Saravanan, M. et al., 2O19; Kuo et al., 2022). By correlating training data with farmers' performance results, we were able to measure the effectiveness of training programs and identify areas for improvement. In addition, precise tracking of seeds and fertilizers distributed ensured equitable distribution and prevented wastage. We also contributed to a rigorous financial analysis to ensure optimal use of the NGO's resources. By evaluating the costs of different interventions in relation to the benefits obtained, we were able to recommend budget adjustments to maximize the impact of spending. The integration of financial data into the dashboard enabled real-time monitoring of expenditure, ensuring transparent and efficient financial management.

4. METHODOLOGY

A researcher frequently fixes the current situation "As is" and the target situation "To be" without knowing the approach to follow or the techniques to use to achieve the target situation (Flick, U. 2022). In fact, scientific research resembles the search for means and methods to leave and/or modify the source to achieve the goal, whatever the field. This is why we define a methodology as an organized and systematic method for completing a specific task, project or study. It includes steps, procedures and methods for organizing the conduction of an activity. In this study, we are using the same four-phase methodology as in the agricultural sector, just as in the financial sector where we are BI analyst. Firstly, we identify the business processes before looking at the hardware and software tools needed to support the business activities. Next, based on our personal experience, we organize the management and storage of the data produced by IT before analyzing it to calculate specific decision support performance indicators. Before continuing, we think it useful to examine each of these stages in detail.

4.1 Mapping of Business Processes

Farming without processes is difficult, if not impossible. Farming is a complex activity involving many steps and organized actions to grow crops or raise livestock efficiently and productively. Farming methods aim to increase crop yields while reducing risks and losses. The type of crop, the farming techniques used, the climate, the geographical region and other factors can all influence agricultural processes. There are tacit processes that guide farming activities, even in traditional forms of agriculture, where the emphasis is more on practical knowledge passed down from generation to generation. Digital farming involves the use of modern technologies, such as sensors, drones, crop management tools and so on. However, here is a general list of processes commonly used in agriculture: Soil preparation, sowing, irrigation, crop management, harvesting, storage, post-harvest processing, sales and marketing, livestock management (if necessary), crop rotation, natural resource management, farm waste management, farm equipment maintenance, training and education and financial management. It is important to note that these processes can differ depending on the type of farming, whether it is large-scale farming, organic farming, agroforestry or other specific farming models.

4.2 IT Choice

With the modernity that accompanies farming activities, the above-mentioned processes are supported by IT tools. Indeed, the role of information technology (IT) is becoming increasingly important in the agricultural sector, as it has a significant impact on the way farmers manage their farms, make decisions and optimize their processes. The appropriate use of these technologies can increase the efficiency, sustainability and profitability of contemporary agriculture. However, it is crucial to consider the unique requirements of each farm and tailor technological solutions accordingly. Here are some of the areas of IT used in agriculture, often referred to as 'digital farming': sensors and the Internet of Things, remote sensing and drones, geographic information systems, precision agriculture, farm management systems, blockchain, water technologies, data analytics and big data, mobile applications, agricultural robotics or livestock technologies. In addition, there is a wide range of software used in the agricultural sector, from farm accounting to crop management. It is important to note that software selection depends on the unique requirements of each farm. A combination of these software packages may be useful for some farmers to meet their specific farm management needs. Although it is not exhaustive, the table below lists some useful software in the agricultural environment.

Table 1. Some useful agricultural software

Software types	Functionalities	Examples
Farm management software	This software helps to manage all agricultural operations, including crop planning, livestock management, financial management and so on.	FarmLogs, Granular, Trimble Ag Software.
Crop planning and monitoring software	This software helps to plan crops, monitor their growth and make decisions based on data.	Climate FieldView, Agworld, Farmer's Edge.
Irrigation management software	For precise irrigation management, optimising water use	Hortau, IrriSoft, CropX.
Fertilizer management	For planning and monitoring fertiliser use	NutrientStar, Adapt-N, Agworld
Blockchain applications	To ensure traceability and transparency in the food supply chain	IBM Food Trust, TE-FOOD,
Farm fleet management	To monitor and manage the use of agricultural machinery	John Deere Operations Center, AgCommand, Trimble Ag Software
Big data analytics	For analysing large quantities of agricultural data and extracting insights	FarmWise, Conservis, Aglytix
Livestock management software	For monitoring health, reproduction and other aspects of livestock farmin	CattleMax, Ceres Tag, HerdMASTER.
Geographic Information Systems (GIS)	For mapping and spatial analysis..	ArcGIS, QGIS, Google Earth Engine
Agricultural weather platforms	Monitor weather conditions and make decisions based on forecasts	The Weather Company, AgWeatherNet, Pessl Instruments
Farm financial	Management Software: For accounting and budget planning	QuickBooks for Farming, AgCinect, CenterPoint Accounting for Agriculture

The use of IT equipment in agriculture has evolved as technology has advanced and the business processes of agricultural producers have become more complex. These typically include sensors, drones, GPS (Global

Positioning System), intelligent farm machinery, on-board computers, automation systems, tablets and smartphones, wireless communication systems, desktops and laptops, computer networks, data storage technologies, touch-sensitive displays, RFID (Radio-Frequency Identification) tags and others. These materials need to be chosen carefully and maintained regularly. Producers are influenced by key success factors to choose the best hardware and software to achieve their objectives as part of a BI study.

4.3 Data Management

To take full advantage of the information generated by various sources mentioned above, such as drones, farm machinery and sensors, structuring agricultural data is essential. A good data structure facilitates management, analysis and decision-making. It is an innovative idea to start by establishing objectives and requirements for the collection and use of agricultural data. A list will help identify potential sources of data, such as sensors, drones, farm machinery, mobile applications, etc., to avoid mixing apples and pears. However, it is important to ensure that data is standardized to guarantee consistency in the way it is recorded and stored. Standards for units of measurement and date formats should also be established before creating a database architecture that reflects the structure and relationships between different entities (e.g., crops, fields, plots, sensors). Depending on specific needs, a relational, geographic or other type of database would be chosen. The best approach is to use popular database management systems to efficiently store, organize and retrieve data in the context of a relational database, such as MySQL, DB2, PostgreSQL, Microsoft SQL Server or MongoDB. It is also advisable to adopt industry standards to ensure greater compatibility and interoperability. Hierarchical data structuring can also simplify data management and traceability. Access management, regular data backup and IT security protocols should all be part of the security measures required to protect sensitive data. Finally, data systems must be consistently integrated, cleansed (data cleansing, validation and correction), standardized and documented.

4.4 BI Benefits

In the context of agricultural data, BI offers several advantages. Those involved in the agricultural sector can make the most of data generated by various sources, such as drones, farm machinery and sensors, by using BI tools. As a result, agricultural data can be analyzed and visualised in a clear and comprehensible way using BI. This helps farmers to make smarter decisions using accurate information in real time. It also helps to optimize the use of resources such as water, fertilizers, pesticides and so on. This cuts costs and reduces environmental impact. Depending on the type of crop, the geographical region and the specific farming practices, BI helps to assess farming performance and to make judicious choices to improve practices and yields. These include, but are not limited to, yield per hectare, yield per plant, irrigation efficiency, fertilizer use, crop growth rate, post-harvest loss rate, cultural health index, crop profitability, crop rotation, cost per unit of output, soil fertility rate, farm machinery efficiency, leaf mass index (LMI), water management rate or leaf growth rate, the agricultural product quality index is used to assess the quality of agricultural products according to criteria such as size, color, flavour, etc.

5. TECHNOLOGY DESCRIPTION

Companies seeking to remain competitive in a complex business environment need BI. Organizations can make more informed strategic decisions, anticipate market changes and improve performance by using intelligent data. In other words, in the business world, BI is crucial because it enables organizations to make informed strategic decisions based on data analysis. Here are three of the many reasons why BI is considered essential.

5.1 Informed Decision-Making

Businesses can make decisions based on facts rather than intuition, thanks to the data analysis tools and techniques provided by BI. This reduces risk while increasing opportunity. In other words, BI helps managers make smarter decisions, anticipate market changes, and stay competitive by transforming raw data into actionable information using a powerful analytical framework. It aggregates data from different sources across the organization, consolidating it in one place. This gives decision-makers a complete, unified view of information, eliminating information silos (Brown M.C, 2020; Chen J. Han J. & Yu P.S, 2012; Daan V. B., 2021; Williams P. D., 2016). BI enables the creation of customized reports for users and teams. Reports can be automated for regular generation, providing constant visibility of business performance. Finally, BI uses BI dashboards to visualize data in the form of graphs, charts and other visualizations. These interactive dashboards enable decision-makers to quickly understand important information and make decisions based on visual understanding. In addition, predictive modelling capabilities can be integrated into certain BI tools to forecast future movements. This helps managers to make strategic decisions based on informed forecasts. BI also helps to align operational decisions with the company's strategic objectives. Decision-makers can assess how each decision contributes to the organization's long-term objectives.

5.2 Optimizing Performance

BI helps organizations identify where improvements can be made by monitoring and analyzing key performance indicators (KPIs). This can lead to improved operations management and process optimization. It is widely accepted that BI is an optimization tool for organizations. A systematic approach to collecting, analyzing and presenting essential business information enables companies to make more informed decisions and maximize their performance (Larson R. R. & Chang V., 2016; Power D. J., 2007, Watson H. J. & Wixom B.H., 2007; Wixom B.H. & Watson H. J., 2010). Business processes can be tracked and analyzed using BI, enabling defects, obstacles and opportunities for improvement to be identified. Organizations can use this information to maximize efficiency. BI improves the quality of decision-making by providing relevant data and in-depth analysis. Managers can make informed decisions using real-time information, reducing the risk of costly errors. BI makes it possible to monitor the use of resources such as finance, raw materials and personnel. As a result, businesses can manage their budgets to maximize operational efficiency. With BI, reports are no longer drawn up on a line-by-line basis, but on a multi-dimensional basis, with the help of a fact table and a dimension table. This eliminates the need to search for two related pieces of information in additional reports. The "drill up" and "drill down" functions can be used to increase or decrease the granularity (hierarchy of information from highest to lowest, and vice versa) to navigate from the most synthetic to the most detailed. The "extract" function can be used to link to another report page to the specified page to obtain information filtered according to the selected data point (Eckerson, W. W, 2010, Smith J. A., 2019; Wu, D. & Zhang J, 2010).

5.3 Cost Reduction

Data management (BI) can help you monitor budgets, identify unnecessary costs and optimize spending. This improves financial management and operational efficiency. Companies can find hidden trends and reduce costs. However, this involves significant costs, complex tools to use and complex data analysis skills. While there is nothing difficult to overcome, it is important to make a thorough assessment before taking the plunge. It is worth remembering that cost reduction is a set of methods aimed at significantly reducing a company's expenditure. This mainly concerns expenditure that is not necessary or that can be eliminated. A company can operate in many different areas, including production, marketing and distribution. The main aim of cost reduction is to reduce the cost of items that are not necessary to the business. An internal audit can be carried out before any improvements are made. By implementing a cost-cutting strategy, it is possible to optimise productivity, a key factor. Improving productivity will inevitably increase profits. Managers who wish to use such a strategy are aware that their resources are limited and must therefore maximize them.

6. DEVELOPMENTS

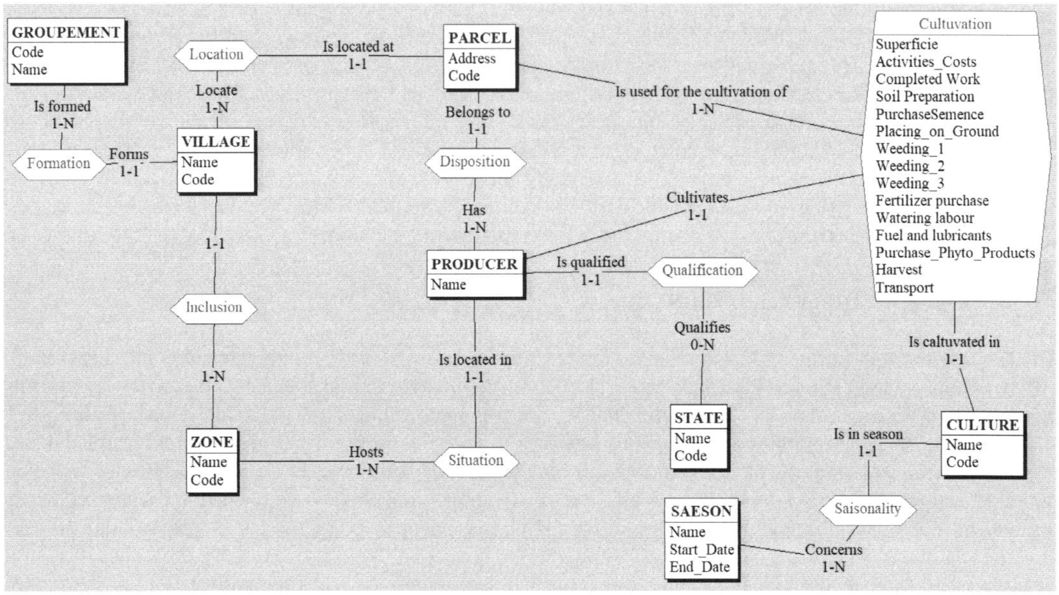

Figure 1. NGO's entity-association model

We have taken a systematic approach to implementing Business Intelligence (BI) for the NGO's activities supporting farmers in Lubumbashi, DRC. Let's discuss the three steps involved in more detail: **(1) Entity-Association Model:** We started by structuring the data to arrive at a relational model. This model is crucial for understanding the various entities involved in the project and how they relate to each other. It captures concepts such as farmers, plots, crops, and costs incurred, providing a comprehensive view of the project's data structure. We used the DBMain Tool to obtain the conceptual model and, after transformation, the logical model and finally the physical model, which we implemented using SQL Server as our Database Management System. **(2) Data Collection and Management:** The NGO managed its historical data in Excel files, which compiled information provided by agronomists and contained key details of farmers' activities with associated costs. Using the above data model, we wrote SQL queries and stored procedures to load the database from the Excel files. Today, a man-machine interface automates data entry directly into the database. **(3) Multidimensional Analysis using Star Model:** With a view to applying business intelligence, we designed a star model to organize data in a data warehouse. To put it simply, we created a specific schema in our database to house the fact table, surrounded by dimension tables. In this way, we were able to take advantage of this model by analyzing the data from different angles, for example, in relation to time, location or crop type. In this way, we were able to obtain information and make informed decisions. We then connected the database to Power BI DeskTop to produce reports, calculate indicators and implement dashboards.

Despite the page limit, we are committed to presenting some of the results of our investigations. Indeed, following the data structuring described above, we have harnessed the software Power BI to analyze and optimize the activities of the NGO supporting farmers in Lubumbashi. The insights gained from data analysis can lead to informed decision-making, leading to better results for farmers and the organization as a whole.

7. RESULTS

To calculate the few indicators we present below, we've used a view of our database deduced from the fact table, where foreign keys are replaced by the values of useful columns. This view thus contains 87,6900 rows with 89 columns. Given the constraints associated with the publication of a scientific article, we plan to detail the data from this NGO in a book to be published very shortly. In summary, we have identified 2,566 farmers producing ten crops supported by the NGO. The first table below shows the expenditure required for each of these ten crops. It should also be noted that the NGO divides farmers into two groups: relay farmers and direct beneficiaries. A relay farmer is a farmer who has received training in new farming methods, technologies or crop management techniques, and who has a good command of the techniques and better performance in terms of production and distribution. Having accumulated this knowledge, the relay farmer acts as a mediator within his community, exchanging his knowledge with other farmers. Farmers qualified as direct beneficiaries are those who receive aid from an NGO and need constant monitoring of their activities.

Table 2. Cost of activities

Culture	Activity Cost	
Amaranth	29000$	3%
Aubergine	39000$	4%
Carrot	14000$	1%
Cabbage	494800$	46%
Chives	12000$	1%
Okra	13500$	1%
Onion	46500$	4%
Chilli	0$	0%
Pepper	1000$	0%
Tomato	420800$	39%
Grand total	1070600$	100%

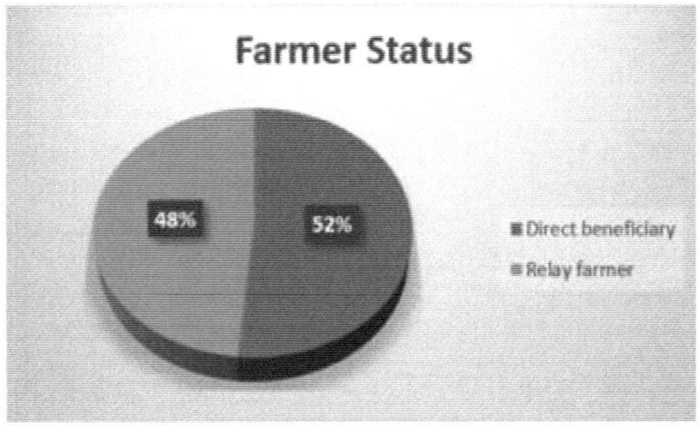

Figure 2. Two categories of farmers

The following table shows the costs of different crops. The percentage of activity is compared with the maximum percentage using the total cost. Overruns are shown in red. Those that need to be monitored in orange and those that are being managed correctly in green.

Table 3. Cost indicator

Activities	Cost	Indicator	Max Target
Soil preparation	472000$	44%	40%
Purchase of seeds	2000$	0%	1%
Setting up the plot	143000$	13%	11%
Weeding 1	64000$	6%	5%
Weeding 2	17000$	2%	3%
Weeding 3	13000$	1%	1%
Purchase of fertilizer	0$	0%	1%
Purchase of manure	0$	0%	1%
Watering labour	0$	0%	1%
Fuel and lubricants	78500$	7%	6%
Purchase of plant protection products	7700$	1%	1%
Phyto treatment	0$	0%	2%
Harvesting	56300$	5%	5%
Transport	217100$	20%	22%

We note that of the fourteen indicators, three are in orange, and therefore worth watching. Five are in red, meaning that they are bad and need to be allocated so as not to exceed the limits. Nevertheless, six indicators are green, but three are not to be considered as no amounts have been committed. In short, the NGO's management is not performing well. However, given the increasing demands from farmers, the NGO's managers are appealing to their donors to raise the maximum thresholds, in the hope of improving their indicators.

8. BUSINESS BENEFITS

The results of these analyses led to several strategic decisions aimed at improving the NGO's performance and farmers' conditions: (1) Recommendations for Crop Rotation: Based on the analysis of yields and soil conditions, specific recommendations were made for crop rotation, to maintain soil fertility and optimize yields; (2) Development of New Training Programs: Identifying gaps in farmers' knowledge, we developed targeted training programs to meet these needs, and, (3) Logistics Optimization: By analyzing transport and distribution data, we proposed improvements to reduce logistics costs and increase the efficiency of resource distribution.

9. CONCLUSIONS

This study rightly demonstrates the importance of BI in the agricultural sector. Indeed, we have first demonstrated theoretically how BI is highly beneficial to agriculture. We have sufficiently explained how and why farmers and industry professionals derive numerous benefits from the use of BI in agriculture, also known as digital agriculture or precision agriculture. BI enables in-depth analysis of agricultural data such as weather, soil, crops, irrigation and other aspects. By understanding this data, farmers can optimize the use of resources such as water, fertilizers and pesticides, contributing to more sustainable agriculture. In addition, farmers can anticipate risks such as plant diseases and adverse weather conditions by using BI tools to analyze historical and real-time data. This enables strategic planning to reduce negative effects. Secondly, the analysis and structuring of data from the NGO working with farmers in Lubumbashi has enabled us to highlight a few useful indicators for the smooth running of our activities. These values have enabled the NGO's managers to redirect their strategies and management to improve their activities. We are working to publish a book detailing the data and indicator calculations, and even dashboards, for a better understanding of the role of BI not only in the NGO's activities, but also in the evolution of modern agriculture.

REFERENCES

Brown, M. C. (2020). Advanced Analytics for Predictive Business Intelligence. New York: Springer.

Cai, H., Chen, H., Wu, L., & Liu, H. (2018). Research on Agricultural Internet of Things and Cloud Computing Integration Service Platform. In 2018 15th International Conference on Service Systems and Service Management (ICSSSM) (pp. 1-4). IEEE.

Chen, J., Han, J., & Yu, P. S. (2012). Data mining for the internet of things: literature review and challenges. International Journal of Information Management, 34(3), 383-401.

Chen, L., & Kim, Y. J. (2017). The Role of Predictive Analytics in Modern Business Intelligence. Journal of Predictive Analytics, 5(3), 189-205.

Collectif, Cultiver la terre avec des algorithmes: Agriculture, numerique et écologie, Bord de l'eau, 2023

Daan V. B. and Charesa C. (2021). Data Science for Decision Makers & Data Professionals: Creating an Intelligent, Data-Driven Organization with AI, BI & Big Data, Passionned Publishers

Eckerson, W. W. (2010). Performance Dashboards: Measuring, Monitoring, and Managing Your Business. John Wiley & Sons.

Flick, U. (2022). Introducing Research Methodology: Thinking Your Way Through Your Research Project (3rd ed.). Sage Publications.

Gebbers, R., & Adamchuk, V. I. (2010). Precision agriculture and food security. Science, 327(5967), 828-831.

Gebbers, R., & Adamchuk, V. I. (2018). Precision agriculture and food security. Science, 359(6379), 716-718.

Islam, A., He, X., & Chong, W. K. (2021). A Survey of Data Mining Techniques for Precision Agriculture. IEEE Access, 9, 26720-26734.

Johnson, R. L., & Davis, S. K. (2018). Business Intelligence and Predictive Modeling: A Comprehensive Guide. Harvard Business Review, 76(4), 56-68.

Koldehofe, B., Herzog, O., Sachs, J., & Weise, C. (2017). Business intelligence in agriculture: a market research. In 2017 20th Conference on Innovations in Clouds, Internet and Networks (ICIN) (pp. 138-143). IEEE.

Kuo, C. H., Tsai, C. H., & Chen, C. L. (2022). Implementing Business Intelligence in Smart Agriculture: A Case Study in Taiwan. IEEE Access, 10, 42012-42025.

Larson, R. R., & Chang, V. (2016). A review and future direction of agile, business intelligence, analytics and data science. International Journal of Information Management, 36(5), 700-710.

Liu, L., Jin, Z., Yang, Q., & Liu, Y. (2017). Application of Big Data and Data Mining Technology in Agricultural IOT. In 2017 12th International Conference on Computer Science & Education (ICCSE) (pp. 207-211). IEEE.

Liu, Y., Wang, S., Wu, Q., & Fu, L. (2021). Big data and business intelligence in agriculture: A systematic review

Martinez, P., Jimenez, M., & Burgos, M. (2016). Big data and business intelligence in agriculture. In 2016 IEEE Global Engineering Education Conference

Olszak, C. M., & Ziemba, E. (2006). Key factors for successful business intelligence implementation. Proceedings of the 2006 Informing Science and IT Education Joint Conference, 125-138.

Raut, R. D., Gardas, B. B., & Narkhede, B. E. (2021). Adoption of Business Intelligence in Indian Agriculture: A Conceptual Framework. Technology in Society, 65, 101582. https://doi.org/10.1016/j.techsoc.2021.101582

Saravanan, M., & Subramanian, K. (2019). Enhancing Agricultural Productivity through Business Intelligence Tools. Journal of Applied Research on Industrial Engineering, 6(3), 167-180. https://doi.org/10.22105/jarie.2019.191948.1105

Sharda, R., Delen, D., & Turban, E. (2014). Business Intelligence and Analytics: Systems for Decision Support. Pearson.

Smith, J. A. (2019). Predictive Analytics in Business Intelligence. Journal of Business Intelligence Research, 10(2), 123-145.

Sugiura, K., & Tanaka, M. (2019). Development of Precision Agriculture System for Sustainable Farming by IoT, Big Data, and Artificial Intelligence Technologies. In 2019 12th International Conference on Human System Interaction (HSI) (pp. 55-60). IEEE.

Watson, H. J., & Wixom, B. H. (2007). The current state of business intelligence. IEEE Computer Society, 40(9), 96-99.

Williams, P. D. (2016). Data Science and Predictive Analytics: A Practical Guide. Boston: Pearson.

Williams, S., Williams, N., & Ferrier, G. (2013). Using Business Intelligence to Support Strategic Decision Making. Journal of Decision Systems, 22(1), 1-17.

Wixom, B., & Watson, H. J. (2010). The BI-based organization. International Journal of Business Intelligence Research, 1(1), 1-11.

Wu, D., & Zhang, J. (2010). Research on business intelligence in financial industry. 2010 International Conference on E-Business and E-Government, 1-4.

E-VOTING IN THE LEBANESE PARLIAMENT: AN INVESTIGATIVE STUDY

Bassima Issa[1] and Bassam Hussein[2]
[1] *Department of Communication Arts, Lebanese International University, Bekaa, Lebanon*
[2] *Department of Industrial Engineering, International University of Beirut, Beirut, Lebanon*

ABSTRACT

The study focused on researching how the electronic voting system is being used in legislative work in the Lebanese Parliament in terms of recommending draft laws and proposals submitted by members of parliament. The study examined the use of electronic voting as a method in legislative work within the Lebanese Parliament and aimed to present an electronic voting system (e-voting). The findings showed that electronic voting as a software has been available in the Lebanese Parliament since 2013, but it has never been used in any legislative stage. It became clear that the electronic voting system is the least used among the seven main applications and tools available to Lebanese parliamentarians work in the various stages and different levels of the legislative process. One of the most important reasons for not using this application is the presence of major obstacles in the Lebanese constitution, as the constitution does not recognize digital voting tools in the legislative process. Legislative work as such has been limited to traditional voting methods, such as raising hands or using a ballot box. The research methodologies deployed in this research include literature review, quantitative data analysis, and case study approach.

KEYWORDS

The Lebanese Parliament, E-voting, Digital Communication Technology, Voting System, Lebanon

1. INTRODUCTION

Despite the advantages of electronic voting in parliaments, the average of its use across the globe is still limited. A negative application appeared on many levels such as: the legislative, the systematic, the politician and the technology (Hajjar et al., 2006). E-voting system was designed for electorates through computers programmed with convivial Graphical User Interfaces. The complex treatments and features are achieved at the levels of application layer and database. Electronic voting, or e-voting, refers to the use of digital technologies to deliver government services and information to MPs. The voting process should be functional and simple since voters have little knowledge of the e-voting process (Heinl et al., 2022). However, e-voting aims to improve the efficiency, transparency, and accountability of government, it has become increasingly important in the digital age, as MPs demand more accessible and user-friendly government services and information. The implementation of the e-voting system raises several issues related directly to elections such as legal, social, technical, political, administrative, and financial issues (, 2002). Otherwise, benefiting from the positive aspects of e-voting requests the implementation of security measures in order to repair the lack of transparency and to regain the trust of electorates and liable authorities (Alonso et al., 2018).

2. LITERATURE REVIEW

Voting theorists have proposed a wide range of election methods using a wide range of ballot types. Alonso (2018) restricted the attention to methods which can be conducted with ballots on which each voter assigns a rank to each candidate, and no other information is indicated on the ballot for the purpose of determining the election outcome (Small, 2010). E-voting is still unpopular and therefore rarely used exceptionally in some countries that are starting to adopt it. Also, Gerlach and Gasser (2009) showed that the Swiss government has actively pursued the implementation of electronic voting "e-voting" in its elections since 1998, their case study examines how these systems have worked in the test cantons of Geneva and Zurich (Gerlach and Gasser, 2009). Having a supportive ICT ecosystem is integral to the success of technology-driven processes including e-voting (Moussalem et al., 2023).

Some countries have rejected the use of internet voting, Kohno et al. (2004) confirmed that the Netherlands was one of the earliest adopters of e-voting (Kohno et al., 2004) (Gibson et al., 2016). KOA was trailed in the European 2004 elections the original system was designed by Logica CMG and a fully open-source version was later developed (Kohno et al., 2004). Cardoso et al. (2004) presented a case study of MPs from Portugal, Germany, the Netherlands, and Scotland, with regard to the effectiveness of using the Internet in their parliamentary work, followed by a detailed analysis of technology. In the study, information and communication technology tools were analysed as a means of communication, in terms of using the internet as a means of accessing information, the figures range from the lowest in Portugal at 30.8% to the highest in Scotland at 89.2%. Similarly, Portugal also scores the lowest for personal web pages for MPs to introduce themselves and communicate with other Internet users (5.1% or fifteen deputies) compared to the highest scorer in Germany at 63.2%. Participation in chat groups ranges from Portugal's low level of 2.6% to Scotland's high of 21.6% (Cardoso et al., 2009).

3. PROS AND CONS OF LEGISLATIVE E-VOTING SYSTEMS

Introducing and using technology-driven applications and tools in the legislative work enables transparency and has important advantages including:

1. **Efficiency and Speed**: E-voting systems can significantly speed up the voting process in legislative bodies. This allows for quicker decision-making and the handling of a larger volume of bills or motions within a limited timeframe (Hajjar et al., 2006).
2. **Accuracy and Reduced Errors:** Electronic systems can minimize human errors in vote counting and recording, thereby enhancing the accuracy of the voting process (Small, 2010). This helps in maintaining the integrity of legislative outcomes.
3. **Accessibility**: E-voting systems can facilitate participation for lawmakers who may not be physically present due to travel constraints, illness, or other reasons. This increases the overall accessibility and inclusivity of the legislative process (Oladoyinbo, 2024).
4. **Transparency and Accountability**: These systems can provide detailed records of voting patterns, making it easier to trace individual votes. This transparency can enhance accountability among legislators and enable constituents to track their representatives' voting behaviour (Hajjar et al., 2006).
5. **Flexibility and Remote Participation**: E-voting systems allow lawmakers to participate remotely, enabling them to engage in legislative activities from distant locations without the need for physical presence in the assembly (Issa and Hussein, 2021).

Despite the important advantages of using voting in legislative bodies, there are some key disadvantages that must be remedied and paid attention to including:

1. **Security Concerns**: E-voting systems are susceptible to hacking, manipulation, or cyberattacks that could compromise the integrity of the voting process (Issa and Hussein, 2021). Ensuring robust security measures becomes crucial to prevent unauthorized access or tampering.
2. **Technical Issues**: Technical glitches or system failures could disrupt the voting process, leading to delays or erroneous results. Reliability and stability of the e-voting infrastructure are critical factors to consider (Gibson et al., 2016).
3. **Potential for Coercion or Vote Selling**: In some cases, electronic voting systems may increase the potential for coercion or vote selling, as lawmakers may be pressured or tempted to share their login credentials or vote in a certain way against their will (Gerlach and Gasser, 2009).
4. **Cost and Infrastructure Requirements**: Implementing and maintaining an effective e-voting system can require significant financial investment for acquiring and maintaining the necessary technological infrastructure. This can pose a challenge for less financially equipped legislative bodies (Hajjar et al., 2006).
5. **Resistance to Change**: Introducing e-voting systems may face resistance from lawmakers accustomed to traditional voting methods. Some may be sceptical of the new technology or concerned about its implications, leading to initial hesitancy in adopting these systems (Gerlach and Gasser, 2009).

Balancing the advantages of efficiency, accuracy, and accessibility with the potential challenges related to security, technical issues, and cost is essential when considering the implementation of legislative e-voting systems. A careful evaluation of these factors is necessary to ensure the successful integration and operation of such systems within legislative processes.

4. VOTING SYSTEM IN THE LEBANESE PARLIAMENT

Sweden was one of the pioneering countries in the work of e-parliament, followed by Denmark and Norway. Conversely, there is a large gap between developed and developing countries in this regard (Wolton, 1989). Like other legislative bodies around the world, it has become necessary for the Lebanese Parliament to deal with modern technology using various tools, as modern media, and information systems (Basheir, 2003). In this regard, the Lebanese Parliament has owned a very recent system of electronic voting in terms of technology since 2005, and the devices and material for this system have been installed in the Parliament, and it has been valid for work since that time in the public hall of the Parliament (Dhaini, 2022). It was updated in 2011.

Moreover, a large screen was received in the public hall of the Parliament, connected to this program, but it was greatly damaged by the port's explosion in 2020. The work of this system was not activated as a result of several obstacles, the most important of which is that the Lebanese constitution stipulated in the Clauses of the law No. (36) - that 'opinions are given by the lips vote or the way of standing and sitting except in the case in which the election is intended, and it is given (The Lebanese Constitution, 2018). Opinions in the way of secret voting. ' The duty here is constitutionally increasing the word 'electronic vote' until the text becomes clear and constitutional, and it is practically done within the Parliament (Moaawad, 2022). All attempts by some MPs to put forward the provision to amend the constitution at this particular point were not successful. The last amendment to the Lebanese Constitution was in 1990 after the adoption of the National Accord Document (Taif Agreement), and its texts have not been affected since that time.

5. RESULTS AND FINDINGS

This study examined the role that technology plays in the legislative work in the Lebanese Parliament and its impact on the development of legislative work, and the voting system was one of the studied sectors. 35 out of 128 MPs participated in the questionnaire with a response rate of 27%. The questionnaire was divided into two basic parts of the following way:

The first part: Personal information about the MPs included in the field of demographic research variables (age, type, educational level, years of experience), and this part also included a census of the parliamentary committees during the legislative period between 2018-2022, and the parliamentary committees that participated in the study.

The second part: It includes questions related to the use of information technology in the Lebanese parliament to serve the legislative work, and this part contains the basic parts that represent the changes of study, according to the following:

1. Using nominal communication means in the various stages of legislative work.
2. The most used northern applications of deputies in their legislative work.
3. The functional performance of the MPs.

Accordingly, the results showed that the MPs do not believe that technology and voting system can improve and develop legislative work, which indicates that the Lebanese MP prefers the traditional method instead of introducing technology in the legislative work in terms of proposing laws and the stages of its passage until the final stage of voting and approving the law. Furthermore, email was the most application used for legislative work. Most of the MP were familiar with Email and Mobile (31.7% and 23.2% respectively) as illustrated in Table 1.

Table 1. Used applications in the Lebanese Parliament legislative work

Tools	Number of PMs	Percentage %
Email	26	31.7
Mobile App	11	13.4
Parliament Website	11	13.4
Digital Recording System	12	14.6
Mobile	19	23.2
BTS	1	1.2
Zoom and Teams	2	2.4

Figure 1 provides a histogram visualization of the findings of the survey regarding the use of the Lebanese MPs of various technology-based tools and applications:

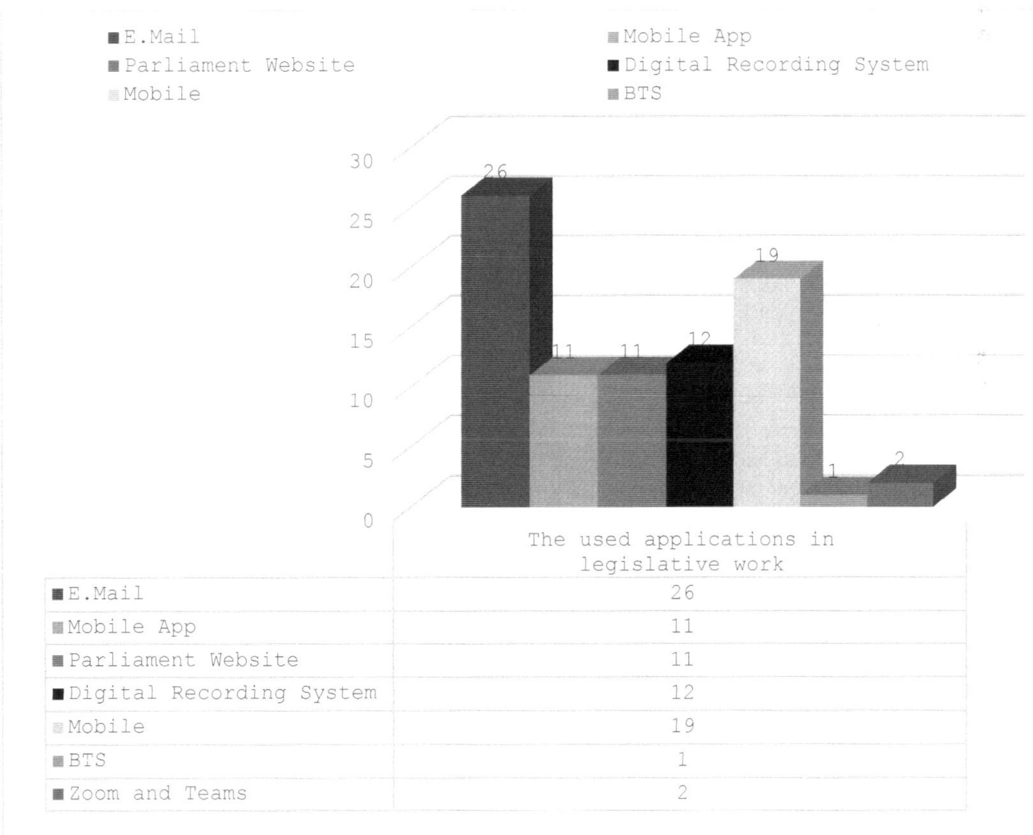

Figure 1. Lebanese MPs applications use in legislative work

Based on the findings, the study reveals that the voting system is not really being used during the legislative process. The highest percentage of usage is for "not used in this process" which indicates that the Lebanese MPs prefer to use traditional means for voting, although, the Lebanese Parliament has an advanced system to track the laws called BTS "Bill Tracking System" through the use of this program, the MPs can follow the stages of the arrival of the laws electronically, but this program is not used in full form, so that it has stopped working completely recently for technical and other financial reasons. A summary of these findings is summarized in Table 2 and depicted in Figure 2 respectively.

Table 2. Distribution of use of technology tools

Process | Tool	**Email**	**Mobile App**	**BTS**	**Mobile Phone**	**Website**	**Digital Recording system**	**Voting system**	**Paper**
Law Proposal	7		1	6	3	1		25
Council Registry		1		2	1			28
Transfer law proposal to President of the Parliament		1		4	1			26
Relevant Committees	9	11	3	10	5	7		24
General Assembly	4	4	3	4	1	14		23
Transfer the law to the Prime Minister	0	0	2	2				20
Transfer the law to the President of the Republic	1			1				19
Official Gazette	3		2	1	7			13
Don't use Technology	21	23	32	23	22	19	35	5
Total	*45*	*40*	*43*	*53*	*40*	*41*	*35*	*183*

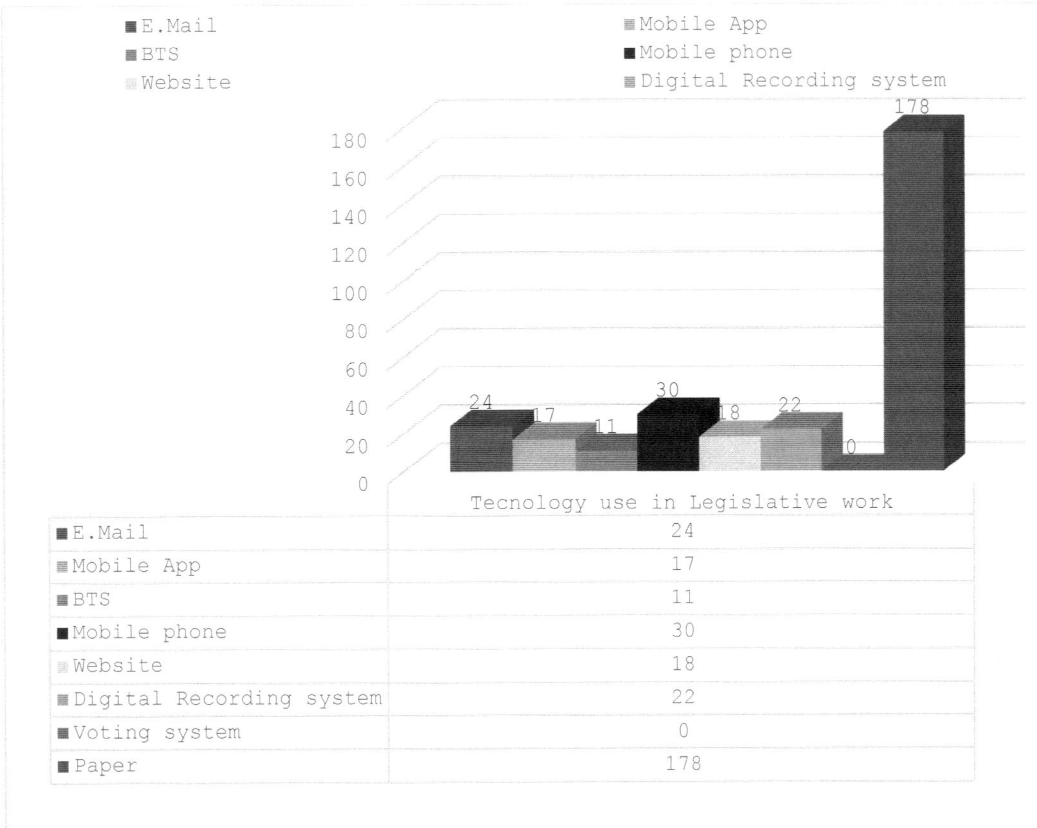

Figure 2. The technology tools use in legislative work by Lebanese MPs

Similarly, the trends of results, grades percentages and curves, and course enrolment over the years may be displayed to monitor variations. The administration's approval of grades may also be displayed.

6. CONCLUSION

This project reveals that although there is a will in the Lebanese Parliament to develop parliamentary work, by striving to provide modern digital programs and applications, the results showed that the most digital application used by parliamentarians is e-mail with a rate of 31% compared to other digital applications, and no use of the electronic voting system at all. However, the use of technology tools in parliament does not exceed 25%. The average use of available ICT tools and applications in the Lebanese parliamentarian averages a lame 6% which is considered low.

Undoubtably, the adoption of ICT can greatly enhance the efficiency, transparency, and effectiveness of organizational work including legislative ones. There are several recommendations to increase and improve the use of Information and Communication Technology (ICT) in the Lebanese Parliament, including:

1. Developing an e-voting strategy: by investment in ICT infrastructure and systems.
2. Activating the electronic voting system because of its importance in adding an element of transparency and credibility in voting on laws.
3. Enhancing transparency: voting systems can enhance transparency by providing access to information, facilitating public participation in the legislative process.

REFERENCES

Alonso, L. P., Gasco, M., Del Blanco, D. Y. M., Alonso, J. Á. H., Barrat, J., & Moreton, H. A. (2018). E-voting system evaluation based on the Council of Europe recommendations: Helios Voting. IEEE Transactions on Emerging Topics in Computing, 9(1), 161-173.

Basheir, I. (2003). Media and Parliamentary Decision Making. Beirut: Lebanese Parliament and Parliamentary Dialogue Forum.

Cardoso, G., Cunha, C., & Nascimento, S. (2004). Ministers of parliament and information and communication technologies as a means of horizontal and vertical communication in Western Europe. *Information Polity*, *9* (1-2), 29-40.

Dhaini, B. (2022). Head of the Department of Information Technology in the Lebanese Parliament". (B. Issa, Interviewer), September 14th, 2022.

Gerlach, J., & Gasser, U. (2009). Three case studies from Switzerland: E-voting. *Berkman Center Research Publication No*, *3* (2009), 2020-2021.

Gibson, J. P., Krimmer, R., Teague, V., & Pomares, J. (2016). A review of e-voting: the past, present and future. *Annals of Telecommunications*, *71*, 279-286.

Hajjar, M., Daya, B., Ismail, A., & Hajjar, H. (2006). An e-voting system for Lebanese elections. Journal of Theoretical and Applied Information Technology, 2(1), 21-29.

Heinl, M. P., Gölz, S., & Bösch, C. (2022). Remote electronic voting in uncontrolled environments: A classifying survey. ACM Computing Surveys, 55(8), 1-44.

Issa, B., & Hussein, B. (2021). *The Evolution of Technology Use in the Lebanese Parliament after COVID-19 Pandemic* (No. 6996). EasyChair.

Kohno, T., Stubblefield, A., Rubin, A. D., & Wallach, D. S. (2004, May). Analysis of an electronic voting system. In *IEEE Symposium on Security and Privacy, 2004. Proceedings. 2004* (pp. 27-40). IEEE.

Moaawad, S. (2022). General Manager of Lebanese Parliament. (B. Issa, Interviewer), August 31st, 2022.

Moussalem, H., Hajj-Hassan, M., Hage-Diab, A., Haj-Ali, A., & Hussein, B. (2023, August). Digital Transformation of University Course Filing Using Information and Communication Technologies (ICT): A Sustainable Approach. In International conference on WorldS4 (pp. 29-35). Singapore: Springer Nature Singapore.

Oladoyinbo, T. O. (2024). The effect of data information security in digital voting and electoral processes. *Current Journal of International Organization of Scientific Research Journal of Computer Engineering (IOSR-JCE)*, *13*(2), 11-16.

Small, A. (2010). Geometric construction of voting methods that protect voters' first choices. arXiv preprint arXiv:1008.4331.

The Lebanese Constitution (2018). Beirut, Lebanon, Zein Legal Library.

Wolton, D. (1989). La communication politique : construction d'un modèle. *Hermès*, (1), 27-42.

THE POTENTIAL OF USING THE BLENDED LEARNING FORMAT IN SOCIAL UNIVERSITIES IN ST. PETERSBURG

Olga Ignatjeva[1], Iuliia Platonova[2] and Alexander Pletnev[2]
[1]Saint Petersburg State University, 7-9 Universitetskaya Emb., St Petersburg 199034, Russia
[2]Saint Petersburg State Institute of Psychology and Social Work, 13a 12th line of Vasilyevskiy Island, St Petersburg 199178, Russia

ABSTRACT

Studying the implementation of the blended learning format in higher education is currently an interesting and relevant topic. This article contains a study of the development potential of blended learning within a social university. The research question is determined, on the one hand, by the popularity and rapid spread of the distant learning component, and on the other hand, by its obvious limitations. The study was conducted using a survey method. The obtained data were processed using factor and regression analysis with the aid the R programming language. Regression analysis made it possible to identify latent learning factors that affect the effectiveness of the blended learning format. The study revealed that distant learning does not allow one to fully develop communication skills and provide students with tacit knowledge. The authors of the article discovered and substantiated the need to use classical learning to transfer tacit knowledge, soft skills. It was also revealed that the Socratic method, which has proven itself in the field of teaching the humanities, cannot be applied in an online format. Based on the results of the study, recommendations were made for the development of the blended learning format in social universities.

KEYWORDS

Blended Learning, Education, Communication Skills, Helping Professions, Tacit Knowledge

1. INTRODUCTION

The spread of digital communication and the emergence of many software solutions for distant learning raise the issue of the prospects for using blended learning technologies in the process of obtaining higher education. A sharp actualization of this issue in the scientific and professional literature has been observed after the 2019 coronavirus pandemic (Aristovnik, 2023), when most universities were forced to switch to a distant learning format.

A study of the effectiveness of using elements of distance learning during the COVID-19 pandemic showed that it can also be an effective way to develop independent thinking and responsibility of students in general (Ferrer et al., 2023). However, for socially oriented universities, the introduction of distant learning technologies into the educational process is problematic, since training in social specialties involves mastering effective communication skills, which can only be developed within the traditional format of full-time education. The authors of the article discovered and substantiated the need to use classical learning to transfer tacit knowledge. It was also revealed that the Socratic method, which has proven itself in the field of teaching the humanities, cannot be applied in an online format that was not mentioned in previous studies of blended learning for helping professions (Niu et al., 2023, Achmad et al., 2023).

The contradiction between the trends towards the universal introduction of distant education and the limitations of this format has necessitated the need to conduct an empirical study of the practice of using the blended learning format in the current educational process.

2. USING THE BLENDED LEARNING FORMAT IN THE CURRENT EDUCATIONAL PROCESS

In our study, the use of the "blended learning" format in the educational process was studied on the basis of the St. Petersburg State Institute of Psychology and Social Work. This university specializes in social programs and trains social workers, conflict specialists and psychologists. The institute implements both distant learning technologies via video communication and asynchronous distant learning technologies. At the same time, training in each of the institute's programs necessarily includes a full-time training format. In essence, the institute implements a blended learning format "blended learning", which can be defined as "a combination of face-to-face classes and distant online learning, that is, autonomous a/synchronous learning, enhanced by digital technologies, conducted individually or in pairs, in groups from home "(Simonova 2023. P. 5093). The COVID-19 pandemic has contributed to a deeper implementation of distant learning in the educational program of the institute and the emergence of educational programs primarily focused on distant learning.

In most cases, both students and teachers positively assess the introduction of distant learning technologies into the educational process, since the combination of face-to-face and online learning formats is more convenient for both the teacher and the student. The introduction of distant learning elements in education allows those participants in the educational process to attend classes who, for various reasons, cannot participate in person. Distant education allows you to save time, which is necessary to physically arrive at the institute. Similar positive assessments prevail in the scientific literature. According to a number of scientific publications, the blended learning format "not only offers more opportunities in the learning process, but is also more effective. Blended learning environments support individual student learning through collaborative efforts in a virtual environment and help students and teachers communicate more" (Tonbuloglu, 2023. P.13988).

However, the widespread introduction of the digital learning format into practice has led to the identification of some shortcomings of this format. Despite the overall positive assessment of distant learning, some representatives of the professional community express concerns that e-learning will hinder the development of students' interpersonal skills, which are indispensable for members of the helping professions. Even face-to-face video communication cannot fully prepare a specialist for real interaction with colleagues and clients. When implementing distant education, students do not engage in full social interaction (Sirotova, 2023) and this can make them feel like they are participating in a simulacrum of education.

An important aspect of the implementation of the "blended learning" format is to increase the role of the student as an active learner under the guidance of teachers. In distant learning, the student has more control over the learning process on their own and "the most important responsibility falls on the students" (Duman, 2023. P. 60). This situation creates difficulties for the least organized students.

The described opportunities provided by the implementation of the "blended learning" format and the limitations of this format led to the need to conduct an empirical study of the problem on the basis of the institute.

3. FACTOR AND REGRESSION ANALYSIS OF BLENDED LEARNING POTENTIAL IN SOCIAL UNIVERSITIES OF ST PETERSBURG

In September 2023, in St. Petersburg State Institute of Psychology and Social Work (St. Petersburg, Russia), a study was conducted among senior students to test the effectiveness of using blended learning during the coronavirus pandemic. Blended learning involves the use of traditional and e-learning formats. There are 204 respondents in this survey. The age and gender balance of sample was made in accordance with the gender and age structure of the population of the Russian Federation for the age category 20-24 (https://rosstat.gov.ru/compendium/document/13284). This balance is 51% men and 49% women. The survey was conducted in online format. The questionnaire was formed based on scientific literature and consultations with the specialists-practitioners in this sphere. The questionnaire is available at the link https://vk.com/sociologica?w=wall-4718166_116%2Fall. The survey was aimed at testing two hypotheses:

H1: Students' inclination towards blended learning is determined by a number of factors to be identified in this study.

H2: Blended learning is a more effective format for teaching students at a social university than traditional learning.

To process the questionnaire data, factor analysis based on SPSS and a logistic regression model using the R programming language were used.

Testing hypothesis 1 involved the use of factor analysis. The survey was conducted using Google forms, the data of which were coded according to the binary principle: 1 - a clearly expressed characteristic, 0 - a characteristic that is weakly expressed or not expressed at all.

Preliminary testing of the data made it possible to verify their suitability for factor analysis. For this purpose, the Kaiser-Meier-Olkin (KMO) criterion of sampling adequacy and Bartlett's criterion of sphericity were used. The sampling adequacy criterion is 0.611, approaching 1, which is an indicator of the quality of this criterion. The sphericity test has statistical significance at a level of less than 0.0001. This means that the correlation in the correlation matrix is statistically significantly different from zero, which means that this matrix is suitable for factor analysis. Through factor analysis, it was possible to discover five latent factors associated with the use of blended learning (Table 1). The variables included in each factor have a factor loading of at least 0.4. A number of variables included in the identified latent factors have a negative sign, which affects the sign of the predictors in regression analysis.

Table 1. Component matrix after rotation

	Components				
	1	2	3	4	5
satisf_ed	,798				
satisf_discipline	,797				
teacher_books	,503			-,393	
ed_policy		,756			
employer_policy		,671			
ed_work			,617		
work_plan	,385		,554		
distant2020	,342		-,552		
self_development				,685	
trajectory				,669	-,395
group_work					,760
private relations			,370		,653

The first factor includes such variables as "Satisfaction with the organization of the educational process", "Satisfaction with the content of the disciplines", "Use of sources recommended by the teacher". This factor can be designated as "Satisfaction with the acquired profession." All variables included in this factor have a positive sign.

The second identified factor contains two variables "Satisfaction with state educational policy", "Cooperation of universities with employers". They also have a positive sign. This factor can be designated as "Practice-oriented learning."

The third factor includes the variables "The relationship between a good job and the quality of education", "Work in a specialty after graduation", "Satisfaction with training during a pandemic" (with a negative sign). This factor can be designated "Formation of professional competencies."

The fourth factor contains two variables – "Tendency towards self-development", "Choice of an individual trajectory". Both variables have a positive sign. This factor can be designated "Formation of the personality of a university graduate."

The fifth factor includes two variables "Group work in the classroom, "Formation of personal connections in the learning process." This factor can be designated as "Quality of graduate socialization."

Using the results of factor analysis, we will construct a logistic regression equation. Checking the applicability conditions for building a logistic regression model in R gives a positive result. The results of logistic regression calculations are shown in table. 2. They show that only two factors "Formation of professional competencies" (FAC3_1) and "Quality of graduate socialization" (FAC5_1) are statistically significant.

Table 2. Results of logistic regression for binary data

Predictors	Estimates	Std. error	z value	p-level
Intercept	2.3905	0.2898	8.250	<2e-16 ***
Satisfaction with the acquired profession (FAC1_1)	0.2373	0.2341	1.014	0.3107
Practice-oriented learning (FAC2_1)	-0.3314	0.2345	-1.413	0.1576
Formation of professional competencies (FAC3_1)	-0.6306	0.2561	-2.463	0.0138 *
Formation of the personality of a university graduate (FAC4_1)	0.1398	0.2105	0.664	0.5067
Quality of graduate socialization (FAC5_1)	-0.6130	0.2952	-2.076	0.0378 *

Thus, after removing factors that did not reach the level of statistical significance, we can write the resulting logistic regression equation:

Probability of using blended learning~Binomial (n=1, πi)
Mathematical expectation E (Efficiency of blended learning)= πi
The logit link function converts probabilities into logits when interpreting regression coefficients.

$$\mathrm{Ln}\left(\frac{\pi i}{1-\pi i}\right)= \eta i$$

$$\eta i = 2{,}35 - 0{,}67 * FAC3\_1 - 0{,}69 * FAC5\_1 \quad (1)$$

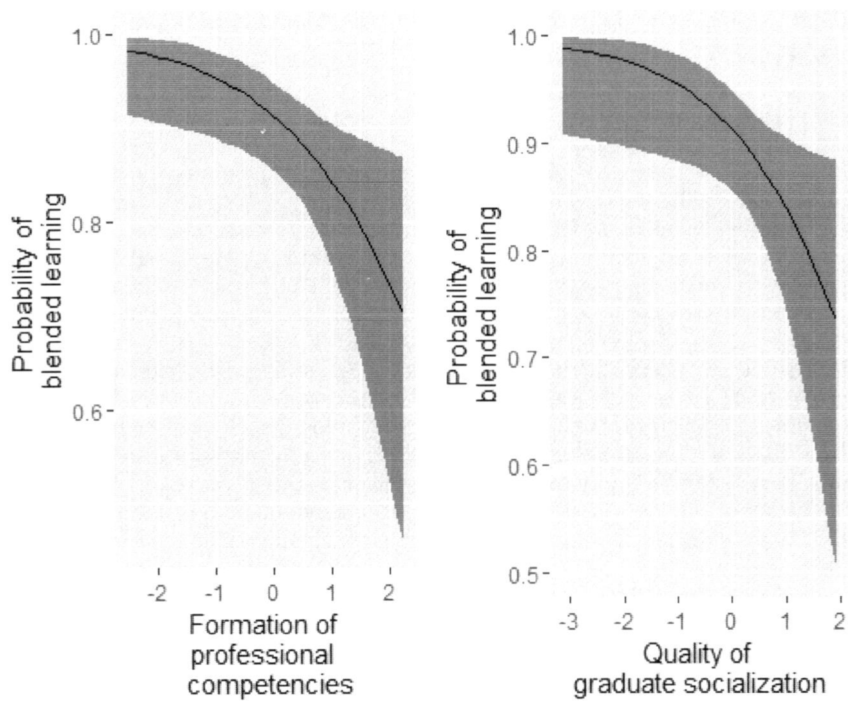

Figure 1. The resulting graphs of the dependence of the probability of using the implementation of the blended learning model on the predictors (factors FAC3_1, FAC5_1).

The logistic regression equation shows the inverse relationship between the factor FAC3_1 ("Formation of professional competencies") and the probability of using blended learning, as well as between the factor FAC5_1 ("Quality of socialization of a graduate") and the dependent variable. Both factors have approximately the same coefficients, so we can talk about approximately the same strength of their impact on the dependent variable "Probability of using blended learning". In Fig. 1 presents graphs that show the relationship between the selected factors and the dependent variable. When interpreting the visual reflections of the relationships, we can conclude that when the factor changes by one positive standard deviation, the probability of using the blended learning model decreases. When moving backwards along the graphs, the probability of using the blended learning model increases.

The interpretation of the logistic regression coefficients allows us to conclude that when the factor FAC3_1 ("Formation of professional competencies") changes by one unit, the probability of using the blended learning model decreases by 0.51 times with the factor FAC5_1 unchanged. When the factor FAC5_1 ("Quality of socialization of a graduate") increases by one unit, the probability of implementing the blended learning model decreases by 0.50 times, with the factor FAC3_1 remaining unchanged. To obtain these results, we raise the Euler number (2.71) to the power of the coefficient associated with the independent variable.

This logistic regression equation shows that the factors "Formation of professional competencies" and "Quality of socialization of the graduate" have a decisive influence on the probability of using the blended learning model in training. These qualities are better formed in the process of traditional full-time education, which allows us to conclude that the administration of a social university should be more careful about introducing elements of distant learning into the educational process. Thus, hypothesis 2 about the effectiveness of blended learning in studying of helping professions was not confirmed.

4. INTERPRETATION OF REGRESSION ANALYSIS RESULTS AND DISCUSSION

The presented results of the questionnaire indicate that the most motivated and most purposeful students intuitively feel the limitations of the distant education format. Students who demonstrate the most developed professional competencies are aware of the need to train to solve emerging professional problems in conditions of real interpersonal interaction. Working in the field of helping professions means the need to be able to resolve conflicts, respond to non-verbal signals in the communication process, and lead the work of a group. Students reasonably wish to acquire these competencies in the format of traditional full-time education. Similarly, students who demonstrate the achievement of the best quality of socialization already have developed communication skills and are convinced of the need to improve them in the process of seminars and trainings.

The results obtained are extremely interesting because they challenge the traditional, predominantly positive perception of digital enhancement in the learning process. When discussing online learning in scientific and professional literature, the emphasis is usually on the digital competencies of teachers and students (Aldhaen, 2024). It is declared that digital competencies are the key to success both in training and in subsequent professional activities. At the same time, it is obvious that an increase in the share of digital interaction in learning will negatively affect the development of abilities for effective communication in real social interaction. With the increasing share of online learning, traditional communication is actually being replaced by digital communication and researchers tend to look for positive aspects in this. Learners are encouraged to participate in digital learning communities, which are believed to "have the potential to improve learning outcomes through improved communication" (Cao, 2023. P. 866). However, for a specialist in helping professions, such a replacement of communication is not equivalent. A specialist in helping professions must be able to respond to non-verbal signals, take into account the situation when communicating, achieve a confidential dialogue with the interlocutor and be able to implement other communication skills, the development of which can only be fully realized in a face-to-face format.

An essential aspect of learning in the digital environment is a special format for assessing knowledge, which includes tests and other tools for remote assessment of a student's knowledge and skills. At the same time, assessment in a remote format makes it difficult for the teacher to perceive the student. In addition to obtaining the correct answer, it is necessary to evaluate the ways in which the student sought an answer to the question. If a student provides an incorrect answer, you can find that he has deep knowledge of the problem and tried to find an independent, creative way to solve it. At the same time, the correct answer may be the result of superficial knowledge, memorizing material without a deep understanding of the essence of what was read, mastering the material without gaining the ability to creatively comprehend and use it. The full-time format of training makes it possible to ask additional questions to find out how much the student correctly understands professional terms and how much he is able to connect the issues under consideration with other topics of the course. For a student, an in-person assessment of knowledge provides the opportunity to receive feedback from the teacher and clarify various subtle aspects of the material being studied. Communication in a remote format gives the student fewer opportunities to receive feedback from the teacher.

Another equally important aspect of full-time education is the ability to transfer to students not only formalized knowledge recorded in educational materials, but also latent knowledge and skills. Such knowledge and skills can be no less important for the graduate's subsequent construction of a successful career in the social sphere. As Sternberg notes, "the terms "professional intuition" and "professional instinct" suggest that the knowledge that is associated with successful performance is tacit in nature" (Sternberg, 2000. P. 104). Teachers pass on to students not only knowledge, but also communication standards in the professional field, patterns of behavior when communicating with clients, and options for solving non-standard problems. Such knowledge is difficult to operationalize and measure, but plays a huge role in successful professional activity. This phenomenon has been called "tacit knowledge" in the scientific literature and since the 60s of the last century has been understood as "knowledge that we rely on while doing work (for example, driving a car or teaching), but which is difficult to express in language or comprehend" (Mitchell, 2022. P. 1664). Tacit knowledge determines a graduate's ability to be more successful in their professional activities because it is an indicator of "how you organize your work, how you get along with other people and how you organize your life in general" (Sternberg, 1997. P. 92). Without obtaining such knowledge, a student cannot become a full-fledged specialist and member of the professional community. In general, tacit knowledge is extremely important and difficult to define and study. There are no attempts in the scientific literature to study the problem of transferring tacit knowledge in the context of introducing e-learning. This is an extremely promising and extremely important topic for further scientific study.

The conducted research allows us to confidently assert that in the system of helping professions it is necessary to maintain the basic format of full-time education, which contributes to the development of the necessary professional skills. Digital learning can help this process and is a good, effective addition to traditional classical education. Therefore, the authors of the article discovered and substantiated the need to use classical learning to transfer tacit knowledge. It was also revealed that the Socratic method, which has proven itself in the field of teaching the humanities, cannot be applied in an online format.

5. CONCLUSION

The empirical data obtained as a result of the study have signs of scientific novelty and allow us to reconsider generally accepted approaches to blended learning. The current discourse on e-learning is entirely positive and ignores the many disadvantages that inevitably accompany distant learning. Increasing the share of distant learning in education is becoming increasingly popular among students and teachers. And therefore, it is overlooked that distant learning is associated with the need for student self-organization and is a good choice for responsible students. Education in a distant format does not allow students to develop full-fledged communication skills, as well as gain tacit knowledge necessary for success in subsequent professional development. The implementation of the blended learning format must be carried out in such a way as to fully preserve all the advantages of face-to-face training. Particular attention to combining full-time and distant learning formats must be paid when training specialists in helping professions, as well as other specialists for whom the ability to communicate effectively face-to-face is extremely important. Effective teaching in the helping professions requires the use of a classical format to convey tacit knowledge. The Socratic method, which has proven itself in the field of teaching the humanities, can only be applied through face-to-face interaction between teacher and student. The topic we have considered is relevant, interesting and has the characteristics of scientific novelty. However, we recognize the limitations of our study. The topic has significant potential and its development can be continued by conducting similar research for other specialties that also require developed communication skills.

REFERENCES

Achmad, B.F., Fitriawan, A.S., Kurniawan, D. & Chen, H-M. (2023). Mediating effect of self-esteem on the relationship between academic self-efficacy and depression symptoms among nursing students participating in blended learning. *Heliyon*, 9(11), e225526. https://doi.org/10.1016/j.heliyon.2023.e22526

Aldhaen, E. (2024). The influence of digital competence of academicians on students' engagement at university level: moderating effect of the pandemic outbreak. *Competitiveness Review*, 34(1), pp. 51-71. https://doi.org/10.1108/CR-01-2023-0008

Aristovnik, A, Karampelas, K, Umek, L. & Ravšelj, D. (2023). Impact of the COVID-19 pandemic on online learning in higher education: a bibliometric analysis. *Frontiers in Education*, 8, 1225834. https://doi.org/10.3389/feduc.2023.1225834

Cao, W., Yu, Z. (2023). Exploring learning outcomes, communication, anxiety, and motivation in learning communities: a systematic review. *Humanities and Social Sciences Communications*, 10, 866. https://doi.org/10.1057/s41599-023-02325-2

Duman, E. (2023). The challenges of distance education and evidence-based solution suggestions. *International Journal of Academic Studies in Technology and Education,* 1(1), 50-64. https://doi.org/10.55549/ijaste.2

Ferrer, J., Iglesias, E., Blanco-Gutierrez, I. & Estavillo, J. (2023). Analyzing the impact of COVID-19 on the grades of university education: a case study with economics students. *Social Sciences & Humanities Open,* 7(1), 100428. https://doi.org/10.1016/j.ssaho.2023.100428.

Mitchell, V.W. & Harvey, W.S. (2022). Where does all the 'know how' go? The role of tacit knowledge in research impact *Higher Education Research and Development*, 41 (5), 1664–1678. https://doi.org/10.1080/07294360.2021.1937066

Niu, J., Xi, H., Liu, J., Sui, X., Li, F., Xu, H., Zhao, L., Li, Y., Zhang, Sh. & Guo, L. (2023). Effects of blended learning on undergraduate nursing students' knowledge, skills, critical thinking ability and mental health: A systematic review and meta-analysis. *Nurse Education in Practice*, 72, 103786. https://doi.org/10.1016/j.nepr.2023.103786

Population of the Russian Federation by gender and age. Retrieved from https://rosstat.gov.ru/compendium/document/13284

Simonova, I., Faltynkova, L. & Kostolanyova, K. (2023). New Blended Learning Enriched after the COVID-19 Experience? Students' Opinions". *Sustainability*, 15(6), 5093. https://doi.org/10.3390/su15065093

Sirotova, M. & Lukas, P. (2023). Positives and Negatives of Distance Education from the Perspective of Teachers with Practical Experience. *Educational Studies Review,* 1(41), 121-138. https://doi.org/10.12775/PBE.2023.006

Sternberg, R. J. (2000). *Practical intelligence in everyday life*. Cambridge: Cambridge University Press.

Sternberg, R. J. (1997). *Successful Intelligence: How Practical and Creative Intelligence Determine Success in Life*. New York: Plume.

Tonbuloglu, B., Tonbuloglu, I. (2023). Trends and patterns in blended learning research (1965–2022). *Education and Information Technologies*, 28, 13987–14018. https://doi.org/10.1007/s10639-023-11754-0

THE EFFECTS OF ECONOMIC STATUS ON ACADEMIC ACHIEVEMENT - BASED ON PISA 2018

Kyung Sook Lee
Korea University, South Korea

ABSTRACT

Based on PISA 2018 data, this study analyzed the differences in reading proficiency, math and science achievement, and global competency among Korean students according to the use of ICT as a predictive factor. The study also examined the differences in these variables based on the socioeconomic and cultural background of students' households (ESCS). The study had three main focuses: first, using ICT proficiency as an independent variable and reading proficiency, math and science achievement, and global competency as dependent variables to produce results. Second, dividing households into high, middle, and low socioeconomic groups and analyzing the differences. Third, using the random forest method to analyze the static and non-static effects of predictive factors on the importance of characteristics and the degree of prediction with partial dependence plots. The results were presented visually through data visualization to make the differences more easily recognizable. The results of the analysis showed that school accessibility to ICT and interest in ICT were ranked as the most important features in terms of their correlation with achievement, regardless of the specific proficiency. The predictive factors of ICTHOME, ICTSCH, and HOMESCH had a static impact, while ENTUSE and USESCH had a non-static impact. The results also showed that in the high socioeconomic group, ENTUSE had the highest value for feature importance, while in the low socioeconomic group, INTICT, AUTICT, and ICTCLASS had the highest feature importance values. The results indicate that in the low socioeconomic group, ICT usage in schools is a statically important factor affecting academic achievement more than in the high socioeconomic group.

KEYWORDS

PISA2018, Science Achievement, ICT Utilization, Random Forest, ESCS

1. INTRODUCTION

Over the past three years, during the experience of the COVID-19 pandemic, it has been apparent that the gap in academic achievement among students has been exacerbated by socioeconomic disparities within families. While previous disparities were known based on numerical data, this period allowed for experiencing how the presence of caregivers influences students' academic achievement through social articles during online classes (Shin, Nam, & Choi, 2022). The social support and parent-child relationship in the home are factors that influence a child's academic achievement (Shin et al., 2022). In terms of ICT accessibility, the presence of caregivers guiding students to actively participate in classes using ICT can influence students' learning attitudes.

The OECD PISA has been measuring reading literacy, mathematical and scientific achievement of students in various countries every three years since 2000, including ICT usage-related surveys from 2003. The survey targets adolescents aged 15 and older in each country. PISA data analysis presents research results regarding predictive variables of reading literacy, mathematical achievement, scientific achievement, and global competence based on PISA data. ICT usage is reported as one of the predictive variables of students' academic achievement in previous studies (Jung & Park, 2022). Research on differences between ICT factors is still lacking. Over the past three years, due to the COVID-19 pandemic, online classes based on ICT were conducted when regular classes could not be held. Although data from this period are not available, it is necessary to analyze the importance of differences in the socioeconomic, cultural, and environmental backgrounds of households in ICT-based classes as predictive variables of reading literacy, mathematical achievement, scientific achievement, and global competence and to study the static and dynamic effects of their impact.

OECD (2018) suggests that students who achieve better results within individual countries are more likely to obtain higher-income jobs after college and have a higher likelihood of future social mobility based on relatively superior achievements, even if they are socioeconomically disadvantaged. This indicates the importance of research on educational environments that can help alleviate socioeconomic inequality and equip students with the competencies needed in society, along with the necessity of ICT-related research.

2. THEORETICAL BACKGROUND AND RESEARCH QUESTIONS

2.1 ICT Usage and Academic Achievement According to Socioeconomic Cultural Background

PISA provides the ESCS (Economic, Social, and Cultural Status) as a derived variable to understand the detailed aspects of socioeconomic cultural backgrounds. ESCS is composed of factors such as parental occupation, family assets, and parental education level. According to research by Choi et al. (2021), the achievement gap based on parental education level increased slightly more from PISA 2009 to PISA 2018. The achievement level according to parental education level decreased at all levels. The achievement gap according to family assets was relatively large in South Korea and Singapore. Mathematics achievement was most affected by ESCS, while reading literacy and scientific achievement were similarly affected. Shin (2010) reported differences in educational values, aspirations, and parenting practices between middle-class families with high parental education levels and low-income families in a comparison study of admission to prestigious universities in South Korea. Even in the case of students from disadvantaged backgrounds who overcome adversity, it was found that they show relatively lower levels of ICT utilization and reading diversity compared to the group with high ESCS and excellent achievements (Jeong & Cho, 2013). South Korea showed an increasing tendency in the dispersion of ESCS effects between schools from PISA 2009 to PISA 2018 compared to other countries. When analyzing the relationship between ESCS and academic achievement, South Korea showed a decrease in both the upper and lower 10% (Choi et al., 2021). It was found that ESCS significantly influences the use of computers for learning purposes in schools (Heo, 2013). Research on the relationship between ICT variables and academic achievement shows different results depending on students' socioeconomic status (SES) and the cultural and social situation of each country. Even if the relationship between ICT variables and academic achievement is objectively presented as a statically significant relationship, it cannot be concluded that ICT variables alone are predictive factors of academic achievement.

2.2 ICT Usage and Academic Achievement and Global Competence

ICT (Information and Communication Technology) is a technology used in society, schools, and homes. PISA investigates adolescents' levels of ICT usage through 11 derived variables. Academic achievement has been evaluated in reading literacy, mathematics, and science, and since 2018, global competence has been added as a new assessment area.When examining accessibility to ICT usage in schools and homes, South Korea has shown an increasing trend in school accessibility since 2015, while home accessibility has been continuously increasing since 2019, but both are lower than the OECD average. ICT accessibility and digital competencies have been found to statically influence academic achievement (Wastiau et al., 2013). It was found that the earlier students start using computers and the more frequently they use them, the higher their ICT literacy (Kim et al., 2012; Nam & Shin, 2014). The use of ICT for information acquisition has decreased, while the use for entertainment and social networking services (SNS) has increased.

This study aims to investigate the relationship between ICT-based educational environments accelerated by the COVID-19 pandemic and academic achievement and global competence, as well as how socioeconomic differences in households affect ICT usage, academic achievement, and global competence. This is a foundational study to prepare for the need for online classes based on ICT in the future and to study the time series changes in student learning achievement data during the COVID-19 period. This study aims to examine how ICT-related variables differ as predictive variables of reading literacy, mathematical achievement, scientific achievement, and global competence and to study differences in the impact of ICT-related variables on reading literacy, mathematical achievement, scientific achievement, and global competence according to the socioeconomic index of households presented as derived variables. The following research questions were set:

Research: How do ICT-related variables differ as predictive variables of reading literacy, mathematical achievement, scientific achievement, and global competence according to the socioeconomic background of households?

3. RESEARCH METHOD

Research Subjects This study compared differences in 11 ICT usage variables as predictive factors of reading literacy, mathematical achievement, scientific achievement, and global competence according to the socioeconomic cultural background (ESCS) of households. The data used in this study were from the 2018 Programme for International Student Assessment (PISA). PISA data is conducted by the OECD every three years, targeting 15-year-old students in each country to assess reading literacy, mathematical and scientific achievement. The data used in this study were derived from a 2-stage sample design using the target population of middle school students aged 15 in each country. To make appropriate inferences, sampling weights should be considered. This study only used derived variables provided by PISA to derive more objective research results.

Data and Sample The reading literacy, mathematical achievement, scientific achievement, and global competence data of PISA are estimated through 10 plausible values (PV) derived from item response theory, which are randomly selected values. PISA data provides derived variables based on survey results to indirectly measure factors that cannot be directly observed, such as by recoding items or scaling to compose them into one indicator (OECD, 2017). In this study, only derived variables provided by PISA 2018 were used for data analysis. This study analyzed data from 6,649 South Korean students surveyed in 2018. The 11 ICT derived variables are as follows: ICTHOME, ICTSCH, ENTUSE, HOMESCH, USESCH, INTICT, COMPICT, AUTICT, SOIAICT, ICTCLASS, ICTOUTSIDE.

The derived variable ESCS reflects the socioeconomic, cultural, and educational level of households, based on parental education level, family assets, parental occupational status, and the number of books owned in the home, as provided by PISA. This study classified the ESCS derived variable presented by PISA into three groups and investigated the differences between these groups. For adolescents, factors such as the accessibility and types of ICT usage are influenced by the socioeconomic and cultural environment of the household. This study divided the ESCS into three groups: Group 3 for the top 10%, Group 1 for the bottom 10%, and Group 2 for the in-between, following the same intervals used in a study analyzing the characteristics of top-performing countries in PISA 2018 by Choi et al. (2020).

Random forest analysis, developed by Breiman (2001) based on the decision tree technique for classification/prediction, assesses the importance of predictor variables using an importance index and visualizes the relationship between predictor and response variables using partial dependence plots (Yoo & Jin, 2015). In this study, the RandomForestRegressor function from the scikit-learn library in Python was utilized for analysis. Multivariate data analysis was conducted using the Lmer function from the Pymer4 library. Prior to analysis, missing data were imputed with the mode. When imputing missing values with the mean of observed values for categorical data, the mode is used (Choi & Kim, 2018). The feature importance index indicates the degree of prediction, and partial dependence plots were used to visually demonstrate the static and dynamic effects of prediction.

4. RESULTS

In machine learning analysis using the random forest method, the importance of predictor variables is assessed using the feature importance index, and the relationship between predictor and response variables is visualized using partial dependence plots (Yoo & Jin, 2015). ICT proficiency is measured both as a direct and indirect predictor variable. The purpose of this study is to compare the degree and static and dynamic effects of 11 ICT proficiency variables on reading literacy, mathematical and scientific achievement, and global competence. Lastly, the study aims to demonstrate how the impact of ICT usage on academic achievement varies according to the socioeconomic and cultural differences among households.

The prediction degree of ICT variables as predictor variables and the direction of static and dynamic effects were analyzed using the feature importance index and partial dependence plots.

Academic Achievement and Global Competence Based on ESCS Groups

1)Feature Importance According to ESCS Groups

To facilitate comparison, feature importance was visualized based on dividing ESCS into three groups: Group 1 representing the bottom 10%, Group 3 representing the top 10%, and the rest categorized as Group 2) The differences in feature importance of ICT-related variables in predicting reading literacy, mathematical achievement, scientific achievement, and global competence across these three groups were examined. First, the feature importance of ESCS Group 3 (top 10%) is presented in [Figure 1]. In the top group, ENTUSE showed the highest importance. The feature importance of ESCS Group 2 (middle group) is shown in Figure 2, where HOMESCH emerged as the highest. Since the middle group constitutes 80% of the total, these results are representative of the overall feature importance across all groups. The feature importance of ESCS Group 1 (bottom 10%) is depicted in [Figure 3]. In the bottom group, there were slight differences depending on the achievement level, but notably, ICTCLASS showed higher feature importance compared to other groups. ICTCLASS represents the extent of using ICT in classroom instruction, indicating that ICT usage in school lessons is a significant factor influencing achievement in the bottom group. This underscores the importance of school roles in ICT-based instruction, indicating its significance in future ICT-based classes.

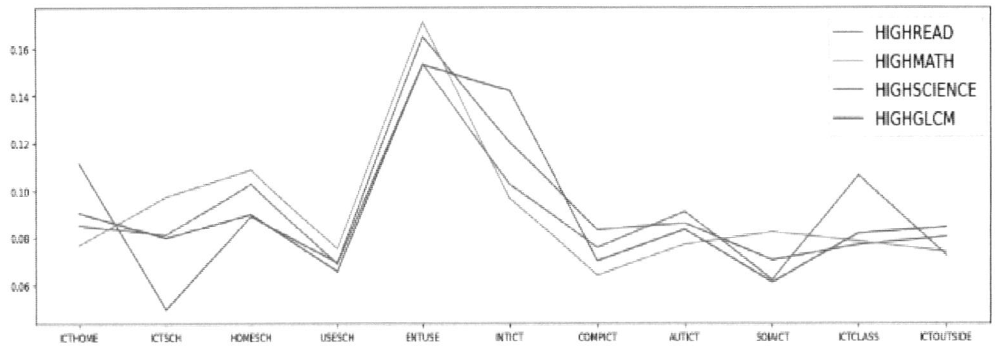

Figure 1. ESCS top 10%

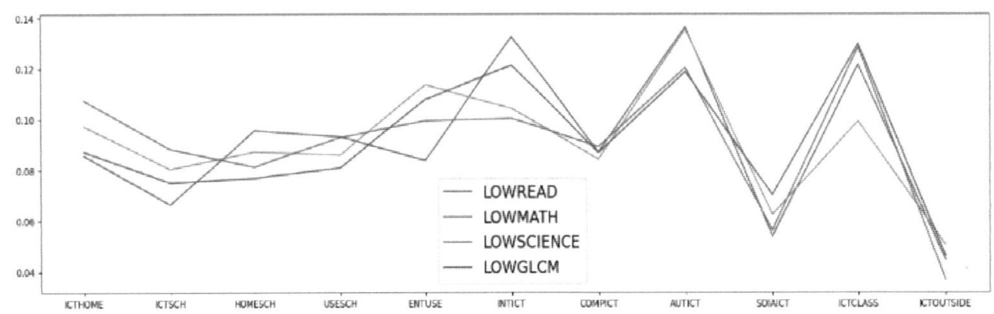

Figure 2. ESCS middle

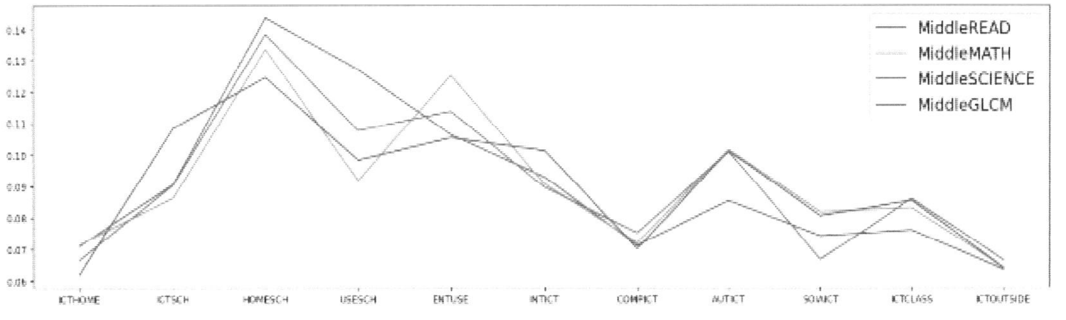

Figure 3. ESCS bottom 10%

Partial Dependence Plots According to ESCS Groups Partial dependence plots are an analytical method that visually demonstrates the static/counteractive direction of the independent variables' influence on the dependent variable. In order to analyze the differences in the static/counteractive effects of ICT factors across ESCS groups, partial dependence plots according to ESCS groups are presented. Below, Figure 6 presents the partial dependence plot for reading literacy. Overall, the factors exerting a static influence are as follows: As ICT access at home increases, reading literacy remains relatively constant until a certain point, after which it sharply changes direction counteractively. This counteractive effect is observed more rapidly in the lowest subgroup. ICTSCH shows a static increase until a certain point, particularly distinct in the lower subgroup compared to the other two. HOMESCH generally increases statically until a certain level, but in the lowest subgroup, it shifts direction counteractively. USESCH remains constant until a certain level, then shifts counteractively. INTICT shows an increase followed by stability. AUTICT increases steeply in all groups. ICTCLASS increases gradually in a static direction, with the lowest subgroup exhibiting the steepest increase. Although ICTOUTSIDE generally remains constant, there is a steep change at a certain point in the lowest subgroup. Factors indicating counteractive effects include ENTUSE, COMPICT, and SOIAICT. ENTUSE exhibits the steepest decrease in the top group. COMPICT, representing confidence in ICT use, shows a larger decrease in the lower subgroup, indicating a more significant counteractive effect on reading literacy. SOIAICT, indicating the level of interaction using ICT, shows a lesser decrease in the lower subgroup.

Overall, the factors exerting a static influence are similar to those in reading literacy, including ICTHOME, ICTSCH, HOMESCH, USESCH, INTICT, AUTICT, ICTCLASS, and ICTOUTSIDE. These factors show similar patterns of change as reading literacy. Additionally, factors exhibiting different characteristics include HOMESCH, representing the extent of ICT use for school assignments outside of school premises, which demonstrates a sharp counteractive effect at a certain point in the top group. USESCH, representing ICT use for school assignments within school premises, exhibits a quantitative increase after a certain point in the top group, unlike other groups. Factors indicating counteractive effects include ENTUSE, COMPICT, and SOIAICT, showing similar changes across groups as observed in reading literacy. The partial dependence plot for science achievement according to ESCS groups is presented in Figure 4. Overall, the factors exerting a static influence are as follows: Similar to mathematical achievement, the factors include ICTHOME, ICTSCH, HOMESCH, USESCH, AUTICT, ICTCLASS, and ICTOUTSIDE. The changes in variables show a similar pattern to mathematical achievement. The variations in HOMESCH and USESCH also resemble those observed in mathematical achievement. Factors indicating counteractive effects include INTICT, ENTUSE, COMPICT, and SOIAICT. These factors show changes across groups similar to those observed in mathematical achievement. A notable characteristic of science achievement is INTICT, representing the level of interest in ICT, which exhibits a counteractive effect. Overall, the factors exerting a static influence are ICTHOME, ICTSCH, HOMESCH, USESCH, AUTICT, ICTCLASS, and ICTOUTSIDE. Factors indicating counteractive effects include ENTUSE, INTICT, COMPICT, and SOIAICT. Global competence shows results similar to those observed in science achievement.

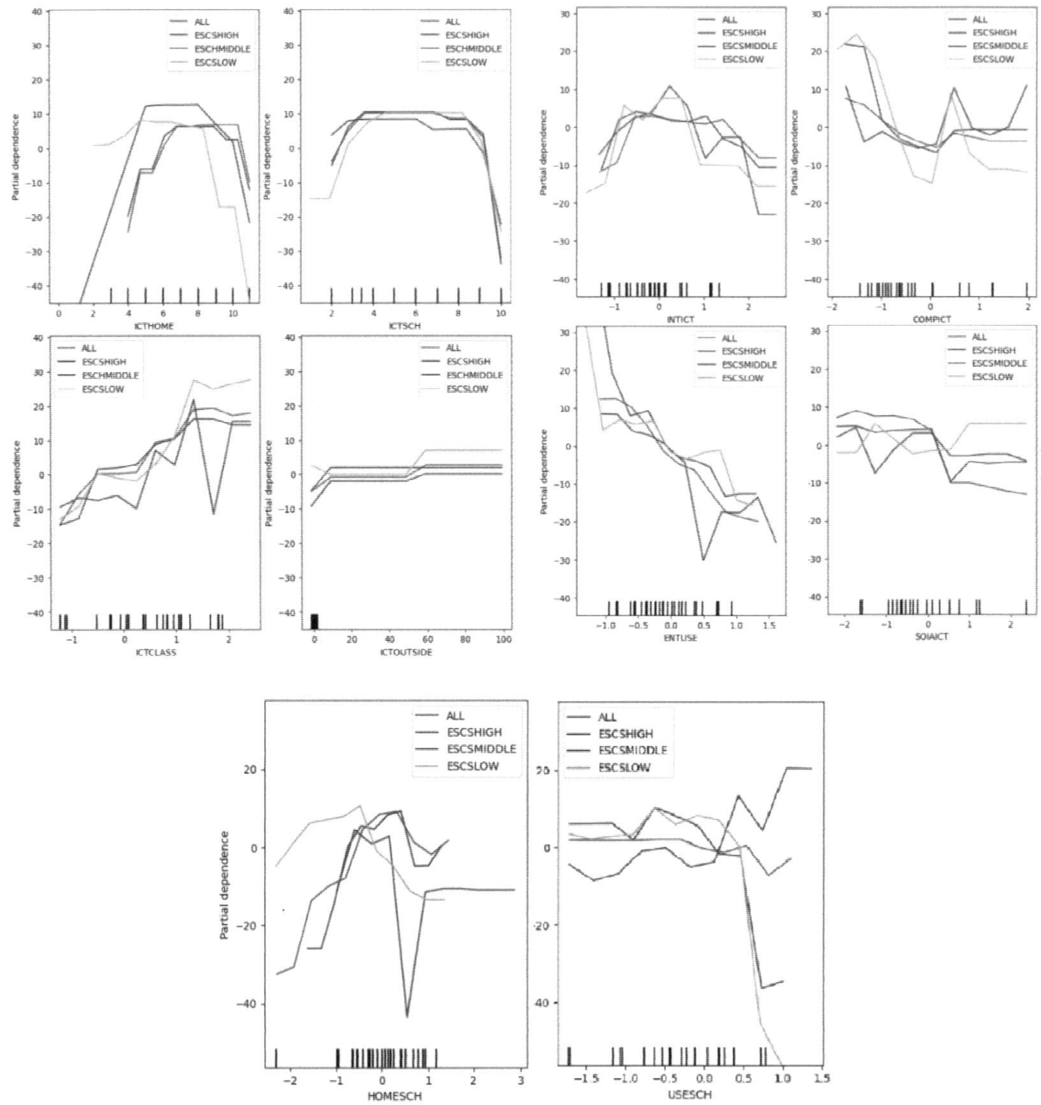

Figure 4. ICTHOME, ICTSCH, ICTCLASS, ICTOUTSIDE, HOMESCH, USESCH, AUTICT, COMPICT, ENTUSE,

REFERENCES

Kim, S., Nam, C., & Jang, S. Y. (2012). The impact of students' EBS and computer utilization and teachers' ICT utilization on learners' academic achievement. *Educational Technology Research*, 28(4), 849-877.

Nam, C., & Shin, S. Y. (2014). The effects of students' ICT-related variables on attitude toward ICT use and problem-solving ability. *Educational Evaluation Research*, 27(5), 1265-1286.

Shin, D. M., Nam, C., & Choi, J. A. (2022). Analysis of middle school creative convergence education performance factors for future education in Busan in the post-COVID-19 era. *Journal of Teacher Education Research*, 61(1), 1-14.

Shin, M. H. (2010). A study on the impact of parental socioeconomic status on children's academic achievement. *Journal of Social Welfare Research*, 41(2), 217-246.

Lee, Y. H., Ku, D. H., & Lim, H. J. (2017). ICT factors at student and school levels affecting computer-based problem-solving skills: Focused on Korea and Japan. *Journal of Information Education Society*, 21(4), 425-435.

Yoo, J. E. (2015). Random forest: A data mining technique as an alternative to decision trees. *Educational Evaluation Research*, 28(2), 427-448.

Jung, H. K., & Cho, J. M. (2013). Analysis of students' overcoming adversity based on PISA 2009 reading and socio-economic background variables. *Journal of Curriculum and Evaluation Studies*, 16(1), 161-184.

Jung, H. W., & Park, S. Y. (2022). Exploration of major predictor variables influencing adolescents' reading, mathematics, and science achievement. *Journal of Curriculum and Evaluation Studies*, 25(1), 223-245.

Choi, I. S., Kim, M. H., Kim, S. J., Kim, H. J., & Lee, S. Y. (2021). OECD international academic achievement assessment study: Analysis of the relationship between achievement characteristics of top-performing countries in PISA 2018 and contextual variables. *Chungbuk Province: Korea Institute for Curriculum and Evaluation.*

Choi, J. Y., & Kim, M. G. (2018). Improvement of heart disease diagnosis based on missing value treatment of data using support vector machine. *Proceedings of the Korean Institute of Communication Sciences Conference*, 862-863.

Heo, K. (2013). Multilevel analysis of ICT utilization ability and effects of computer use for learning purposes in PISA 2009. *Journal of Computer Education Society*, 16(1), 51-61.

Hong, S. J., & Kim, C. H. (2017). Analysis of the PISA 2018 evaluation system for enhancing global competency education. *Journal of Learner-Centered Curriculum and Instruction Research*, 17(1), 65-91.

Aypay, A. (2010). The Adaptation Study of General Self-Efficacy (GSE) Scale to Turkish. *Inonu University Journal of the Faculty of Education (INUJFE)*, 11(2).

Breiman, L. (2001). Random Forests. *Machine Learning*, 45(1), 5-32.

Kuhlemeier, H., & Hemker, B. (2007). The Impact of Computer Use at Home on Students' Internet Skills. *Computers and Education*, 49(2), 460-480.

Liaw, A., & Wiener, M. (2002). Classification and regression by randomForest. *R News*, 2(3), 18-22.

OECD. (2017). PISA 2015 technical report. OECD Publishing.

Papanastasiou, E. C., Zembylas, M., & Vrasidas, C. (2003). Can Computer Use hurt Science Achievement? The USA Results from PISA. *Journal of Science Education and Technology*, 12(3), 325-332.

Wastiau, P., Blamire, R., Kearney, C., Quittre, V., Van de Gaer, E., & Monseur, C. (2013). The Use of ICT in Education: A Survey of Schools in Europe. *European Journal of Education*, 48(1), 11-27.

DETERMINANTS OF INTENTION TO DONATE THROUGH CROWDFUNDING PLATFORMS

Dekar Urumsah and Andi Agung Kurniawan Arifuddin
Department of Accounting, Universitas Islam Indonesia, Indonesia

ABSTRACT

This study aims to analyse the effects of performance expectancy, effort expectancy, social influence, facilitating conditions, empathy, and trust on the intention to donate through crowdfunding platforms. In addition, this research is also to find the influences of information quality, security and privacy on trust. In this research, the Unified of Acceptance and Use of Technology (UTAUT) theory was employed alongside a quantitative method to analyse primary data collected through online questionnaires using Google Forms. The sample contained 220 respondents who made donation for charity through a crowdfunding platform. SEM-PLS was used to analyse the data with the help of SmartPLS 4. The study results show that effort expectancy, empathy, and trust positively influence the intention to donate. Similarly, information quality and security also have positive effects on trust. Meanwhile, performance expectancy, social influence, and facilitating conditions do not affect the intention to donate. Privacy also does not influence trust. The results of this study can be used by the government as a regulator and the providers of crowdfunding platforms to innovate for the betterment.

KEYWORDS

Crowdfunding, Empathy, Trust, Information Quality, Security, Privacy

1. INTRODUCTION

The advancement of technology, especially the internet, has revolutionized financial technology (fintech), making it easier and more efficient for individuals to donate online through platforms like crowdfunding (Wicks, 2013). Statistics Indonesia (BPS) states that Indonesia experienced a recession after its economic growth contracted for two consecutive quarters, in the second quarter by –5.32% and in the third quarter by –3.49% (Kusuma, 2020). Along with the decreasing growth of the national economy, a number of providers for digital donation in Indonesia reported an increase in traffic since the pandemic. Putri Dianita from LinkAja and Budi Gandasoebrata from GoPay reported a doubling in digital donation traffic since the pandemic began (Bisnis.com, 2020).

Republika (2020) also reported that during the pandemic, one of the crowdfunding established by Rumah Zakat, Sharing Happiness, gained a rise in the number of donors reaching 280 thousand people. Another popular name, Kitabisa, also experienced a significant traffic hike in March 2020 with 3.5 million visits compared to the number of visits in February as many as 2.1 million (Nabila, 2020). Thus, it can be inferred that during the pandemic which resulted in economic recession, many people were moved to make donation digitally. This phenomenon appeals the researcher to find the reasons why more people were attracted to make digital donation through crowdfunding instead of direct donation. Research on crowdfunding has been previously conducted using several theories, one of which is Unified of Acceptance and Use of Technology (UTAUT). Some research which relates UTAUT theory and crowdfunding platforms includes Li et al. (2018), Kim and Hall (2020), as well as Moon and Hwang (2018). UTAUT is an evaluation result of eight notable user acceptance models which are integrated into a new model (Nasir, 2013). For that reason, the researcher is interested in using UTAUT model as a reference for research model framework. The constructs which will be adapted from UTAUT model encompass performance expectancy, effort expectancy, social influence, and facilitating conditions as the starting point to study the behaviour intention of an individual to donate through crowdfunding platforms.

The researcher expands the model by adding empathy and trust which directly affect one's intention to donate using crowdfunding platforms. The construct of trust itself is influenced by information quality, security, and privacy. In addition, different from the previous research, this study focuses on crowdfunding activity during the Covid-19 pandemic. Meanwhile, the previous studies mostly examined the general causes related to individual intention to donate. In Indonesia, only few studies connect crowdfunding with a particular condition or event. This article will be started with an introduction which is followed by literature review and hypothesis development. The research model was measured quantitatively. The next part is hypothesis presentation entailed by research methodology which presents research sample, data analysis using PLS, and study results. This article is closed by discussion and conclusion.

2. LITERATURE REVIEW AND HYPOTHESIS DEVELOPMENT

2.1 Unified of Acceptance and Use of Technology (UTAUT) and Crowdfunding Platform

The UTAUT model emphasizes that performance expectations, effort expectations, and social influence users' intention to adopt technology, while facilitating conditions and behavioral intention directly affect technology users (Venkatesh et al., 2003). This study adopts the UTAUT constructs by adding factors of empathy, trust, information quality, security, and privacy. Crowdfunding, which aims to raise funds through the internet for commercial or charitable purposes, utilizes web technology and online payment portals to connect project owners and donors (Choy & Schlagwein, 2016). Crowdfunding services encompass various types such as equity-based crowdfunding, debt-based crowdfunding, donation-based crowdfunding, and reward-based crowdfunding (Kuti & Madarász, 2014). The focus of this research is on donation-based crowdfunding.

2.2 Effect of Performance Expectancy on Intention to Donate using Crowdfunding Platforms

Performance expectancy is the extent to which an individual believes that his performance will improve after using a particular system (Venkatesh et al., 2003). In the context of this study, if an individual believes that crowdfunding platforms can improve his performance, his intention to donate using crowdfunding platforms will also increase. Previous research on crowdfunding has shown that performance expectancy has a significant influence on the intention to use or adopt crowdfunding services (Kim & Hall, 2020; Tariqul, 2019). Thus, the hypothesis is drawn, as follows.

H1: Performance expectancy positively influences the intention to donate through crowdfunding platforms.

2.3 Effect of Effort Expectancy on Intention to Donate using Crowdfunding Platforms

Effort expectancy indicates the level of ease perceived by an individual in using a particular system (Venkatesh et al., 2003). Previous study conducted by Palau-Saumell et al. (2019) shows the positive relation between effort expectancy and intention. A person will have the intention to adopt Mobile Applications for Restaurant Searches and/or Reservations (MARSR) if he perceives that the application is deemed efficient for easy search and time saving. In this study context, if a person finds that the crowdfunding platform is easy to use, it will increase the intention for making donation using the crowdfunding platform. Therefore, the hypothesis is formulated as follows.

H2: Effort expectancy positively influences the intention to donate through crowdfunding platforms.

2.4 Effect of Social Influence on Intention to Donate using Crowdfunding Platforms

Social influence is an individual of the importance of other individuals perceiving that he must use a new system (Venkatesh et al., 2003). In this study, the existence of social influence where other surrounding people use the crowdfunding platforms will increase the intention of an individual to use the platforms as well. Social influence is one of the factors affecting the intention of an individual to invest. The influence comes from the people around the person which later results in his intention to invest (Kim & Hall, 2020). Accordingly, the hypothesis proposed is as follows.

H3: Social influence positively affects the intention to donate through crowdfunding platforms.

2.5 Effect of Facilitating Conditions on Intention to Donate using Crowdfunding Platforms

Facilitating conditions are an individual belief in the availability of his organizational and technical infrastructure to facilitate the use of a system (Venkatesh et al., 2003). In this research, the individual belief that the crowdfunding platforms can provide the infrastructure needed will enhance the intention to donate using the platforms. Kurfalı et al. (2017) shows that facilitating conditions have a positive effect on behaviour intention to use e-government services. Nevertheless, Sulaeman and Ninglasari (2020) prove that facilitating conditions do not affect the intention to donate using alms-based crowdfunding platforms. The hypothesis is constructed as follows.

H4: Facilitating conditions positively influence the intention to donate through crowdfunding platforms.

2.6 Effect of Empathy on Intention to Donate using Crowdfunding Platforms

Empathy is the ability to understand and share others' emotions which plays a crucial role in a charity project (Eisenberg & Miller, 1987; Li et al., 2019). Research by Li et al., (2019) indicates that empathy mediates the relationship between social experiences and donation intentions. In the context of crowdfunding, higher levels of empathy are linked to increased donation intentions (Smith et al., 2019). Hence, the hypothesis is devised as follows.

H5: Empathy positively influences the intention to donate through crowdfunding platforms.

2.7 Effect of Trust on Intention to Donate using Crowdfunding Platforms

Trust is the belief that technology providers can fulfill their obligations (Gefen, 2000). In the context of this study, an individual trust in a crowdfunding platform can increase his intention to donate through the crowdfunding platform. Kim et al. (2020) argue that a potential donor has high level of trust in a crowdfunding platform if the platform presents the strong attributions including accreditations, guarantees, and valid license from third parties. Hence, the hypothesis is drawn as follows.

H6: Trust positively influences the intention to donate through crowdfunding platforms.

2.8 Effects of Information Quality, Security and Privacy on Trust

Information quality, encompassing aspects of accuracy, completeness, clarity, understanding, utility, and reliability of output data in an information system, plays a key role in building user trust in crowdfunding platforms (Chen & Chang, 2018; Kim et al., 2008). Research also indicates that good information quality can increase public trust in using social media for e-government services (Khan et al., 2021). User security, assessing the extent to which users are protected from potential risks, also plays a crucial role in enhancing user trust in crowdfunding platforms (Kim et al., 2010; Nguyen & Le, 2021).

User trust in the security of crowdfunding platforms, involving user protection from potential risks, can increase users' intention to use the platform for donations (Zhang et al., 2020; Normalini & Ramayah, 2017; Vega, 2015). Meanwhile, privacy, related to the potential misuse of personal information, also impacts user trust in crowdfunding platforms (Vega, 2015). Although individual privacy concerns may decrease the intention to donate using crowdfunding platforms, there is research showing that privacy does not affect customers' trust in internet banking services (Normalini & Ramayah, 2017). The proposed hypotheses are as follows.

H7: Information quality positively influences trust.

H8: Security positively influences trust.

H9: Privacy negatively influences trust.

3. RESEARCH METHODS

This study employs quantitative method using primary data which were collected by a survey using questionnaire technique. The research population is individuals who use financial technology services, especially the users of crowdfunding platforms. According to Hair et al. (2019), the minimum number of samples from the unknown population number can be drawn from the total number of research indicators multiplied by 5-10. The number of indicators in this research is 42. By multiplying it with 5, the number of samples should be collected is 210. There were 220 respondents participating in this research. The questionnaire was distributed online using Google Form, and the data were analyzed using Partial Least Square (PLS) with the help of *Smart*PLS 4 program.

4. RESULTS AND DISCUSSION

4.1 Description of Respondents

There were 220 respondents in this research who can be classified as follows: (1) 46 (20.9%) males and 174 (79.1%) females; (2) 101 (45.9%) high-school graduates, 12 (5.5%) undergraduates, 94 (42.7%) D-3 graduates, 11 (5%) master's graduates, and 2 (0.9%) doctoral graduates; (3) donation frequency through online crowdfunding platforms: 188 (85.5%) respondents doing 1-3 times in a month, 14 (6.4%) respondents doing 4-6 times in a month, and 18 (8.2%) respondents doing more than 6 times in a month.

Table 1. Heterotrait-Monotrait Ratio (HTMT), Composite Reliability (CR), and R-Square

	EP	PE	EE	TR	FC	IQ	ID	SI	SC	PV
EP										
PE	0,623 CI85(0,469;0,796)									
EE	0,273 (0,117;0,450)	0,659 (0,483;0,821)								
TR	0,496 (0,372;0,622)	0,623 (0,456;0,781)	0,635 (0,515;0,732)							
FC	0,485 (0,266;0,586)	0,580 (0,370;0,785)	0,550 (0,339;0,630)	0,628 (0,398;0,712)						
IQ	0,515 (0,380;0,647)	0,626 (0,457;0,810)	0,559 (0,383;0,647)	0,790 (0,702;0,866)	0,624 (0,382;0,711)					
ID	0,466 (0,334;0,334)	0,497 (0,290;0,706)	0,426 (0,291;0,551)	0,505 (0,373;0,628)	0,460 (0,235;0,593)	0,441 (0,296;0,581)				
SI	0,756 (0,640;0,892)	0,640 (0,430;0,883)	0,395 (0,206;0,590)	0,653 (0,493;0,805)	0,665 (0,400;0,798)	0,726 (0,553;0,898)	0,534 (0,355;715)			
SC	0,495 (0,340;0,645)	0,603 (0,429;0,772)	0,520 (0,353;0,672)	0,791 (0,698;0,683)	0,635 (0,391;0,708)	0,830 (0,755;0,889)	0,512 (0,380;0,632)	0,714 (0,570;0,852)		
PV	0,041 (0,038;0,182)	0,063 (0,046;0,237)	0,179 (0,073;0,303)	0,241 (0,102;0,375)	0,075 (0,081;0,275)	0,166 (0,058;0,309)	0,154 (0,57;0,305)	0,174 (0,052;0,343)	0,228 (0,088;0,365)	
CR	0,941	0,812	0,931	0,943	0,791	0,927	0,900	0,832	0,935	0,976
R-Squared				0,601			0,277			

4.2 Outer Model Measurement

4.2.1 Validity Test

The validity test used was convergent validity which is fulfilled if the rule of thumbs of AVE is more than 0.50 (Wong, 2013). In this research, all variables have met the criteria for AVE values. The performance expectancy variable has an AVE value of 0.684, effort expectancy 0.770; social influence 0.713, facilitating conditions 0.558, empathy 0.761, trust 0.805, information quality 0.719, security 0.827, privacy 0.912, and intention to donate 0.693. It indicates that the total AVE values of each variable exceed 0.50, confirming the minimum value of convergent validity. Discriminant validity testing was conducted using HTMT, which is more sensitive than traditional methods. Discriminant validity is met if the HTMT value is < 1 (Hair et al., 2019). The results of the HTMT test are listed in Table 2. Table 2 shows that the HTMT values are less than 0.85, with the highest value reaching only 0.830 and the upper confidence interval (CI) threshold less than 1, where the highest value is 0.892. Therefore, the research constructs pass the discriminant validity test and are declared valid.

4.2.2 Reliability Test

This research construct reliability is shown by the value of composite reliability. If the value of composite reliability is more than 0.70, the construct is reliable (Bagozzi & Yi, 1988). Table 2 shows that all instrument items of this research are reliable indicated by the value of composite reliability > 0.7.

4.3 Hypothesis Test Results

The structural model used to test the hypotheses was path coefficient and T-test (P value). The results show that performance expectancy (H1), social influence (H3), and facilitating conditions (H4) do not influence the intention to donate through crowdfunding platforms. Meanwhile, effort expectancy (H2), empathy (H5), and trust (H6) positively influence the intention to donate using crowdfunding platforms. Also, information quality (H7) and security performance (H8) have positive effects on trust. In contrast, privacy (H9) does not affect trust. The summary of the hypothesis test can be seen in Table 2.

Table 2. Hypothesis Test Result

Hypothesis	Relation	Path Coefficient	P Value	Result
H1 (+)	PE → ID	0.042	0.613	Not supported
H2 (+)	EE → ID	0.168	0.021*	Supported
H3 (+)	SI → ID	0.109	0.158	Not supported
H4 (+)	FC → ID	0.052	0.464	Not supported
H5 (+)	EP →ID	0.197	0.008**	Supported
H6 (+)	TR → ID	0.167	0.035*	Supported
H7 (+)	IQ → TR	0.417	0.000***	Supported
H8 (+)	SC → TR	0.395	0.000***	Supported
H9 (-)	PV → TR	-0.078	0.093	Not supported

Significance: *$p < 0.05$; **$p<0.01$; ***$p<0.001$

4.4 Structural Model (Inner Model)

SEM PLS is a predictive / explorative modelling which is needed to estimate a PLS model which has been examined as having good predictive power. There are numerous researchers who assume that R-squared test can be used to predict the strength of a model. Hair et al. (2019) state that the interpretation is not all correct because R-squared test only shows the model strength within the sample but does not explain anything related to the prediction strength of the model outside the sample. To overcome this, Shmueli et al. (2019) propose a series of procedures to make a prediction outside the sample using PLS predict analysis.

4.4.1 R-Squared (R^2) Test

R-squared value shows a model ability to describe the dependent research variable. If the value of R^2 is >0.10, the model is deemed a better fit (Falk & Miller, 1992). Table 1 indicates that the research model can explain the variables of trust and intention to donate as much as 0.601% and 0.277 respectively. Since the values are >0.10, the model is supported.

4.4.2 Goodness of Fit (GoF) Test

GoF criteria include 0.10 denoting small, 0.25 denoting medium, and 0.36 denoting large (Cohen, 1988) . Table 3 displays the average values of R-squared and communality 0.439 and 0.748 respectively. The calculation result shows GoF value of 0.573 which is categorized into large, so this research model is robust.

4.4.3 PLS Predict

PLS analysis in prediction-based SEM evaluates model strength, especially in prediction-oriented models, by comparing PLS predictions with linear regression (LM) using RMSE or MAE. According to Shmueli (2019), high prediction strength occurs if all PLS indicators surpass LM, medium if most do, and low if only a few does.

Table 3. PLS Predict Test

	PLS-SEM_RMSE	PLS-SEM_MAE	LM_RMSE	LM_MAE
ID1	0.935	0.740	1.018	0.829
ID2	0.930	0.718	1.015	0.788
ID3	0.868	0.666	0.958	0.736
ID4	0.766	0.603	0.798	0.619
TR1	0.611	0.396	0.638	0.435
TR2	0.556	0.414	0.587	0.426
TR3	0.617	0.414	0.681	0.476
TR4	**0.513**	**0.388**	0.501	0.383

Table 3 shows that most of the indicators (7 out of 8 measurements) of PLS SEM have lower RMSE and MAE scores compared to those of linear regression model (LM). Thus, it can be concluded that this PLS SEM model has medium predictive power.

4.5 Discussion

Based on research results, performance expectations do not significantly influence the intention to donate on crowdfunding platforms, indicating that contributors tend to prioritize altruistic reasons over personal satisfaction regarding performance after using the platform (Venkatesh et al., 2003; Moon & Hwang, 2018). These findings are in line with previous research regarding Mobile Health Service Applications (Utomo et al., 2021), but differ from the results of a study by Butarbutar et al. (2022) and Holzmann et al. (2020) who found the influence of performance expectations in technology adoption. This research highlights that users of donation-based crowdfunding platforms tend to focus more on helping others than personal gain, emphasizing the importance of service providers meeting users' expectations of project success to increase satisfaction and engagement. Up-to-date information on project progress, disbursement of funds and results is key to building donor trust and meeting their goals in supporting crowdfunding initiatives. In addition, research findings also show a positive influence of effort expectations on donation intentions on crowdfunding platforms, with user-friendly experiences proven to increase donation intentions (Venkatesh et al., 2003). Recommendations for service providers include prioritizing user interface simplicity and providing a variety of payment channels to increase users' convenience in donating through these platforms, which will ultimately strengthen their donation intentions.

Other results from this study show that social influence has no significant effect on intention to donate via crowdfunding platforms, in contrast to previous research which linked social influence with intention to donate (Li et al., 2018; Kim & Hall, 2020; Moon & Hwang, 2018). These findings indicate that the motivation of donors during the Covid-19 pandemic is based more on personal altruism than external influences, strengthening a sense of social responsibility and encouraging donation activities. Although social influences were shown to influence intentions to use 3D printing technology in research by Holzmann et al. (2020), this study emphasizes the importance of understanding users' intrinsic motivation for donating. On the other hand, this study proves that facilitation conditions do not influence the intention to donate via crowdfunding platforms, in line with other research which found that facilitation conditions are not the key factor influencing donor intentions on crowdfunding platforms (Sulaeman & Ninglasari, 2020; Moon & Hwang, 2018), but in contrast to previous research by Li et al. (2018), Kim and Hall (2020). Even though the facilitation conditions do not have a significant effect on the intention to donate, crowdfunding service providers should still provide the best facilities to users, such as adequate information regarding the background and objectives of the fundraising project to strengthen the intention to participate in crowdfunding activities. Additionally, technical support such as complaint handling and responses to questions should always be available via social media or email.

Empathy and trust play an important role in driving the intention to donate via crowdfunding platforms. Research shows that empathy has a positive impact on individuals' willingness to help through donations, especially in crisis contexts such as the COVID-19 pandemic, in line with previous findings (Liu et al., 2018; Kuo et al., 2020). The credibility of a crowdfunding project also influences donation intentions, with clear and honest information being key, especially in the wake of disasters affecting individuals driven by empathy. Meanwhile, trust was shown to have a positive impact on donation intentions, with donors tending to be more willing to contribute if they believe in the reliability of the crowdfunding platform. These findings support the importance of building trust and maintaining a good reputation in increasing donor participation and contributions (Li et al., 2018; Moon & Hwang, 2018; Zhang et al., 2020). Alharbey and Van Hemmen's (2021) study confirms that trust in crowdfunding platforms has a significant influence on investors' decisions to invest, highlighting that increased trust ultimately contributes to increased intentions to donate via the platform.

The research findings highlight the significant impact of information quality and security on trust in crowdfunding platforms. Information quality, which includes aspects such as accuracy and usefulness, plays a crucial role in increasing users' trust in these platforms (Chen & Chang, 2018), in line with previous research by Zhang et al. (2020). Assisted by Najib et al. (2022), perceived information quality influences trust, as seen in the context of purchasing dietary supplements during the Covid-19 outbreak. It is important for crowdfunding platforms to provide comprehensive and transparent project information to strengthen donors' trust and subsequently influence their donation intentions. In addition, user security, defined as the level of protection against risk, positively influences trust in using crowdfunding platforms (Nguyen and Le, 2021). Understanding the security measures implemented by these platforms instills a sense of security in users during the donation process, further strengthening their intent to engage with the platform. This study confirms the importance of security in shaping user trust, in line with findings from previous research (Zhang et al., 2020; Normalini & Ramayah, 2017; Vega, 2015). Ensuring strong security measures not only increases donor safety but also increases the level of trust, ultimately influencing users' willingness to donate via crowdfunding platforms.

The results of the study also found that privacy does not have a significant impact on trust. Privacy related to the potential misuse of personal information, also impacts user trust in crowdfunding platforms (Vega, 2015). The results of this study explain that a person's concerns about the possibility of their privacy being misused when using a crowdfunding platform cannot reduce trust in using the platform. Researchers argue that this happens because people are still less aware of privacy security, so respondents in this study did not have concerns about the possibility of their privacy being misused by crowdfunding platform providers. This finding supports previous research conducted by Normalini and Ramayah (2017) which stated that privacy does not have a significant impact on user trust. Even though privacy does not have a positive effect on trust, crowdfunding platform providers still need to convince users that the crowdfunding platform is safe from the risk of misuse of privacy data, thereby increasing user trust in the crowdfunding platform.

5. CONCLUSION

The statistical analysis in this study proves that performance expectancy, social influence, and facilitating conditions do not influence the intention to donate through crowdfunding platforms. Meanwhile, effort expectancy, empathy, and trust positively influence the intention to donate. Also, information quality and security have positive effects in trust, while privacy does not affect trust. The theoretical contributions of this study include the potential to become a reference for further research related to information technology adoption, enriching information technology adoption models by integrating constructs such as empathy, trust, information quality, security and privacy, as well as enriching understanding related to information technology adoption, especially in crowdfunding platform context.

This research has significant implications for both regulators and service providers. Regulators, particularly government bodies, are urged to update policies to promote the use of crowdfunding services and collaborate with stakeholders to enhance service quality and infrastructure. Meanwhile, service providers should prioritize factors that bolster public trust, such as ensuring security, protecting personal information, and maintaining high information quality. Moreover, simplifying platform usage and effectively promoting crowdfunding projects via social media and interpersonal channels can encourage greater community engagement. Despite these insights, the study acknowledges limitations, including variations in platform assessments due to diverse respondent experiences and the exclusion of certain variables beyond the UTAUT model. Based on these limitations, future research is suggested to include platform classification, additional variables such as customer satisfaction and costs, and conduct qualitative investigations.

REFERENCES

Alharbey, M., & Van Hemmen, S. (2021). Investor Intention in Equity Crowdfunding. Does Trust Matter? *Journal of Risk and Financial Management, 14*(2), 53-73.

Bagozzi, R. P., & Yi, Y. (1988). On the evaluation of structural equation models. Journal of the Academy of Marketing Science, 16(1), 74–94.

Bisnis.com. (2020). *Donasi Digital Meningkat Selama Pandemi Covid-19.* Retrieved July 25, 2022, from https://finansial.bisnis.com/read/20200519/563/1242695/donasi-digital- meningkat-selama-pandemi-covid-19

Butarbutar, N., Lie, D., Bagenda, C., Hendrayani, E., & Sudirman, A. (2022). Analysis of the Effect of Performance Expectancy, Effort Expectancy, and Lifestyle Compatibility on Behavioral Intention QRIS in Indonesia. *International Journal of Scientific Research and Management (IJSRM), 10(11),* 4203-4211.

Chen, C.-C., & Chang, Y.-C. (2018). What drives purchase intention on Airbnb? Perspectives of consumer reviews, information quality, and media richness.*Telematics and Informatics, 35*(5), 1512-1523.

Choy, K., & Schlagwein, D. (2016). Crowdsourcing for a better world: On the relation between IT affordances and donor motivations in charitable crowdfunding. *Information Technology & People, 29*(1), 221-247.

Cohen, J. (1988). *Statistical Power Analysis for the Behavioral Sciences* (2nd ed.). Lawrence Erlbaum Associates.

Eisenberg, N., & Miller, P. A. (1987). The Relation of Empathy to Prosocial and Related Behaviors. *Psychological Bulletin, 101*(1), 91-119.

Falk, R. F., & Miller, N. B. (1992). A Primer for Soft Modeling. *The University of Akron Press, Akron.*

Hair, J. F., Risher, J. J., Sarstedt, M., & Ringle, C. M. (2019). When to use and how to report the results of PLS-SEM. *European Business Review, 31*(1), 2–24. https://doi.org/10.1108/EBR-11-2018-0203

Hair, J. F., Black, W. C., Babin, B. J., & Anderson, R. E. (2019). *Multivariate DataAnalysis.* Hampshire: Cengage Learning.

Holzmann, P., Schwarz, E. J., & Audretsch, D. B. (2020). Understanding the determinants of novel technology adoption among teachers: the case of 3D printing. *The Journal of Technology Transfer, 45,* 259-275.

Khan, S., Umer, R., Umer, S., & Naqvi, S. (2021). Antecedents of trust in using social media for E-government services: An empirical study in Pakistan. *Technology in Society, 64*, 1-13.

Kim, C., Tao, W., Shin, N., & Kim, K.-S. (2010). An empirical study of customers's of security and trust. *Electronic Commerce Research and Applications, 9*(1), 84-95.

Kim, D. J., Ferrin, D. L., & Rao, H. R. (2008). A trust-based consumer decision- making model in electronic commerce: The role of trust, perceived risk, andtheir antecedents. *Decision Support System, 44*(2), 544-564.

Kim, M. J., & Hall, C. M. (2020). What drives visitor economy crowdfunding? Theeffect of digital storytelling on unified theory of acceptance and use of technology. *Tourism Management Perspectives, 34*, 100638.

Kuo, Y.-F., Lin, C. S., & Wu, C.-H. (2020). Why do People Intend to Back Crowdfunding Projects? a Perspective on Social Cognitive Theory. *Journalof Electronic Commerce Research, 21*(3), 180-196.

Kurfalı, M., Arifoglu, A., Tokdemir, G., & Paçin, Y. (2017). Adoption of e- government services in Turkey. *Computers in Human Behavior, 66*, 168- 178.

Kusuma, H. (2020, November 7). *Indonesia Resmi Resesi, Apakah BerujungKrisis?* Diambil Kembali dari finance.detik.com: https://finance.detik.com/berita-ekonomi-bisnis/d-5245302/indonesia- resmi-resesi-apakah-berujung-krisis

Kuti, M., & Madarász, G. (2014). Crowdfunding. *Public Finance Quarterly, 59*(3),355-366.

Li, B., Hou, F., Guan, Z., & Chong, A. (2019). How Social Experience EncouragesDonation Intention to Charitable Crowdfunding Projects on Social Media: Empathy and Personal Impulsiveness. *PACIS 2019 Proceedings*, (p. 195).

Li, Y. Z., He, T. L., Song, Y. R., Yang, Z., & Zhou, R. T. (2018). Factors impactingdonors' intention to donate to charitable crowd-funding projects in China: aUTAUT-based model. *Information, Communication & Society, 21*(3), 404–415.

Liu, L., Suh, A., & Wagner, C. (2018). Empathy or perceived credibility? An empirical study on individual donation behavior in charitable crowdfunding. *Internet Research, 28*(3), 623-651.

Moon, Y., & Hwang, J. (2018). Crowdfunding as an Alternative Means for FundingSustainable Appropriate Technology: Acceptance Determinants of Backers.*Sustainability, 10*(5), 1456.

Nabila, M. (2020, April 8). *Kekuatan Orang Baik, Kunci Tenarnya Platform "SocialCrowdfunding".* Diambil kembali dari dailysocial.id: https://dailysocial.id/post/kekuatan-orang-baik-kunci-tenarnya-platform-social-crowdfunding

Najib, M., Fahma, F., Suhartanto, D., Sumardi, R. S., & Sabri, M. F. (2022). The role of information quality, trust and anxiety on intention to buy food supplements at the time of COVID-19 outbreak. *International Journal of Pharmaceutical and Healthcare Marketing,* 1-20.

Nasir, M. (2023). Evaluasi Penerimaan Teknologi Informasi Mahasiswa di Palembang Menggunakan Model UTAUT. *Seminar Nasional Aplikasi Teknologi Informai (SNATI),* 36-40.

Nguyen, T.-D., & Le, K.-D. (2021). PLS-SEM approach in measuring the impact of PLS-SEM approach in measuring the impact of in e-payment – The caseof rural areas in Vietnam. *International Journal of Scientific and Research Publications, 11*(4), 357-364.

Normalini, M. K., & Ramayah, T. (2017). Trust in Internet Banking in Malaysia and the Moderating Influence of Perceived Effectiveness of Biometrics Technology on Perceived Privacy and Security. *Journal of Management Sciences, 4*(1), 3-26.

Palau-Saumell, R., Forgas-Coll, S., Sánchez-García, J., & Robres, E. (2019). User Acceptance of Mobile Apps for Restaurants: An Expanded and Extended UTAUT-2. *Sustainability, 11*(4), 1210.

Republika. (2020). *Donatur Sharing Happiness Rumah Zakat Naik Hingga 280 Ribu.* Retrieved July 25, 2022, from republika.co.id:https://republika.co.id/berita/qjl0eq396/donatur-sharing-happiness-rumah- zakat-naik-hingga-280-ribu

Shmueli, G., Sarstedt, M., Hair, J. F., Cheah, J. H., Ting, H., Vaithilingam, S., & Ringle, C. M. (2019). Predictive model assessment in PLS-SEM: guidelines for using PLSpredict. European Journal of Marketing, 53(11), 2322–2347

Smith, K. E., Norman, G. J., & Decety, J. (2019). Medical students' empathy positively predicts charitable donation behavior. *The Journal of Positive Psychology, 15*(6), 734-742.

Sulaeman, & Ninglasari, S. Y. (2020). Analysing the Behavioral Intention Factorsin Using Zakat-Based Crowdfunding Platform in Indonesia: A QuantitativeStudy. *International Journal of Zakat, 5*(3), 1-19.

Tariqul, I. M. (2019). Factors Influencing the Adoption of Crowdfunding in Bangladesh: a Study on Start-Up Entrepreneurs. *Doctoral dissertation,Ritsumeikan Asia Pacific University.*

Utomo, P., Kurniasari, F., & Purnamaningsih, P. (2021). The Effects of Performance Expectancy, Effort Expectancy, Facilitating Condition, and Habit on Behavior Intention in Using Mobile Healthcare Application. *International Journal of Community Service & Engagement, 2(4),* 183-197.

Vega, J. A. (2015). Determiners of Consumer Trust towards Electronic Commerce:An Application to Puerto Rico. *Esic Market Economics and BusinessJournal, 46*(1), 125-147.

Venkatesh, V., Morris, M. G., Davis, G. B., & Davis, F. D. (2003). User acceptanceof information technology: Toward a unified view. *MIS Quarterly, 27*(3), 425-478.

Wong, K. K.-K. (2013). Partial Least Squares Structural Equation Modeling (PLS-SEM) Techniques Using SmartPLS. *Marketing Bulletin, 24*(1), 1–32.

Wicks, M. (2013). *Crowdfunding: An introduction.* Victoria: Blue Beetle Books Inc.

Zhang, Y., Tan, C. D., Sun, J., & Yang, Z. (2020). Why do people patronize donation-based crowdfunding platforms? An activity perspective of criticalsuccess factors. *Computers in Human Behavior, 112.*

DIDACTIC GAME ABOUT RENEWABLE AND SUSTAINABLE ENERGIES

Pedro Simões and Piedade Carvalho
GILT, ISEP, IPP
Porto, Portugal

ABSTRACT

Renewable sources play a crucial role in addressing global energy challenges and mitigating environmental impacts associated with conventional energy sources. In response to the growing need for effective educational tools in this field, Sustainable Energy Centers of Vocational Excellence (SECOVE) issued a challenge to create a game that would teach the players about sustainable energies while capturing their attention. This project aims to provide an enhanced way for the subject to be taught to students in a class environment while also being prepared to teach people outside of that environment about the subject. To achieve this goal, a multi-phase approach was developed, integrating research, design, and deployment. Games with similar themes, such as "Power Up" and "Siemens Energy Island", were studied, along with techniques identified to enhance game development. The resulting game was designed to engage players while providing relevant information about renewable energies, their advantages, and their importance. While it was reported to have a strong teaching component and engaging gameplay experience, feedback on the player actions fell short of expectations. Nonetheless, the game holds potential for further development to incorporate reported feedback and expand on existing teaching content. In summary, this research aims to introduce a novel approach to teaching about renewable energies, leveraging familiar technology (games) to captivate a younger audience.

KEYWORDS

Didactic, Serious Game, Renewable Energies, Educational

1. INTRODUCTION

In today's digital era, video games have become increasingly captivating for young people, sometimes to the detriment of their academic performance (Staff, 2022). This project seeks to address this challenge by leveraging the immersive nature of games to not only motivate players to excel, but also educate them on crucial topics, especially renewable energy. The instructional approach integrates questionnaires as a primary teaching method with the aim of guiding students during the learning process (Salas-Morera, Arauzo-Azofra and Garcia-Hernandez, 2012). This paper details the study behind this serious game, including its development and the decisions made to optimize its results. Supported by several studies that defend the advantages of gamification as a teaching measure, our work seeks to integrate serious games as a scientifically based tool in the teaching process of renewable energies.

Carried out within the scope of the European project SECOVE (Centers of Professional Excellence in Sustainable Energy), this study aims to integrate serious games as a scientifically based tool in the teaching process of renewable energies.

The paper is organized into distinct sections that cover various aspects, including exploring relevant learning theories establishing guidelines for developing educational games, examining the flow experience, comparative analysis of similar games, detailed presentation of the design process, and solution development, comprehensively evaluating game performance and offering insightful suggestions for future research and improvements.

2. STATE OF ART

To develop this game, a study on the important characteristics most games should contain was made. This was also accompanied by a study on important characteristics of didactic games as well as actual didactic games developed by other people.

2.1 Learning Theories

There are many effective ways to teach students about a specific topic. An effective method to improve the students' learning is using quizzes, which takes advantage of the "testing effect" (Sanchez, 2020). This effect suggests that the students experience increased retention of learned knowledge and/or skills by retrieving material through testing (Larsen, 2013). Having this in mind, a game can be designed around the use of quizzes as a learning tool so that the average student can learn from playing the game. This approach also allows the game to be easily adapted to the students, as the quizzes can be created by their teacher, who is familiar with their class and their knowledge on the subject, making it easier to introduce in a classroom environment.

2.2 General Game Development Guidelines

When designing a Digital Educational Game (DEG), there are some characteristics that help making the game objectively better and more attractive to the player. These points were established as sort of guidelines when designing the game so that the average player has a better time playing the game and, because of that, learn more about the subject. (Balci, 2015). These guidelines are:

- Challengeability: Provide the player with difficulty so that he does not get bored;
- Effectiveness: How effective the game is at teaching the subject;
- Engageability: How much game captures and holds the player's attention;
- Enjoyability: Make the game fun and enjoyable to play;
- Interactivity: How much the player interacts with the game;
- Transformativeness: The game could be adapted to various types of players according to their skills and knowledge;
- Usability: How easy the game is to use and provide a player-friendly experience;

These were believed to be some of the most important aspects to consider when developing this game. As mentioned, they were used as guidelines but also as metrics to measure the final product and its various characteristics.

2.3 Flow Experience

Another important characteristic of a game is the flow experience. When playing a game, the intention is for the player to become immersed in it. This immersion can be characterized as "flow". During the state of "flow", the player tends to become concentrated, lose track of time, lose self-awareness, and have an overall positive experience. For example, in sports, although winning is important, "flow" does not depend solely on it, "flow" offers more than just victory. Similarly, in games, what matters is not only the outcome but also the experience of playing the game itself. "Flow" acts like a rope that binds players and encourages them to play the game repeatedly (Kiilia, 2012).

Figure 1 illustrates that a game needs to strike a good balance between challenge and skill for the player to engage effectively. For instance, if the game presents a significant challenge that the player struggles to overcome, they may experience anxiety, but if the game is too easy, the player becomes bored. Therefore, achieving a good balance between these two elements is crucial for the player to enter the flow state.

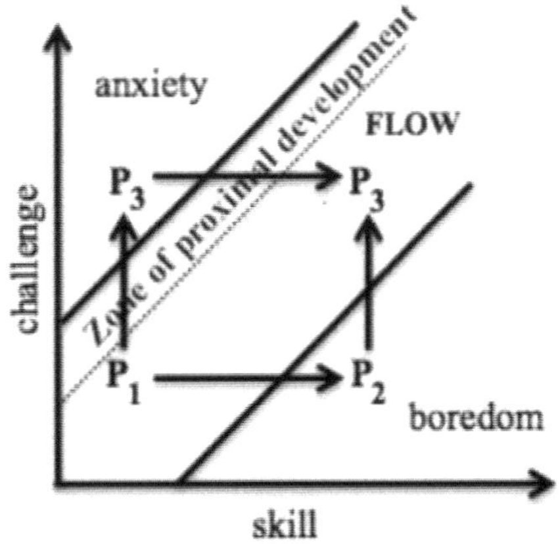

Figure 1. Graph about skill and challenge proportions (Kiilia, 2012)

2.4 Related Work

Before an elaborative approach, some games which have similar content to the intended one were studied. By examining these works, valuable insights into effective mechanics and innovative ideas were gained, thereby informing, and enriching the approach towards developing the intended game. The studied games were "Power Up" and "Siemens Energy Island" which are two games focused on teaching the player about renewable and sustainable energies.

2.4.1 Power Up

This game simulates the role of an "Energy Engineer" tasked with restoring energy to a country facing shortages, prioritizing environmentally friendly methods. While the game concept is promising, its execution feels disjointed and lacks coherence, leaving players confused. Although the player learns to choose appropriate energy sources for each state, the primary learning component revolves around answering end-of-level questions for additional points. However, the game itself provides limited educational content and information.

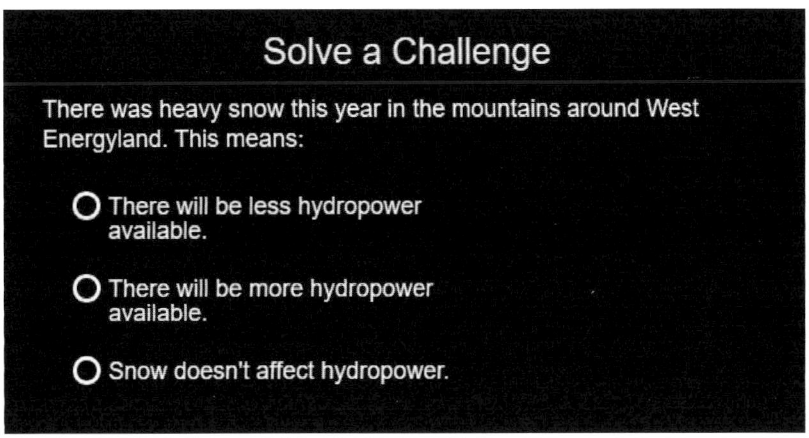

Figure 2. Example of question (Source: Power Up)

The questions component feels good to use as some source of learning in a game. It gives the player a need to get the answer right and provides some type of challenge. The questions can also spite some interest on the player about the topic, making him search on his own and learn more about it.

2.4.2 Siemens Energy Island

Siemens Energy Island (see Figure 3) is another game designed to educate players about renewable energies. In this game, players place various energy sources strategically on an island to power up a city. However, the gameplay is simplistic and requires little strategic thinking. While the game introduces renewable energy sources with brief descriptions, it lacks depth in teaching the topic. Nevertheless, the game's layout shows potential for improvement if approached differently.

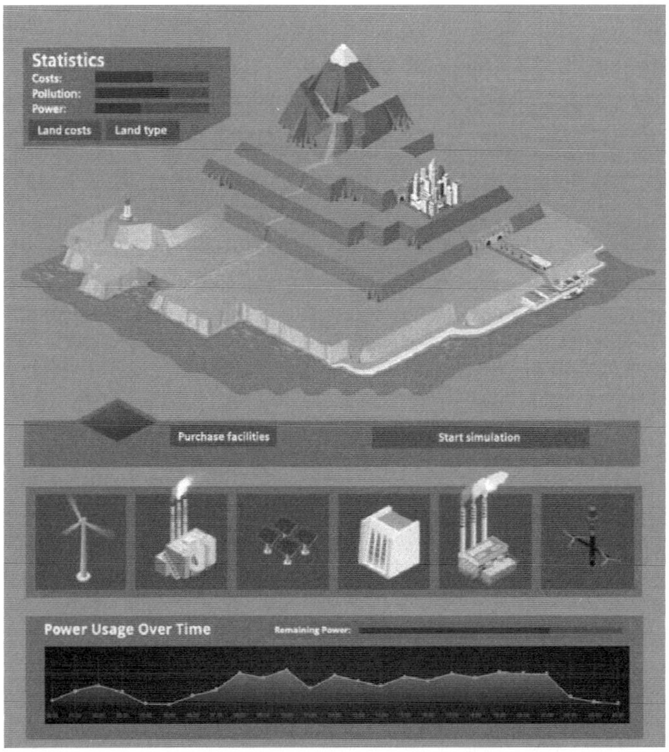

Figure 3. Layout of the game Siemens Energy Island (Source: Siemens Energy Island)

The gameplay feels satisfying, only needing a little bit more challengeability for it to be more entertaining. The learning component from this game is the small description of each energy source, as well as the optimal locations for each one of them.

2.5 Conclusion

To summarize, both games present their own merits and demerits, serving as valuable educational tools for players. Siemens Energy Island excels with its core gameplay and comprehensive explanations of energy sources, offering engaging mechanics that enhance learning. Conversely, Power Up stands out with its thought-provoking questions, enriching players' knowledge and sparking curiosity. These essential aspects were thoroughly evaluated during the project's development, alongside other significant factors.

3. METHODOLOGY

The methodology used in this study covered several stages, from the analysis of the state of the art to the development and evaluation of the didactic game on renewable and sustainable energy.

To develop the game, comprehensive research was carried out on the essential features that most games should contain, as well as on the specific features of existing teaching games. This analysis included an in-depth review of similar games such as "Power Up" and "Siemens Energy Island" to gain insights into effective mechanics and innovative ideas.

Several learning theories relevant to game development were explored. In particular, the use of quizzes as a teaching method was highlighted to take advantage of the "testing effect", which improves knowledge retention through active retrieval of studied material.

Guidelines for game development were established, including aspects such as challenge, effectiveness, involvement, fun, interactivity, transformation, and usability. These guidelines were used as a reference throughout the game design process.

The importance of experience flow in games and its impact on player immersion and the quality of the overall experience while playing was recognized. Efforts were made to appropriately balance game challenges with player skills to promote entry into flow state.

An in-depth study of similar games was conducted to gain insights into effective mechanics and innovative ideas that could enrich the development of our teaching game on renewable and sustainable energy.

Furthermore, the choices made during the solution design and development process prioritized the game's educational objectives over technical issues, and the testing and evaluation process was detailed, including the validation of the game's effectiveness as an educational tool with university students.

The game was evaluated using a form created to collect information about various aspects of the game and the user experience. The points evaluated included:

- Game mechanics: Assessment of the effectiveness of game mechanics in providing an engaging and challenging experience.
- Gameplay Experience: Overall assessment of the user experience when playing the game, including ease of use, clarity of instructions, and quality of the user interface.
- Teaching component: Assessment of the game's ability to teach players about renewable energy, including the relevance and accuracy of the information provided.
- User feedback: Collecting feedback from players about their perceptions and suggestions for game improvements.
- Replayability: Assessment of the game's ability to motivate players to play again, considering different strategies and challenges.

The evaluation was made by a class of participants who were mostly male and university students. Their ages ranged between 18 and 22 years old and possessed basic knowledge on the topic of renewable energies. After playing the game, they filled out the evaluation form, providing their opinions and suggestions for future improvements. The evaluation results were analyzed to identify the game's strengths and areas for improvement, guiding the development of future versions.

This comprehensive methodology allowed the development of an adaptable educational game, designed to teach about renewable and sustainable energy in an effective and attractive way.

4. DESIGN AND DEVELOPMENT OF THE SOLUTION

Taking advantage of the last chapter, a solution was devised, incorporating most of the elements discussed there.

4.1 Proposed Solution

The solution designed for this problem is a game called Energy Valley, a strategy game that combines elements from Siemens Energy Island and questions like those on the game Power Up. In Energy Valley (see Figures 4 and 5), the player's objective is to supply increasing energy demands to a city each day. The player must strategically place available energy sources across the map, with each tile possessing unique characteristics. Careful placement is crucial to meet daily energy requirements. Upon placing an energy source, the player faces a topic-related question which, if answered correctly, provides an energy boost.

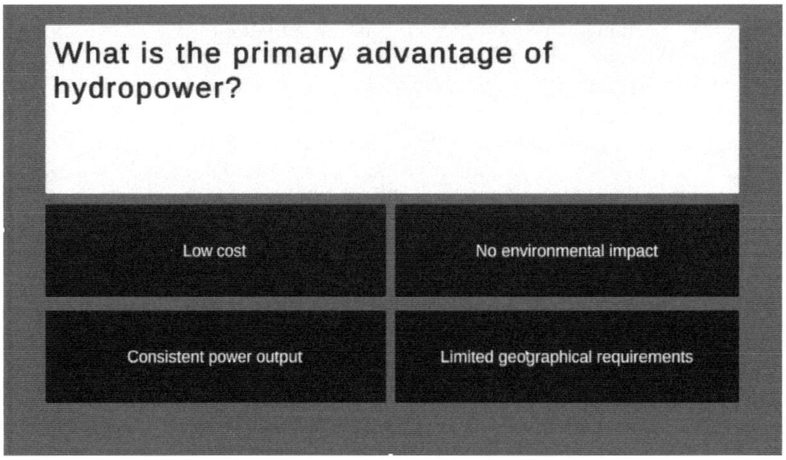

Figure 4. Question example (Source: Energy Valley)

The player operates within a limited budget, aiming to meet the energy quota. Successful completion of each day grants additional funds and changes the climate on each tile, introducing new challenges. If the player fails to meet the energy quota, the game ends, and the player's score, based on the number of days with sustained energy and the total energy provided each day, is saved in a global database. This competitive aspect motivates players to strive for better performance.

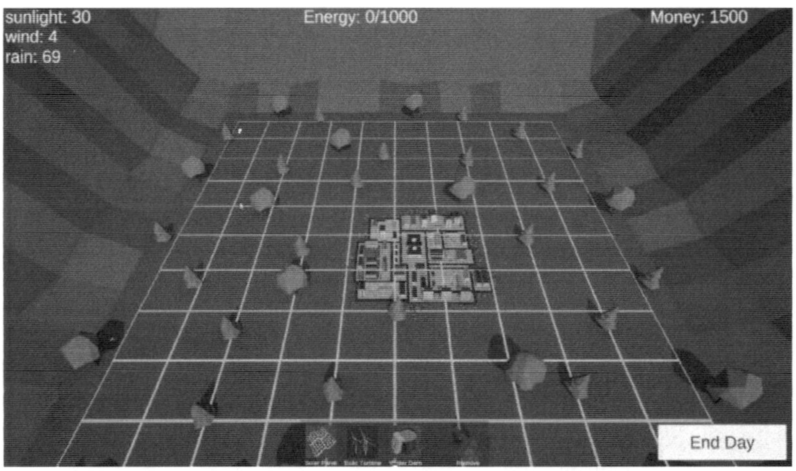

Figure 5. Print from the game's prototype (Source: Energy Valley)

This game aims to provide players with a challenging experience of managing resources while imparting diverse knowledge on the chosen topic. By giving players limited funds and an explanation of the game mechanics, they immerse themselves in the gameplay, striving to optimize energy placements within their budget constraints. Throughout the game, players are periodically prompted to answer questions about renewable energies, including their pros, cons, and other relevant facts. This solution also considers players' varying levels of knowledge by allowing certified individuals to customize questions based on each player's proficiency in the topic which makes it more suitable for classroom use.

Overall, this game serves not only as a form of gamified education but also as an innovative tool for classroom instruction on renewable energies. It aims to assist teachers in guiding their students through the learning process on this important topic.

4.2 Development of the Solution

To develop this solution, certain choices were made that prioritize the game's objectives over engineering efficiency. For instance, instead of saving questions in online databases, they are saved locally to allow offline gameplay (excluding access to the leaderboard) and ensure that altered questions are specific to each teacher's class. In Figure 6, we observe the game's question menu, sourced directly from Energy Valley.

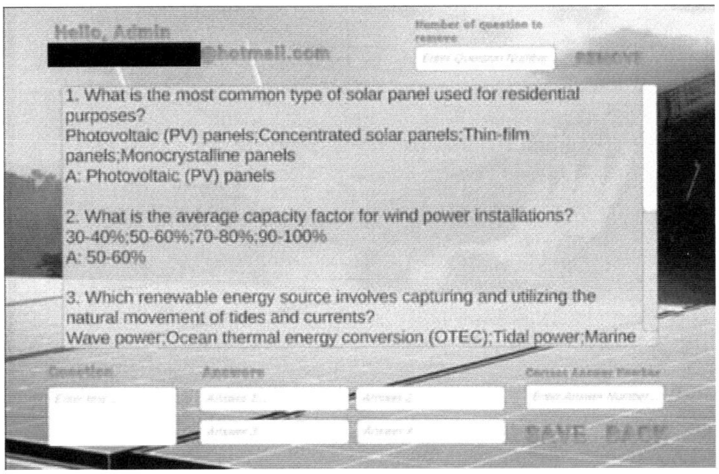

Figure 6. Print from the game's question menu (Source: Energy Valley)

The game features a grid where players place selected objects, triggering a question with multiple-choice answers. Upon selection, the answer is revealed, and the object appears on the grid, with total energy recalculated based on the player's response. Certain individuals can access a menu containing game questions, allowing the questions to be changed. These are the main features from the game. There is also a simple leaderboard where the players can see the top 10 results from everyone who played the game from all around the world.

5. SOLUTION EVALUATION

To evaluate the solution, a form was created to evaluate a few points from the ones previously mentioned on the research, such as the game mechanics, the gameplay experience by the user, the teaching component of the game, the feedback the user felt from what he was doing and the replayability of the game. The solution was tested by university students with basic knowledge on the topic, who played the game and reported their experience on the form. Most of those points received a good score overall with an average of 4.2 out of 5 on categories such as game mechanics, gameplay experience and teaching component. These parts were classified as the better components of the game from the students who tested the game. On the other hand, the feedback component was reported to be lacking as the game appeared to not provide enough feedback to the player about the result of his actions. This means that when the players performed an action (for example placing an energy source and answering a question), they were left with little clue of the impact of their actions. This also applied to the instructions for the game that, in their opinion, were not as clear as expected. For future work, the game could be more developed so that it could have a more diverse set and style of questions, as well as improving the existing ones. It could also accommodate some requests from the players such as a clearer feedback system to the player, a better layout for the game's UI and the possibility to choose the questions' difficulty. The map could also be expanded and with even more possibilities for different maps which could improve the replayability of the game even more.

ACKNOWLEDGEMENT

This project was developed as part of the European project with the reference number 101056201—SECOVE-ERASMUS-EDU-2021-PEX-COVE.ERASMUS-LS.

REFERENCES

Balci, S. A., (2015), March 2). SIMULATION. GAMED: digital educational game development methodology, pp. 307 - 319.

Csikszentmihalyi, M., (1990). FLOW: The Psychology of Optimal Experience. Harper and Row. Retrieved from Flow (psychology): https://en.wikipedia.org/wiki/Flow_(psychology)

D, L., (2013). When I say ... test-enhanced learning. Medical Education, 961.

Kiilia, K., (2012). The Design Principles for Flow Experience in Educational Games. Virtual Worlds for Serious Applications (VS-GAMES'12), p. 14.

Salas-Morera, Loernzo & Arauzo-Azofra, Antonio & Garcia-Hernandez, Laura., (2012). Analysis of online quizzes as a teaching and assessment tool. Journal of Technology and Science Education. 2. 39-45. 10.3926/jotse.30.

My American Farm., n.d.. Power Up. Retrieved from http://www.myamericanfarm.org/games/power-up

Sanchez D, L. M., (2020). Gamification in the classroom: Examining the impact of gamified quizzes on student learning. Computers and Education, 144.

Siemens Energy., n.d.. Siemens Energy Island. Retrieved from https://energyislandgame.co.uk/

Staff, I., (2022). THE GOOD AND THE BAD EFFECTS OF VIDEO GAMES ON CHILDREN. Retrieved from Institute for Educational Advancement: https://educationaladvancement.org/blog-the-good-and-the-bad-effects-of-video-games-on-children/

DIGITAL LEGACY IN A DIGITAL WORLD

Thomas Keller, Mirella Moser and Hugo Bossi
ZHAW School of Management and Law, Winterthur, Switzerland

ABSTRACT

This paper explores the evolving concept of digital legacies within the context of rapidly advancing technologies. Acknowledging the human desire to be remembered, it probes the transformative potential of digital "memory boxes" which, fueled by the digital footprints left behind, could extend interaction with the deceased beyond traditional remembrance methods. With the proliferation of large language models and AI-driven creativity tools in 2023, the research delves into the psychological and societal implications of sustaining post-mortem communication through digital avatars, chatbots, and holograms. The objective is to delineate the imaginable from the desirable, bridging the gap between technological feasibility and personal or societal acceptance. Employing science fiction prototyping, the study gauges public sentiment on digital legacies before and after exposure to immersive, multilinear narratives that simulate potential future experiences. This approach aims to discern whether direct engagement with such scenarios alters perceptions and desires around digital inheritance. Methodologically, the study commences with forecasting technological advancements likely to impact digital legacies. Participants' pre- and post-experience attitudes were then measured, focusing on their openness to various digital legacy technologies and their reactions to the ethical and emotional complexities presented. Results revealed that while futuristic digital legacies are broadly conceivable, they are not uniformly desired, with preferences not varying by demographic factors such as age and education level. Notably, the experience of the multilinear narrative influenced attitudes, enhancing both the imaginability and the desirability of such technologies, although to varying degrees. The discussion posits that while conceivable digital legacies are not universally appealing, the act of experiencing multilinear narratives shifts perceptions. Consequently, this indicates a potential misalignment between technological trajectories and public aspirations. The conclusion calls for an inclusive discourse to actively shape a future in alignment with collective values, rather than passively inheriting a future shaped solely by technological advances. The study underscores the importance of public engagement in the development and adoption of emerging technologies, particularly those with profound personal and cultural implications.

KEYWORDS

Digital Legacy, Science Fiction Prototyping, Multilinear Narratives, Digital Avatars, Chatbots, Holograms

1. INTRODUCTION

Harari (2018) describes the pursuit of eternal life as one of humanity's great projects. Eternal life is - at least today - not yet possible. Every person is therefore mortal - "unless they are remembered" (Meise, 2017, p. 158). There are various ways and means of remembering a deceased person. For example, one website that aims to provide guidance on this says: "There may be videos, sound recordings and certainly photos that have been collected over a lifetime; they become a documentation of life. Objects can be stored in a "memory box". A photo album is created with the collected photos. [...] Later, looking at it brings back memories" (*Grief - Loving Remembrance And Commemoration*, n.d.). Looking at today's and, above all, future technological possibilities, this "memory box" could look significantly different than in the past. For example, it could take the form of a chatbot, an avatar in the metaverse, a hologram or a humanoid robot.

Looking back, 2023 seems to be the year of artificial intelligence. With Large Language Models, writing and image programs based on artificial intelligence, which require a certain kind of creativity, became known to a wider public worldwide. The possibilities that are opening up here are probably just the beginning.

In the area of digital estates, there are already initial examples of applications that can have a disturbing effect. Would I like to be able to continue talking to my deceased father after his death, as James Vlahos (Deutschlandfunk Nova, 2017) can with his "Dadbot"? Or is it desirable for parents to be able to meet their dead child again in a virtual world, as a South Korean TV show enabled a mother to do? (BILD, 2020)

In any case, the first start-ups have recognized the potential of offering services for interacting with deceased people beyond their death (Huber, 2022).

What are still isolated cases today are likely to become more widespread in the future as technology develops.

"Too often, technological progress is described as fate. As a fate that befalls us, or as one that redeems us. Don't let that fool you. Artificial intelligence is not a destiny, but a tool. The time has come to look at what this tool can do. [...] because now the rules of the game are being made for the time to come." (Fulterer, 2022)

2. RESEARCH OBJECTIVES

Increasing digitization is generating ever larger amounts of data, including a lot of personal data that is generated and stored consciously or unconsciously. This can be used to construct personal digital "memory boxes" - possibly even without the knowledge or consent of the persons concerned.

This work is intended to explore the question of what such possible "memory boxes" could be and which of them are desirable. The aim is to initiate a discourse on this topic, which in turn should serve to shape the future as we would like it to be - so that we do not suddenly find ourselves in a future that we never wanted.

This work aims to investigate the potential gap between imaginability and desirability and actual behavior using sci-fi prototyping. It explores the question of people's attitudes towards a possible future digital legacy and what they would like to see in this regard.

The research questions of this thesis are:

1. What are conceivable future digital legacies?
2. What is desirable and what is rejected?
3. Does the attitude change if someone can experience the consequences of his/her decision as an example?

3. RELATED WORK

Many works that deal with the topic of "digital inheritance" look at it primarily from a legal perspective, often supplemented by a technical view. However, they also address the question of what the digital legacy is about and what it entails (Frauenhofer SIT, 2019; Brucker-Kley et al., 2013). This includes, for example, online accounts and who has the rights to these accounts after death and how access is regulated or how they can be deleted. The handling of digital contracts, social media accounts, online bank accounts and digital currencies is also considered. From this, it can be deduced what to look out for in digital estate planning (Lötscher, 2021; Frauenhofer SIT, 2019; Hrubesch-Hrubesch-Millauer et al., 2021).

In addition to presenting the rights and obligations as well as the legal framework, Brucker-Kley et al. (2013) aimed to sensitize internet users to the topic of digital legacy. In this context, the tension between the right to be forgotten and the preservation of a digital memory is discussed, among other things.

The UNESCO Charter on Digital Heritage adopted in 2003 has a different focus (UNESCO, 2003). This was issued due to the concern that information resources are increasingly available in digital form, are often ephemeral and require targeted production, maintenance and management in order to be preserved. The aim of the Charter is to make digital information accessible to future generations.

The website dead.work draws attention to the fact that people can "come back to life" after their death through the use of technology. Digital employment after death is on the rise. The website therefore offers the option of declaring whether you allow - or not - personal data to be used and used with AI after death (*D.E.A.D. Digital Employment After Death*, 2020).

TA-Swiss, which has the task of investigating the opportunities and risks of new technologies, is currently conducting a project entitled "Death in the digital age". According to the project tender, this interdisciplinary study "aims to assess the opportunities and risks of technologies in the areas of end-of-life care, management of digital data of the deceased and mourning work" (TA-Swiss, 2021a). Beyond the legal context, the study will shed light on ethical aspects, intellectual property and new norms and rituals in bereavement work. In addition to raising awareness, it is also planned to formulate recommendations for action for politicians, funeral professionals and the general public.

Savin-Baden (2022) examines the topic of AI from various angles in her book "AI for Death and Dying". Among other things, she addresses the topic of digital immortality. However, she focuses on current developments in the field of artificial intelligence, such as the technical creation of a digital human - and less on conceivable future, imaginable or desirable developments (Savin-Baden, 2022, pp. 148-152).

In summary, it can be said that a significant proportion of the articles that deal with the topic of digital inheritance do so from a legal perspective. They place a strong emphasis on technologies that have emerged in recent years. However, no study could be found that deals with which future technologies are conceivable for the population in this context or which form of digital inheritance people would like to see.

4. METHODOLOGY

To create the conditions for answering the first research question, research was carried out to investigate which technological developments are currently underway or can be expected in the foreseeable future that could have an impact on the topic of digital legacies. From this, the possible future digital legacies were derived. A selection had already been made which will represent the technological leaps in the narrative later in the study. Various people were asked what they personally can imagine and what they would like or reject.

With the help of multilinear stories, the interviewees then immersed themselves in the future world, where they experienced how their decisions for or against a technology (or one or other form of digital legacy) can have an impact. The third research question is intended to answer whether people's attitudes towards the imaginable legacies have changed or solidified as a result of the experience - i.e. whether there are deviations from the survey before the experience.

The procedure and methodology for this work are shown in Figure 1 and described below.

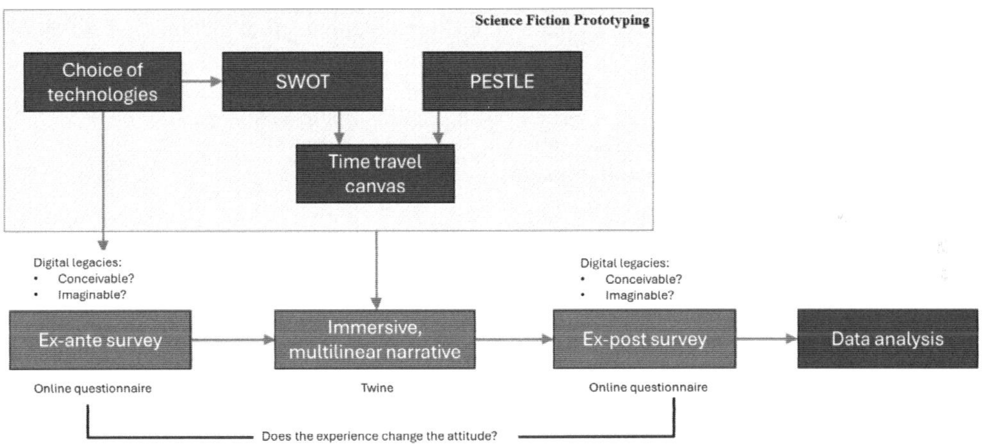

Figure 1. Methodology

Based on research, possible technologies that could have an impact on future forms of a digital legacy were identified and analyzed using a SWOT analysis (Nagel et al., 2020). These technologies then served as the basis for further work. A preselection of technologies was therefore made, which are then presented to the participants in the survey as possible digital legacies.

PESTEL analysis (Nagel et al., 2020) was used to describe the influencing factors that affect the environment of the story and its scenarios. The different scenarios (Steinmüller, 2012; Kosow & Gaßner, 2008) for the multilinear story were developed using the science fiction prototyping method (Brucker-Kley, 2023; Johnson et al., 2011; Merrie et al., 2018). The story should make the possible futures tangible for the interviewees and show them the possible consequences of their decisions. The multilinear story was implemented using a twine[1].

By means of a standardized online survey (Wagner-Schelewsky & Hering, 2019) people were asked about their attitude to possible forms of digital legacy (ex-ante survey). What do they consider desirable, what do they reject (Helmrich & Zika, 2019)? They then had the opportunity to create a multilinear story (Brucker-Kley & Keller, 2019) in which they reach different points where they have to decide for or against a technology. Depending on the decision, the story continues differently, but can also lead back together again. This story should enable the test subjects to immerse themselves in the future and experience it and the effects of their decisions.

After the end of the story, the participants were asked again about their attitude towards the various forms of digital legacy. This ex-post survey was compared with the one before the story so that it can be determined whether attitudes have changed or not due to the fact that the test subjects were placed in the future and presented with possible consequences of their decisions.

5. THE MULTILINEAR NARRATIVE

5.1 Conceptualization

"Key technologies are technical prerequisites or enablers (devices, components, applications, processes, algorithms, etc.) that implement a technological concept now and in the future for a specific application domain" (Keller, 2022).

In order to find out which key technologies are relevant to the issue and the scenario field, various trend analyses were reviewed for this study in addition to a literature review and internet search, with the focus on these three:

- Megatrends of the Zukunftsinstitut (*The Megatrend Map*, 2022)
- Technology Predictions Report of the IEEE Computer Society (Technology Predictions, 2022)
- TA-Swiss call for projects on "Death in the digital age" (TA-Swiss, 2021b)

These trend analyses were analyzed with a focus on which of them could have a connection to the digital legacy. Based on the questions formulated for this thesis, the following key technologies were classified as particularly relevant:

- Next Gen Remote Presence, includes augmented reality, virtual reality, holograms, etc.
- Social networks, communication networks
- Artificial intelligence
- Big data (and data storage)
- Humanoid robots and chatbots, incl. NLP
- Brain-Copy

In a second step, a time travel canvas is created based on a SWOT and PESTEL analysis. This time travel canvas represents a morphological box and is therefore a creativity technique (Schawel & Billing, 2018). It provides a basic framework for developing the scenarios for the multi-linear story. The canvas contains three different temporal levels:

- Stage 1: Near future
- Stage 2: Distant future
- Stage 3: Far future

In terms of time, it is not precisely defined in how many years which future is to be classified. The respective stages are not primarily characterized by leaps in time, but by leaps in technology. Different scenes are created for the individual technological leaps in which the story will take place. The following technological leaps were selected for the development of the story:

- Chatbot
- Avatar in augmented reality
- Humanoid robot with a brain trained on humans

[1] https://twinery.org/

In a third step, the narrative is developed as a science fiction prototype. According to Johnson et al. (2011, p. 7) a science fiction (SF) prototype is a short story, movie or comic created based on real science and technology. What is special about science fiction prototypes is that they explicitly use fictional entities as a step or input in the development process. In the present work, the SF prototype is a multi-linear story.

The aim of SF prototypes "is to start a conversation about technology and the future." (Johnson et al., 2011, p. 23). The process of creating an SF prototype according to Johnson et al. (2011, pp. 50-62) can be divided into 5 steps:

- Step 1: Pick Your Science and Build Your World: this is about choosing the technology for the story, defining the setting and the protagonists.
- Step 2: The Scientific Inflection Point: Introduction and explanation of the technology to be explored in the prototype.
- Step 3: Ramification of the Science on People: What are the effects of technology and what impact does it have on people's lives?
- Step 4: The Human Inflection Point: What can we learn from seeing the technology used in a realistic environment? Does anything need to be changed?
- Step 5: What Did We Learn? What are the impacts on people? Solutions and impacts from step 4 should be investigated.

5.2 Implementation

The creation of the artifact represents an iterative process in which a version of the prototype is created, evaluated and further improved. Schematically, this procedure is based on that of the Building, Intervention and Evaluation (BIE) cycle, which is used in the context of Action Design Research (ADR).

The tool used is Twinery, an open source software for interactive, multilinear storytelling. For the present work, the artifact was created using version 2.6.2 and the Harlowe 3.3.5 story format. The story can be exported as an html file and thus made online accessible to readers at (Bossi et al., 2024).

The final version of the story comprises 49 sections. These can be summarized according to the course of the story in the following sections:

1. **Introduction and pre-test**: greeting, instructions for readers, collection of personal data, survey on attitudes towards technology, selection of the name for the story
2. **Near future**: Introduction to the setting, technology is a chatbot; reader:in visits father in hospital; he is suffering from incurable cancer and then dies.
3. **Distant future**: time jump and introduction to the setting; technology is a so-called Future Companion, an AR application. Reader is married and has a young daughter. The spouse has a fatal accident.
4. **Far future**: time jump and introduction to the scenery. The technology is a humanoid robot. Reader is about to retire; he/she remarried a few years ago. The partner dies.
5. **Post-test and conclusion**: Survey on attitudes to technology, opportunity to submit comments, data transfer to Limesurvey.

At the end of each section, the reader is given the choice of how the story should continue. The choice is about whether the person decides in favor of or against the use of a technology. In some cases, it is also possible to return to decisions made earlier and decide against or in favor of a technology. The possible decision points are shown in Figure 2 illustrated.

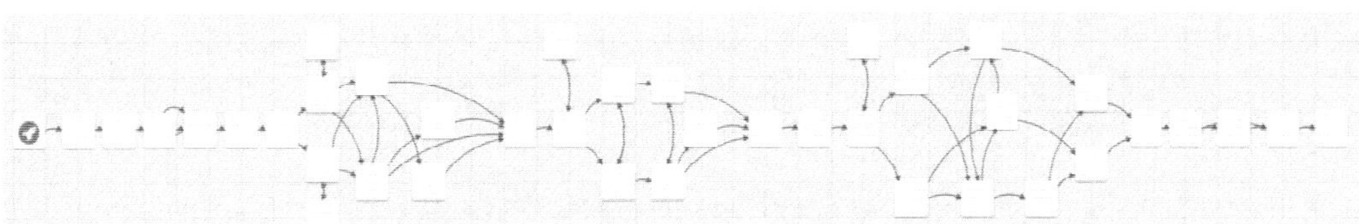

Figure 2. Structure of the multilinear narrative

6. THE SURVEY

Figure 3 provides an initial overview of the results of the survey on the conceivability and desirability of the various technologies. The "chatbot" technology is used as an example to illustrate the figure: The participants in the survey were asked both before and after going through the multilinear story whether this technology is conceivable for them. Accordingly, the results before and after the survey are shown below. It can be seen that the results of the ex-ante survey are not identical to those of the ex-post survey. The green shares have increased, which means that respondents were more likely to imagine the "chatbot" technology after the story. They were also asked how desirable they considered this technology to be. Here too, this has changed for the chatbot to the effect that desirability has increased for the respondents. However, it can also be seen from the figure that chatbot technology was rated much higher in terms of conceivability than desirability.

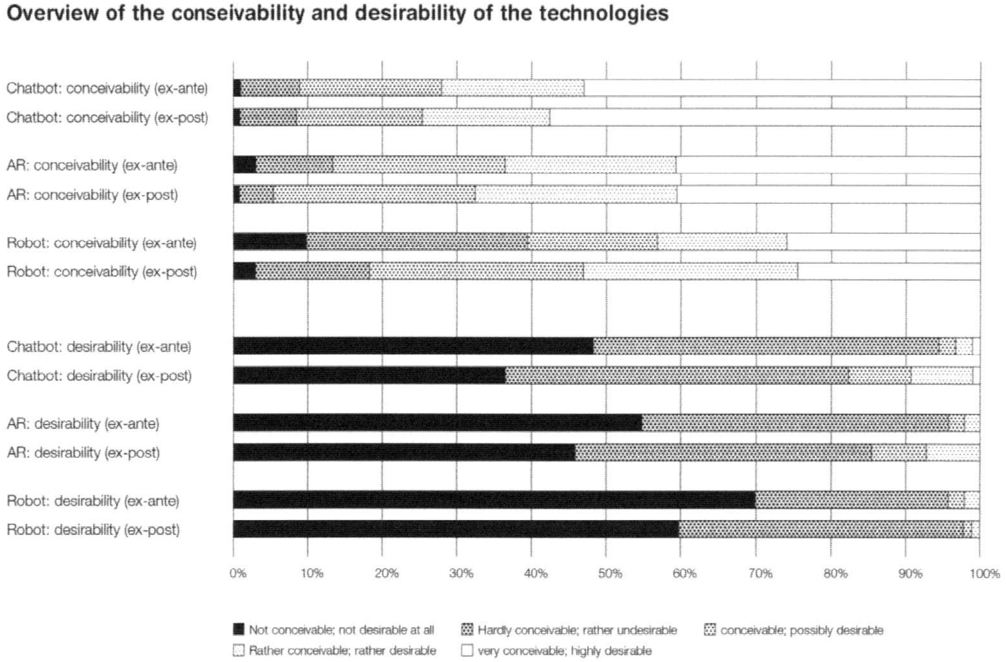

Figure 3. Overview of survey results

From Figure 3 the following two statements can be derived:

1. The people surveyed can imagine the technologies quite well. However, they were rated between "not at all desirable" and "rather undesirable".
2. There is a recognizable difference between the ex-ante and ex-post survey. Both imaginability and desirability increased after playing through the story.

7. DISCUSSION

What are conceivable future digital legacies?

Based on research work, the following technologies were selected as digital legacies for further work and the survey:

- Chatbot with AI (digital assistant) and the voice of the deceased person
- Future Companion (AR application) as a digital image of the deceased person, can be used with AR glasses.

- Humanoid robot, with the appearance of the deceased person and trained on that person's brain.

Survey results indicate these concepts are within the realm of imagination for most participants. The further the technology is in the future (i.e. chatbot -> future companion/AR -> robot), the more the conceivability decreases somewhat, but is still quite high. These technologies are therefore rated as fairly realistic overall.

However, there are hardly any differences between the various groups of people in this respect. Only in relation to the level of education was it found that people with a higher (tertiary) level of education were more likely to be able to imagine the technologies than others.

What is desirable and what is rejected?

Although the forms of digital legacy mentioned above are conceivable, they are largely not considered desirable. The least rejected technology is the chatbot. But the further we look into the future, the more the technology is rejected.

There were also hardly any differences between the various groups of people in terms of desirability. The only difference was in age: younger people considered the technologies to be slightly more desirable overall than older people.

Does the attitude change if someone can experience the consequences of his/her decision as an example?

It could be shown that the attitude towards the conceivability and desirability of the technologies was different before the story than after playing through the multilinear story. This is attributed to the fact that the people were able to experience both the technologies themselves and the effects of their decisions.

The changes took place in such a way that the readers were both more able to imagine the forms of digital legacy presented after the story and also considered them more desirable. This applies not only on an aggregated level, but also for the individual technologies. Only for the imaginability of the chatbot and the desirability of the robot no significant change could be demonstrated. The fact that no such change took place here may be due to the fact that this concerns the most pronounced aspects: the chatbot was already the most imaginable before the story; and the robot was considered the least desirable.

In addition, two areas that are not directly related to the research question but can provide clues for its interpretation should be briefly discussed here. These are, firstly, the path that the readers took and, secondly, the comments that they were able to leave as free text. In the narrative, it was possible at certain points to choose a technology (chatbot, AR application) without it taking on the voice or appearance of the deceased person. The path shows that this option was chosen more often than the personalized variant (but still less than the low-tech variant). It is possible that a "copy" of a deceased person (or parts of them) simply goes a little too far for respondents in terms of what is desirable. This is confirmed, for example, by the following comment: "I would probably find non-human assistants helpful, but not in the form of loved ones."

In summary, it can be said that the forms of digital legacy presented are quite conceivable. However, they are not considered desirable. And experiencing them through the multi-linear story has led to a change in attitude in that the technologies have become more imaginable and slightly more desirable.

8. CONCLUSION

This work has revealed a discrepancy that can be pointedly expressed as follows: the digital legacies shown are realistic, but not desired. This raises the question of how this realization can and should be dealt with. There will hardly be a simple solution. A broad-based debate on future technologies and their desirability seems appropriate. In addition to this discrepancy between what is feasible and what is desirable, there are still many unanswered questions in this context that have not been addressed in this paper. These include religious, legal, psychological, social and various other issues.

Individual comments from respondents are quoted here to illustrate this. One person said: "It would be nice if people were actually asked so openly about future developments and could thus actively influence them - but the reality will once again be that everything that is technically possible will come anyway." The statement contains two components. Firstly, the suggestion that people should be more involved in such discussions about future technical developments. On the other hand, it also has a resigned character, which is expressed in the belief that everything that is technically possible will come anyway. It will probably be up to everyone to decide for themselves whether they want to use these technologies and to make these decisions consciously. However, these technologies are often simply used, as another comment suggests: "I don't think it's desirable for such technologies to be used, but I believe that they would be used and that I would use them if they existed." In addition to the individual level, politicians will also be called upon to lead this discourse, as will private, public and non-profit organizations.

What the work has shown is that there is no divide between the different groups of people (e.g. in terms of gender, age). This can be seen as positive and can be interpreted as meaning that society as a whole is challenged - and not just individual groups of people.

"I notice that the gap between what is feasible and what is desirable is widening," someone commented in the survey. Realizing this is a first step towards helping to shape the future. Because, as mentioned at the beginning of the work, without debate and discourse, we suddenly find ourselves in a future that we never wanted. The aim of this work was to initiate this discourse. As the concluding quote from another comment shows, this has been achieved, at least on a small scale: "Thanks for the suggestion!"

REFERENCES

Borg, I. (2003). *Management instrument employee survey: Theorien, Tools und Praxiserfahrungen (*3rd, revised and expanded ed.). Hogrefe, Publ. for Psychology.

Bossi, H., & Keller, T. (2024, March 20). MyDigitalLegacy. Retrieved from osf.io/9f3aw

Brucker-Kley, E. (2023, November 28). *Experience friendship with AI immersively - science fiction prototyping for responsible innovation* [Event Dissemination]. ZHAW Information Systems. https://www.zhaw.ch/de/linguistik/institute-zentren/iam/veranstaltungen/iam-veranstaltungen-detailansicht/event-news/freundschaft-mit-ki-immersiv-erleben-science-fiction-prototyping-fuer-verantwortungsvolle-innovationen/

Brucker-Kley, E., & Keller, T. (2019). *Exploring the potential of immersive narrative scenarios to identify design criteria for our digital future(s)*. 499–504. https://doi.org/10.1109/IIAI-AAI.2019.00108

Brucker-Kley, E., Keller, T., Kurtz, L., Pärli, K., Schweizer, M., & Studer, M. (2013). *Sterben und Erben in der digitalen Welt* (ZHAW, Ed.). vdf Hochschulverlag AG. https://doi.org/10.3218/3546-9

D.E.A.D. Digital Employment After Death. (2020). https://dead.work/en/

Deutschlandfunk Nova. (2017, November 27). *Chatbot: Talking on after death*. Deutschlandfunk Nova. https://www.deutschlandfunknova.de/beitrag/kuenstliche-intelligenz-vater-als-chatbot

Frauenhofer SIT. (2019). *The digital legacy. An investigation from a legal and technical perspective.* Fraunhofer-Gesellschaft. https://publica.fraunhofer.de/handle/publica/300017

Fulterer, R. (2022, December 17). What remains for man? *NZZ*, 1.

Harari, Y. N. (2018). *Homo Deus: A History of Tomorrow* (A. Wirthensohn, Trans.; 13th ed.). C.H. Beck.

Helmrich, R., & Zika, G. (2019). Forecasts, projections and scenarios. In N. Baur & J. Blasius (Eds.), *Handbook of methods in empirical social research* (pp. 231-246). Springer Fachmedien Wiesbaden. https://doi.org/10.1007/978-3-658-21308-4_15

Hrubesch-Millauer, S., Wolf, S., & Eggel, M. (Eds.). (2021). *Digital Inheritance Law - Perspectives from Switzerland: Contributions on the Influence of the "Digital" on Inheritance Law and Inheritance Planning*. Nomos.

Huber, D. (2022, November 6). *When the dead talk - start-ups create virtual versions of the deceased*. watson.ch. https://www.watson.ch/!446276751

IEEE (Ed.). (2022). *Technology Predictions*. IEEE Computer Society. https://ieeecs-media.computer.org/media/tech-news/tech-predictions-report-2022.pdf

IMAGE (Director). (2020, February 13). *Mother meets her deceased daughter again.* https://www.youtube.com/watch?v=mB6h18_lg3I

Johnson, B. D., Frenkel, J., Doctorow, C., Warner, C., & Perkowitz, S. (2011). *Science fiction prototyping: Designing the future with science fiction*. Springer International Publishing AG.

Keller, T. (2022). *Digital Society key technologies and factors*. Lecture notes in Information Systems, Winterthur.

Kosow, H., & Gaßner, R. (2008). *Methods of future and scenario analysis: Overview, assessment, and selection criteria.*

Lötscher, C. (2021). *The digital legacy*. Schulthess.

Meise, N. (2017). The we does not forget. Carrier media of collective memory of the deceased. In N. Jakoby & M. Thönnes (Eds.), *On the sociology of dying* (pp. 157-172). Springer Fachmedien Wiesbaden. https://doi.org/10.1007/978-3-658-11874-7_9

Merrie, A., Keys, P., Metian, M., & Österblom, H. (2018). Radical ocean futures-scenario development using science fiction prototyping. *Futures*, *95*, 22-32. https://doi.org/10.1016/j.futures.2017.09.005

Nagel, M., Mieke, C., & Teuber, S. (2020). *Methodenhandbuch der Betriebswirtschaft* (2nd ed.). utb GmbH. https://doi.org/10.36198/9783838587615

Savin-Baden, M. (2022). *AI for death and dying*. CRC Press.

Schawel, C., & Billing, F. (2018). Morphological box: (Creativity techniques). In C. Schawel & F. Billing, *Top 100 Management Tools* (pp. 219-221). Springer Fachmedien Wiesbaden. https://doi.org/10.1007/978-3-658-18917-4_57

Statista Research Department. (2023, February 16). *Topic page: Children and young people in Switzerland*. Statista. https://de.statista.com/themen/6513/kinder-und-jugendliche-in-der-schweiz/

Steinmüller, K. (2012). Scenarios - A complex of methods between scientific claim and zeitgeisty bricolage. In R. Popp (Ed.), *Future and science* (pp. 101-137). Springer Berlin Heidelberg. https://doi.org/10.1007/978-3-642-28954-5_6

TA-Swiss. (2021a). *Call for tenders for a technology assessment study on the topic of "Death in the digital age"*. https://www.ta-swiss.ch/tod-im-digitalen-zeitalter

TA-Swiss. (2021b). Death in the digital age. *TA-SWISS*. https://www.ta-swiss.ch/tod-im-digitalen-zeitalter

The megatrend map. (2022, October 31). zukunftsinstitut.de. https://www.zukunftsinstitut.de/artikel/die-megatrend-map/

Mourning-Loving remembrance and commemoration. (n.d.). Retrieved November 27, 2022, from https://www.abschiedstrauer.de/erinnern-an-verstorbene.htm

UNESCO. (2003, October 15). *Charter on the Preservation of Digital Heritage*. https://www.unesco.org/en/legal-affairs/charter-preservation-digital-heritage

Wagner-Schelewsky, P., & Hering, L. (2019). Online survey. In N. Baur & J. Blasius (Eds.), *Handbook of methods of empirical social research* (pp. 787-800). Springer Fachmedien Wiesbaden. https://doi.org/10.1007/978-3-658-21308-4_54

FAKE NEWS IN THE KNOWLEDGE SOCIETY: A QUANTITATIVE ANALYSIS IN PORTUGAL

Natália Gomes, Pedro Tadeu, Carlos Brigas and Elisabete Brito
CI&DEI - Polytechnic University of Guarda, Guarda, Portugal

ABSTRACT

Different reports have recently indicated that fake news can constitute one of society's biggest problems in achieving the objectives proposed by the worldwide governments for an information society. This article aims to understand how the Portuguese population uses social networks to validate that the information is disseminated on the networks and how they verify the integrity of the information received. The survey results provide a comprehensive view of social media consumption and the perception of misinformation among Portuguese residents. Several key insights emerged by examining the demographics, social media habits, and attitudes toward misinformation. The primary purpose is to underline some of the abstract concepts of fake news and present a descriptive exploratory study. The results of a survey applied in this study provide valuable insights into the social media behaviours and attitudes of Portuguese residents. It highlights a pervasive use of social media, significant concerns about misinformation, and varying levels of trust in the information encountered online.

KEYWORDS

Fake News, Disinformation, Information Society, Social Media, Internet

1. INTRODUCTION

In recent decades, we have witnessed an explosion of information; this phenomenon has been accentuated due to several factors, such as the development of democracy, informational pluralism, decentralisation of powers, and technological evolution. With the spread of ICT, and the Internet in particular, the growth of these information channels has become more accessible, as has the public's participation and eagerness for information, causing a progressive saturation of information.

Flore et al. (2019) stated that factors contribute to this information saturation: font manipulation, insufficient mediation between message source and receiver, and user difficulty in managing the mass of available information, to name a few. Other studies reveal that this type of information/disinformation has immense potential for rapid dissemination compared to reliable information, often aided by its virality (Vosoughi et al., 2018). The online spreading of fake news and misinformation has been recently identified as a significant issue. It constitutes a potential threat to all areas of society, much of which is enabled by social networks and online media sites.

The information society has stimulated information creation, development, and distribution. Conversely, the design and massive data distribution in social networks have given rise to an enormous amount of misinformation, disinformation, and Fake News (Pennycook & Rand, 2021).

According to studies carried out within the scope of the European Union's (EU) action, the data obtained in these studies are alarming and indicate that about 71% of EU citizens find fake news online several times a month; if we analyse these numbers from another perspective, we find that about 30% of the EU population residing are faced with news or information that they believe distorts reality every day or almost every day.

From the same studies, we found that one of the groups most likely to be influenced, such as young people, is 63% of EU youth facing fake news more than once a week (European Commission, 2020).

However, the spread of false information in the digital age is not only a technological problem but also has social, cultural, and even political implications. Marvick (2018) mentioned that the sociotechnical model explains how individuals interpret, and share information is closely linked to their social positioning, identity, discursive resources, and competencies. In addition, the material configurations of different media - such as newspapers, television, or social media - have technical peculiarities that affect the creation of meaning and the exchange or sharing of information. This implies that fake news can be widely shared on digital platforms due to their sociotechnical characteristics, such as the ease of sharing, viral nature of content, and recommendation algorithms prioritising engagement and virality over accuracy and truthfulness.

The scientific community is becoming increasingly concerned about the proliferation of fake news, disinformation created by social media networks, and, currently, by artificial intelligence software. It is now time to find ways to determine the best practices for teaching and informing users about the extent to which they can distinguish truth from false information and the problems associated with disseminating false information. Fake news, by its nature, content, and objective, prevents the construction of a rational and well-formed judgment (Comunicación, 2018).

The indiscriminate use of the term "fake news" can be highly detrimental as it can create confusion among citizens attempting to differentiate between legitimate news and fabricated information in the age of digital media (Allcott & Gentzkow, 2017; UNESCO, 2018). Furthermore, recent research suggests that individuals often label news as "fake" if it challenges their preconceived notions. This leads to a blurring of the distinction between factual reporting and subjective opinions in the increasingly complex digital landscape (Nielsen & Grave, 2017).

Having critical and independent thinking is vital for making decisions freely. Questions like how, when, for what purpose, and who created this false information are increasingly challenging because of rapid social media replication. According to the Guardian (2020), everyone from academic and industrial researchers to amateur enthusiasts, visual effects studios, and porn producers can produce and distribute Fake News. The media frequency of fake news has increased dramatically, interfering negatively in various sectors of society, such as politics, health, and security.

The abundance of (tentative) definitions that have been floated has led some to worry that the term 'fake news' 's heterogeneity results in it becoming "a catch-all term with multiple definitions" (Lilleker, 2017).

Popular terms such as fake news, post-truth, and disinformation have brought to light a massive problem of how humans can verify the veracity and reliability of the information disseminated on the Internet (Sintra, 2019).

Fake news has also been defined as "a news article that is intentionally and verifiably false" (Shu et al., 2017; Allcott & Gentzkow, 2017) and also the "information presented as a news story that is factually incorrect and designed to deceive the consumers into believing as true" (Goldbeck et al., 2018). Fake news can be considered a form of press that deliberately distributes false information to promote misinformation and mislead people (Fallis, 2015; Kaplan, 2010). We need to stress again that the mention of the term Fake News was only enhanced by the growth of technologies and access to platforms associated with the Internet, verifying documented records of its existence since the Roman Empire (Social, 2022; Posetti & Mathews, 2018). According to these studies, disseminating false information (disinformation) has always been part of humanity.

This is a significant problem today, especially regarding educating people. Fake news can influence public opinion, negatively impact idea formation, and damage trust in government institutions and the media. Related to this, people must be educated about "fake news" and learn to identify and avoid it; the literature provides several strategies.

One of the main strategies is media literacy, which involves teaching skills to assess the quality and credibility of information sources. This approach includes teaching people to evaluate the integrity of information based on criteria such as the source of information, the quality of the content, the context, and the objectivity of the message. This will allow people to make more informed choices when seeking information and help prevent the spread of "fake news." In addition, it is crucial to encourage intellectual curiosity and promote a culture of questioning and inquiry. This may include promoting reliable sources of information, such as academic journals, quality newspapers, and independent news organisations.

However, educating about "fake news" is only one part of the solution; we still have essential actors playing in this society with a considerable role.

So, social media platforms and governments also have this obligation to reduce the spread of "fake news" and increase information transparency so that they can implement fact-checking and fake news identification policies and promote access to trusted sources of information. Governments can implement policies encouraging transparency and accountability of information and promoting education about "fake news" in schools and other educational institutions.

The use of new technologies, the massive access to the Internet, the new habits of information consumption, and its easy exchange, provided by different platforms, allows its users to distribute any information through a simple "click". This type of news does not require rigours in its production and enables different actors' participation (Fallis, 2015).

The spread of disinformation and misinformation is made possible mainly through social networks and messaging. Today, social media is fueled by personal and political content (UNESCO, 2018).

In the present era, social media platforms are significant sources of information distribution, and people believe it without knowing their source and authenticity. Social media has captivated people worldwide, facilitating the widespread dissemination of fake news due to its easy accessibility, affordability, and effortless information sharing.

The rapid way fake news spreads on social networks instantly enables the dissemination of misleading statements. The algorithms this platform uses give users access to the most relevant content, ensuring that the information shown to each person is conditioned and filtered. On the other hand, different political or partisan interests, or simply confusion, become reasons for more frequent dissemination of misleading content (IFJ, 2022). The previous paradigm, in which the media possessed the informative primacy, has changed dramatically (Comunicación, 2018).

Some studies suggest that there seems to be some association between related emotion and fake news and found that false news was more novel than trustworthy news, which indicates that people were more likely to share novel information. Whereas false stories inspired fear, disgust, and surprise in replies, true stories inspired anticipation, sadness, joy, and trust (Vosoughi et al., 2018). Findings also provide some tentative evidence that the effect of emotion on perceptions of accuracy is specific to fake news.

The significant correlational interaction between self-reported use of emotion and the type of news headline (fake, real) suggests that heightened reliance on emotion decreases people's ability to discern between real and fake news (Martel et al., 2020).

In another study analysing Twitter social media, falsehood diffused significantly further, faster, deeper, and more broadly than the truth in all categories of information. They also concluded that false news was more novel than true news, suggesting people were likelier to share novel information (Vosoughi et al., 2018).

The latest Reuters Digital News Report survey has concluded that the Portuguese population trusts the news more than its counterparts in other countries. In 2021, with OberCom (Communication Observatory), this organisation presented a new report that identified that television and the Internet (including social networks) continue to be Portugal's primary source of information. Facebook and YouTube are still the most used social networks by the Portuguese community (73.2% and 65.6%, respectively).

Concerning social networks and the consumption of information, 47.7% of the Portuguese use Facebook, 20.9% WhatsApp, and 19.9% use YouTube (Posetti & Mathews, 2018).

The different studies analysed in the scope of this work allow us to conclude that social networks have not, so far, taken enough measures to verify the integrity of the information and whether the source is reliable or not. Facebook and other tech platforms must create ways and legal politics to adopt more robust measures to combat misinformation, disinformation, and fake news.

2. MATERIALS AND METHODS

The study used a descriptive exploratory study framed in a research design with a quantitative questionnaire methodology. The questionnaire, structured with 16 items and designed ad hoc, collected information about media and information consumption, social network use, and relationships with fake news. Data gathering was arranged using an instrument adapted from some Reuters Institute for the Study of Journalism—Digital News Report reports. A Google Form was used to develop the questionnaire.

The methodological phases in the present study were developed and applied according to the following:

1. Exploratory and design phase -the instrument's preparation following the objectives. The design phase begins with identifying the instrument's goals and developing a specifications table.

2. Validation phase: The researchers conducted a quantitative pilot study and analysed the data collected and the participants' feedback. Ten students and five professors of the Polytechnic of Guarda-Portugal participated in the pilot study.

3. Results analysis - Data were analysed using SPSS Statistics for Windows 26 (IBM SPSS Statistics for Windows, Version 63.0. Armonk, NY: IBM Corp). Descriptive data were compared using Chi-Square and Mann-Whitney U tests to calculate descriptive statistics (e.g. frequencies, percentages, measures of central tendency and dispersion) and inferential statistics (Chi-square test of independence between two variables). Data privacy and confidentiality were guaranteed at all times.

An important motivation for the study is that its sample should best reflect the sociodemographic variation of the Portuguese population at any age and gender.

The purpose of the descriptive study is not to test a particular hypothesis but to summarise what is discovered about how the Portuguese population uses social networks to validate that the information is disseminated on the networks and how they verify the integrity of the information received. Furthermore, it aims to draw well-grounded conclusions aligned with the phenomena observed throughout the research process.

2.1 Sample

The survey gathered socially relevant and statistically representative information on the population of residents in Portugal, including the autonomous island regions. The sample conceived as the set of elements of the population asked to participate in the investigation corresponded to Facebook users from different parts of Portugal regions, as shown in Figure 1. The study was applied, achieving a total sample of 1018 Portuguese Internet users chosen randomly. The distribution was as follows in Figure 1 and Figure 2, with most of the sample being from Castelo Branco District (N = 441; 43.3%), Guarda District (N = 303; 29.8%), and Viseu (N = 79 7.8%).

Figure 1. Sample frequency distribution

Adapted from: https://pt.wikipedia.org/wiki/Ficheiro:Portuguese_Districts_Map_With_Names.svg

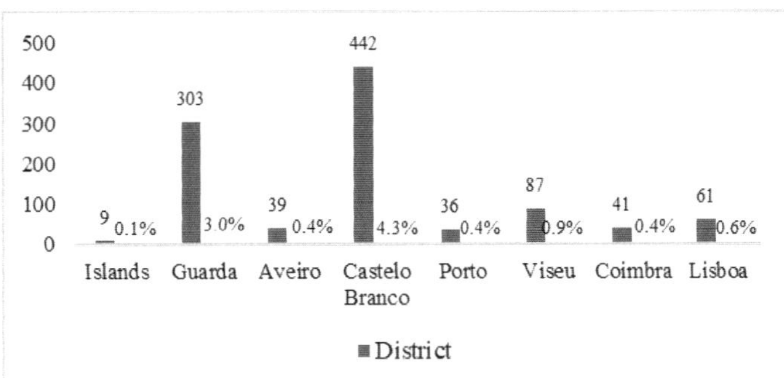

Figure 2. Sample highest frequency distribution by regions

The sample composition was as follows: 61.7% of the sample (N = 628) was female, 37.3% (N = 377) was male, and 1.3% (N=13) preferred not to answer.

The respondent was given alternatives with eleven-year intervals. The first interval reached a population under or equal to 14 years, the second from 15 to 19, and so on until older or equal to 60 years old. The 15-19 interval included 23.9% of the respondents. The second to most included 15.4% of the respondents and was the <=14 interval. The third to most included 12.4% of the respondents, who were 20-24. If we analysed all the age divisions proposed on the questionnaire, we could analyse the following %of respondents: The interval of age between 25-29 with 6%; the interval between 30-34 with 3.9%; interval of 35-39 with 5.9%; 45-49 with 11.3%; 50-54 with 6.3%; 50-59 with 3.2% and population with 60 years old or older with 2.7% of respondents.

Regardless of academic degrees the distribution of respondents was 22.69% (N=231) having an elementary school degree, 34.5% (N=353) having a secondary school degree, 1.08% (N=11) having a short cycle, 23.18% (N=236) having a Bachelor's degree, 10.22% (N=104) having a Master's Degree, and 8.15% (N=83) having a Doctoral degree.

3. RESULTS AND DISCUSSION

The results will now be presented to check the research objectives corresponding to the different constructs of the study.

3.1 Social Media Consumption

The results for the first study construct - Social Media Consumption - The variables were qualitative categorical, as observed in the following tables. Table 1 shows the relationship between gender and the frequency of use of social networks.

Table 1. The distribution between gender and frequency regarding the use of social networks

Frequency	Gender		
	Female	**Male**	**Total**
One or two in a week	28 46,7% 4,5%	32 53,3% 8,2%	60 100,0% 5,9%
Three or five a week	48 56,5% 7,6%	37 43,5% 9,5%	85 100,0% 8,3%
Every day	552 63,2% 87,9%	321 36,8% 82,3%	873 100,0% 85,8%
Total	628	390	1018

χ=7,586; ρ =0,022. *The frequency of use of social networks is statistically associated with gender.*

The results show that women use social networks for over two hours (Table 2). The average time of connection for 58.0% of respondents is between 1 to 4 hours per day; from the users connected between 4 and 6 hours a day, 75% are female.

The data allows us to assert that Women use social media more frequently and also use social networks longer than men, presenting statistically significant results; one other way we can affirm this dependence is statistically significant.

Table 2. Distribution of the number of hours per day according to gender

User Time	Gender Female n % line %column	Total n % line % column Male n % line %column
Less than 1 hour	99 - 47,6% 15,8%	109 – 52,4% 27,9%
Between 1 and two hours	205 - 58,7% 32,6%	144 - 41,3% 36,9%
Between 2 and 4 hours	163 - 67,6% 26,0%	78 - 32,4% 20,0%
Between 4 and 6 hours	93 - 75,0% 14,8%	31 - 25,0% 7,9%
More than 6 hours	68 - 70,8% 10,8%	28 - 29,2% 7,2%
Total	628 - 61,7%	390 - 38,3%

χ=35,063; ρ =0,000; *The frequency of the number of hours per day is statistically associated with gender*

Young people and adults use social networks longer than theoretically expected (more than 4 hours). Children who use social networks for less than 1 hour per day exceed expectations (Table 3).

Table 3. Verification of the trustworthiness of a publication

		Time spent using social media					
		Less than 1hour	**Between 1 and 2 hours**	**Between 2 and 4 hours**	**Between 4 and 6 hours**	**More than 6 hours**	**Total**
Degree	**Primary education**	56	73	53	26	23	231
		26,9%	20,9%	22,0%	21,0%	24,0%	22,7%
	Secondary school	41	109	101	54	48	353
		19,7%	31,2%	41,9%	43,5%	50,0%	34,7%
	TESP	3	3	2	2	1	11
		1,4%	0,9%	0,8%	1,6%	1,0%	1,1%
	Bachelor	47	89	52	36	12	236
		22,6%	25,5%	21,6%	29,0%	12,5%	23,2%
	Master	27	38	31	4	4	104
		13,0%	10,9%	12,9%	3,2%	4,2%	10,2%
	PhD	34	37	2	2	8	83
		16,3%	10,6%	0,8%	1,6%	8,3%	8,2%
Total		208	349	241	124	96	1018
		100,0%	100,0%	100,0%	100,0%	100,0%	100,0%

χ=93.313; ρ =0.000. *The time spent using social networks is statistically associated with educational qualifications*

Individuals with secondary education and a bachelor use social networks more frequently (every day), exceeding what was theoretically expected.

Individuals with a third cycle, master's degree, and doctorate who use social networks daily for less than 1 hour exceed what was theoretically expected. In contrast, those with secondary education or a degree who use social networks for more extended periods (at least 4 hours) per day exceed expected.

Regarding the type of social network most used by those surveyed, it has been verified that there is no more major network than another. However, Instagram, YouTube, Facebook, and WhatsApp are the most indicated (Table 4).

Table 4. Social Networks

Social Network	Positive answers	Total % (n=1018)
	n	%
Instagram	553	23,1%
YouTube	417	17,4%
Facebook	504	21,0%
WhatsApp	522	21,8%
Twitter	140	5,8%
TikTok	93	3,9%
Pinterest	65	2,7%
Snapchat	101	4,2%
	2395	100,0%

Educational attainment appears to influence social media behaviour. Those with secondary education or a bachelor's degree are more likely to use social media extensively, whereas individuals with higher degrees (master's and doctoral) tend to use it less frequently. This could suggest that higher educational levels are associated with more discerning or time-constrained use of social media, possibly due to professional commitments or a greater inclination towards other forms of information consumption.

3.2 Misinformation and Fake News - Trust in Social Networks, Misinformation and Fake News

Social media are increasingly being used as an information source. Social media platforms have morphed into public information utilities that control how most people view the world in a misinformation information society. In the opinion of the participants, 49.4% (N=503) consider social media networks to be a good source of information, 33.1% (N=337) considered social media not a good source to get valid information, and 17.5% (N= 178) did not have an opinion about that. These results are significantly associated with gender (χ=14.642; ρ =0.000), age group (χ=53.843; ρ =0.000) and educational qualifications (χ=35.719; ρ =0.000). It was found that the respondents who exceeded what was theoretically expected in their good opinion of social networks as a source of information were women, those aged between 35 and 49, and/or with secondary education or a degree.

This high level of concern is likely driven by the proliferation of misleading content on social platforms, impacting users' perception of the information's reliability. Despite this, many users do not consistently verify the information they encounter. This gap between concern and action suggests that users need better digital literacy and critical evaluation skills to navigate the information landscape more effectively.

The second result addressed was related to social media's trust and veracity of information. 41.0% believe that information is doubtful or false, 42.6% believe it is accurate, and 0.1% consider the information in social media authentic. It appears that 41.7% (n=424) of respondents consider the information shared on social networks to be true, and 40.2% (n=409) consider it to be somewhat untrue. This opinion is significantly associated with gender (χ=20.439; ρ =0.000), age group (χ=59.666; ρ =0.000) and educational qualifications (χ=41.764; ρ =0.000). It was concluded that the respondents who exceeded what was theoretically expected in the true opinion were women, those aged between 30 and 44 years old, and/or with secondary education.

Regarding the concern about having misinformation or fake news on social networks, 86.2% (N=878) of the respondents are very concerned about the spread of misinformation /fake news, consequently showing much distrust about social networks. This concern (having misinformation or fake news on social networks) is significantly associated with gender (χ=34.418; ρ =0.000), age group (χ=53.843; ρ =0.000), and educational qualifications (χ=87.692; ρ =0.000). It was found that the respondents who exceeded what was theoretically expected in terms of concern about fake news were women, those aged between 20 and 54 years old, and/or with secondary education or a degree.

The last question regarding the second construct analyses the percentage of sharing information posteriorly identified as fake news or misinformation. Even if the number of persons who did not share is significant at 67,4% (N=686), there is still a relatively high percentage of 20,4% (N=208) that share fake news or misinformation on social media. It appears that the majority, 67.4% (n=686) of respondents, do not share comments or publish information about content that later turned out to be false; only 20.4% (n=208) admitted that they did so. This attitude is not significantly associated with gender (χ=1.624; ρ =0.444), but it was with age group (χ=43.238; ρ =0.000) and educational qualifications (χ=40.601; ρ =0.000). It was concluded that the respondents who exceeded what was theoretically expected in making a comment or subsequent publication were those over 35 years old and/or had a degree. This discrepancy might indicate a lack of awareness about misinformation or a retrospective realisation of sharing false information. The tendency to share information without thorough verification underscores the challenges in combating misinformation on social media.

3.3 Identify Fake News on Social Media

Regarding verifying the trustworthiness of a publication, the majority of respondents, 35.2% (N=358), say that they occasionally check the veracity of the published information. In comparison, 26.8% (N=273) say they do it frequently, and 14.5% (N=148) refer to consistently verifying the veracity of the published information.

When asked if when they react to a publication, respondents check whether it is reliable, 27.4% (N=279) say they do it only occasionally, and 24.8% (N=252) say they frequently check if the information is accurate, a significant percentage of respondents 20.9% (N=213) say they always do it. However, 14.5% (N=148) say they rarely care for it. When asked if, when they share a publication, they check whether it is trustworthy, most of the respondents, 42.8% (N=436), report having this concern whenever they share information. 21.4% (N=218) do it frequently, and 16.4% check it occasionally.

Table 5. Verification of the trustworthiness of a publication

Questions	Never n (%)	Rarely n (%)	Occasionally n (%)	Frequently n (%)	Always n (%)	I do not know how to do it n (%)
When you see/read a publication, do you verify trustworthily	53 (5,2%)	122 (12,0%)	358 (35,2%)	273 (26,8%)	148 (14,5%)	64 (6,3%)
When you react to a publication, do you verify trustworthily	63 (6,2%)	148 (14,5%)	279 (27,4%)	252 (24,8%)	213 (20,9%)	63 (6,2%)
When you share a publication, do you verify trustworthily	46 (4,5%)	81 (8,0%)	167 (16,4%)	218 (21,4%)	436 (42,8%)	70 (6,9%)

When asked about the procedures and resources they use to validate the information, only 20.6% (N=252) mentioned that they used traditional sources of information to validate the data obtained.

Table 6. Resources used to validate the information

Veracity	Positive answers regarding the use	% from total respondents (n=1018)
Confirm the source (e.g. journals or reviews)	252	20,6%
Check other sources	720	59,0%
Without no opinion	186	15,2%
Other	63	5,2%
	1221	100,0%

The table below shows that 24.8% (n=252) of those interviewed search newspapers and magazines to confirm the veracity of the news they read on social media, and 70.7% (n=720) do so on other websites. It should be noted that 18.3% (n=186) had no opinion. Considering the items with the highest frequency of use, search on other internet sites and look in newspapers and magazines, and proceed with applying the chi-square independence test to investigate a possible association of this behaviour with gender, age, and/or qualifications of respondents. Regarding searches on other internet sites, it was concluded that this behaviour was not significantly associated with gender (χ=2.971; ρ =0.085) but was significantly associated with age group (χ=33.069; ρ =0.000) and educational qualifications. (χ=27.099; ρ=0.000). It was found that people aged between 20 and 44 who had qualifications such as a bachelor's or master's degree most demonstrated this behaviour. Regarding search behaviour in newspapers and magazines, it was found that it was not significantly associated with gender (χ=0.047; ρ =0.828), but it was significantly associated with age group (χ=43.238; ρ =0.000) and educational qualifications (χ=38.120; ρ=0.000). It was found that people aged between 20 and 44 with qualifications of at least a bachelor's degree were those who most demonstrated this behaviour.

In resumes, 59% of respondents check other sources for information, and 20.6% rely on traditional sources like journals or reviews. However, a notable proportion (15.2%) have no opinion, indicating either apathy or uncertainty about verification methods. The reliance on multiple sources for verification reflects a cautious approach among some users, but the overall practices suggest room for improvement in media literacy.

4. CONCLUSIONS

As we mentioned earlier, several works indicate that fake news can be one of the biggest problems for society. With this study, we had the ambition to characterise the behaviour of the Portuguese population regarding the use of social networks as a source of information. The results obtained through the application of a survey on the use of social networks, the relationship with knowledge, integrity, trust, and validation show that:

- Women use social networks for a more significant number of hours.
- The survey shows that it is not a significant network that is more used than another. However, the inquiries indicate Instagram, YouTube, Facebook, and WhatsApp.

When asked about trust in social networks, misinformation, and fake news, the results obtained show:

- Most participants, around 50%, consider social networks to be a good source of information; a third of the participants indicated that social networks are not an excellent source for obtaining valid data.
- However, 40.2% of the participants believe that the information is dubious or false, 41.7% believe it is accurate, and only 2.3% considered that the information on social networks is authentic.
- Most respondents indicated concern about misinformation or fake news on social media. About 87% of respondents are very concerned about disinformation news spread, consequently showing much distrust towards social networks.

When asked how they validate the information obtained through social networks and what care they have in sharing content through social networks, the results indicate that:

- Most respondents (35.2%) say they only occasionally check the integrity of the information obtained. In comparison, around 30% (say they do it frequently, and only 15% say they always inspect the integrity of the information published);
- Regarding their care when sharing a publication, around 50% indicated that they check if it is reliable.

The results show how intensive use of social networks would be expected, with a slight difference in use if you consider gender. There is also diversity in the types of platforms used.

The study clearly shows that fake news is a problem today. Most respondents are very concerned about the misinformation/ fake news broadcast, consequently distrusting social networks. In the universe of respondents in this study, there is not always a concern about verifying the integrity of information circulating on social networks, which seems contradictory.

This study allows us to conclude that the education sector urgently needs to define ways and competencies for learning how to find and share trustworthy information. In the same way, social media platforms need to develop new solutions that allow users to filter and detect sites containing false and misleading information by creating automated algorithms that locate fake news. The study clearly shows that fake news is a problem today. Most respondents are very concerned about the misinformation/fake news transmitted, consequently distrusting social networks. However, in the universe of respondents in this study, there is not always a concern about verifying the integrity of the information circulating on social networks, which is contradictory. On the one hand, we see the general mass use of social networks and the daily proliferation of Fake News without much concern for the information disseminated; on the other hand, users show concern about this issue.

Therefore, serious investment is needed to develop users' skills and learn how to find and share severe and reliable information. Likewise, social media platforms should develop new solutions that allow users to filter and detect sites containing false and misleading information, creating automated algorithms that locate fake news. On the other hand, it is also important to remember that the pervasive spread of AI-generated fake news critically undermines public trust, deepens societal divides, poses significant challenges for detection and regulation, and highlights the urgent necessity for cutting-edge technological solutions and robust media literacy education.

This study allows us to conclude that educating on the proper use of social networks and creating help mechanisms for users must be a priority in the knowledge society. Ultimately, education about "fake news" is vital to protect the integrity of information and prevent the spread of false and misleading information. By implementing effective media literacy strategies and fostering a culture of questioning and inquiry, people can better critically evaluate the information they receive and make informed decisions based on accurate facts.

In summary, the results underscore the need for enhanced digital literacy programs to equip users with the skills to evaluate information critically and reduce the spread of misinformation. Additionally, understanding the demographic influences on social media usage can help tailor more effective communication strategies to different population segments.

ACKNOWLEDGEMENT

This work is funded by National Funds through the FCT - Foundation for Science and Technology, I.P., within the scope of the project Refª UIDB/05507/2020 and DOI identifier https://doi.org/10.54499/UIDB/05507/2020. Furthermore, we would like to thank the Centre for Studies in Education and Innovation (Ci&DEI) and the Polytechnic of Guarda for their support.

REFERENCES

Allcott, H., & Gentzkow, M. (2017). *Social Media and Fake News in the 2016 Election.* Journal of Economic Perspectives. 31, 211-236. https://doi.org/10.1257/jep.31.2.211

Comunicación, E. d. (2018). *Influencia de las noticias falsas en la opinión pública.* España: Servimedia. 2018.

European Commission (2020). *Shaping Europe's digital future: Eurobarometer survey supports sustainability and data sharing.* https://ec.europa.eu/commission/presscorner/detail/en/IP_20_383, (11/05/2023).

Fallis, D. (2015). *What Is Disinformation? Library Trends 63*(3), 401–426. https://doi.org/10.1353/lib.2015.0014.

Flore, M.; Balahur, A.; Podavini, A.; Verile, M. (2019). *Understanding citizens' vulnerabilities to disinformation and data-driven propaganda.* EUR 29741 EN, Publications Office of the European Union, Luxembourg, 2019, ISBN 978-92-76-03320-2, doi:10.2760/919835, JRC116009.

The Guardian. (2020). *What are deepfakes – and how can you spot them?* (T. Guardian, Ed.)). Available online: https://www.theguardian.com/technology/2020/jan/13/what-are-deepfakes-and-how-can-you-spot-them (05/04/2022)

International Federation of Journalist-IFJ. *¿Qué son las fake news? Guía para combatir la desinformación?.* n.d from International Federation of Journalists. Available online: https://www.ifj.org/fileadmin/user_upload/Fake_News_-_FIP_AmLat.pdf (05/06/2022)

J. Golbeck et al. (2018). *Fake news vs satire: A dataset and analysis.* Proc. 10th ACM Conf. Web Sci., pp. 17-21, 2018.

Journalism, O. —R. (2021). *Digital News Report Portugal (2021).* OberCom — Reuters Institute for the Study of Journalism. Available online: https://obercom.pt/wp-content/uploads/2021/06/DNR_PT_2021_final.pdf (12/06/2022).

K. Shu, A. Sliva, S. Wang, J. Tang and H. Liu (2017). *Fake news detection on social media: A data mining perspective*. ACM SIGKDD Explore. Newsletter., vol. 19, no. 1, pp. 22-36, 2017.

Kaplan, A. (2020). *Social Media and Fake News: Is this the end of democracy?* Artificial Intelligence, Social Media, and Digital Transformation in Media & Society. doi:10.26650/B/SS07.2020.013.09

Lilleker, D., (2017). *Evidence to the Culture, Media and Sport Committee 'Fake news' inquiry presented by the Faculty for Media & Communication, Bournemouth University*. Documentation. Bournemouth University.

Martel, C., Pennycook, G. & Rand, D.G. (2020). *Reliance on emotion promotes belief in fake news*. https://doi.org/10.1186/s41235-020-00252-3

Marwick, A. E. (2018). *Why do people share fake news? A sociotechnical model of media effects*. Georgetown Law Technology Review, 2018, 2(2), 474–512.

Nielsen, R.K., & Graves, L. (2017). *News you don't believe: Audience perspectives on fake news*. Available online: https://reutersinstitute.politics.ox.ac.uk/sites/default/files/2017-10/Nielsen&Graves_factsheet_1710v3_FINAL_download.pdf (05/04/2021)

Pennycook, G., & Rand, D. G. (2021). *The psychology of fake news*. Trends in Cognitive Sciences, 2021,25(5), 388–402. https://doi.org/10.1016/j.tics.2021.02.007

Posetti, J., & Matthews, A. (2018). *A short guide to the history of 'fake news' and disinformation*. International Center of Journalists. Available online: https://www.icfj.org/sites/default/files/2018-07/A%20Short%20Guide%20to%20History%20of%20Fake%20News%20and%20Disinformation_ICFJ%20Final.pdf (05/06/2022)

Sintra, M. C. (2019). *Fake News e a Desinformação: Perspetivar comportamentos e estratégias informacionais*. Lisboa: NOVAFCSH (2019, 06).

Social, C. (Ed.). *O surgimento das fake news*. Available online: http://contextosocial.com.br/o-surgimento-das-fake-news (05/06/2022)

UNESCO. (2018). *Journalism, fake news & disinformation: handbook for journalism education and training*. 2018. doi:978-92-3-100281-6

Vosoughi S, Roy D, Aral S. (2018). *The spread of true and false news online*. Science. Mar 9;359(6380):1146-1151. doi: 10.1126/science.aap9559. PMID: 29590045.

TECHNOLOGICAL CITIZENSHIP IN THE DIGITAL AGE

Anne Marte Gardenier and Lambèr Royakkers
Eindhoven University of Technology
PO Box 513, 5600 MB Eindhoven, The Netherlands

ABSTRACT

This article examines the concept of 'technological citizenship' in the context of today's digital challenges, including misinformation, cybercrime, and privacy erosion. Highlighting the World Economic Forum's identification of misinformation as a critical threat, it advocates for empowering citizens to navigate the digital landscape responsibly and informatively. The notion of 'technological citizenship,' introduced by Frankenfeld in 1992, is explored as a framework for leveraging digital technology's benefits while mitigating its risks. Through two case studies, the article illustrates the complex interplay between digital technology, regulatory frameworks, and citizen engagement. The first case addresses a significant data breach within the Dutch Public Health Services during the COVID-19 pandemic, underscoring the consequences of insufficient governmental oversight. The second case focuses on the debate surrounding the proposed Child Sexual Abuse Regulation by the European Commission, highlighting the tension between privacy and child protection. The discussion extends to the legal, political, and sociological dimensions of technological citizenship, emphasizing the importance of citizen participation in shaping digital policies. By advocating for a dynamic democracy and a secure, equitable digital society, the article calls for policies that enable citizens to actively contribute to societal well-being in the digital age.

KEYWORDS

Technological Citizenship, Public Values, Digital Rights, Citizen Empowerment, Digital Society

1. INTRODUCTION

The World Economic Forum (2024) has identified misinformation and disinformation as paramount societal threats, surpassing the risks of extreme weather and international conflicts. This assertion is timely, as misinformation's potential to influence electoral outcomes and public perception on pivotal issues like public health, climate change, and social justice becomes increasingly evident. Such a landscape accentuates the essential role of citizens in the digital era, emphasizing the need for access to accurate information and the liberty to disseminate it. In the context where digital technology plays a central role in mediating societal interactions, the imperative for citizens to make informed decisions is undeniable. This requirement goes beyond countering misinformation to encompass addressing the opportunities and risks presented by the digital age, including cybercrime, espionage, and the impact of social media on mental health. Addressing these challenges calls for citizens' comprehensive understanding and active participation.

The notion of 'technological citizenship,' introduced by Frankenfeld in 1992, advocates for a societal framework that empowers citizens to harness digital technology's benefits while minimizing its risks. This concept proposes a societal contract for the responsible use and development of technology, emphasizing the right of individuals to be informed about, and participate in, decisions affecting technological impacts on their lives. Frankenfeld's discussion, although initially focused on ecological risks, extends to the broader implications of technology on society, suggesting that active citizen participation in technology-related decision-making can balance its potential benefits and harms.

Contrasting the World Economic Forum's focus on misinformation, this article argues for a broader understanding of citizens' roles in shaping the digital society. It suggests that citizens' influence extends beyond electoral participation to include raising awareness, challenging policies, and innovating solutions to address governmental or market failures. Everyday decisions, such as disengaging from certain platforms or adopting digital technologies for health, demonstrate citizens' active role in defining the digital landscape's norms and values.

Recognizing the critical role of citizens in navigating the digital age's complexities, this article underscores the importance of enhancing their digital literacy and creating supportive environments for informed decision-making. It posits technological citizenship as crucial for developing a secure and equitable digital society, requiring a social contract that addresses misinformation and empowers citizens to shape the digital age actively.

Through an examination of two case studies – one with a local and the other with an international focus – this article demonstrates the perception that facilitating technological citizenship is a state responsibility. It argues that the state must establish rights and duties for its citizens, enabling them to act in society's best interest. These rights and duties, emerging from democratic processes and political efforts, highlight the importance of civic engagement in evaluating and influencing government policies. Such engagement is essential for steering the digitization of society in a direction that aligns with democratic values and societal well-being.

2. CASE STUDIES ON CITIZENSHIP IN THE AGE OF DIGITIZATION

In this section, we will discuss two case studies. The first case study considers a data breach within a local context. The second one demonstrates a digitization issue in an international context.

2.1 GGD's Data Mishandling during Covid-19

The COVID-19 pandemic required rapid and extensive public health responses globally. In the Netherlands, the (municipal) Public Health Services (GGDs) were at the forefront of testing and contact tracing efforts. However, a significant challenge emerged during the first wave of the pandemic when a major data breach was reported, affecting potentially 6.5 million citizens.

To manage the increasing demand for COVID-19 testing and tracing, the Ministry of Health expanded the GGD staff significantly. This expansion involved hiring temporary workers through partner organizations, including call centers and IT suppliers. Due to the urgency, outdated IT systems, which were originally accessible to only a small team of physicians, were made accessible to approximately 26,000 GGD employees. This access inadvertently exposed the sensitive personal data of 6.5 million Dutch citizens, which might have fallen into criminal hands and can be misused, e.g., for identity fraud.

The breach came to light in early 2021 by the Dutch television news service *RTL Nieuws* when it was discovered that GGD employees were extracting private data from the systems and selling it on underground marketplaces. These data included home addresses, phone numbers, social security numbers, test results, and contact tracing information. Some employees sold this privacy-sensitive and confidential data through channels such as Telegram and Snapchat. Notably, the data of public figures and celebrities were also compromised and shared via messaging platforms like WhatsApp. Following the disclosure, police arrested some of the involved GGD employees, and the GGDs enhanced their system security.

However, a group of citizens, represented by the ICAM foundation – a non-profit organization created to protect the interests of large groups of individuals when they suffer damages due to wrongful acts of large (government) organizations – held the Ministry of Health accountable for the data breach and filed a mass damage claim against the ministry. The Ministry of Health had tasked the GGDs with expediting testing and monitoring virus spread among citizens. The lawsuit accused the ministry of negligence in the design of the IT systems and the lack of proper employee screening and data access monitoring. They demanded the government to structurally embed privacy and information security in policy and sought compensation for those whose personal information was compromised: 500 euros for everyone who was included in the database, and 1250 euros for the 1250 victims whose personal data was actually stolen.

2.2 Proposed European CSA Regulation Causing a Controversy

In 2022, the European Commission introduced a draft legislation aimed at combating child sexual abuse – the Child Sexual Abuse (CSA) Regulation. This proposed law mandates that communication service providers monitor their platforms (e.g., WhatsApp) for content related to child abuse, removing and reporting such content as necessary. Experts have raised concerns that this legislation may undermine privacy standards, notably end-to-end encryption, thereby establishing a precedent for mass surveillance (Mullin, 2022; Neroni Rezende, 2024). Furthermore, it is anticipated that providers may resort to employing third-party automated scanning tools to identify CSA content. Such entities have reportedly advocated for the enactment of this legislation (Stavinoha, 2023), shifting the onus onto providers to ensure a secure online environment. Critics argue that this technical solution is inadequate for addressing the complexities of the issue at hand. Overall, opponents argue that curtailing the privacy of communications is disproportional as the law will harm all internet users' fundamental rights such as privacy, including of those who are aimed to be protected.

In response, human rights organizations, non-governmental organizations (NGOs), and concerned citizens are actively protesting and lobbying against the enactment of this regulation. They propose alternative methods to address child abuse, emphasizing that CSA constitutes a multifaceted social issue best tackled through the concerted efforts of local law enforcement, social service agencies, educational institutions, and families – parties best positioned to detect and report such incidents (European Digital Rights, 2022). Several European Union member states, including the Netherlands, Germany, Italy, Malta, and Poland, have expressed reservations regarding this legislation (General Secretariat of the Council, 2023).

These two cases underscore the unpredictable impacts of digital technology on society. Everyone aims to benefit from digital technology, using, applying, and developing it to make life faster, more efficient, and more valuable. Yet, it is imperative to ensure the safety and privacy of all involved. The growing awareness of digitization's challenges across academia (see, e.g., Isin & Ruppert, 2015), politics, and the public prompts a critical inquiry: How can we apply digital technology so that its benefits are maximized without disadvantaging anyone, and what roles do the state and citizens play in this context? And in what ways will digitization reshape civic engagement and political action, emphasizing the emergence of new forms of rights, duties, and identities? The concept of 'technological citizenship' addresses these questions.

3. CITIZENSHIP

Frankenfeld uses 'citizenship' to indicate a connection among a group of people, endowed with certain rights and duties, overseen by an authority. In this sense, the conceptualization of 'technological citizenship' closely aligns with the general understanding of 'citizenship': as a citizen, you are part of a society within a state, enjoy the rights and duties of that state, and an authority oversees the enforcement of these rights and duties. However, citizenship encompasses more than this. Various disciplines offer different approaches to citizenship, providing insights into the digitization issue.

3.1 Legal Approach

From a legal perspective, citizenship involves defining who qualifies as citizens, what their rights and duties are, and who or what oversees their enforcement. National citizenship typically requires birth in the country, employment, or financial investment. Rights and duties include protection and political participation rights and the duty to comply with the law, regulated by the country's government and its agencies.

In defining 'technological citizenship,' Frankenfeld applies similar criteria, substituting national borders with the impact range of specific technology. A state authority is necessary to regulate this technology's impact and provide citizens affected by this technology with certain rights and duties. These 'technological citizens' are entitled to rights such as information and participation, informed consent, and a 'maximum level of danger,' alongside duties like participation, critical thinking, and acting responsibly in society. These rights and duties aim to prevent mutual endangerment while allowing freedom to experiment and innovate with technology. Part of the 'critical thinking' duty, for example, involves not hastily opposing technological innovation without considering its potential societal benefits. Thus, citizens are expected to behave responsibly when allowed to contribute to decisions on technology development or application in society. These rights and duties should ideally address the issues arising from digitization; problems typically emerge when technology impacts others unexpectedly and adversely, as seen in the two case studies.

3.1.1 Digital Rights and Authority

The concept that citizens are entitled to specific rights concerning technology is not an idea propagated exclusively by Frankenfeld. Numerous activist collectives and advocacy organizations fervently support the agenda for 'digital rights' – rights pertaining to citizens' interactions with digital technologies. These rights frequently serve as adaptations or expansions of established Universal or European human rights or civil liberties. Karppinen & Puukko (2020) have delineated these into two categories: positive rights, which enable citizens to engage actively with digital technology, and negative rights, designed to protect individuals from governmental overreach affecting privacy and freedom of expression. Furthermore, the advocacy for digital rights is posited as a pathway to distributive justice, offering the prospect of liberating marginalized groups from the constraints imposed by dominant societal structures.

Redeker et al. (2015) have situated the initiatives calling for new digital rights under the concept of 'digital constitutionalism.' They articulate that the constitutionalization of digital technology transcends merely establishing a set of rules and laws; it constitutes a process in which technology continuously innovates and precipitates new societal challenges, necessitating ongoing regulatory responses. The call for new legislation is perceived as the initial phase of constitutionalization, preceding their actual legal institutionalization.

These advocates for digital rights encounter a dilemma, which lacks a clear resolution, regarding the type of authority required to implement and enforce these rights (Redeker et al., 2015). Given the universal and international development and usage of digital technologies like the internet, there is a demand by some groups for universal rights that supersede state influence. Similar to early internet pioneers, they resist state attempts to impose regulations limiting freedom of expression and privacy online (Barlow, 1996; Karppinen & Puukko, 2020). The enforcement of such universal rights remains uncertain, raising the question of what kind of universal enforcer is needed to oversee the adherence to these rights. Even Frankenfeld does not provide a definitive answer, suggesting the necessity for a "statist Leviathan" whose authority extends beyond or is greater than the scope of technology's impact (Frankenfeld, 1992), without specifying whether this overseer operates within or beyond national boundaries.

3.1.2 The Responsible Authority in the EU Case

Nonetheless, recent advancements in internet activism and technology policy indicate a paradigm shift towards an expanded role for states and local governments in regulating digital technologies and the internet. State entities are increasingly acknowledged as pivotal regulators within the digital realm. This evolving perspective is notably gaining momentum within the European Union, as illustrated by the case study related to the drafting of legislation aimed at combating online child abuse. Through this legislative proposal, the European Union assigns a clear responsibility to its member states to address child abuse online, thereby affirming its authoritative influence in sculpting the digital legal landscape, with potential global legislative implications.

Digital rights activists and NGOs acknowledge this authoritative stance of the EU, recognizing both the risks it poses to digital rights and the opportunities it presents. By engaging in advocacy at the EU level, activist groups such as Bits of Freedom and the Electronic Frontier Foundation can significantly influence the development of European legislation to align with their objectives. A key tactic involves lobbying during the drafting phases of new laws pertaining to the digital sphere. This approach is currently being applied in the context of the proposed Child Sexual Abuse (CSA) regulation, and has previously demonstrated its efficacy, as seen with the GDPR (Jang & Newman, 2022).

Moreover, citizen-led initiatives, exemplified by "The Code" in the Netherlands (code.impakt.nl), showcase innovative forms of activism. Through these initiatives, citizens actively encourage local politicians and Members of the European Parliament to support legislation that safeguards fundamental online rights.

Accordingly, calls for digital rights can be interpreted as advocating for the facilitation of technological citizenship within a state or group of states, such as the EU. Technological citizenship, therefore, overlaps with existing forms of citizenship, with the overseeing "state Leviathan" remaining the same. Consequently, states are held accountable for enabling technological citizenship for their citizens, necessitating the establishment of rights and duties related to technology that empower citizens to act in the best interest of society.

3.1.3 The Responsible Authority in the GGD Case

This is also evident in the GGD case, where the plaintiffs hold the Dutch government accountable for the data breach. This is notable, considering the involvement of multiple parties. The GGD rapidly hired many new employees, occasionally neglecting to verify whether these employees had a certificate of conduct, which is a formal requirement for working in a government agency. Furthermore, new employees received inadequate training and monitoring, especially as they worked remotely from home. Notably, it was these new GGD employees who exploited the situation by downloading and selling information on the black market. Nevertheless, the plaintiffs hold the government responsible for failing to establish conditions necessary for 'good' citizenship. The government, focusing on efficiency and accessibility, should have also prioritized privacy and information security as fundamental conditions when instructing the GGD to scale up testing capacity. According to the plaintiffs, this clearly did not happen, leading to employees knowingly and unknowingly abusing the situation. One of the detainees cited the ease of database access as a reason for their actions, unaware of its illegality.

Moreover, the lawsuit addresses a more systemic failure of the government regarding the implementation of information security and privacy in policy. The Dutch equivalent of the GDPR (the 'AVG') mandates the protection of citizens' personal information privacy and data security within organizational databases. In this case, the AVG applied to the GGD as the proprietor of the IT systems storing personal data, making the GGD the accountable entity for securely managing this information, which they failed to do.

The enforcement of the AVG is monitored by the Personal Data Authority (AP), which should have identified the GGD's improper privacy practices, issued warnings, and, if unimproved, imposed fines. However, the AP has faced capacity issues for years. In 2021, 9,800 complaints from the previous year remained unaddressed, and only 0.3% of reported data breaches were investigated (Autoriteit Persoonsgegevens, 2021). Several consultancy firms have explored the AP's failures, concluding that it lacks sufficient financial support and staff to fulfill its responsibilities. This appears to be a political decision, with the ruling party in the Netherlands favoring individual company responsibility for personal data management and over-allocating resources to an authority that ensures compliance. This approach has left citizens vulnerable, exemplifying the Dutch government's structural failure to secure information privacy and security through its policies.

The revelation of this data breach prompted politicians to leverage the case to advocate for increased financial resources for the AP. Subsequently, a decision was made to augment its budget. Nevertheless, according to the AP and critics, the allocation remains insufficient. Consequently, the plaintiffs demand that the government assume greater responsibility for ensuring citizens' privacy and information security in the future. In essence, the government must enable citizens to act appropriately when dealing with digital technology, facilitating technological citizenship for its citizens.

3.2 Political/Sociological Approach

The legal approach has defined relevant groups and their responsibilities: citizens have rights and duties, and the state oversees their enforcement. These rights and duties enable citizens to act correctly for society. However, what rights and duties are necessary for 'good' citizenship? How are they defined, and by whom? These questions are addressed from a political/sociological perspective (see, e.g., Marshall, 1950; Theiss-Morse, 1993).

Various rights and duties related to technological citizenship have been discussed. In the GGD case, plaintiffs demand the government structurally embed privacy and information security in future policy. In the CSA case, the necessity to uphold private communications on the Internet is emphasized. Digital rights sought by internet activists primarily aim to protect internet freedom of expression. The diversity of these focuses is unsurprising, given technology's continually changing impact on society. The challenges posed by digitization did not exist when Frankenfeld wrote his article in 1992, and current issues may become irrelevant in twenty years. New laws and rights are continuously needed to address technology-induced problems in society. Citizen input is essential for defining these rights and laws, with the political/sociological approach to citizenship examining how citizens strive to obtain new rights and duties, their implementation in policy, and their practical execution.

3.2.1 Democracy as a Dynamic Process

Political scientist Dewey (2016) views democracy as a dynamic process, where the state's origin and purpose are to address citizens' problems. A democratic state must remain vigilant to its citizens' issues. Dewey uses the analogy of a shoemaker: although the shoemaker is the repair expert, the shoe wearer best understands where the shoe pinches. Without the shoe wearer's input, it is impossible to know precisely what problems the shoemaker, or government, must solve. Thus, citizens' political efforts are crucial for bringing problems to the political agenda, leading to new policies that enable good citizenship.

Sociologist Marshall describes citizens' political efforts as a "never-ending struggle," as governments within a democracy always protect the rights of the previously dominant group (Bellamy, 2008, p 49; see also Marshall, 1950). When citizens encounter new problems, such as those arising from new technology, it is up to them to make these issues known to the government and ensure they are addressed. This often occurs through civil rights movements where citizens advocate for their rights or demand new ones. These movements frequently involve emancipation, striving for a full place in society from a disadvantaged position, or demanding equality for a minority against the dominant group. This endeavor requires constant renewal as new problems emerge due to (technological) developments, necessitating ongoing policy redesign. Hence, laws, rules, and institutions are not fixed but continuously evolve – democracy is a dynamic process.

3.2.2 Forms of Counterpower

It is clear that within a democracy, laws and regulations are not solely devised by the government in isolation. This occurs in conjunction with citizens who experience policy implementation, respond to it, and strive to ensure it is adjusted to better address their problems. Citizens in a democracy have various political participation opportunities to make their problems and desires known to the state, including voting, participating in referendums, and forming lobbying groups to persuade politicians. However, political participation extends beyond these methods. Rosanvallon (2008) describes these additional forms under the concept of 'counter-democracy,' asserting that a well-functioning democracy must also include various forms of counterpower. Although not institutionalized like regular voting, counterpower is a vital component of a democratic society. Rosanvallon identifies three ways citizens exercise counterpower: judgment, oversight, and prevention.

Judgment

The GGD case particularly exemplifies the first form of counterpower: citizens can sue the state, thus evaluating its performance. Lawsuits between citizens and the state can correct government policy in two ways: by identifying misconduct and generating jurisprudence that serves as a framework for future legislation.

In the GGD case, the group of citizens took the Ministry of Health to court because it oversaw the COVID-19 response and instructed GGDs to use poorly secured IT systems. This is problematic as the plaintiffs argue that digital security is a crucial government responsibility. Additionally, it remains unclear whether millions of citizens' personal data have fallen into criminal hands. According to the plaintiffs, the government must take responsibility and clarify the extent of the leak. The lawsuit aims to restore trust in the government, requiring the structural embedding of privacy and information security in policy. The plaintiffs hope the lawsuit will provide the necessary incentives to prevent future data breaches.

If the lawsuit reveals that the government indeed neglected its responsibilities, a significant policy implementation error is highlighted. This establishes the government's accountability regarding digital technology, serving as guidance when new technology is introduced. If the government repeats a similar mistake in the future, potentially related to other or new digital technology, citizens will be better positioned to hold it accountable based on this case. Through this form of counterpower, citizens significantly influence government policy.

In the CSA case, this form of counterpower is also relevant, as opponents of the proposed law argue that the law might turn out disproportionally when a court would have to judge a conflict in the future. Therefore, they warn for creating an unlawful law that might be operationalized by citizens to sue the European government in the case of a fundamental rights breach.

Oversight

The second form of counterpower is evident in both cases: citizens play a crucial role in overseeing government performance. A functioning media landscape is essential for this purpose. Journalism can expose misconduct and societal issues, placing topics on the public and political agenda.

In the GGD case, several GGD employees were concerned about the database's easy accessibility. Some attempted to report the leak to their employer but were ignored. A whistleblower platform revealed that employees were searching for and sharing information about public figures. This caused some commotion but had no repercussions. Only when an investigative journalist discovered personal information from the database being sold on the online black market did the issue gain enough attention to become politically relevant, and the Minister of Health praised the journalist who brought the case to light.

In the CSA case, a well-functioning media landscape is essential for citizens to be informed about the misconduct of online child abuse while at the same time being aware of responsible solutions to solve this issue. This is necessary to fulfill the duty of 'critical thinking' as laid out by Frankenfeld, and to hold the government accountable for developing and implementing equitable policies and laws. Citizens have a critical responsibility to monitor government performance and bring misconduct to the political agenda, especially regarding digital technology, whose impact can be challenging to predict.

Prevention

The third form of counterpower involves blocking government decisions, especially when citizens feel insufficiently involved in the decision-making process. In the CSA case, this form of counter-power is particularly demonstrated. Concerned by the far-reaching implications of this law, citizens and NGOs have united to collectively voice their opposing views. An open letter was presented, which was signed by 134 national, European, and international civil society organizations (Civil Society Open Letter 2022). An open letter criticizing the law by 300 scientists around the world has also been presented (Scientists Open Letter, 2023). Finally, the NGO European Digital Rights initiated a petition against the law, which was signed by 200.000 citizens and 133 NGOs, and published a white paper that presents alternatives that would provide more responsible solutions (see https://stopscanningme.eu/en).

This case demonstrates that new international laws for the digital domain can have a major and direct impact on the lives of citizens, but might also have global consequences. This bill outlines the responsibilities of private parties in detecting child sexual abuse material and therefore sets the norm for how to deal with such problems in the digital domain. To protect one right – the protection of children – another fundamental right – privacy of communications – is about to be jeopardized. The role of NGOs and the actions of citizens by signing petitions and protesting to address the problematic consequences of this bill might crucially impact the implementation of this bill.

4. CONCLUSION

The exploration of 'technological citizenship' in this article reveals the intricate relationship between citizens, states, and the digital realm. The case studies of the GGD's data breach and the proposed European CSA regulation illustrate the multifaceted challenges and responsibilities that arise in the age of digitization. These instances underscore the necessity for a dynamic and participatory approach to citizenship, where individuals are not only informed and protected but also actively involved in shaping the policies and technologies that influence their lives.

Moreover, the discussion highlights the evolving nature of citizenship in the digital era, marked by the emergence of new rights, duties, and forms of engagement. As we navigate the complexities of digital technology, the principles of 'technological citizenship' offer a framework for ensuring that the benefits of digitization are harnessed ethically and equitably, without compromising the fundamental rights and well-being of citizens.

The imperative role of states in facilitating this form of citizenship is clear, necessitating policies that empower citizens to participate meaningfully in the digital society. Simultaneously, the collective actions of citizens, through advocacy, oversight, and innovation, play a crucial role in steering the digital transformation toward a more inclusive, secure, and democratic future. As we move forward, the collaborative efforts of governments, civil society, and citizens will be vital in realizing the full potential of technological citizenship, ensuring that the digital age is marked by advancement, not at the cost of rights and freedom, but in their enhancement and protection.

ACKNOWLEDGEMENT

This publication is part of the project "Strengthening Cyber Resilience by Technological Citizenship (with project number 410.19.004 of the research programme "Digital Society – The Informed Citizen" which is financed by the Dutch Research Council (NWO).

REFERENCES

Autoriteit Persoonsgegevens, (2021). *Klachtenrapportage AP 2020*. AP, The Hague (https://www.autoriteitpersoonsgegevens.nl/documenten/klachtenrapportage-ap-2020).

Barlow, J. P., (1996). *A Declaration of the Independence of Cyberspace*. https://www.eff.org/cyberspace-independence.

Bellamy, R., (2008). *Citizenship: A Very Short Introduction*. Oxford University Press, Oxford.

Civil Society Open Letter, (2022). *European Commission: Uphold Privacy, Security and Free Expression by Withdrawing New Law* (https://edri.org/wp-content/uploads/2022/06/04.2023_ENG_Open-letter-to-the-European-Commission-on-the-proposed-CSA-Regulation.pdf).

Dewey, J., (2016). *The Public and Its Problems: An Essay in Political Inquiry*. Swallow Press, Athens.

European Digital Rights, (2022). *A Safe Internet for All. Upholding Private and Secure Communications* (https://edri.org/wp-content/uploads/2022/10/EDRi-Position-Paper-CSAR.pdf).

Frankenfeld, P. J., (1992). Technological Citizenship: A Normative Framework for Risk Studies. *Science, Technology, & Human Values*, Vol. 17, No. 4, pp 459–484.

General Secretariat of the Council, (2023). *Proposal for a Regulation of the European Parliament and of the Council Laying down Rules to Prevent and Combat Child Sexual Abuse - Comments from Delegations on Articles 12 to 15*. Council of the European Union, Brussels.

Hintz, A., et al, (2019). *Digital Citizenship in a Datafied Society*. Polity, Cambridge.

Jang, W., & Newman, A. L., (2022). Enforcing European Privacy Regulations from Below: Transnational Fire Alarms and the General Data Protection Regulation. *JCMS: Journal of Common Market Studies*, Vol. 60, No. 2, pp 283–300.

Isin, E, & Ruppert, E., (2015). *Being Digital Citizens*. Rowman & Littlefield International, London.

Karppinen, K., & Puukko, O., (2020). Four Discourses of Digital Rights: Promises and Problems of Rights-Based Politics. *Journal of Information Policy*, Vol. 10, pp 304–328.

Marshall, T H., (1950). *Citizenship and Social Class: And Other Essays*. Cambridge University Press, Cambridge.

Mullin, J., (2022). EFF Tells E.U. Commission: Don't Break Encryption. *Electronic Frontier Foundation* (https://www.eff.org/deeplinks/2022/03/eff-tells-eu-commission-dont-break-encryption).

Neroni Rezende, I., (2024). The Proposed Regulation to Fight Online Child Sexual Abuse: An Appraisal of Privacy, Data Protection and Criminal Justice Issues. *International Review of Law, Computers & Technology*, doi: 10.1080/13600869.2024.2324548.

Redeker, D. et al, (2015). Towards Digital Constitutionalism? Mapping Attempts to Craft an Internet Bill of Rights. *International Communication Gazette*, Vol. 80, No. 4, pp 302–319.

Rosanvallon, P., (2008). *Counter-Democracy. Politics in an Age of Distrust*. Cambridge University Press, Cambridge.

Scientists Open Letter, (2023). *Joint Statement of Scientists and Researchers on EU's Proposed Child Sexual Abuse Regulation*. https://edri.org/wp-content/uploads/2023/07/Open-Letter-CSA-Scientific-community.pdf

Theiss-Morse, E., (1993). Conceptualizations of Good Citizenship and Political Participation. *Political Behavior*, Vol. 15, No. 4, pp 355-380.

World Economic Forum, (2024). *The Global Risks Report 2024*. World Economic Forum, Geneva.

WHEN YOU SAY DISCRIMINATION, DO YOU MEAN...?: COMMUNICATION CHALLENGES AND CROSS-DISCIPLINARY TRANSLATION RISKS IN ARTIFICIAL INTELLIGENCE

Hilde G. Corneliussen[1], Gilda Seddighi[2] and Cheshta Arora[1]
[1]Western Norway Research Institute, Box 163, 6851 Sogndal, Norway
[2]Norwegian Research Centre (NORCE), Postboks 22 Nygårdstangen, 5838 Bergen, Norway

ABSTRACT

The paper addresses the challenges of translating socially relevant concepts related to artificial intelligence (AI) across different disciplines and discursive contexts. Based on a survey of around 500 organisations in the public sector in Norway as well as 19 in-depth interviews, we map how the risk of discrimination associated with AI is perceived and translated by the representatives of the public sector in Norway. The paper foregrounds six discursive responses to the risk of discrimination associated with the development and deployment of AI in the public sector. Based on the findings, we recommend that AI developers remain critically aware of the dynamic and emergent nature of discrimination without replacing it with ancillary concepts such as bias, differentiation, privacy, or other mainstream concepts such as justice or ethics.

KEYWORDS

Artificial Intelligence, Public Sector, Risk of Discrimination, Inter-Disciplinary Challenges

1. INTRODUCTION

There's an increasing interest among public administrators in Norway and the EU to explore the potentials of data-driven technologies such as artificial intelligence (AI) for a more efficient public sector, more value creation in the business sector and a simpler everyday life for most people (Kommunal- og moderniseringsdepartementet (KMD, 2020). While AI can bring notable benefits to the operations of various actors in the public sector (Alhosani & Alhashmi, 2024; Chiariello, 2021; Wirtz et al., 2019), it also brings risks of producing unfair results and discrimination against different demographic groups (Jørgensen, 2023; Kuziemski & Misuraca, 2020). In the interviews with representatives of AI development in the public sector in Norway, our initial question about the risks of discrimination according to the Equality and Anti-discrimination Act in Norway was translated into various other concepts, such as bias, fairness, explainability, openness, transparency, ethics, and privacy, or, in some cases, it was not on the agenda. In this paper, we foreground that although there is increasing awareness of various types of negative consequences and risks of AI, one of the barriers to counteract such risks is the challenge of translating concepts and communicating across disciplines. This challenge became apparent in our study of plans for introducing AI in the public sector in Norway and the risks of discrimination therein (Corneliussen et al., 2022).

Using the interviews from this previous study with public sector representatives engaged in the development of AI as our starting point, we will discuss how the concept of discrimination was translated and communicated and what effects and consequences this might have for the use of AI in the public sector. The research question we will pursue here is: How is the question of discrimination perceived and translated in the public sector and what are its consequences?

Developing our understanding of how the notion of discrimination is received in the field of AI development and innovation in the public sector will help identify better strategies for counteracting the harmful effects of AI. The Norwegian government's endeavours concerning data-driven AI are still in its nascent stage (Broomfield & Reutter, 2021) and the journey from ideation to implementation is best described as a "hop-on, hop-off" ride with several challenges producing unwanted stops and exit points (Corneliussen et al., 2024, p.1). Previous research has examined different aspects underpinning this gap between ideation and implementation and its consequences while noting the need for more studies that can identify the "issues that are largely unseen by both policymakers and practitioners" (Broomfield & Reutter, 2021, p.73). The list of societal harms and risks associated with AI is continuously growing (*AIAAIC - AI Algorithmic Risks Harms Taxonomy*, n.d.), highlighting an urgent need to reimagine ethical, participatory designs and actively interrogate normative values and practices that inform the development of data-driven technologies. Several examples and case studies have noted how AI models mirror existing discriminatory patterns in society with the risk of further amplifying and accelerating them (Birhane, 2021). Among the many infamous examples so far include deploying AI to identify a new employee or a new top leader for a company, both of which are prone to favour the demographic group stereotypically considered to be more suitable over other demographic groups (Drage & Mackereth, 2022; Srinivasan & Chander, 2021).

The concern with AI becomes more acute when it's discussed in the context of the public sector which relies on mining personal data to deliver essential welfare services. Norway has a long history of registering data about citizens, which can provide a valuable dataset for developing AI-based services (Broomfield and Rutter, 2021). However, the public sector's access to data has made researchers ask whether Norway risks "Stumbling into an Algorithmic Welfare Dystopia" in which predictive models can increase the risk of discrimination against certain demographic groups (Broomfield & Lintvedt, 2022, p.1). While the vast amount of data that the Norwegian state holds about citizens could provide important input for developing AI, this also introduces risks and is challenged by the privacy provisions under GDPR and its principle of data minimization which states that as little data as possible is stored for as short a time as possible (Malek, 2021). Thus, uncritical use of AI in the public sector can deny essential services to vulnerable and marginalized groups, cause discrimination at scale and give legitimacy to societal issues such as racism, discrimination, and inequality (Keyes et al., 2021). It is within this context that the translation of the concept of discrimination, as outlined in legislation, into concepts and practices that are meaningful to public sector employees becomes particularly important and requires critical unpacking.

Below we will present the empirical data from the study of AI in the Public sector in Norway and the methodological framework for this paper before presenting the findings regarding various translations of the concept of discrimination. Thereafter, we will discuss the connotations of these translations for AI development in the public sector before concluding with a discussion on the consequences of the translation.

We foreground the implications that the translations across disciplines have on the discourse of inclusion and discrimination in the context of AI development in the public sector in Norway. We understand translation not just as a search for equivalence or loss of 'correct' meaning but translations as sites of judgement and continuous contestation (Law & Lin, 2017) that generate meaning (Sarukkai, 2013), actions, and weave partial connections (Strathern, 2004). In doing so, we shift the focus from the individual beliefs and value systems of interviewees. Instead, we aim to highlight that the design and development of emerging technologies, such as AI systems and their socio-technical imaginaries, involves a dynamic interplay of forces and circumstances of different situations and disciplines. Within this interdisciplinary framework, actors may translate concepts suddenly or without careful consideration. However, an awareness of these processes can direct us towards more 'careful' (de la Bellacasa, 2011) practices concerning the development and deployment of AI in the public sector.

2. METHODS

The empirical data we use for this paper originates from a research project commissioned by the Norwegian Directorate for Children, Youth and Family Affairs to provide a better knowledge base for efforts to prevent discriminatory effects when using artificial intelligence in the public sector in Norway (Corneliussen et al., 2022). To learn more about how AI is used and understood in the public sector in Norway, we invited, together with other partners (ibid.), 500 public sector organisations to respond to a survey. States and municipal enterprises from sectors such as healthcare, education, employment and welfare administration, tax, customs and police were invited to respond to the survey which covered questions related to their use and plans for using AI and risks of discrimination.

The study was particularly focused on how public sector organisations perceived and dealt with risks of discrimination when developing AI and therefore a total of 19 in-depth interviews were subsequently conducted with organisations that had an AI system or project that involved the use of personal data which intensifies the risk of discrimination against certain demographic groups. It was during the in-depth interviews, where the question concerning discrimination was discussed with the interviewees, that the key moment of translation appeared – when discrimination was translated and understood by the respondents as a question concerning bias or through other ancillary concepts.

3. THEORETICAL FRAMEWORK

While the original study (Corneliussen et al., 2022) aimed to explore the extent of public sector organisations' use or plan to use AI, this paper takes as its starting point the translations experienced during the interviews when the interviewer asked questions about discrimination. In the study, it was explicitly stated that we used the concept of discrimination in accordance with the Equality and Anti-discrimination Act (EAD). EAD accounts for unlawful discrimination of certain demographic groups, with the particular awareness of discrimination as a result of gender, pregnancy, care responsibility, ethnicity, religion, disability, sexuality, gender identity and age. Despite this clear frame of reference for the concept, in most of the 19 interviews, the interviewers observed instances where the concept of discrimination was substituted with some of the other concepts that we will outline below. To make sense of this moment, where the initial concept was moved into a different frame of reference, we engage with the concept of discursive resources (Dick, 2004; Corneliussen & Seddighi, 2020), which points to how organisations and individuals embedded therein use their own discursive context to understand and make sense of, for instance, external requests to follow rules regarding gender equality. This means that instead of identifying how certain translations are misplaced within the framework of the EAD, we aim to widen our understanding of how such translations involve a different set of discourses from which the interviewees speak. The analysis below thus aims to deepen our understanding of how AI developers in the public sector perceive the risk of discrimination in different ways, which will help identify strategies to counteract this risk in the development of AI in the public as well as private sectors.

While the framework of discursive resources supports the analysis of how interviewees address discrimination, emphasizing the contextual, and discipline-based relevance of certain concepts over 'discrimination', a feminist perspective supports examining how discourses also involve elements of hierarchical relations and power struggles (Livholts & Tamboukou, 2015). The concepts that we choose to use when discussing for instance the risk of discrimination, will affect not only how this risk is perceived but also the ability to deal with such risks. These two theoretical perspectives will guide our analysis: first, in understanding the discursive context of the translations encountered in the interviews, and second, in pointing towards the effects and consequences of such translations for the development of AI for the public sector.

4. FINDINGS

In the survey as well as the interviews, the issue of discrimination was presented within a framework of the Norwegian Anti-Discrimination Act (EAD) in the following manner: "According to the Norwegian Equality and Anti-Discrimination Act, it is not permitted to discriminate based on the categories listed below. Which of these are relevant to or handled by AI in your organisation? Gender, pregnancy, leave in connection with childbirth or adoption, caregiving responsibilities, ethnicity, religion/belief, disability, sexual orientation, gender identity, gender expression, age". By explicitly associating our understanding of discrimination with EAD, we wanted to emphasize that we were interested in the risk of unlawful discrimination which could lead to directly or indirectly treating certain demographic groups differently or unfairly compared to others. However, even though the starting point within the framework of the EAD was made clear from the start, the interviewees often responded directly through other concepts, such as bias, as the basis for understanding the question. Furthermore, most of the interviews were made in Norwegian, making this moment of translation even more peculiar. The Norwegian equivalent for 'discrimination' is 'diskriminering' but the English term 'bias' has no Norwegian equivalent apart from the imported term 'bias', and some of the concepts introduced rather reflected a disciplinary terminology from computer science or data science. Below we have grouped the responses under six headings that reflect slightly different contexts or discursive resources.

Discrimination: Only in a couple of interviews did the respondents speak about discrimination as 'unlawful discrimination' following the EAD act. These respondents were part of AI projects that had interdisciplinary expertise on discrimination either within the group or at the organisation level. Other respondents frequently invoked discrimination through other ancillary concepts such as:

Bias: Most respondents evoked 'bias' in response to the question concerning discrimination. This mainly reflected a computer science or a data scientist's epistemic universe where the concept of bias is used to talk about how algorithms, AI models, and data can produce unfair results (Srinivasan & Chander, 2021).

Mainstream concepts: The second most common way of responding to questions about discrimination was to respond within a reference frame of one or more of a series of concepts that often appear in discussions of harmful results of AI, thus what we have labelled as mainstream concepts here. These were concepts such as fairness, openness, transparency, explainability, representativity, justice, and ethics. These concepts were used to talk about the challenges of avoiding harmful results with the use of AI and machine learning in particular and reflect concepts dominating these debates today (Birhane et al., 2022).

GDPR: The General Data Protection Law, GDPR, received a lot of attention when it was introduced and, in particular for the public sector, draws up a hard boundary not to be crossed. In the interviews, this was frequently reflected in concerns around dealing with personal data where the main focus was on compliance and the need to operate within the limits of this law. The law itself poses some challenges to AI development such as requesting to collect as little data as possible, and storing it for as short as possible. However, in some cases, GDPR appeared to take the place of related laws such as the EAD.

Differentiation: The concept of differentiation was used interchangeably with discrimination by some of the interviewees. In one of the interviews, the interviewee responded to the question about discrimination by saying "Of course we discriminate. We need to differentiate between different people such as men and women" (paraphrased). This informant spoke within the framework of mathematics, statistics, and computer science, where it is necessary to differentiate between different entities (Friedman, 1997).

Unaddressed: In a couple of our interviews, it was made clear that the issue of unlawful discrimination against certain demographic groups was not on the agenda of the project. One of the informants simply replied by saying, "We haven't thought about that. Thank you for reminding us". They illustrate a group of AI developers who had not had access to competence about discrimination in the development process, and therefore they had not come to think of this as an important perspective to include in the process.

5. DISCUSSION: EFFECTS AND CONSEQUENCES

The discursive universe encountered when asking AI developers in the public sector about the risk of discrimination with AI reflects how this question has a variable status in the different AI projects. In this section, we discuss the consequences of each of the discursive responses:

Bias: Given that computer scientists were prominent in the interviews, bias was the language most familiar to them when questions of discrimination were raised. Bias and discrimination are, however, not synonyms and the jump from bias to discrimination is not straightforward. The concept of 'bias' in the Anglo-phone philosophy of science has witnessed a series of reformulations. It is no longer sufficient to merely understand bias as preferences, deviations, inclinations or prejudices that can be accounted for to arrive at a value-free or neutral science. Bias has a moral import which can have discriminatory effects. Feminist approaches to techno-science have played a leading role in interrogating how different types of bias underpinning knowledge-making practices might have discriminatory effects (Longino & Doell, 1983). This helped debunk the common myths of science such as objectivity, universality and value-neutrality by foregrounding that technoscience is often situated and partial. Thus, it is important to account for the discriminatory effects when accounting for bias in science.

More recently, the question of bias has emerged as central to interrogating the theory and practice of data science and consequently how the discourse around AI performs the same modern myths of objectivity and value-neutrality that were earlier identified in the practice of science. These mythologies of scientific practice that data science mimics co-produce bias as a problem that can be treated through methodological fixes. The perspective of a technological fix to bias in society can make it challenging to address the discriminatory outcomes of AI. This is because it creates the illusion that simple technological solutions can make the problem disappear. The foundation for bias in sight might be limited to easily recognized variables such as gender, age, and sexuality while failing to explore and deal with the fact that discrimination is dynamic and all attempts at AI-related monitoring, predicting, automating, and profiling can lead to several discriminatory outcomes. This was apparent in some of the methods used to 'wash' the data, such as anonymizing it and removing basic features like gender and age. However, it remains an open question to consider whether other pieces of data could also potentially lead to discriminatory AI results. Furthermore, the concept of bias was most often used to refer to unconscious bias, that is, discrimination that we are not aware of (Suveren, 2022). In the interviews this appeared as a translation from the risk of discrimination with AI to a general risk of discrimination in society, often combined with the questioning of whether AI can be better than society. The findings from the interviews were supported by the results of the survey, where less than a third of the survey respondents reported that the main challenge of dealing with discrimination is demographic bias in the data, while two-thirds of respondents answered that the main challenge was to anonymize the data (ref (Corneliussen et al., 2022), Figure 3.1).

Mainstream concepts: The mainstream concepts and values such as fairness, openness, transparency, explainability, representativity, justice, and ethics have a critical role in the development of AI. However, they do not cover the responsibilities covered under EAD. Furthermore, it seems that these concepts, due to their prominent role in the discourses and policies about AI, are not only concepts that AI developers in Norway are more familiar with than EAD's version of discrimination but also appear as more tangible and accessible tools for dealing with harmful effects of AI. In the interviews, this was illustrated with these concepts not only replacing the concept of discrimination but also representing a solution. However, these mainstream concepts do not always align with the aims of the EAD. Concerns around discrimination are not always implied in these mainstream concepts, and AI developers relying on these mainstream concepts still need to develop a careful understanding of the risk of discrimination underpinning their AI projects.

GDPR: GDPR was introduced in Norway as an unyielding framework with mechanisms for ensuring that companies fulfil their obligations according to the law. On the other hand, the EAD, although recognised and accepted in society in general, does not have a mechanism for ensuring that organisations comply with the law or follow-up guidance for organisations in need (Nordberg, 2019).

Differentiation: The translation of discrimination into differentiation also changes the meaning from the EAD targeting unlawful discrimination, to a lawful differential treatment. This translation thus makes it very difficult to talk about discrimination according to the EAD.

Unaddressed: It should be sufficient to foreground that not putting questions relating to discrimination on the agenda does not promote or facilitate any strategies or ways of dealing with issues of discrimination.

Table 1 sums up the different translations, their discursive context and meaning, and the effects and consequences they might have.

Table 1. Translations of the concept of discrimination referring to the Equality and Anti-Discrimination Act

Translation of discrimination	Discursive context and meaning	Effects and consequences
Discrimination	Equality and Anti-Discrimination Act	Ability to deal with unwanted discrimination.
Bias	Commonly used in computer science for referring to differences between demographic groups in society	Dealing with demographic differences through a technological fix. Risk of simplifying both problem and solution
Mainstream Concepts	Common concepts to talk about challenges of producing fair results with the use of AI.	Alternative frameworks talk about harm and justice, without engaging with the dynamic and emergent nature of discrimination.
GDPR	Legal framework for working with personal data	Taking precedence before other considerations such as EAD.
Differentiation	A mathematical concept for distinguishing between variables.	Replacing discrimination for differentiation erases the core principle of unwanted

		discrimination targeted by the EAD.
Unaddressed	The issue of discrimination was not on the agenda for the AI project.	Not having discrimination on the agenda makes it difficult to deal with such issues.

6. CONCLUSION

The paper presents communication challenges in interviews with AI developers in the public sector in Norway. When asked about their views on the risk of discrimination, most informants exchanged this concept for other concepts. As discussed above, it is possible to understand this translation in terms of the discursive resources that the informants were talking from. However, these translations also have effects.

The biggest challenge is that perspectives that can help nuance our understanding of unlawful discrimination were weakly represented among AI developers in the public sector in Norway. Not including this perspective will make it more difficult to fully understand the risk of discrimination, and thus also to develop strategies to avoid further producing or reproducing discrimination. While the mainstream concepts, as well as GDPR, are important tools for AI development, an uncritical recourse to them will not fully capture the ambition of the EAD, and thus they cannot fully substitute the necessary critical work required in any development and deployment of AI projects. Unfortunately, it seems the mainstream concepts in some cases appear as a fully adequate solution to any challenges of reducing harmful results with AI. Thus, while we appreciate these mainstream concepts' frameworks as highly relevant for AI development, we will encourage AI developers to also include a critical perspective on discrimination along with the understanding that the EAD is premised upon, which is discrimination against certain demographic groups for reasons that are unlawful and thus not legitimate.

This above analysis illustrates that we lack a common language to communicate across disciplines and fields of expertise. One example is the exchange of discrimination with the concept of differentiation, moving away from unlawful discrimination to deliberately identifying differences between individuals.

This further illustrates how knowledge about discrimination in terms of EAD is necessary to be involved in AI development. In other words, AI development needs to happen in interdisciplinary groups that can critically unpack the existing as well as emergent risks of discrimination associated with AI.

Bias is the most used concept that AI developers talk about to avoid the harmful effects of AI models. As we have argued above, this will not cover the need to focus on unlawful and emergent discrimination in accordance with the EAD. It has been argued that most data-based AI models are error-prone (Pasquinelli & Joler, 2021) and harms (such as discrimination, and exclusion) can be introduced throughout the ML life (Suresh & Guttag, 2021) in the way data is collected, curated, and annotated, or how the AI system is designed, by whom, pivoting on which values, and to achieve what goals. Given this, an evocation of 'bias' plays a performative role in the practice of data science. Critical perspectives on data-driven approaches have underscored how reliance on bias reinforces the notion of neutrality and objectivity in data science (Birhane et al., 2022). This reliance reproduces a false sense of security, or strengthens the hope that we can develop technologies for good if we can fix its inherent bias and align it with abstract principles such as transparency or fairness (Powell et al., 2022). Further, it shifts the focus away from systemic harms of technologies we build to individual perception. Within critical work on AI and data-driven practices, several authors have argued for a move away from shallow, technical, methodological considerations of bias to its social, and ethical considerations where bias ought to be understood in relation to AI harms such as discrimination, exclusion and inequality (Birhane, 2021; Dancy & Saucier, 2022; Draude et al., 2018, 2019). Thus, nurturing an attitude of responsibility concerning bias in AI needs a sociotechnical approach that addresses the cultures of algorithm (Draude et al., 2019), and a stronger, interdisciplinary and critical focus on how these systems are designed, developed, and deployed (Dancy & Saucier, 2022). It also demands deep insights into individual and organisational behaviour, economic incentives, as well as complex dynamics of the sociotechnical systems (Adomavicius & Yang, 2022). This requires improving disciplinary skills or fostering interdisciplinarity within teams working on data-driven solutions in fields as varied as hate speech, agriculture or climate (Doman & Garrison, 2021). These interventions underscore responsibility and response-ability vis-a-vis bias (Feinberg, 2007).

In Norway, discrimination is addressed through the Equality and Anti-discrimination Act (EAD) which has been in the making for more than four decades and has directed social change via the "transformative potential of law" (Hellum et al., 2024, p.135). While more critical legal research is needed to understand if EAD is enough to tackle AI or data-based discrimination, it's important to note that the act's emphasis on discrimination and on avoiding new and emergent discrimination gets obfuscated in the practice of developing AI for the public sector.

The findings of our study illustrate that discrimination is not on the agenda of AI developers in Norway and is often side-stepped by evoking other ancillary concerns such as difference, bias, privacy, transparency etc. While it's important to ensure that AI models are fair, transparent and privacy-respecting, encoding these values doesn't guarantee that the model will not have discriminating effects.

ACKNOWLEDGEMENT

The research project referred to in this paper was funded by the Directorate for Children, Youth and Family Affairs. We want to thank our colleagues Aisha Iqbal and Rudolf Andersen at Rambøll Management Consulting who also participated in the data collection, for collaborating on the project. The elaborate discussion of the translation challenges is original for this paper produced by the authors.

REFERENCES

Adomavicius, G., & Yang, M., (2022). Integrating Behavioral, Economic, and Technical Insights to Understand and Address Algorithmic Bias: A Human-Centric Perspective. *ACM Transactions on Management Information Systems*, Vol. 13, No. 3, pp. 1–27. https://doi.org/10.1145/3519420

AIAAIC - AI algorithmic risks harms taxonomy., n.d.. [dataset]. Retrieved 30 October 2023, from https://www.aiaaic.org/projects/ai-algorithmic-risks-harms-taxonomy

Alhosani, K., & Alhashmi, S. M., (2024). Opportunities, challenges, and benefits of AI innovation in government services: A review. *Discover Artificial Intelligence,* Vol. 4, No. 1, pp. 18. https://doi.org/10.1007/s44163-024-00111-w

Birhane, A., (2021). Algorithmic injustice: A relational ethics approach. *Patterns,* Vol. 2, No. 2, pp. 100205. https://doi.org/10.1016/j.patter.2021.100205

Birhane, A., Ruane, E., Laurent, T., S. Brown, M., Flowers, J., Ventresque, A., & L. Dancy, C., (2022). The Forgotten Margins of AI Ethics. *Proceedings of the 2022 ACM Conference on Fairness, Accountability, and Transparency.* Seoul, Republic of Korea, pp. 948–958. https://doi.org/10.1145/3531146.3533157

Broomfield, H., Lintvedt, M.N., (2022). Is Norway Stumbling into an Algorithmic Welfare Dystopia? Snubler Norge inn i en algoritmisk velferdsdystopi? *Tidsskrift for velferdsforskning*, Vol. 25, No. 3. pp 1-15. https://doi.org/10.18261/tfv.25.3.2

Broomfield, H., & Reutter, L., (2021). Towards a Data-Driven Public Administration: An Empirical Analysis of Nascent Phase Implementation. *Scandinavian Journal of Public Administration*, Vol. 25, No. 2, pp. 73–97.

Chiariello, A. M., (2021). European Review of Digital Administration & Law | AI and Public Services: A Challenging Relationship Between Benefits, Risks and Compliance with Unavoidable Principles. *European Review of Digital Administration & Law - Erdal*, Vol. 2, No. 2, pp. 185–203. https://doi.org/9791259947529 16

Corneliussen, H. G., Iqbal, A., Seddighi, G., & Andersen, R., (2022). Bruk av kunstig intelligens i offentlig sektor og risiko for diskriminering. *Vestlandsforsking,* 7–2022, pp. 80. https://www.vestforsk.no/sites/default/files/2023-03/VFrapport7_2022_KI_i_offentlig_sektor.pdf

Corneliussen, H., Seddighi, G., Iqbal, A., & Andersen, R., (2024). Artificial Intelligence in the Public Sector in Norway: AI Development as a Hop-on-Hop-off Journey. *AI, Data, and Digitalization. SAIDD 2023. Communications in Computer and Information Science,* Vol. 1810. Springer, Cham., pp. 160-172 https://doi.org/10.1007/978-3-031-53770-7_11

de la Bellacasa, M. P., (2011). Matters of care in technoscience: Assembling neglected things. *Social Studies of Science*, Vol. 41, No. 1, pp. 85–106.

Doman, M., & Garrison, C., (2021). Introducing algorithmic bias considerations in an introductory CS course. *Journal of Computing Sciences in Colleges*, Vol. 37, No. 5, pp. 31–42.

Drage, E., & Mackereth, K., (2022). Does AI Debias Recruitment? Race, Gender, and AI's "Eradication of Difference". *Philosophy & Technology*, Vol. 35, No. 4, pp. 89. https://doi.org/10.1007/s13347-022-00543-1

Draude, C., Klumbyte, G., Lücking, P., & Treusch, P., (2019). Situated algorithms: A sociotechnical systemic approach to bias. *Online Information Review,* Vol. 44, No. 2, pp. 325–342. https://doi.org/10.1108/OIR-10-2018-0332

Draude, C., Klumbytė, G., & Treusch, P. (2018). Re-Considering Bias: What Could Bringing Gender Studies and Computing Together Teach Us About Bias in Information Systems? *CEUR Workshop Proceedings*, Vol.1-2103, Paper No. 3. *https://ceur-ws.org/Vol-2103/paper_3.pdf*

Feinberg, M., (2007). Hidden Bias to Responsible Bias: An Approach to Information Systems Based on Haraway's Situated Knowledges. *Information Research: Proceedings of the Sixth International Conference on Conceptions of Library and Information Science—"Featuring the Future"*, Vol. 12, No. 4. https://informationr.net/ir/12-4/colis07.html

Friedman, J.H., (1997). On Bias, Variance, 0/1—Loss, and the Curse-of-Dimensionality. *Data Mining and Knowledge Discovery, Vol. 1*, pp. 55–77. https://doi.org/10.1023/A:1009778005914

Hellum, A. et al., (Eds.)., (2023). *Nordic Equality and Anti-Discrimination Laws in the Throes of Change: Legal developments in Sweden, Finland, Norway, and Iceland.* Routledge, London.

Jørgensen, R. F., (2023). Data and rights in the digital welfare state: The case of Denmark. *Information, Communication & Society*, Vol. 26, No. 1, pp. 123–138. https://doi.org/10.1080/1369118X.2021.1934069

Keyes, O., Hitzig, Z., & Blell, M., (2021). Truth from the machine: Artificial intelligence and the materialization of identity. *Interdisciplinary Science Reviews*, Vol. 46, Nos. 1–2, pp. 158–175. https://doi.org/10.1080/03080188.2020.1840224

Kommunal- og moderniseringsdepartementet (KMD), (2020). *Nasjonal strategi for kunstig intelligens*. Kommunal- og moderniseringsdepartementet (KMD). https://www.regjeringen.no/contentassets/1febbbb2c4fd4b7d92c67ddd353b6ae8/no/pdfs/ki-strategi.pdf

Kuziemski, M., & Misuraca, G., (2020). AI governance in the public sector: Three tales from the frontiers of automated decision-making in democratic settings. *Telecommunications Policy*, Vol. 44, No. 6, pp. 101976. https://doi.org/10.1016/j.telpol.2020.101976

Law, J., & Lin, W., (2017). The Stickiness of Knowing: Translation, Postcoloniality, and STS. *East Asian Science, Technology and Society: An International Journal*, Vol. 11, No. 2, pp. 257–269.

Livholts, M., & Tamboukou, M., (2015). *Discourse and Narrative Methods: Theoretical Departures, Analytical Strategies and Situated Writings*. SAGE Publications, USA. ISBN: 9781446269701

Longino, H., & Doell, R., (1983). Body, Bias, and Behavior: A Comparative Analysis of Reasoning in Two Areas of Biological Science. *Signs: Journal of Women in Culture and Society*. Vol. 9, No. 2, pp. 206-227 https://doi.org/10.1086/494044

Malek, M. A., (2021). Bigger Is Always Not Better; less Is More, Sometimes: The Concept of Data Minimization in the Context of Big Data. *European Journal of Privacy Law & Technologies (EJPLT)*, Vol. 1, pp. 212.

Nordberg, T. H., (2019). Arbeidsgivers ansvar for likestilling i arbeidslivet. *Tidsskrift for Kjønnsforskning*, Vol. 43, No. 2, pp. 90–107. https://doi.org/10.18261/issn.1891-1781-2019-02-03

Pasquinelli, M., & Joler, V., (2021). The Nooscope manifested: AI as instrument of knowledge extractivism. *AI & Society*, Vol. 36, No. 4, pp. 1263–1280. https://doi.org/10.1007/s00146-020-01097-6

Powell, A. B., Ustek-Spilda, F., Lehuedé, S., & Shklovski, I., (2022). Addressing ethical gaps in 'Technology for Good': Foregrounding care and capabilities. *Big Data & Society*, Vol. 9, No. 2, pp. 1–12. https://doi.org/10.1177/20539517221113774

Sarukkai, S., (2013). Translation as Method: Implications for History of Science. *The Circulation of Knowledge Between Britain, India and China*, pp. 309–329. Brill, Netherlands. https://doi.org/10.1163/9789004251410_014

Srinivasan, R., & Chander, A., 2021. Biases in AI Systems: A survey for practitioners. *Artificial Intelligence and Machine Learning:* Communications of the ACM, Vol. 64, No. 8, pp. 44-49. https://10.1145/3464903

Strathern, M., (2004). *Partial Connections*. Altamira Press, UK.

Suresh, H., & Guttag, J. V., (2021). A Framework for Understanding Sources of Harm throughout the Machine Learning Life Cycle. *EAAMO '21: Proceedings of the 1st ACM Conference on Equity and Access in Algorithms, Mechanisms, and Optimization*, No. 17, pp. 1–9. https://doi.org/10.1145/3465416.3483305

Suveren, Y., (2022). Bilinçsiz Önyargı: Tanımı ve Önemi. *Psikiyatride Güncel Yaklaşımlar*, Vol. 14, No. 3, pp. 414–426. https://doi.org/10.18863/pgy.1026607

Wirtz, B. W., Weyerer, J. C., & Geyer, C., (2019). Artificial Intelligence and the Public Sector—Applications and Challenges. *International Journal of Public Administration*, Vol. 42, No. 7, pp. 596–615. https://doi.org/10.1080/01900692.2018.1498103

THE SUSTAINABILITY OF SOCIAL NETWORKS: "SMALL-WORLD" NETWORKS AS A MEDIA COUNCIL

Gunjidmaa Gongor and Bolormaa Battsogt
Media Council of Mongolia
Mongolia, Ulaanbaatar

ABSTRACT

The structure of the Media Council was established, and 45 people were elected from 5 sectors to represent the media industry including 18 owner representatives, 18 journalist representatives, and 9 community/initiator group representatives in Mongolia. This study examines the current situation and sustainability of media self-regulation in Mongolia. We consider social networks, which explain individual network and the forms of mutual relationships between individuals, as social entities and research objects. Therefore, first, we review the previous sociological studies on social networks as a concept. Based on these concepts, we highlight the necessity of understanding social networks as entities, making them the research objects. Finally, we analyze the form of social networks as social entities based on the organizational formation of Media Council of Mongolia and its sustainability. In other words, this study presents a relational model function for sustainability by dividing the analysis into two levels: the relationships between individuals within the network and the network as a whole.

KEYWORDS

Media Council, Network Theory, Solidarity, Sustainability

1. INTRODUCTION

Mongolia transitioned to a democratic system in the 1990s, and the constitution guaranteed the rights of its citizens to have faith and belief, freely express their opinions, and publish and obtain information. Any kind of censorship was prohibited.

However, even though 30 years have passed since the birth of free democratic journalism, efforts to ensure the freedom and independence of the media in Mongolia remain insufficient. As of now, there are more than 500 media outlets for the small market of over 3 million people. The country is ranked 90th out of 180 countries in the "World Press Freedom Index" in 2022, declining sharply by twenty-two places from 2021 (Reporters without Borders n.d.). The report noted that "in Mongolia, more than half of the criminal cases related to slander and insults are filed against journalists and editors, which is stirring self-censorship."

At first glance, about 500 media outlets are operating in Mongolia; they are rapidly moving to the digital environment, and pluralism seems to exist. However, 74.36 percent of the media organizations are owned and controlled by politicians, or business groups with political ties because of legal conflicts, and economic and financial conditions (Press Institute of Mongolia 2016). In addition, media outlets hide their subscription and sales information, the market share of consumers, real ownership, and affiliations to generate financial resources. In other words, the concentration of media outlets "in one hand" encourages editorial censorship, thereby stifling freedom of the press, weakening pluralism, and adversely affecting the quality of information.

Therefore, the studies highlight the advantages and possibilities of self-regulation in media concentration, as the need to promote journalistic freedom, independence, and media pluralism and diversity is paramount (Humphreys and Seamus 2018, pp.130-63). In practice, each country recognizes and implements media self-regulation at different levels depending on its political culture, legal status, economy, media development, and maturity. Democratic countries' aim to protect the independence of journalistic media by creating independent self-regulatory bodies. In Mongolia, the media self-regulatory organization, the "Media Council (hereinafter: "MCM") was established with a wide representation of journalists, editors, media owners, journalistic associations and citizens in 2015. Currently, all members of the Ethical Committees are unpaid volunteers. The MCM agreed that the biggest challenge to the successful operation of the council is the lack of an adequate funding system (Bolormaa and Gunjidmaa 2024). Financial sustainability is a key challenge for the MCM, independent self-regulation bodies (Per and Anand 2023).

2. SOCIAL NETWORKS AS A CONCEPT IN SOCIAL SCIENCE

An overview of the changes in the structural principles of social studies can be considered using the scientific explanationism or decision-making principles (rational decision-making, social consensus formation, open value formation, rational thought formation, and social formation) and social participation. Since the 1960s, various theories regarding universal value standards have been introduced in social anthropology and have started to be gradually used in sociology as well. For example, Cassirer (1944) pointed out that human activity is regulated by signals and symbols. According to Cassirer, "Signals are part of the world of physical being," and "symbols are part of the world of human meaning". Besides humans, signal is a means of communication used with animals as well as between animals. Cassirer considered the symbols that regulate human behavior in religious, artistic, dream, and fantasy worlds that extend beyond scientific language or physical being (Cassirer 1944). Subsequently, studies performed by cultural anthropologists Lévi-Strauss (1963), Turner (1978), and Barthes (1972) were influenced by Cassirer. The range of human cosmology and imagination (temporal and spatial independence from the physical world) largely determines human behavior as a social network, in some cases by using ideologically constructed symbols.

Moreover, Mitchell argued that the social relationships in which ordinary people are embedded can be considered social networks. He systematically organized human social relationships using networks as an analytical concept and schematized social relationships. Reachability is the extent to which a particular individual can reach others who are important to him or her, and the concept of range or network size refers to the extent to which a focal individual can reach important others. In other words, a network is the number of people with whom one has regular contact (Mitchell 1969). Mitchell's concept of networks is based on understanding the characteristics of the connections between individuals to understand their social behavior and then assume social networks as specific connections between specific individuals. This was the first attempt to quantify and schematize human social relationships. Mitchell's basic concept of networks has played a pioneering role in the subsequent development of network theory. This is because using networks as an analytical tool allows us to express human social behavior in much more detail through mathematical methods. This approach has been widely applied since Mitchell.

An analysis of social behavior using the concept of social networks can also be found in Fisher's work. Fisher used a network approach to analyze human relationships in an urban society. According to Fisher, a network radiating from an individual connects that individual to society. Therefore, society can be thought of as a messy web made up of countless networks (Fischer 1977, pp.17). Furthermore, through econometric analysis using network concepts, Fischer clarified that, for residents of modern urban society to enjoy psychological well-being, they must connect to their neighbors (Fischer 1977, pp.163). This approach has made it possible to draw a diagram of human behavior by filling in the deficiencies of traditional structure-function analysis.

In sum, network research is more commonly treated as an analytical approach in sociology, and it can be said to be effective. However, the concept of social network itself remains unclear. Therefore, it is necessary to go beyond network theory as a definition and the analytical approach that defines social structure as a network of existing social relationships to reconsider social networks.

2.1 Social Networks Defined as Social Entities

If it becomes necessary to redefine social networks at the level of society as a whole, these networks should go beyond being mere means and the current limits of existing analytical approaches and should be considered as concrete social networks. We must reconsider this as a real entity and an object of sociological research. Therefore, by selecting and considering the following two points among the several characteristics of social networks s, it is possible to dispel the vagueness of the network concept. Social networks can be viewed as unified bodies of spiritual and material solidarity. This is because social networks are not vertical organizational relationships based on institutionally created hierarchical relationships, but rather mutual relationships between people based on horizontal and voluntary relationships. As such, they carry supporting information.

A social network is the unity of solidarity between individuals or between individuals and groups. Traditionally, the concept of solidarity has been understood in various ways. For example, Durkheim proposed the concepts of mechanical and organic solidarity regarding the division of labor in the industrial society (Durkheim, É. and Davy, G., 2014). For him, society was a moral entity that constrained individuals from the outside and collective consciousness, which could not be reduced to individual consciousness; this was viewed as a social fact. Solidarity is made possible by the external expression of some social result or condition.

Furthermore, Tönnies' concepts of Gemeinschaft and Gesellschaft include the meanings of spiritual and material solidarity. Specifically, Gemeinschaft is a combination of emotional fusion, mutual love, intimacy, talking, and thinking. Gesellschaft, however, is a union of interests in which each person regards the other as a self-interested or self-based and does not give to others unless it is in exchange for counter-benefits or reciprocation. However, Tönnies emphasizes that the two are essentially separate, regardless of the connections between them. For this reason, he cites families based on blood ties, villages based on geographical ties, and medieval cities based on friendships as examples of Gemeinschaft and life in large cities as examples of Gesellschaft (Tönnies 2012, pp.28).

In Durkheim's concepts of mechanical solidarity and organic solidarity and Tönnies' concepts of Gemeinschaft and Gesellschaft, changes in the form of people's interconnectedness are central to the changes in social structure due to the emergence of industrial civilization. However, this approach is considered problematic. In other words, fundamental changes in society are made possible by external expressions.

There are various ways to understand solidarity other than the concept proposed by Durkheim and Tönnies, but it is often argued that the unity of solidarity includes both spiritual and material solidarity. Spiritual solidarity refers to the conceptual, value-based, and intrinsic interconnectedness and interdependence of people, whereas material solidarity refers to reciprocal and beneficial exchange relationships. Both exist simultaneously and can be transformed into each other. However, social networks are the sum total of the interpenetration and mutual transformation of spiritual and material solidarity.

Social networks are connected through attributes and habitual, exchange, and symbolic relationships. There is no guarantee that these relationships, once formed, will change their nature. Human emotions and desires are constantly changing and, accordingly, the information posted on social networks is also constantly changing. Material solidarity exists as spiritual solidarity. Furthermore, whether a person performs a certain action is determined not only by considering the profit and loss of doing so, but also the moral pros and cons of doing so.

3. THE SUSTAINABILITY OF SOCIAL NETWORKS

Given the diversity of the analyses regarding networks, the entire picture is difficult to grasp. Research based on social network theory has two main streams, depending on the nature of interpersonal relationships and networks that are of interest. Coleman (1988) argued for the effect of strong ties, representing one stream. The other stream of research focuses on short-term and accidental social contacts, the most famous of which is Granovetter's weak ties theory (1973). Granovetter confirmed previous claims that weak ties are used more than strong ties in acquiring job change information, and lamented the way many conventional network models place too much emphasis on strong ties. Granovetter pointed out that information transmitted only through strong ties is likely to remain in a small group, and as such, only small, well-defined groups have been studied. Compared with strong ties, weak ties represent a flexible relationship with a high frequency of aggregation and dispersion.

Given that strong ties have high sustainability, whereas weak ties have low sustainability, the network as a whole is partially open. Continuous and relatively closed exchanges with strong ties have great advantages, but they often lead to fixed business content, technology, sales channels, etc. (Guimera et al. 2004). Meanwhile, weak ties are suitable for generating innovative business ideas but often lack the power to gather the management resources necessary to realize them. The two interactions should be considered complementary.

Therefore, "small-world" networks (Watts and Strogatz 1998), have been attracting increasing attention. From this perspective, a regional economic zone in which networks with the characteristics of small-world networks can be translated as one that enables high growth of the knowledge industry. Small-world networks are defined as clustering coefficients that indicate the degree of grouping, even though the average distance from one node to another is similar to that of a random network. It also refers to a network with the characteristic of high C. A high degree of grouping indicates superiority in strong ties. Meanwhile, short average path lengths are favorable for weak ties. Therefore, a network with small-world characteristics can be considered to be superior in both strong and weak ties.

Recently, Watts and Strogatz (1998) proposed the concept of a superposition of networks with small-world properties: a highly clustered sub-network consisting of the "local acquaintances" of nodes, together with a collection of random long-range shortcuts that help produce short paths. In addition to empirical studies of social, technological, and biological networks, Watts and Strogatz considered the following simple model system: Start with a d-dimensional lattice network and add a small number of long-range links out of each node to destinations chosen uniformly at random. A network created by this superposition will have local clustering and short paths, comparable to many real-world networks.

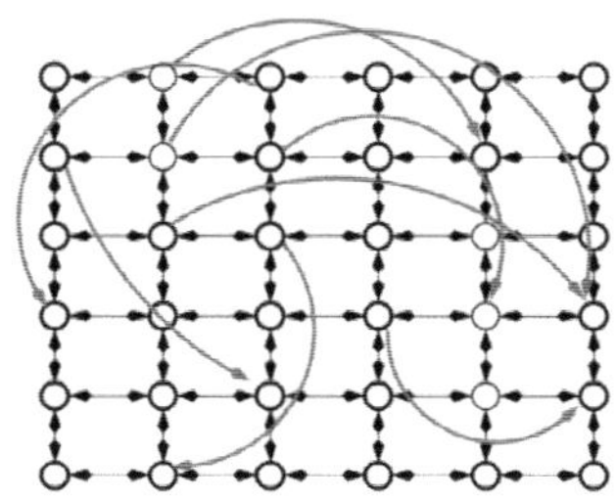

Figure 1. Two-dimensional grid with many random shortcuts superimposed (as in the Watts-Strogatz model)

4. "SMALL-WORLD" NETWORKS AS A MEDIA COUNCIL

In the previous section, we discussed how social networks can be viewed as unified bodies of spiritual and material solidarity. Moreover, a social network with small-world characteristics can be considered superior in terms of both strong and weak ties. Therefore, in this section, we discuss the organizational formation of MCM and its sustainability based on small-world networks with solidarity.

In the last two decades, the President of Mongolia, the Government of Mongolia, and some members of Parliament have taken the initiative to update the Media Freedom Law (1998) and have submitted several revised drafts to the Parliament. However, none of these revised drafts have been confirmed to date.

In contrast to the legislative framework that regulates the structures of the media industry, journalistic output is safeguarded from state regulation (Puppis 2009, pp.57-61). In January 2013, the President of Mongolia withdrew the revised draft of the Media Freedom Law, which was submitted and discussed in Parliament. However, legislators faced strong opposition from media owners. The owners strongly objected to the provision of disclosure of ownership shares of the media owners and investors and ensuring the independence of the editorial rooms.

At the same time, a group of Mongolia journalists, editors, and media experts started a voluntary initiative to establish the first independent self-regulation body in Mongolia.

Consequently, in the beginning of 2014 a group of Mongolia journalists and media civic actors set up a voluntary "Media Council Club" (hereinafter: "Club"). The Club aimed to promote the importance and need for a self-regulatory body among media professionals, advocating that all media stakeholders collaborate. The Club led the process of reaching consensus in all stages of setting up a media self-regulation body and establishing a foundation for creating an independent MCM. After the approval of the Statute of the Club, the first 12 journalists and editors were registered as volunteer members of the Club on February 11, 2014.

Mongolia journalists emphasized the need to establish a regulatory body, the MCM, for practical reasons, such as protecting the reputation and trust of journalism, not being called to court and being interrogated for accidental mistakes in the course of professional work, and preventing media owners or other influential parties from censoring the content of public information and editorial work.

The establishment process of the MCM was not easy, and necessitated overcoming many challenges and struggles, such as disunity in the media industry, misunderstanding of media self-regulation, denial, suspicion, mistrust of initiators, and conflicts of interest among several groups of people.

5. THE PRINCIPLE OF EQUAL QUOTAS OF MEDIA OWNERS AND JOURNALISTS

Most importantly, when there was "consensus built" from all stakeholders, the MCM is effectively established. The consensus-building was based on the following aspects: 1) Uniting for "fairness" among media owners and journalists; and 2) When media audience strongly criticizes the journalism for being unethical, irresponsible, and engaging in negative practices such as paid stories and blackmail. The Mongolia media had already faced the second condition, but it was faced with the need to quickly find a way out. More than 70% of the respondents in a national public opinion poll stated that they did not trust the media (Press Institute of Mongolia 2011). It is most important to help owners understand this situation and involve them in forming alliances.

The first consensus was that the principle of a self-regulatory body should be fully represented by an equitable number of media owners and journalists. The second consensus was to have representatives in the MCM in appreciation of the group of initiators, but it should be fewer than the representatives of media owners and journalists. Media self-regulation is, more narrowly, a process of setting, implementing, and sanctioning rules by members of the profession themselves (Puppis 2009, pp.36).

More than 30 coalitions and associations with different functions were operating when the MCM was being established in Mongolia. Moreover, approximately 2000 journalists and editors were working for a total of 522 media outlets (135 newspapers, 99 magazines, 166 televisions, 84 radio stations, and 68 online sites). Due to the lack of solidarity in the media sector and the recognition and representativeness of the associations, independent media outlets refused to join any coalitions or associations. In addition, there was massive criticism against having a small number of interests, people, or certain groups that represented the unity of journalists.

For these reasons, it was difficult to establish the MCM in consultation and consensus with media owners and journalists' associations, and it was difficult to gain acceptance in the industry by ensuring the participation of many parties. Influential editors were not members of the coalition. The biggest challenge in setting up the MCM was ensuring the participation of media owners and solidarity in the media industry. In terms of providing information and equal participation to all stakeholders, regardless of whether they are members of an association, has become the main task of the Club. The Club's main advantage is that some active members are famous and influential journalists and editors in the media industry and society. The biggest impetus for this was the confidence of Mongolia journalists that they would make their own regulations for the industry, not relying upon law.

The Club takes leadership in organizing actvitities with the goal of setting up a professional, independent self-regulatory body. The Club organizes more than 50 training sessions, consultancy meetings, and debates. These discussions included topics such as ethical dilemmas in Mongolia journalistic practices, the self-regulating body's structure, strategic objectives and planning, and the common ethical principles of professionalism. Moreover, leaders of the Club held meetings and seminars with legal and policy decision-makers (politicians and government representatives) in terms of informing a goal and process for setting up the independent media self-regulation body and raising awareness of the importance of journalists' and media owners' engagement in this initiative. The Club's activities have continued to attract the attention and interest of an increasing number of journalists. Therefore, the number of media practitioners interested in supporting the process has been steadily growing.

To ensure diverse participation, each member of the Club invited friends and other journalists from their editorial office to a wedge-day meeting. In this manner, journalists' participation expanded naturally. However, reaching owners, especially those involved in owners' associations, remained difficult. The Association of Daily Newspapers was of the opinion that "it does not support but does not condemn the initiative of creating a MCM," and the Association of TVs continued to argue that "the MCM should be based only on the associations, but not to include representatives who are registered electronically, who are not members of the association." However, after several joint meetings, the three site associations agreed to participate under the condition that their quotas would be divided equally.

The main basis for creating unity and reaching a consensus in the media sector was to choose club leaders and coordinators to spread information, visit editorial offices to make presentations and influence work, and constantly encourage them to openly present what is going on in the industry and what they are aiming for. It was understood that all parties should be treated equally and be free from the vested interests of any individual or any organization.

In this way, a multi-faceted club was established and a volunteer group was formed to carry out visible and tangible tasks, continuously volunteer until the goal was achieved, and lead the process, which gave many people the confidence that "this initiative will work."

Between November 5 and 15, 2014, more than 360 people registered, almost 70 percent of whom were journalists. It is also noteworthy that the representatives of the owners participated in the electronic registration. They supported the industry's initiative to create self-regulation, and participated in the creation of the MCM by requesting a mandate to participate in the registration process. As journalists' participation increased, the coalition representing owners began to pay more attention to the development of the process. They continued to remind the initiators that their main demand was a board with full industry representation and equal participation.

Finally, the initiators' groups and site associations held branch meetings of owners and journalists, and local media associations held branch meetings of owners and journalists and sent their representatives. Thus, in December 2014, nine branch meetings of five sectors were organized by the Club members in collaboration with the group of initiators.

At the end of all this, on January 28, 2015, the structure of the MCM was established, and 45 people were elected from 5 sectors to represent the media industry, and the first 45 members were identified, including 18 owner representatives, 18 journalist representatives, and 9 community/initiator group representatives, and to lead the founding assembly. The Board of Directors (15 members), the Ethical Committee of Newspapers, Magazines and Websites (15 members), and the Ethical Committee of Radio and Television (15 members) were established.

6. CHALLENGES

Although it was important to establish the MCM by reaching a joint consensus, sustainably managing the organization was the next big challenge. As a result of constant discussions and consensus meetings within the industry for one year, the MCM was established with the participation of representatives from all sectors of the industry.

The 45 newly-elected members of MCM represented five sectors: broadcasting, print media, electronic media, local media, and groups of initiators. Thus, a diverse group of representatives had emerged. First, it was important to unite the knowledge and understanding of journalistic ethics and media self-regulation among these diverse people, work together, have a mutual understanding, and have common interests and unified values. For this purpose, capacity-building training was continuously organized.

Since the first training session was held on November, 2015, 16 empowerment training sessions have been conducted for ethics committee members. In the first training session, cases of complaints received by The German Press Council and the conclusions that were discussed and resolved were presented as examples. Later, the MCM continued to learn from their mistakes by discussing the cases they had solved.

The MCM has two separate ethics committees, each with 15 members, for a total of 30 people. During 2015-2023, i.e. 8 years, 555 complaints were received by the MCM. Of these, 323 complaints (59 %) were discussed and resolved at the quarterly meetings of the Ethics Committees. The MCM continuously organized 54 ethics committee meetings every quarter, and committee members voluntarily participated in these meetings for free.

Additionally, 15 members of the Board of Directors introduced the establishment of the MCM and proposals for cooperation in physical meetings with media organizations. For example, presenting to the associations that did not actively participate in the process of establishing the MCM, such as the Mongolian TV Association, Mongolian Cable Channels Association, and Mongolian Daily Newspaper Association, are important strategic steps, such as sharing information openly, providing equal opportunities for all, and ensuring equal participation. was happening. As a result, by following the policy of including representatives of the unions in the by-election of members, it was possible to reduce rejection, opposition, and mistrust of the MCM.

Unlike other coalitions, elected members of the MCM are voluntary, but have certain responsibilities and work for a fixed period. For example, each member of the ethics committee should personally participate in quarterly committee meetings, be familiar with all the materials regarding the complaints to be discussed when coming to the meeting, express their position with a clear conclusion on whether the case involves an ethical error, and make the right decision, if necessary. requires active and informed participation, including debates with other members. Therefore, because each member is required to participate effectively and continuously in the self-regulation of the sector, the attendance records of each member are kept regularly. Being a member of the MCM is a voluntary act, and exemption is also a voluntary act of one's own conscience. Industry self-regulation refers to the voluntary activities of a group of people united by shared values. This way, it was intended to establish a standard based on the awareness and responsibility of the member, and not on a mandatory basis, to give the opportunity to the next person if they were unable to complete volunteer work. The by-election of exempted members shall be notified in writing to the relevant branch associations and requested to send a representative, or if not sent, an open notice shall be issued to provide an opportunity to interested parties.

The Board of Directors discussed and approved the implementation of the MCM's operating procedures, procedures for accepting and settling complaints to the Ethics Committee, and the Code of Ethics for the members of the Ethics Committee. However, the function of developing, discussing, and approving the ethical principles of Mongolia media, which has 10 general chapters and 33 detailed provisions, is under the authority of the Ethics Committees.

In this way, the direction of the activities of the Board of Directors and Ethics Committees were clearly defined by the rules, which formed a system of fair distribution of powers, mutual balance, and control.

7. CONCLUSION

This study discusses how social networks can be viewed as unified bodies of spiritual and material solidarity. Moreover, social networks with small-world characteristics can be considered superior in strong and weak ties. Therefore, this section discusses the organizational formation of the MCM and its sustainability based on small-world networks with solidarity.

The most important factor in ensuring the independence and stability of the media self-regulatory organization was the unity of the actors in the industry, the collective agreement of the stakeholders, and the structure of the organization representing it. In this structure, the representation of media stakeholders, number of quotas, period of representation, and byelection process are included in the rules. Therefore, the organization could conduct its activities independently, free from the biased interests of any party.

The factors affecting the stability are as follows: In the future, the structure/balance and distribution of powers, equal numbers of lords, and journalists represent so that no one's interests are left out of the circle, the policymaker and the ethics committee have independent activities according to the rules, and the Secretariat works in connection with them. These rules determine the distribution of the balance of power. Industry stakeholders are regularly updated through multiple advocacy meetings, and participation opportunities are always open. Empowering experiences are regularly conducted on a large scale, providing an opportunity to consolidate and strengthen values and accumulate experiences. This contributed to the independence of the MCM's judgment. Maintaining unity, increasing power and financial resources is necessary to ensure long-term sustainable development. Therefore, studying the statutory self-regulation system, assessing its appropriateness for Mongolia, and consulting with policymakers are necessary.

REFERENCES

Barabasi, A. L. (2003). *Linked: How everything is connected to everything else and what it means*. Plume.

Barthes, R. (1972). Mythologies. 1957. *Trans. Annette Lavers. New York: Hill and Wang*, pp.302-06.

Bolormaa, B. and Gunjidmaa G. (2024). The Media Council in Mongolia: A Study on the Cooperation between a Self-Regulatory System and Network Theory. *The Journal of Communication and Media Studies* 9 (1): 85-98. doi:10.18848/2470-9247/CGP/v09i01/85-98.

Cassirer, E. (1944). The concept of group and the theory of perception. *Philosophy and phenomenological research*, *5*(1), pp.1-36.

Coleman, J. S. (1988). Social capital in the creation of human capital. *American journal of sociology*, *94*, pp.S95-S120.

Durkheim, É. and Davy, G. (2014). *Émile Durkheim* (p. 48). Louis-Michaud.

Fischer, S. (1977). Long-term contracts, rational expectations, and the optimal money supply rule. *Journal of political economy*, *85*(1), pp.191-205.

Globe International Center. (2022). *Media Freedom Report*. Globe International Center Press

Granovetter, M. S. (1973). The strength of weak ties. *American journal of sociology*, *78*(6), pp.1360-1380. https://doi.org/10.1086/225469

Guimera, R., Sales-Pardo, M. and Amaral, L. A. N. (2004). Modularity from fluctuations in random graphs and complex networks. *Physical Review E*, *70*(2), pp.025101.

Humphreys, P. and Simpson, S. (2018). *Regulation, governance and convergence in the media*. Edward Elgar Publishing.

Lévi-Strauss, C. (1963). The bear and the barber. *The Journal of the Royal Anthropological Institute of Great Britain and Ireland*, *93*(1), pp.1-11.

Mitchell Jr, J. V. (1969). 9: Education's Challenge to Psychology: The Prediction of Behavior From Person-Environment Interactions. *Review of educational research*, *39*(5), pp.695-721.

Per, O., & Anand,T. (2023). *Media Council of Mongolia impact study*. DW Akedemie: Germany.

Press Institute of Mongolia. (2016). *Media Ownership Monitor Mongolia*. Press Institute of Mongolia. Retrieved May 12, 2023, from https://mongolia.mom-rsf.org/en/findings/affiliations/

Puppis, M. (2009). Media regulation in small states. *International communication gazette*, *71*(1-2), pp.7-17.

RSF. (2023). *Press Freedom Index: Mongolia*. RSF Reporters without Borders. Retrieved May 20, 2023, from https://rsf.org/en/country/mongolia.

Tönnies, F. (2012). " Community and Society": From CP Loomis (ed.), Community and Society (1963)[1887]. In *The urban sociology reader* (pp. 16-22). Routledge.

Turner, R. H. (1978). The role and the person. *American journal of Sociology*, *84*(1), pp.1-23.

Watts, D. J. and Strogatz, S. H. (1998). Collective dynamics of 'small-world'networks. *nature*, *393*(6684), pp.440-442.

AI-DRIVEN TAXONOMY OF DEMOCRATIC SYSTEMS

Žiga Kolar and Matjaž Gams
Department of Intelligent Systems, Jožef Stefan Institute, Jamova 39, 1000 Ljubljana, Slovenia

ABSTRACT

This study employs machine learning techniques to present an in-depth analysis and comparison of various forms of democracies, designs a robust taxonomy. The study first characterizes democracies globally with a focus on key features such as political institutions, electoral systems, citizen participation, and rights and freedoms. It then utilizes machine learning methods on 11 text descriptions of different democracy types to model these diverse democratic structures. The resulting taxonomy offers a more intricate understanding of democratic variations and exemplifies machine learning's capability in political science. It explores which groups of democracies represent sensible similarities and distances to other groups. The outcomes of this research not only contribute to better understanding of democratic forms but also showcase the potential of machine learning, offering a promising methodology for exploring complex political phenomena.

KEYWORDS

Democracy, Natural Language Processing, Data Mining, E-Democracy

1. INTRODUCTION

In recent years, the evolving landscape of political science has seen a growing interest in examining democratic systems. Researchers have explored the diversity of democratic institutions worldwide using various approaches (Dahl, 2020). Democracy, a cornerstone of modern governance, includes models with varying institutional structures, decision-making processes, and citizen participation mechanisms. Understanding these variations is crucial for policymakers, researchers, and citizens to assess their strengths, weaknesses, and potential improvements. Traditional comparisons often rely on qualitative analysis and expert judgment, which may introduce subjectivity and limit scalability (Achen and Bartels, 2017).

This paper proposes a novel approach to comparing and categorizing different types of democracies using artificial intelligence (AI) methods, specifically machine learning (ML) techniques (Kreps and Kriner, 2023). Democracies are treated as abstract models described by text rather than practical forms of governance, though practical democracies can be classified into formal types or their mixtures. The paper aims to address key questions: methodology for detecting similar democratic types and the formulation of a robust taxonomy of democratic models.

This study leverages data from constitutional frameworks, electoral systems, political institutions, socio-economic indicators, and historical records, utilizing ML algorithms such as decision trees to identify patterns and compare democracies. ML offers an objective framework for comparison, reduces biases, enhances scalability, and improves transparency with visual outcomes. The ML-driven taxonomy facilitates systematic, data-driven analysis, aiding in policy analysis, model evaluation, and reform assessments, and supports comparative research to identify best practices and challenges. Ultimately, this paper integrates AI, ML, and political science, creating a comprehensive taxonomy that advances understanding of democracies, supports evidence-based policymaking, and promotes the progress of comparative politics.

The paper is organized as follows: Section 2 describes each type of democracy. Section 3 introduces the ML algorithms used for comparison and the taxonomy construction algorithm. Section 4 summarizes the findings. Finally, conclusion suggests future research directions.

2. TYPES OF DEMOCRACY

This section outlines various types of democracy, detailing their distinct characteristics, historical development, and regional variations. Democracy, as a government form that honors individual freedoms and popular will, manifests differently across diverse political, social, and cultural contexts. The descriptions of democracy originate from an extensive PhD study (Vozlič, 2020) that reviewed 365 references and have been condensed for this presentation. While some terms for these democracies are globally recognized, others remain inconsistently defined.

2.1 Participative Democracy

Participative democracy is a governance model where citizens actively engage in decision-making, rather than delegating this responsibility solely to elected representatives. This model is rooted in the principle that individuals should have a say in decisions that impact their lives. Citizen participation can occur through various means, such as town hall meetings, public forums, and online platforms.

The main advantage of participative democracy is the inclusion of diverse perspectives, which can lead to more informed and balanced decisions, as well as enhanced social cohesion and community involvement. However, it poses challenges, such as being time-consuming and resource-intensive. Ensuring equal representation and preventing dominance by certain groups are also significant concerns.

Despite these issues, participative democracy is a valuable tool for fostering citizen engagement and ensuring responsive governance. It has been effectively implemented in different contexts globally, from local initiatives to national decision-making processes (Smit and Oosthuizen, 2011.).

2.2 Deliberative Democracy

Deliberative democracy is a democratic governance model that prioritizes informed and reasoned discussion among citizens to make collective decisions. It operates on the principle that public deliberation yields better outcomes than simple majority rule or other decision-making methods.

In this model, citizens engage in structured, facilitated discussions on public issues, adhering to rules of civility and respect. These discussions aim to encompass diverse perspectives and foster common ground and understanding.

The primary advantage of deliberative democracy is that it leads to more informed and nuanced decision-making. It also enhances civic engagement and social cohesion, as citizens feel more connected to the decisions affecting their lives. However, challenges include ensuring equal representation of all voices, especially marginalized groups, and reconciling competing interests and values in polarized situations (Gutmann and Thompson, 2004).

2.3 Transdemocracy

Transdemocracy is an emerging concept that extends democratic principles beyond the nation-state to encompass global governance and decision-making. It acknowledges that global challenges like climate change, economic inequality, and pandemics necessitate international cooperation and collective action.

In a transdemocratic system, citizens would directly participate in global decision-making through new institutions and mechanisms, such as global citizen assemblies or online platforms for global deliberation.

The main advantage of transdemocracy is its potential to address the limitations of traditional democratic systems, which often focus on national issues and may be slow to respond to global challenges. By applying democratic principles globally, transdemocracy could foster greater international cooperation and more effective responses to worldwide problems. However, challenges include ensuring equal representation of all voices globally, considering existing power imbalances, and reconciling diverse interests and values across different cultural and political contexts (Neves, 2017).

2.4 Guided Democracy

Guided democracy is an authoritarian governance model where a single leader or group retains control while permitting limited citizen participation. It features centralized power, restricted political parties, and controlled media. Synonyms include illiberal democracy, authoritarian democracy, or delegative democracy.

In guided democracies, citizen participation is monitored and restricted, with limitations on political parties, candidates, freedom of speech, and press. A strong, charismatic leader often uses propaganda and media control to shape public opinion and maintain regime support.

Guided democracy aims to balance political stability and economic development with limited citizen participation. Examples include Singapore, where the ruling party allows some opposition and public involvement while maintaining power. However, it is often criticized for lacking genuine democratic freedoms and civil liberties and is associated with corruption, nepotism, and authoritarianism due to concentrated power and lack of accountability (Christoff, 2003).

2.5 Modern Direct Democracy

Modern direct democracy is a governance model where citizens have direct control over political decision-making through mechanisms like online platforms, electronic voting, and citizen assemblies. It bypasses intermediaries such as elected representatives or political parties, allowing citizens to vote on policy proposals and propose their own initiatives.

Key advantages of modern direct democracy include more responsive decision-making and increased civic engagement. It ensures that citizens' voices are heard and reflected in policies, fostering a sense of ownership and investment in the political system. Additionally, it promotes a more active and informed citizenry. However, challenges include ensuring equal access to the political process, especially for underrepresented or marginalized groups. There is also the difficulty of ensuring decisions are well-informed and based on sound evidence and reasoning (Schiller, 2011).

2.6 E-Democracy

E-democracy, also known as digital or internet democracy, leverages digital technologies to enhance citizen participation in the political process. It includes online voting, social media engagement, digital petitions, and citizen forums using modern e-tools. Examples of e-democracy include crowdsourcing initiatives, online consultations, and virtual town halls.

The main advantage of e-democracy is increased citizen engagement, particularly among younger generations who frequently use digital technologies for social and political activities. It also enhances transparency and accountability by providing greater access to information and enabling citizens to monitor their elected representatives.

However, e-democracy faces challenges such as security and privacy concerns with online voting and other digital initiatives. Issues of digital literacy and access also pose significant barriers, as not all citizens may have the necessary skills or resources to participate effectively (Kneuer, 2016).

2.7 Representative Democracy

Representative democracy involves citizens electing representatives to make decisions on their behalf, recognizing that direct participation in every decision is impractical. Representatives, elected through regular elections to serve specific areas, convene in legislative bodies like parliaments to legislate and make decisions. This system allows citizen participation without needing in-depth knowledge of every issue and provides stability through fixed terms. However, challenges such as ensuring true representation and combating corruption and lobbying persist. Despite these issues, representative democracy is the most common democracy form worldwide, celebrated for fostering participation and democratic governance. (Alonso et al., 2011).

2.8 Liquid Democracy

Liquid democracy, or delegative democracy, merges aspects of direct and representative democracy by allowing citizens to vote directly on issues or delegate their voting power to a trusted individual. This flexible system enables citizens to either participate directly or choose representatives for specific issues, and delegations can be changed at any time.

The primary advantage of liquid democracy is that it empowers citizens to engage in issues they care about while delegating decisions they are less knowledgeable about to trusted experts or individuals. This approach can increase citizen participation and ensure decisions are informed by knowledgeable delegates.

However, challenges include ensuring equal access to the political process, particularly for underrepresented or marginalized groups, and guaranteeing that decisions are well-informed and based on sound reasoning and evidence (Kahng et al., 2021).

2.9 Blockchain Democracy

Blockchain democracy, or blockchain voting, uses blockchain technology to record and verify votes securely and transparently. In this system, citizens cast votes on a blockchain-based platform, with a decentralized network of computers ensuring each vote is accurately recorded and verified.

The primary advantage of blockchain democracy is its high security and transparency, as the decentralized and public ledger makes vote tampering or alteration nearly impossible. It also has the potential to increase voter turnout and participation by allowing voting from anywhere with internet access and reducing the cost and complexity of traditional elections.

However, challenges include security concerns, as vulnerabilities in the blockchain system can be exploited by hackers. Additionally, issues of accessibility and voter privacy may arise, as some citizens might lack the necessary technology or be hesitant to share personal information on a blockchain platform (Racsko, 2019).

2.10 Source Democracy

Source democracy emphasizes the role of the "source code" or the underlying decision-making structures over the individuals or representatives making decisions. It distributes decision-making power among all community members, allowing for direct participation. The aim is to create a transparent, decentralized system grounded in shared values and principles.

The main advantage of source democracy is its promotion of transparency and accountability. With access to the decision-making structure, community members can observe how decisions are made and hold decision-makers accountable. This model also fosters consensus-building and collaboration by incorporating diverse perspectives and ideas. However, challenges include ensuring equal access to the decision-making process, especially for underrepresented or marginalized groups, and ensuring that decisions are well-informed and based on sound evidence and reasoning (Rushkoff, 2003).

2.11 Ideal Typical Democracy

The ideal typical democracy outlines key criteria for a fully democratic system, including universal suffrage, free and fair elections, accountable political representation, and civil liberties like freedom of speech and religion. It emphasizes the rule of law, separation of powers, and demands accountability and transparency from officials. These principles, though not fully met by any democracy, serve as benchmarks for evaluating and enhancing democratic systems (Tully, 2002). This framework aids in developing fairer systems that address all citizens' needs. Additionally, literature on types of democracies, such as AI democracy, explores the impact of AI on democratic processes (Nemitz, 2018).

3. METHODOLOGY

The paper outlines 11 types of democracy, including Blockchain, Liquid, Representative, and others, each described in section 2. Each democratic type is characterized by an English text description containing a maximum of 10,000 words. Each text description was converted to lowercase, and all whitespace and numbers were eliminated. For example, "Apple" and "apple" refer to the same entity but would be treated as different words if case-sensitive. Extra whitespace and numbers can add noise to the data. Removing these can help simplify the text and make it more uniform.

After the conversion, the data was examined to identify similar democracy types and subsequently develop a taxonomy or decision tree that effectively distinguishes the different types of democracies based on specific attributes. One viable method for achieving this is by creating n-grams. N-grams are a crucial tool in natural language processing (NLP) and computational linguistics, denoting consecutive sequences of n elements extracted from a specified text. These elements may be word or characters. The n value sets the sequence length, leading to different n-gram types based on its varying values. For instance, for the word "Democracy", which is the most common word in every text description, a 4-gram for characters would produce "Demo", "emoc", "mocr", "ocra", "crac", "racy". After breaking down the converted text descriptions into n-grams, it's possible to calculate the cosine similarity for each pair of democracy types, thereby gaining a similarity measure between them.

The cosine similarity is a prevalent metric in areas such as information retrieval, text analysis, and NLP, employed to gauge the similarity between two non-zero vectors. It is calculated as the cosine of the angle between the two vectors, which can be determined from the dot product of the vectors divided by their magnitude's product.

Cosine similarity ranges from -1 to 1, with 1 indicating identical vectors, 0 indicating no relation, and -1 indicating opposite vectors. In text analysis and NLP, it measures the similarity between text documents or sentences, represented as vectors in a multi-dimensional space based on terms or n-grams. This measure is ideal for comparing different types of democracy, as it quantifies the correlation between their textual descriptions. After calculating similarity measures, an 11x11 matrix was created (Figure 1), with diagonal elements set to 1, indicating maximum similarity of a democracy type with itself. The matrix values, ranging from 0 to 1, represent the similarity between different democracy types; values close to 1 suggest high similarity, while those near 0 indicate significant differences. Older democracy types, such as Source democracy and Ideal-typical democracy, exhibit the greatest similarity to each other. In contrast, newer democracy types, like Blockchain democracy, show the highest similarity to Representative democracy and Transdemocracy, respectively.

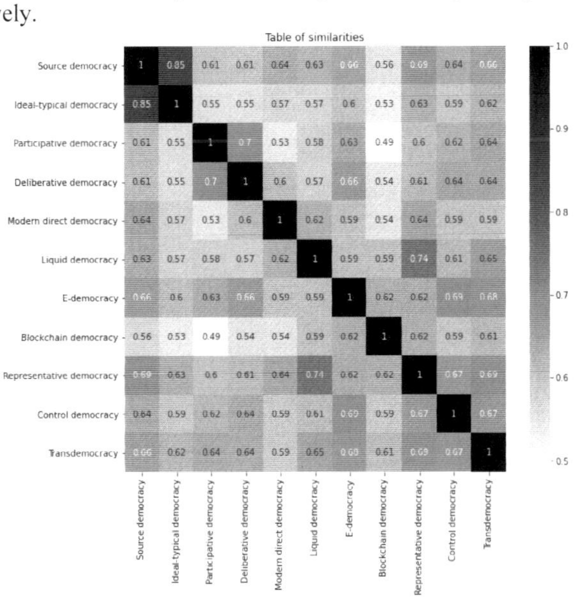

Figure 1. Table of similarities

This study formulates a taxonomy for democratic systems, emphasizing accurate classification. A similarity matrix was initially considered for constructing a decision tree but was deemed inappropriate due to several drawbacks. Similarity matrices rely on pairwise scores rather than direct attributes, complicating rule creation. They also involve interdependent data, whereas decision trees require independent attributes. Additionally, their size can surpass the original dataset, increasing complexity and risks like overfitting. Finally, although numerical, similarity scores do not correspond directly to attribute values, hindering their interpretation by decision trees.

In addition, the study employed 30 distinct attributes for the taxonomy, including Theoretical Understanding, Independence, Stability, Flexibility, and Political Implications, among others. Each attribute had a text value (e.g. "Yes", "No", "Stable", "Unstable", etc.) which had to be converted to a numerical value with binary (1 or 0) or continuous values within the [0, 1] range. Text attributes were presented in an extended PhD study (Vozlič, 2020). This study did not empirically compare types of democracy using a decision tree, a non-parametric algorithm that forms a hierarchical decision-making structure. Constructed to create homogeneous subsets, decision trees provide interpretability and manage both categorical and numerical data. In our taxonomy (Figure 2), democratic typologies are linked to unique leaf nodes, showing distinct characteristics. In the root (first) node, Democracies are categorized based on the "Technical background" attribute: those with a value of 0.5 or less are placed in the left branch, and those over 0.5 in the right, until a specific democracy type is determined. The term "gini" in Figure 2 refers to the Gini impurity, a measure of classification accuracy at each split in the tree. "Fork," often used in technology, denotes a split within a political entity due to differing views or strategies.

This taxonomy allows for a structured understanding of democratic systems, aiding researchers, policymakers, and educators in comprehending their complexities and nuances, facilitating more informed decisions and discussions.

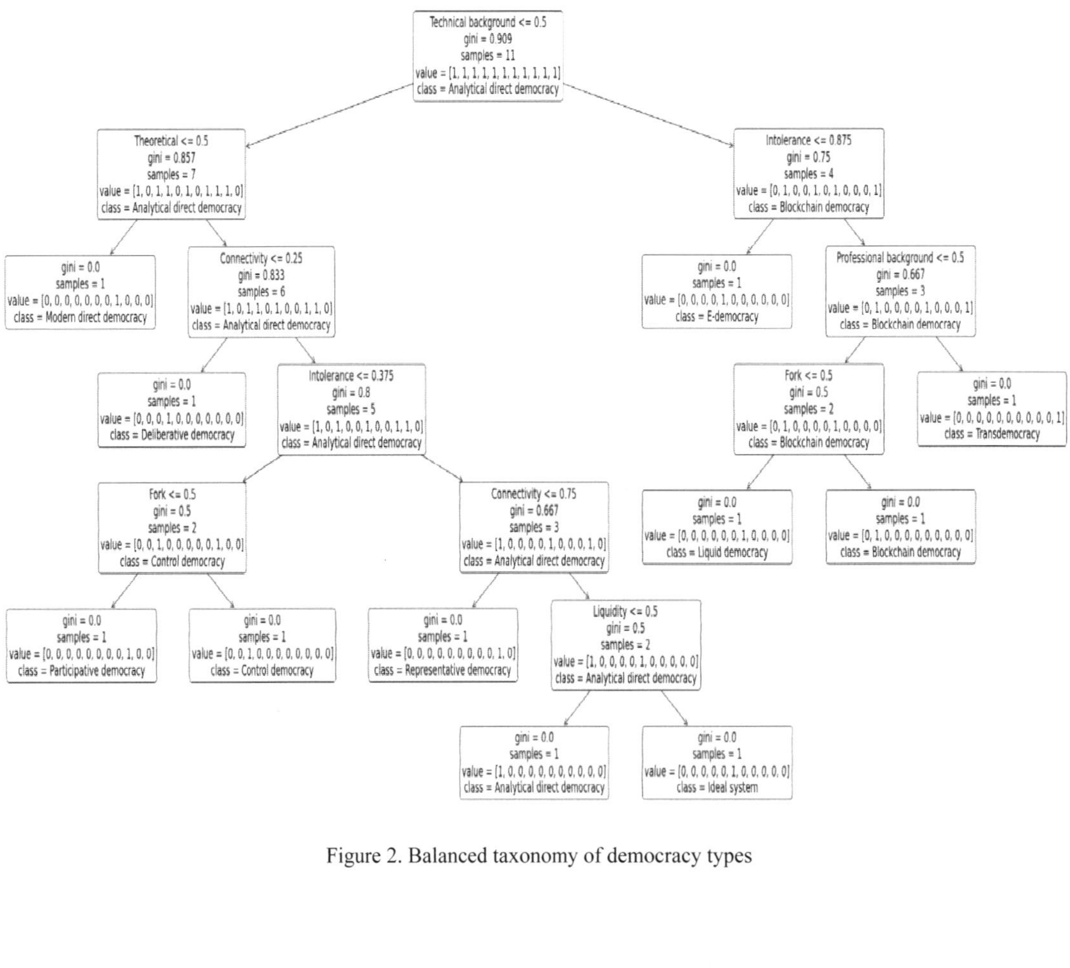

Figure 2. Balanced taxonomy of democracy types

4. FINDINGS

This study provides an algorithm of how to detect similar democracy types. Together with the development of a novel taxonomy it facilitated a more detailed understanding of different democratic systems, highlighting their unique characteristics, patterns, similarities and dissimilarities, and evolution.

The designed ML models distinguish the intricacies of democracies based on numerous attributes including, but not limited to, the nature of electoral systems, the separation of powers, the extent of political participation, and the protection of civil liberties. The taxonomy proposed herein stands as a testament to the power of computational approaches in political science, specifically in democratic studies.

The similarity table presented in Figure 1 suggests that it would maybe make sense to merge only the only the source and ideal-typical democracy, while the others seem sufficiently unique for a meaningful definition. Taxonomy illustrated in Figure 2 effectively demonstrates the distinctions between various democracy types based on the value of the different attributes. At the root of the tree is the attribute "Technical background" which promptly segregates democracy types into two categories based on the attribute value. The process continues until a leaf (terminal) node is reached. Each leaf node represents one democracy type. The application of machine learning decision tree method yields results within microseconds, significantly surpassing the speed and efficiency of human-based grouping.

It should also be noted that while the taxonomies provide a robust framework for analyzing democratic systems, they are not exhaustive or absolute. Democracies are complex and dynamic and although basic principles are thousands of years old, they are constantly evolving and adapting to internal and external changes. Therefore, the constructed taxonomies should be viewed as a tool for understanding and exploration, rather than a definitive absolute classification. It is our hope that future research will build upon this work, refining and expanding the taxonomy to better capture the rich diversity and complexity of democratic systems.

5. CONCLUSION

The value of this study extends beyond the academic realm. It provides critical insights for policymakers and governance professionals, allowing them to recognize democratic patterns and structures in various contexts. Additionally, it can also serve as a foundation for further research aimed at exploring the dynamics of democracies and political systems worldwide.

The application of ML and AI techniques to its study, while promising, comes with its own set of challenges and limitations. The models used in this study are inevitably shaped by the data they are trained on. As such, they might fail to capture the full complexity of some democratic systems, particularly those that have undergone recent changes or are characterized by unique, local dynamics.

One of the examples of the evolution is the emergence of GPT-like systems which can introduce another type of democracy - the AI democracy, where intelligent agents play an important role in it. There is no doubt that generative AI already impacts the democratic processes (Nemitz, 2018). Also, there are other types of democracies that can be added to the proposed ones.

In the future, continuous refinement of the designed models will be essential, incorporating up-to-date data and advancements in ML methods. Furthermore, interdisciplinary collaborations are encouraged to broaden the understanding of democracies. The development of more sophisticated metrics for evaluating the health and efficacy of different democratic models is also advocated.

To summarize, this research marks an important step in employing ML and AI methods in the study of types of democracies. The methods and findings from this research may catalyze future scholarly work, foster a better understanding of democracy, and contribute to the enhancement of democratic systems across the globe.

ACKNOWLEDGEMENT

The author(s) made use of chatGPT to assist with this article. ChatGPT was commonly employed as a tool for enhancing the language of the initial draft, without altering the length of the text. ChatGPT 4 was accessed/obtained from chat.openai.com and used with modification in May 2024.

REFERENCES

Achen, C. and Bartels, L. (2017). *Democracy for realists: Why elections do not produce responsive government.* Princeton University Press.

Alonso, S., Keane, J. and Merkel, W. eds. (2011). *The future of representative democracy*. Cambridge University Press.

Christoff, P. (2003). Ecological citizens and ecologically guided democracy. In *Democracy and green political thought* (pp. 159-176). Routledge.

Dahl, R. A. (2020). *On democracy*. Yale university press.

Gutmann, A. and Thompson, D. F. (2004). *Why deliberative democracy?*. Princeton University Press.

Jungherr, A. (2023). Artificial intelligence and democracy: A conceptual framework. *Social media+ society*, 9(3), p.20563051231186353.

Kahng, A., Mackenzie, S. and Procaccia, A. (2021). Liquid democracy: An algorithmic perspective. *Journal of Artificial Intelligence Research*, 70, pp. 1223-1252.

Kneuer, M. (2016). E-democracy: A new challenge for measuring democracy. *International Political Science Review*, 37(5), pp. 666-678.

Kreps, S. and Kriner, D. (2023). How AI Threatens Democracy. *Journal of Democracy*, 34(4), pp. 122-131.

Nemitz, P. (2018). Constitutional democracy and technology in the age of artificial intelligence. *Philosophical Transactions of the Royal Society A: Mathematical, Physical and Engineering Sciences*, 376(2133), p.20180089.

Neves, M. (2017). From transconstitutionalism to transdemocracy. *European Law Journal*, 23(5), pp. 380-394.

Racsko, P. (2019). Blockchain and democracy. *Society and Economy*, 41(3), pp. 353-369.

Rushkoff, D. (2003). *Open source democracy: How online communication is changing offline politics. Demos.*

Schiller, T. (2011). Local Direct Democracy in Europe–a comparative overview. *Local direct democracy in Europe*, pp. 9-29.

Smit, M.H. and Oosthuizen, I.J., 2011. Improving school governance through participative democracy and the law. *South African Journal of Education*, 31(1), pp. 55-73.

Tully, J., 2002. The unfreedom of the moderns in comparison to their ideals of constitutional democracy. *The Modern Law Review,* 65(2), pp. 204-228.

Vozlič, A., 2020. *Transdemokracija kot rekonceptualizacija demokracije v okolju digitalne države.* Doctoral dissertation. Ljubljana: A. Vozlič. Available at: https://repozitorij.uni-lj.si/IzpisGradiva.php?lang=eng&id=122202 [Accessed May 15, 2024].

Short Papers

DEVELOPMENT OF THE MODEL OF WORKING IN A HYBRID ENVIRONMENT

Pradit Songsangyos[1], Supakorn Iamamporn[2] and Mesith Chaimanee[1]
[1]*Faculty of Engineering and Technology, Shinawatra University, Pathum Thani, Thailand*
[2]*Faculty of Business Administration and Information Technology, Rajamangala University of Technology Suvarnabhumi, Pranakhon Si Ayutthaya, Thailand*

ABSTRACT

The post-COVID-19 stimulated the transition of work from the on-site workplace to remote work. The objectives of the study are to build a model of working in a hybrid environment that combines working both in a physical office and remotely by using information and communication technology. Next, evaluate the appropriateness of the proposed model by five experts. The sample was selected by a purposive selection method. The research is divided into two stages. Stage 1: Design the model of working in a hybrid environment, and Stage 2: The experts evaluated the appropriateness of the proposed model. The model of working in a hybrid environment consists of (1) Information and Communication Technology. (2) Flexible Scheduling. (3) Defined Workspaces. (4) Well-being and Work-Life Balance. (5) Performance and Evaluation Metrics. (6) Hybrid work, including 6.1) On-site work and 6.2) Remote Work. (7) Outcomes. The experts strongly agree on the appropriateness of the proposed model. Information and Communication Technology and Outcomes had the highest score, as Strongly Agree. That refers to Information and Communication Technology are essential to a hybrid work. In addition, Outcomes can be workloads or achievements of desired goals that can be measurable, besides related to an organisation's commitments.

KEYWORDS

Hybrid Work, Hybrid Environment, Remote Work, On-Site Work

1. INTRODUCTION

The outbreak of the COVID-19 pandemic stimulated the transition of work from the traditional on-site workplace to remote work. The employees work from home using communication tools to connect with a remote computer site. A flexible work arrangement means adjusting working time at home for a better work-life balance. In contrast, work-family conflict may occur between the roles undertaken in the separate domains of work and family (Songsangyos, P. and Iamamporn, S., 2020). This is in line with a study by Daroue, M. and Pluut, H. (2021), which indicated that on days when employees worked from home, they experienced less time pressure and, in turn, reported lower levels of work-family conflict on that particular day. Moreover, we found that experiences of work-family conflict predicted individuals' next morning engagement and exhaustion levels and affective states towards the organisation they work for. Then, in the post-COVID-19 pandemic era, it turned into Hybrid working. Hybrid working can be defined as the combination of working both in a physical office (working on-site) and remotely (working off-site) from anywhere, at any time, outside the office, by using information and communication technology (Ateeq, K., 2022) (Busboom, J., 2023).

The study by Khatimah, H. (2022) showed that the hybrid working model affects employee performance significantly. When working in a hybrid environment, employers offer exceptional workplace places and create greater collaboration and community for their employees Kamis, J., et al. (2023). The study by Tran, L. (2022) indicated that hybrid work positively impacts job satisfaction, collaboration, and communication. The study of Duckert, M. (2023) aims to comprehend cooperative engagements across the spectrum of fully collocated and completely virtual, focusing on the placement of hybrid work. A study by Busboom, J. (2023) proposed that (1) understand hybrid work settings and their challenges, (2) create knowledge around possible futures of hybrid work, and (3) investigate the strategic value of participatory Futuring methods in industrial settings.

A study by Akahori, W., et al. (2023) found that hybrid workers who feel subject to strong social norms have lower well-being. Conversely, those more willing to conform to social norms have higher well-being.

A study of Mahfoodh, H., et al. (2021), a tracking system can connect all stakeholders involved in governmental services: citizens, management, and employees. The hybrid environments allow interested parties to communicate digitally and from their offices. The tracking service adopts the traffic light system as follows. (1) Green: Service delivered on time or in advance. (2) Red: Service delayed for more than one week of the estimated time, and it has an option for submitting a complaint. (3) Yellow: Service notification of possible delay between one to three working days. (4) Orange: Stakeholders must contact a given number for further reference or submit more documents. The traffic light can be used as a milestone to monitor the ongoing task or as one evaluation metric. In terms of building hybrid environments, a model has been adopted based on looking into not only the employee but also customer satisfaction by several indicators or evaluation metrics related to the sustainability of work continuity instead of maximising the profit as before the COVID-19 pandemic era.

Hybrid work is a flexible work model that a business might design to offer their employees with their work schedule to be on-site and remote work for a certain number of days. So, a designated workspace at home for remote work might be one factor to consider. Also, the facility to support their work. There are four types of work schedules as follows. (1) Hybrid at-will: Employees can choose which day(s) to come to work in the office. (2) Hybrid split-week: A company assigns specific days for onsite and remote work by team or function. (3) Hybrid manager-scheduling: Managers choose which day(s) their team comes into the office. (4) Hybrid mix: Combining all three options (Kirkham, A. and Fowell, T., 2023). S. Behson, S. (2023) found that for many companies to move to remote or hybrid environments, traditional good management includes frequent goal-setting, peer feedback, and progress reporting. The study of Naqshbandi, M., et al. (2023) shows that flexible work positively affects work engagement, and work engagement significantly mediates the relationship between flexible work and job performance. Prins, N. (2023) suggests the seven hybrid productivity metrics as follows. (1) Planned-to-complete work ratio: Employers divide the number of "planned" tasks employees should have finished by the number they completed, then convert these numbers into percentages. (2) Employee engagement: Some businesses use tools for their employees to share feedback, which entails employees gauging each other's quality of work. (3) Achievement of goals: A hybrid work productivity can be measured by checking whether the employee's outcome contributes to the company's goals. To build these objectives, they must be specific, measurable, attainable, realistic, and time-bound. (4) Productivity by profit: It's about prioritising tasks, setting goals, and future planning. (5) Time management: To compute the amount of money each task makes for the company. (6) Technology use: Using new technologies in the workplace helps employees become more productive and efficient. (7) Communication effectiveness: The ability to communicate clearly and effectively with others so they can complete their work correctly.

The objectives of the study are to build a model of working in a hybrid environment from a review of the previous studies. Next, evaluate the appropriateness of the proposed model by the experts.

2. METHODOLOGY

2.1 Research Processes

The data collection using an assessment form for the model of working in a hybrid environment. The population in the study consisted of the experts in the area of information and communication technologies, besides organisation management. The sample group comprised five experts including three experts who have experience in the area of information and communication technologies, and two experts in the area of organisation management, who either held a doctoral degree or had at least five years' experience in their field for evaluation and suggestions. A purposive selection method was selected. Jamil (as cited in Hamzah, F., et al., 2019) stated that a minimum of five years of working experience would be enough to ensure expertise in their respective fields. Analyse the results of the evaluation of the appropriateness of a proposed model using mean and standard deviation.

The research is divided into two stages as follows. Stage 1: Design the model of working in a hybrid environment: (1.1) Relevant articles and research papers were analysed and synthesised. (1.2) Use the obtained information to synthesise and summarise as the model of working in a hybrid environment. (1.3) The Research instrument was designed as an evaluation form. Stage 2: The experts evaluated the appropriateness of the proposed model: (2.1) Propose the concept idea and the model of working in a hybrid environment to seven experts. (2.2) The proposed model was verified, and the five identified experts filled in appropriate evaluation forms. (2.3) The proposed model was modified based on the advice of the experts. (2.4) Analyse the results of the evaluation of the appropriateness of the proposed model using mean ($\overline{X}$) and standard deviation. Five criteria for assessment were considered using Likert scales anchored with the terms Strongly Agree, Agree, Undecided, Disagree, and Strongly Disagree (Samsudin, S. et al., 2019; Brown, S., 2010).

2.2 Results of the Study

The results of the study are as follows.

Stage 1: The model of working in a hybrid environment was designed as illustrated in Figure 1.

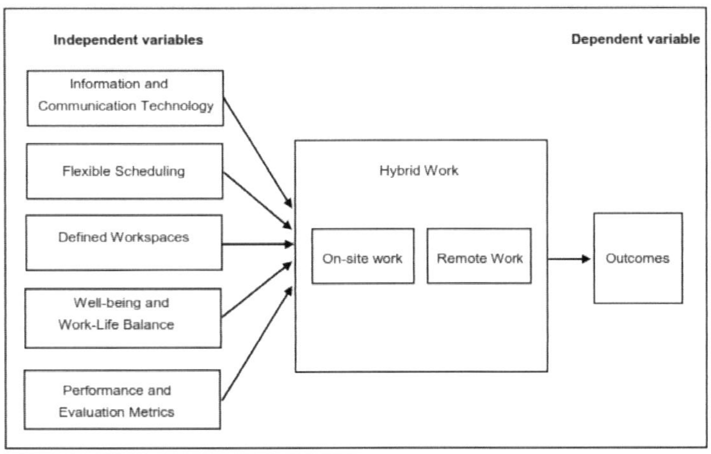

Figure 1. Model of working in a hybrid environment

The model of working in a hybrid environment is characterised by several key components that enable a flexible approach to work. These components include:

1. Information and Communication Technology: Hybrid work heavily relies on technology to facilitate communication, collaboration, and productivity. This includes tools for video conferencing, project management, file sharing, and communication platforms.

2. Flexible Scheduling: Employees often have the autonomy to set their work schedules, which can include flexible start and end times. This flexibility helps individuals manage personal and professional responsibilities more effectively.

3. Defined Workspaces: Employees may have a designated workspace at home for remote work, while office environments may need to be reconfigured to accommodate both in-person and remote work.

4. Well-being and Work-Life Balance: The hybrid work model promotes employee well-being by allowing for a better work-life balance. Organisations often encourage employees to set boundaries to prevent overwork and burnout.

5. Performance and Evaluation Metrics: Organisations need to establish clear performance metrics and evaluation methods that consider both remote and in-person work. These metrics should focus on outcomes and results rather than hours worked.

6. Hybrid work including the following. (6.1) On-site work: In contrast to remote work, there are scheduled or required days when employees work in a physical office or workspace. In-person work facilitates face-to-face interaction, collaboration, and access to on-site resources. (6.2) Remote Work: Employees have

the option to work remotely, typically from their homes or other remote locations. This component allows individuals to avoid daily commutes and work in a location that suits their needs.

7. Outcomes: Outcomes can be workloads or achievements of desired goals with organisation commitment.

Stage 2: Assessment of the model of working in a hybrid environment.

The experts evaluated the appropriateness of the model of working in a hybrid environment, as shown in Table 1.

Table 1 Appropriateness of the model of working in a hybrid environment.

Table 1. Appropriateness of the model of working in a hybrid environment

Descriptions	$\overline{X}$	S.D.	Level of appropriation
1. Information and Communication Technology: Hybrid work relies on technology to facilitate communication, collaboration, and productivity.	.4.60	0.5477	Strongly Agree
2. Flexible Scheduling: Employees have the autonomy to set their work schedules.	4.40	0.8944	Agree
3. Defined Workspaces: Employees have a designated workspace at home for remote work, while the office may reconfigured to accommodate both on-site and remote work.	4.00	0.0000	Agree
4. Well-being and Work-Life Balance: The hybrid work model promotes employee well-being by improving work-life balance.	4.20	0.4472	Agree
5. Performance and Evaluation Metrics: Organizations need to establish clear performance metrics and evaluation methods that focus on outcomes.	4.00	0.7071	Agree
6. On-site work: There are scheduled or required days when employees work in a physical office or workspace.	4.00	0.0000	Agree
7. Remote Work: Employees can work remotely from their homes or other locations.	4.40	0.5477	Agree
8. Outcomes: Outcomes can be workloads or achievements of desired goals.	4.60	0.5477	Strongly Agree
9. The model has a possibility of implementation in practice.	4.40	0.5477	Agree
Overall	***4.29***	***0.5486***	***Agree***

The experts evaluated the appropriateness of the model of working in a hybrid environment overall as Agree, with a mean of 4.29, S.D. = .5486. Whereas they agree that the model has a possibility of implementation in practice with a mean of 4.40, S.D. = .5477. Information and Communication Technology and Outcomes had the highest score, as Strongly Agree, by a mean of 4.60, S.D. = 0.5477. That refers to Information and Communication Technology are essential to working in a digital organization not only for on-site work but also for remote work. In addition, Outcomes can be workloads or achievements of desired goals which can be measurable besides related to an organisation's commitments. By the way, the Defined Workspaces, Performance, and Evaluation Metrics, besides On-site work, had the lowest score, Agree, with a mean of 4.00. The experts suggested defining more descriptive evaluation metrics, which are crucial to measuring the outcomes.

3. CONCLUSION

Shortly, Hybrid work combines both in a physical office and remotely from anywhere, anytime, outside the office, using information and communication technology. It can be applied based on employee consideration as well as customer satisfaction. The organization may consider designated workspaces and schedules, which affect well-being and family conflicts. It also positively impacts work engagement, which mediates the relationship between flexible work and productivity. The model of working in a hybrid environment includes (1) Information and Communication Technology. (2) Flexible Scheduling. (3) Defined Workspaces. (4) Well-being and Work-Life Balance. (5) Performance and Evaluation Metrics. (6) Hybrid work, including 6.1) On-site work and 6.2) Remote Work. (7) Outcomes. The appropriateness assessment of the proposed model by five experts as Strongly Agree. Information and communication technology are critical to on-site work and remote work. In addition, the result may be the workload or achievement of the desired goal which can be measurable and related to an organisation's commitments. Experts recommend defining more descriptive evaluation metrics, which will be crucial to measuring the outcomes.

For further study, the organisation should consider the evaluation metrics suitable to each task or person. Self-evaluation or a desired target could be used, along with organisation standards or expectations. The perception of hybrid work may differ by their work position as the manager versus non-manager or their geographic.

ACKNOWLEDGEMENT

Researchers express deep gratitude to the Shinawatra University for the financial support. We are also grateful to the experts for their valuable evaluation and suggestions.

REFERENCES

Akahori, W., et al., 2023. Impacts of the Strength and Conformity of Social Norms on Well-Being: A Mixed-Method Study Among Hybrid Workers in Japan. *Proceedings of 2023 CHI Conference on Human Factors in Computing Systems*, pp. 1-17. https://doi.org/10.1145/ 3544548.3581383

Ateeq, K., 2022. "Hybrid Working Method: An Integrative Review," *Proceedings of the 2022 International Conference on Business Analytics for Technology and Security (ICBATS)*, Dubai, United Arab Emirates, pp. 1-8. https://doi.org/10.1109/ICBATS54253.2022. 9759041.

Behson, S., 2023. Making Performance Reviews Fairer in a Hybrid Workplace. *Human Resource Management*.

Brown, S., 2010. Likert Scale Examples for Surveys. *In Iowa State University Extension*, pp. 1-4.

Busboom, J., 2023. The Futures of Hybrid Work - Participatory Futuring in Practice. *Proceedings of 2023 ACM International Conference on Supporting Group Work (GROUP '23) Companion (GROUP '23)*, January 8–11, 2023, Hilton Head, USA., pp. 48-50. https://doi.org/10.1145/3565967. 3571753.

Daroue, M. and Pluut, H., 2021. Work from home today for a better tomorrow! How working from home influences work-family conflict and employees' start of the next workday. *In Stress and Health*, Volume 37, pp. 986–999. https://doi.org/10.1002/smi.3053.

Duckert, M., 2023. The Futures of Hybrid Work: A Socio-Technical Framework for Designing Hybrid Environments. *Proceedings of Computer Supported Cooperative Work and Social Computing (CSCW '23 Companion)*, October 14–18, 2023, Minneapolis, USA., pp.1-3. https://doi.org/ 10.1145/3584931.3608921

Hamzah, F., et al., 2019. Rasch Model Analysis for Evaluating Validity and Reliability of Authentic Learning Instruments in Malaysian Polytechnics. *In International Journal of Innovation, Creativity and Change*. Volume 9, Issue 7, pp. 51-62.

Kamis, J., et al., 2023. A Review on Hybrid Work and Work Performance During Post-Pandemic. *Proceedings of Third Economic, Law, Education and Humanities International Conference*, pp. 192-198.

Khatimah, H., 2022. Analysis of Remote Working and Hybrid Models on Employee Performance through Work Life Balance (WLB) at Bkad Barru District. *In The Scientia Journal of Economics Issues*, Volume 1 Issue 1, pp. 55-65.

Kirkham, A. and Fowell, T., 2023. What is hybrid work and why do employees want it? Envoy blog. [On-line] Retrieved October 21, 2023 from https://envoy.com/blog/what-is-a-hybrid-work-model

Mahfoodh, H., et al., 2021. "Sustaining Work Continuity through Hybrid Work Environments: Tracking Systems," *Proceedings of 2021 International Conference on Innovation and Intelligence for Informatics, Computing, and Technologies (3ICT)*, Zallaq, Bahrain, pp. 677-684. https://doi.org/10.1109/3ICT53449.2021.9581371

Naqshbandi, M., et al., 2023. The future of work: work engagement and job performance in the hybrid workplace. *In Emerald Insight*, pp. 1-22.

Prins, N., 2023. 7 Hybrid Work Productivity Metrics Every Business Needs to Look At. [On-line] Retrieved November 5, 2023 from https://gethppy.com/productivity/hybrid-work-productivity-metrics - every-business-needs

Samsudin, S., et al., 2019. Effectiveness of Outdoor Education Program on Physical Education Student Resilience. *In International Journal of Innovation, Creativity and Change*. Volume 9, Issue 12, pp. 218-229.

Songsangyos, P. and Iamamporn, S., 2020. Remote Working with Work-life Balance. *In International Journal of Applied Computer Technology*, Volume 9 Issue 2, pp. 85-88.

Tran, L., 2022. The Impact of Hybrid Work on Productivity: Understanding the Future of Work. Master of Science Thesis: KTH Royal Institute of Technology, Sweden, pp. 1-94.

BUSINESS ANALYTICS EDUCATION: A LITERATURE REVIEW AND IMPLICATIONS

Emrah Bilgic[1], Yanqing Duan[2] and Selman Karagoz[1]
[1]*Leicester Castle Business School, De Montfort University, Leicester, LE19BH, UK*
[2]*University of Bedfordshire Business School, University of Bedfordshire, Luton, LU13JU, UK*

ABSTRACT

The objective of this study is to conduct a comprehensive review of existing academic literature on "business analytics education". This review will facilitate the identification of shortcomings, needs, challenges, and the current status of analytics education within business schools. As known, the proliferation of technology has greatly simplified data collection processes, leading to a significant surge in the volume of data within the contemporary business landscape. This abundant data reservoir presents organizations with opportunities to derive substantial value. Consequently, over the past two decades, there has been an exponential increase in the demand for business analytics experts which led business schools to open analytics-related programs. Upon analysis of the literature utilizing the key term "business analytics education" it becomes evident that this subject has received substantial attention and thorough discussion within the top academic business journals. However, given the rapid development of the domain, there is a pressing need for further research, particularly in the design of contemporary curricula and the utilization of novel teaching methodologies.

KEYWORDS

Business Analytics Education, Business Schools, Curriculum

1. INTRODUCTION

The contemporary phenomenon of Big Data, characterized by its exponential growth and ubiquitous presence, manifests in the accumulation of vast volumes of data, often measured in billions of megabytes, as enterprises progressively transition their operational frameworks into digital realms. The effective management and analysis of both structural and non-structural data hold promise in unveiling critical insights and actionable intelligence for organizational endeavors. Amidst the backdrop of evolving global dynamics, particularly accentuated by the recent COVID-19 pandemic crisis, enterprises have undergone profound transformations in their operational paradigms, witnessing shifts in decision-making modalities and substantial investments in digitalization initiatives. This transformative landscape has catalyzed the emergence of novel roles such as Business Analysts, Data Analysts, and Data Scientists, alongside the establishment of specialized departments dedicated to Data Science, Information Systems, and Business Intelligence.

Concurrently, academic institutions in Europe and the USA have responded to the escalating demand for analytical expertise by introducing specialized programs such as Business Analytics and Data Science. Positioned at the intersection of computer technologies, management science methodologies, and statistical analysis, Business Analytics serves as a pivotal problem-solving mechanism, as articulated by INFORMS. In the contemporary milieu dominated by Big Data, organizations increasingly seek to recruit personnel endowed with proficiencies in these domains, as underscored by reports such as LinkedIn's Workforce Report (2018), which highlights a demand exceeding 150,000 Data Scientists in the United States alone. In its 2023 survey of 803 global companies, the World Economic Forum determined that roles such as 'AI and Machine Learning Specialists' and 'Data Analysts and Scientists' were among the top 10 positions anticipated to experience the most rapid growth between 2023 and 2027 (World Economic Forum, 2023).

This research endeavors to examine the lacunae, requisites, challenges, and prevailing status of analytics education within business schools, employing qualitative inquiry techniques. A comprehensive review of extant literature under the thematic purview of "analytics education" reveals a robust discourse within the top business journals, indicative of the scholarly and practical significance accorded to the subject matter.

Furthermore, insights gleaned from the works of Delen and Zolbanin (2018), Chiang et al. (2012), Turel and Kapoor (2016), Janicki et al. (2014), and Seal et al. (2020) collectively corroborate the persistent inadequacies plaguing university-level analytical programs, thereby impeding the capacity of business researchers and practitioners to assimilate and apply analytical methodologies effectively within their academic pursuits and professional endeavors. This dearth reverberates across industry landscapes and academic forums alike, casting a pall over the holistic advancement of the field of business analytics.

This paper endeavors to address the following research inquiries: What are the prevailing deficiencies and challenges confronting business analytics education? What are the existing problems impeding the efficacy of business analytics education programs? What is the current status of business analytics education within business schools?

To attain these objectives, an extensive literature review will be undertaken first. This comprehensive examination of scholarly works aims to elucidate the multifaceted landscape of analytics education, shedding light on its deficiencies, challenges, and prevailing status. Furthermore, this review will serve as a foundational resource, providing insights and directions for future research endeavors aimed at enhancing the efficacy and relevance of analytics education initiatives.

2. ANALYTICS, BIG DATA ANALYTICS AND BUSINESS ANALYTICS

The evolution of analytics continued through subsequent decades, marked by milestones such as the emergence of Enterprise Resource Planning (ERP) systems in the 1980s and the proliferation of Business Intelligence and Information Technologies in the 1990s (Krishnamoorthi & Mathew, 2018). The late 2000s witnessed the integration of Information Retrieval (IR) as a pivotal analytical component within the realm of Business Intelligence, alongside advancements in Data/Text Mining and Cloud Programming (Delen and Zolbanin, 2018). The advent of the 2010s ushered in an era dominated by the Internet of Things (IoT), precipitating a surge in data generation and necessitating advanced analytics frameworks to extract insights from diverse data sources, notably social networks/media data (Delen & Ram, 2018).

Presently, the term "analytics" predominantly encompasses two distinct domains: Big Data Analytics and Business Analytics. Big Data Analytics (BDA) entails the application of advanced data management, analysis, and visualization techniques to voluminous and complex datasets, often measured in terabytes or exabytes (Chen et al., 2012). Conversely, Business Analytics (BA) is defined as the systematic collection, storage, analysis, and interpretation of data aimed at enhancing organizational performance and facilitating informed decision-making (Davenport, 2006). Furthermore, empirical research underscores the strategic imperatives and competitive advantages conferred by analytics adoption within organizational contexts (Cao et al., 2015; Davenport et al., 2010; Teece et al., 1997). Studies indicate that enterprises leveraging BA techniques exhibit enhanced decision-making process, superior performance, and heightened competitiveness, substantiating the pivotal role of analytics in driving business outcomes (Bronzo et al., 2013; Krishnamoorthi & Mathew, 2018). Notably, managerial perceptions advocate the positive impact of BA on decision-making processes, underscoring the potential dividends accruable from analytics investments in terms of customer satisfaction and profitability (Troilo et al., 2016).

3. EARLY FINDINGS AND DISCUSSIONS ON LITERATURE REVIEW OF BUSINESS ANALYTICS EDUCATION

Upon reviewing the literature in Scopus database under the thematic purview of just "business analytics" AND "education" it becomes evident that this subject has garnered considerable scholarly attention within the top academic journals, particularly in recent years. There are 179 articles in the Scopus database. As depicted in Figure 1, illustrating the co-occurrence of keywords using Voswiever Software (2011) for these articles, several discernible clusters emerge. Notably, one cluster pertains to Business Analytics methodologies, including Text Mining and Data Mining techniques. Concurrently, another cluster encompasses scientific domains associated with Business Analytics, notably Big Data, Business Intelligence, and Decision Support Systems. Moreover, a distinct cluster emerges about educational facets which is the subject of this study, encompassing topics such as skills development, knowledge acquisition, curriculum design, pedagogical strategies, and experimental learning methodologies.

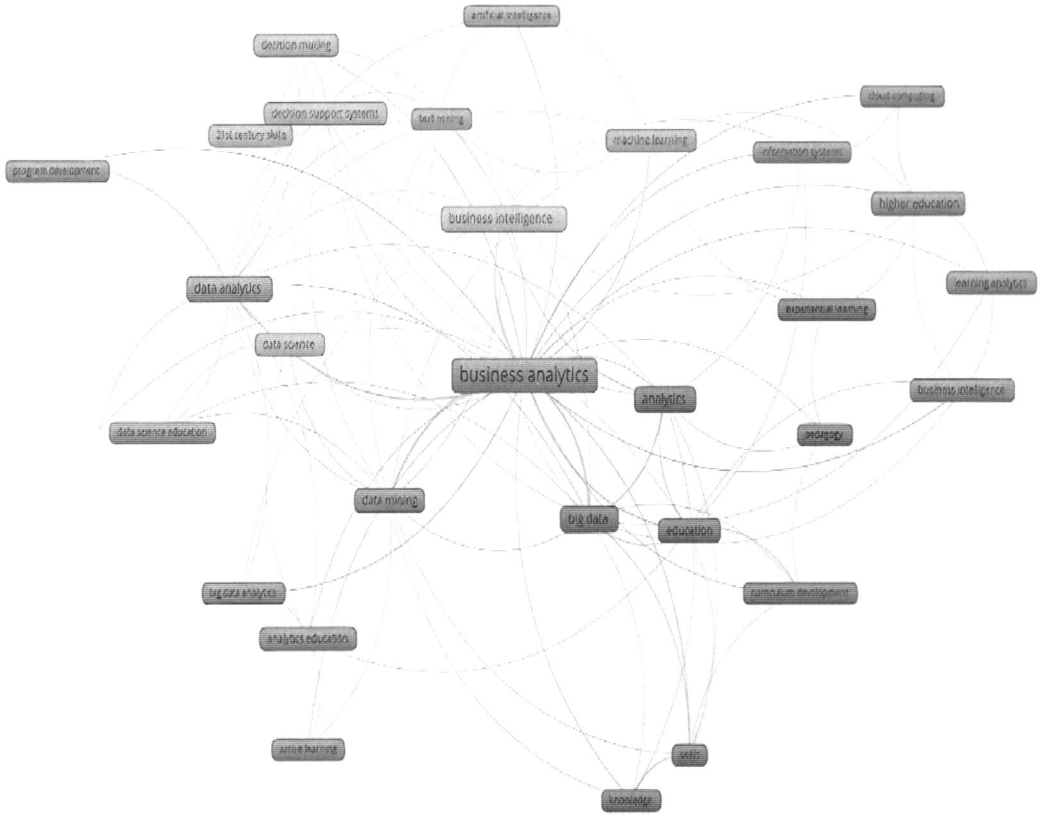

Figure 1. Co-occurrence of keywords within 179 "business analytics education" journal articles
(Source: *VOSviewer* Software)

Upon meticulous examination of articles closely, it becomes evident that authors underscore the deficiencies within the programs. Seminal works by Delen and Zolbanin (2018), Chiang et al. (2012), Turel and Kapoor (2016), Janicki et al. (2014), and Seal et al. (2020) have identified significant deficiencies persisting within related educational programs. These deficiencies impede the acquisition of requisite skills among aspiring business researchers and practitioners, hindering their ability to comprehend and apply analytical methodologies effectively in both academic and professional realms. The deficiencies that authors are pointing out parallels the pervasive "data problem" confronting contemporary enterprises, characterized not by data scarcity but by the challenge of effectively managing and analyzing voluminous datasets sourced from diverse origins. This predicament has garnered attention within academic circles and international conferences, with scholars attributing organizational inadequacies to the perceived shortcomings in the education of students enrolled in relevant graduate programs.

In recent years, the integration of mathematics, statistics, operations research, and numerical methods has culminated in the establishment of programs such as Business Analytics, characterized by a pragmatic and application-oriented pedagogical framework. Notably, graduate programs in Business Analytics have witnessed a surge in popularity in universities across all over the world. Insights gleaned from the 3rd Business Intelligence Congress in 2014 (Wixom et al., 2014) underscore several key findings regarding these programs, as presented in five main findings below. Although the congress was held ten years ago findings of Kumar (2020) in which the author have conveyed the round table discussions with the experts, exhibit many similarities.

1. A marked increase in the proliferation of Business Analytics and Business Intelligence programs has been observed since 2010.

2. Correspondingly, there has been a proliferation of documents, pedagogical resources, and program accessibility.
3. However, the burgeoning demand for these programs outstrips their current supply.
4. Despite the advent of the Big Data era, foundational skills remain paramount in educational discourse.
5. Stakeholders express dissatisfaction with the practical experience garnered by university graduates, indicating a misalignment between educational curricula and industry expectations.

The imperative for universities to augment their offerings with more comprehensive analytical programs has been underscored by Wixom et al. (2014), who advocate for a richer educational landscape supplemented by additional instructional material. Conversely, Sharda et al. (2013) shed light on a disconnection between academia and industry, noting that companies leveraging analytics technologies—such as IBM, Dell, HP, and Oracle—tend to focus on operational processes, infrastructure, and software without substantial engagement with university educators. Notably, Sharda et al.'s (2013) study, conducted approximately a decade ago, reflects an earlier iteration of the landscape. Similarly, Janicki et al. (2014) conducted a study a decade ago, wherein they surveyed 225 industry experts to delineate corporate needs; however, the educational aspect concerning universities remained unexplored. In contrast, Lawler and Molluzzo (2015) directed their attention towards the educational facet, proffering recommendations for curriculum development. Their scholarly endeavor contributes to bridging the gap between theoretical instruction and practical application within academic settings.

Over time, the programs have been evolving, and researchers in business analytics education are increasingly focusing on curricular and pedagogical matters. As Hameed et al. (2021) emphasize, a majority of AACSB-accredited schools, specifically over 65% out of a sample comprising 535 schools, provide degree programs with concentrations in business analytics, available at both undergraduate and graduate levels. Therefore, it has become important to renew and enhance the content of the programs while the supply and demand side of business analytics education are increasing. We observe that research in business analytics education is becoming more specialized compared to the early studies. For instance, Radovilsky and Hegde (2022) identified and compared the frequencies of content and skills within a specific BA technique, Data Mining (DM) module syllabi across various business analytics programs. They systematically categorized DM content and skills present in the analytics job market and compared them with the content and skills outlined in DM syllabi. On the other hand, drawing from their collective experiences, Gharehgozli et al. (2024) formulated a business analytics program. Their research a comprehensive framework encompassing the intricate steps required to devise and execute such an undergraduate Business Analytics program tailored for a business school within a state-funded public university in the US. The paper emphasizes the rationale behind the program and outlines the developmental process. Then it addresses aspects such as program structure, learning objectives, and resource allocation. Lastly, it disseminates the insights gained from the experience. Zhang et al., (2024) approach the issue from a pedagogical standpoint, utilizing student experiences as a foundational basis for the proposition of a novel instructional module. The paper outlines the creation process of an undergraduate business analytics course integrating elements from both active and experiential learning methodologies.

4. CONCLUSION

The landscape surrounding business analytics has indeed undergone significant transformations over time. After over ten years, the supply side, the prevalence of academic programs offering degrees and certificates in analytics continues to rise steadily. In recent times, a multitude of educational programs have emerged across the world offered by both reputable universities and private education companies. The surge in interest in analytics programs primarily stems from the escalating demand from employers. It is evident that there exists a pressing need for further research to inform the design of modules and programs within the realm of business analytics education. Key areas requiring exploration include identifying optimal teaching methods and determining the most suitable software applications for instructional purposes. Addressing these issues represents an ongoing challenge within academia that necessitates concerted efforts and interdisciplinary collaboration to achieve meaningful advancements.

REFERENCES

Bronzo, M., de Resende, P.T.V., de Oliveira, M.P.V., McCormack, K.P., de Sousa, P.R. and Ferreira, R.L., 2013. Improving performance aligning business analytics with process orientation. *International Journal of information management*, *33*(2), pp.300-307.

Cao, G., Duan, Y. and Li, G., 2015. Linking business analytics to decision making effectiveness: A path model analysis. *IEEE Transactions on Engineering Management*, *62*(3), pp.384-395.

Chen, H., Chiang, R.H. and Storey, V.C., 2012. Business intelligence and analytics: From big data to big impact. *MIS quarterly*, pp.1165-1188.

Chiang, R.H., Goes, P. and Stohr, E.A., 2012. Business intelligence and analytics education, and program development: A unique opportunity for the information systems discipline. *ACM Transactions on Management Information Systems (TMIS)*, *3*(3), pp.1-13.

Davenport, T.H., 2006. Competing on analytics. *Harvard business review*, *84*(1), p.98.

Davenport, Thomas H., Jeanne Harris, and Jeremy Shapiro. "Competing on talent analytics. "*Harvard business review* 88, no. 10 (2010): 52-58.

Delen, D. and Ram, S., 2018. Research challenges and opportunities in business analytics. *Journal of Business Analytics*, *1*(1), pp.2-12.

Delen, D. and Zolbanin, H.M., 2018. The analytics paradigm in business research. *Journal of Business Research*, *90*, pp.186-195.

Gharehgozli, A., Gupta, A. and Paik, S.K., 2024. Developing an undergraduate business analytics program for a public state-funded business school. *Journal of Education for Business*, *99*(1), pp.11-19.

Hameed, T., Lavoie, R. and Sendall, P., 2021. An overview of current business analytics programs across US AACSB schools. *Issues in Information Systems*, *22*(2), pp.306-317.

Janicki, T., Cummings, J. and Kline, D.M., 2014. Information technology job skill needs and implications for information technology course content. *Information Systems Education Journal*, *12*(6), p.59.

Krishnamoorthi, S. and Mathew, S.K., 2018. Business analytics and business value: A comparative case study. *Information & Management*, *55*(5), pp.643-666.

Kumar, U.D., 2020. Analytics education. *IIMB Management Review*, *32*(1), pp.108-117.

Lawler, J. and Molluzzo, J.C., 2015. A proposed concentration curriculum design for big data analytics for information systems students. *Information Systems Education Journal*, *13*(1), p.45.

Linkedin Economic Graph, 2018. LinkedIn Workforce Report, *https://economicgraph.linkedin.com/resources/linkedin-workforce-report-august-2018*, accessed: 28.03.2024

Radovilsky, Z. and Hegde, V., 2022. Contents and Skills of Data Mining Courses in Analytics Programs. *Journal of Information Systems Education*, *33*(2), p.182.

Seal, K.C., Leon, L.A., Przasnyski, Z.H. and Lontok, G., 2020. Delivering business analytics competencies and skills: A supply side assessment. *INFORMS Journal on Applied Analytics*, *50*(4), pp.239-254.

Sharda, R., Asamoah, D.A. and Ponna, N., 2013, June. Business analytics: Research and teaching perspectives. In *Proceedings of the ITI 2013 35th international conference on information technology interfaces* (pp. 19-27). IEEE.

Teece, D.J., Pisano, G. and Shuen, A., 1997. Dynamic capabilities and strategic management. *Strategic management journal*, *18*(7), pp. 509-533.

Troilo, M., Bouchet, A., Urban, T.L. and Sutton, W.A., 2016. Perception, reality, and the adoption of business analytics: Evidence from North American professional sport organizations. *Omega*, *59*, pp.72-83.

Turel, O. and Kapoor, B., 2016. A business analytics maturity perspective on the gap between business schools and presumed industry needs. *Communications of the Association for Information Systems*, *39*(1), p.6.

Van Eck, N.J. and Waltman, L., 2011. VOSviewer manual. *Manual for VOSviewer version*, *1*(0).

Wixom, B., Ariyachandra, T., Douglas, D., Goul, M., Gupta, B., Iyer, L., Kulkarni, U., Mooney, J.G., Phillips-Wren, G. and Turetken, O., 2014. The current state of business intelligence in academia: The arrival of big data. *Communications of the Association for information Systems*, *34*(1), p.1.

World Economic Forum, 2023. The future of Jobs Report, *https://www.weforum.org/publications/the-future-of-jobs-report-2023/digest,* accessed: 28.03.2024

Zhang, Y.G., Dang, M.Y. and Albritton, M.D., 2024. Delivering a Business Analytics Course Focused on Data Mining for Both Technical and Non-Technical Students. *Journal of Information Systems Education*, *35*(1), pp.86-98.

UNLOCKING MENTAL WELLNESS: THE VITAL ROLE OF INSURANCE IN DIGITAL MENTAL HEALTH ENGAGEMENT

Nasreen Khan, Anusuyah Subbarao, Shereen Khan, Tan Booi Chen and Rahimah Samsudin
Faculty of Management, Multimedia University, Cyberjaya, 63100, Selangor, Malaysia

ABSTRACT

In recent years, there has been a significant shift towards acknowledging mental health challenges due to increased openness among individuals. The World Health Organization (WHO) has stressed the necessity of improving access to quality mental health care services for everyone, regardless of their financial or social status. Global health experts are advocating the need for digital mental health care due to its accessibility and affordability. Despite this growing awareness, there is still a lack of understanding regarding the effectiveness and accessibility of digital mental health care, especially concerning its integration with existing health insurance schemes. This study aims to investigate the role of insurance in the usage of digital mental health services. This study conducted interviews with 25 individuals experiencing emotional distress, using a semi-structured questionnaire. Employing framework analysis, the study found that flexibility was the most significant factor influencing access to digital mental health care, followed by affordability, accessibility, communication, cultural sensitivity, and government subsidies & funding. The study highlighted the crucial role of insurance coverage in facilitating access to these services, suggesting that incorporating mental health insurance is essential for overcoming financial barriers, improving the well-being of insured individuals, and mitigating the societal impact of untreated mental health issues.

KEYWORDS

Digital Mental Health, Insurance, Engagement

1. INTRODUCTION

Despite the prevalence of mental illnesses, many individuals do not receive treatment, with three out of five adults not accessing care (Wang et al., 2005). High costs are a significant barrier, creating a treatment gap that burdens patients and their families economically and psychosocially (Abdulmalik et al., 2019). Including mental health treatment in insurance coverage is crucial for overcoming these financial barriers, promoting well-being, and reducing societal burdens (Saxena, 2023). Health insurance has increased access to mental health care for young adults (Lee and Kim, 2020). There is a shortage of mental health professionals, especially in public facilities and rural areas. Over the past 25 years, Digital Mental Health Interventions (DMHIs) like tele-psychiatry, tele-therapy, self-help tools, and monitoring platforms have emerged to address this gap (Lattie et al., 2022). However, concerns about the safety, effectiveness, and equity of digital tools persist (Nicole, 2022). Issues like inadequate infrastructure and lack of evidence-based research pose challenges for insurers. To address this, online mental health providers are collaborating with insurers to offer smartphone-based treatments and access to therapists and psychiatrists (Valerie, 2022).

2. RESEARCH BACKGROUND

The urgency of addressing mental health care has intensified, especially due to the global COVID-19 pandemic, which has worsened mental health issues. In Malaysia, the prevalence of mental health problems has significantly increased. The National Health and Morbidity Survey 2015 reported that 29.2% of Malaysians experienced mental health challenges, up from 10.7% in 1996. By 2017, anxiety was the most common issue among adolescents, affecting 39.7%, followed by depression at 18.3%, and stress at 9.6% (Gomes, 2019).

Despite this rise, Malaysia's mental healthcare services, particularly counselor availability, remain insufficient. The alarming increase in suicide cases highlights the urgent need for improved mental healthcare. Mental health expert Synthia Surin noted severe delays in accessing psychiatric care, with wait times of several months for urgent cases (Mok, 2021).

Integrating mental health into broader healthcare and insurance is challenging. The CEO of Etiqa Life Insurance Bhd highlighted the difficulty of establishing universally accepted mental illness diagnoses for underwriting, complicating insurance claims (Shasitiran, 2019). Globally, this issue persists. While countries like the UK, US, Australia, and Hong Kong offer mental health coverage through private insurers, often with higher premiums or limited reimbursement, Malaysia faces a shortage of mental health professionals in public healthcare. This leads to long waits and suboptimal care, with many turning to expensive private healthcare. However, most Malaysian insurance plans do not cover mental health or offer limited reimbursement, exacerbating accessibility issues.

3. AIM OF THE STUDY

This research aims to investigate the advantages of incorporating mental health coverage within existing insurance policies to promote engagement with digital mental health services. Through a review of relevant literature, this paper aims to shed light on the significance of mental health coverage and provide suggestions for improving mental health support.

4. LITERATURE

In today's digital age, healthcare is being transformed by innovation and disruptive technologies, enhancing patient care and wellness. Artificial intelligence (AI) significantly improves physician-patient interactions by optimizing communication, reducing consultation times, and minimizing unnecessary hospital visits, thus benefiting healthcare management, marketing strategies, and corporate reputation (Sheth, 2020). Digital mental health, encompassing telepsychiatry, online counseling, mental health apps, wearables, and AI tools, aims to make mental health care more accessible, convenient, and cost-effective (Magni, 2024).

Health Economic Theory – Health economics, a subfield of economic science, focuses on the financial implications of health and healthcare. It tackles problems with value, effectiveness, efficiency, and behaviour in providing and using healthcare services (Howard, 2020). The size of the healthcare industry, the percentage of public expenditures devoted to healthcare, and the quantity of research on health economics have all grown significantly since Arrow's groundbreaking 1963 article on the subject. Arrow emphasized the part that uncertainty had in driving the need for health insurance.

Factors lead to engagement in digital mental health- Based on the systematic literature review, the factors for engagement in digital mental health can be categorized into accessibility (Sultana & Pagán, 2023), flexibility (Naslund et al., 2017), affordability (Koly et al., 2022), communication (Sultana & Pagán, 2023), cultural sensitivity (Lee et al., 2020), government subsidies/public mechanisms (Li and Marquez, 2023) and stigma (Corrigan, 2004). The cost of mental health services has consistently been a major barrier for individuals seeking care for mental health issues. According to Abdulmalik et al. (2019), patients and their families often face significant financial burdens and struggle to access adequate psychosocial support due to insufficient funding and limited availability of mental healthcare services.

5. METHODS

This qualitative cross-sectional study, conducted in Malaysia from January to March 2024, involved online interviews with 25 individuals experiencing emotional distress, defined as persistent sadness, hopelessness, depression, or anxiety in the past month. Participants, invited via email and given honorary gifts, provided written consent before the interviews. Eligible participants had experienced mental illness and used digital mental health services. Using the framework method (Gale et al., 2013), the study organized and analyzed qualitative data, identifying themes through comparative analysis. The data were categorized to highlight areas of agreement and disagreement regarding factors influencing engagement with digital mental health services and the impact of insurance on this engagement, assessing a range of viewpoints.

6. RESULTS

Most respondents are female, employed, and hold a tertiary education, and their income level ranges between RM 1 – RM 4850. When respondents were asked about barriers preventing them from seeking mental health services, 25% of respondents believed that accessing mental health services is expensive, 22% stated that they do not have insurance coverage, 18% believed that there are insufficient mental health service providers, 14% believe that they have a fear of being labeled, 12% stated that it is shameful to discuss and lastly 9% are not aware of digital mental health services. When questioned about whether their current insurance plan covers mental health services, 63% of respondents indicated that their current insurance plan does not include coverage for mental illness, while 37% expressed uncertainty regarding their insurance coverage in this regard. The study employed the framework analysis method to analyze and interpret the data, focusing on identifying consensus or opposing responses. Table 1 outlines the framework analysis process, which includes four themes and their corresponding analyses.

Table 1. Framework analysis

Variables of Study	Consensus response	Opposite view
Factors that influence engagement in digital mental health services	When questioned about the most crucial factors for participating in digital mental health services, most respondents highlighted flexibility as the top factor, followed by affordability, accessibility, communication, cultural sensitivity, and government policies (subsidize and fund).	However, most respondents do not see stigma as a major factor affecting their use of digital mental health services. This is attributed to the accessibility of such services from any location and the flexibility they offer in engagement.
Role of insurance coverage in engaging in digital mental health services.	One of the primary barriers identified was the high cost of mental health services, which is often unaffordable for many individuals. When inquired about the impact of insurance coverage on their readiness to utilize digital mental health services, a significant majority of respondents emphasized that comprehensive insurance coverage for digital mental health services facilitates convenience and accessibility. When individuals do not have to worry about the financial costs, they are more likely to engage in regular and sustained use of these services, leading to better mental health outcomes.	A few respondents were uncertain about insurance coverage for mental illness. In Malaysia, most medical insurance plans exclude mental health disorders, and those that do offer coverage provide limited reimbursement. Additionally, individuals with pre-existing mental health conditions face challenges in obtaining private health insurance.

6.1 Factors That Influence Engagement in Digital Mental Health Services

Most respondents emphasized flexibility as the primary factor for engaging with digital mental health services, seeking user-friendly, adaptable platforms with easy scheduling. They believed these services should be more affordable than traditional in-person options and highlighted the need for constant accessibility, easy navigation, and effective use of online resources. Seamless communication with experts was also crucial, with respondents wanting to feel comfortable discussing their well-being online. Additionally, respondents stressed that digital mental health services should respect cultural practices and beliefs, offering content and communication in multiple languages. They viewed government policies and subsidies as significant in shaping access to these services. However, they were largely unconcerned about stigma or negative attitudes associated with using digital mental health services.

6.2 Role of Insurance Coverage in Engagement with Digital Mental Health

Most respondents are uncertain about whether their current insurance policies cover mental illness. This limitation in insurance coverage highlights a significant gap in the current healthcare system. However, if their insurance does cover mental illnesses, they are inclined to utilize digital mental health services. Additionally, they expressed a preference for their existing insurance plans to extend coverage to include digital mental health services. This result emphasizes how important insurance coverage is to increasing access to digital mental health services. Insurance plans can greatly lower financial barriers by paying for these services. This is in line with the health economics concept, which stresses lowering out-of-pocket costs to boost healthcare consumption. Thus, expanding insurance coverage for online mental health treatments can improve accessibility and motivate more people to get treatment.

7. POLICY IMPLICATIONS

The study underscores the critical importance of insurance coverage in promoting the use of digital mental health services. It strongly supports policy changes to mandate comprehensive mental health coverage in insurance plans, including a broad range of mental health services, to reduce financial barriers and improve accessibility. The study found significant disparities in access to mental health services based on insurance coverage. To address these inequities, policymakers should implement health policies ensuring all individuals, regardless of financial status or pre-existing conditions, have access to essential mental health services. This may involve regulations requiring insurance providers to cover mental health services without discriminating against those with pre-existing conditions. The study emphasizes the broader implications for health economics and equity, stressing the need for policies that increase access to mental health services while promoting overall well-being and equitable health outcomes. Policymakers should integrate mental health services into the wider healthcare system, ensuring that mental health care is prioritized equally with physical health care.

ACKNOWLEDGEMENT

This research was supported by a grant from the Ministry of Higher Education of Malaysia (FRGS grant MMUE/220034). I am grateful to MMU for their invaluable assistance and support.

REFERENCES

Abdulmalik, J., Olayiwola, S., Docrat, S., Lund, C., Chisholm, D., and Gureje, O. (2019). "Sustainable financing mechanisms for strengthening mental health systems in Nigeria". International Journal of Mental Health Systems, 13(1), 38. https://doi.org/1 0.1186/s12888-017-1352-9

Corrigan, P. (2004). "How Stigma Interferes with Mental Health Care". The American psychologist. 59. 614-25. 10.1037/0003-066X.59.7.614.

Gale, N.K., Heath, G. and Cameron, E. (2013). "Using the framework method for the analysis of qualitative data in multidisciplinary health research". BMC Medical Research Methodology, 13, 117. https://doi.org/10.1186/1471-2288-13-117.

Gomes, V. (2019). Insurance: Providing mental illness coverage. Accessed from https://theedgemalaysia.com/article/insurance-providing-mental-illness-coverage

Howard, Brandon; Health, JH Bloomberg School of Public. "What Is Health Economics?". Johns Hopkins Bloomberg School of Public Health. Retrieved 25 February 2020.

Koly, K.N., Jobaida, S., Rasma, M., Rifath, B.M., Tasdik, H.M., David, C-C., and Narelle, W. (2022). "Exploring the Potential of Delivering Mental Health Care Services Using Digital Technologies in Bangladesh: A Qualitative Analysis." Internet Interventions 29 (September). https://doi.org/10.1016/j.invent.2022.100544

Lattie E.G., Stiles-Shields C., and Graham A.K. (2022). "An overview of and recommendations for more accessible digital mental health services". Nat. Rev. Psychol. 1:87–100. doi 10.1038/s44159-021-00003-1.

Lee, Y.C., Naomi, Y., and Yun, H. (2020). "Designing a Chatbot as a Mediator for Promoting Deep Self-Disclosure to a Real Mental Health Professional." Proceedings of the ACM on Human-Computer Interaction 4 (CSCW1). https://doi.org/10.1145/3392836

Lee, J. and Kim, J. (2020). "The role of health insurance in mental health care for young adults". Applied Economics, 52 (42), 4577-4593. https://doi.org/10.1080/00036846.2020.1738326.

Li, Y., and Marquez, R. (2023). "Can government subsidies and public mechanisms alleviate the physical and mental health vulnerability of China's urban and rural residents?" Int J Equity Health 22, 59. https://doi.org/10.1186/s12939-022-01805-2

Magni, D. (2024). "Revolutionizing Healthcare: Unveiling the Transformative Power of Chatbots Through a Systematic Literature Review". Design and Development of Emerging Chatbot Technology, 199-217.

Mok, O. (2021). Mental healthcare should be covered by insurance in post-pandemic Malaysia. Accessed from https://www.malaymail.com/news/malaysia/2021/10/20/mental-healthcare-should-be-covered-by-insurance-in-post-pandemic-malaysia/2014621

Naslund, J.A., and Kelly A. , Aschbrenner, R.A, Lisa A. M., Jürgen, U, Vikram, P., and Stephen, J. B. (2017). "Digital Technology for Treating and Preventing Mental Disorders in Low-Income and Middle-Income Countries: A Narrative Review of the Literature." The Lancet Psychiatry. Elsevier Ltd. https://doi.org/10.1016/S2215-0366(17)30096-2.

Nicole, M-M. (2022). Envisioning a Path toward Equitable and Effective Digital Mental Health. A job Neuroscience. doi: 10.1080/21507740.2022.2082597

Saxena, A. (2023). The Role of Health Insurance in Mental Health and Wellness. Accessed from https://policyghar.com/blog/the-role-of-health-insurance-in-mental-health-and-wellness/

Shasitiran, J. (2019). Depressing lack of insurance coverage for mental health. Accessed from https://www.freemalaysiatoday.com/category/nation/2019/11/12/depressing-lack-of-insurance-coverage-for-mental-health/.

Sultana, S., and José, A. P. (2023). "Use of Telehealth to Address Depression and Anxiety in Low-Income US Populations: A Narrative Review." Journal of Primary Care and Community Health 14 (January). https://doi.org/10.1177/21501319231168036.

Valerie, A.C. (2022). Online company working with insurers to provide digital therapy. Mental Health Weekly. doi: 10.1002/mhw.33106

Wang, P.S., Lane, M., Olfson, M., Pincus, H.A., Wells, K.B, and Kessler, R.C. (2005). Twelve-month use of mental health services in the United States: results from the National Comorbidity Survey Replication. Arch Gen Psychiatry. 2005;62(6):629–40

DIGITALIZED CITIZENS? A SUCCINCT LITERATURE REVIEW ON CHINA'S SOCIAL CREDIT SYSTEMS

Ariane Ollier-Malaterre
PhD, School of Management (ESG-UQAM)
Université du Québec A Montréal
Case postale 6192, succursale Centre-Ville
Montréal (Québec) Canada H3C 4R2

ABSTRACT

Citizens across the globe are increasingly exposed to digital governance. In China, the government has set up a "social credit system" which has been largely misunderstood in Western media and even scholarship. To remedy this significant knowledge gap, I synthesize and update the review presented in my monograph on digital surveillance in China to introduce readers to the different types of social credit systems, analyze how the blacklists (sanctions) and redlists (rewards) work, and explain that these systems remain more fragmented and less algorithmic than Western analysts sometimes believe.

KEYWORDS

Citizens, China, Social Credit Systems, Blacklists, Digital Surveillance, Governance

1. INTRODUCTION

In many parts of the worlds, citizens are subjected to surveillance when they conduct internet searches, write emails, post on social media, make electronic payments or go by facial recognition cameras. China is a particularly fascinating setting in which to study such surveillance, as the state and other governmental bodies systematically collect data on citizens, in partnerships with commercial companies such as Baidu, Alibaba, Tencent, and Xiaomi (Creemers, 2018, Liang et al., 2018). Several factors explain the broad scope of data collection. First, the use of cash is fast disappearing. Nearly everything requires payment trough Alipay (Alibaba) or WeChat Pay (Tencent): people use these applications to pay for a bus ride, rent a bike, hail a taxi, split the cost of a restaurant meal, shop online, book train or show tickets, settle their taxes and utility bills, and much more (Chen et al., 2018b). Second, social media platforms are the fabric of everyday life for personal, social and work purposes—people look up the news on Weibo and entertain themselves on TikTok, they exchange countless text, audio, and video messages on WeChat daily, and WeChat is considered in many workplaces as easier and faster to use than email (Chen et al., 2018b). Since the 2017 Cybersecurity Law, internet service providers and digital service companies are required to allow the State to monitor their networks and facilitate the identification of their users (Chen et al., 2018a). Whenever someone makes an online purchase, uses WeChat Pay or Alipay, or comments on a social media post, their identity can be traced. Third, China has the highest ratio of closed-circuit television (CCTV) cameras to citizens in the world—one for every 12 people (Ghosh, 2020); it is also a leader in facial recognition cameras, with companies such as Hikvision, Megvii, or Sensetime exporting their technology (Ding, 2021).

Although surveillance is an age-hold practice in China, the 2014–2020 Chinese government plan to set up a social credit system (Creemers, 2018) for businesses and citizens emerged as a significant new step in the implementation of digital surveillance. This initiative was inspired by US credit rating and followed a decade of experiments to restore trust in social and economic relationships (Brussee, 2023). Social credit systems have been much discussed in Western countries, and often erroneously depicted as a dystopian panopticon that would assign a single credit score rating to each Chinese citizen based on efficiently aggregated data (Brussee, 2023). This confusion originates in part in the opacity surrounding the social credit system and in part in its experimental and fragmented nature (Brussee, 2023).

To rectify this misunderstanding that hampers knowledge accumulation on digital surveillance worldwide, this paper presents a succinct literature review on social credit systems in China and how they impact citizens. It does so by synthesizing and updating the literature review proposed in *Living with Digital Surveillance in China: Citizens' Narratives on Technology, Privacy and Governance* (Ollier-Malaterre, 2024).

This paper first introduces readers to the different types of social credit systems and explains that rewards and sanctions systems, rather than scoring, are the most visible components of social credit systems. Then, it analyzes what behaviors can lead a citizen to appear on a blacklist or a redlist, and which sanctions or rewards, respectively, may materialize. In conclusion, it discusses how the pandemic fostered function creep and centralization of data collection and storage, and how these systems nevertheless remain more fragmented and less algorithmic than is sometimes believed in Western countries.

2. THE SOCIAL CREDIT SYSTEMS

As astutely noted by Vincent Brussee (2023), the term social credit system is misleading: it is more a toolbox or policy umbrella than a system; it is more societal, i.e., constructed with and appropriated by social actors, than social; and it is more about trust than credit.

2.1 Types of Social Credit Systems

The social credit systems consist of three interconnected models: (1) municipal and provincial systems (2) commercial systems, and (3) the joint rewards and sanctions system (Zhang, 2020).

Following the publication of the 2014–2020 plan, many local governments piloted social credit systems, more often focused on businesses than citizens (Li and Kostka, 2022). In 2018 the National Development and Reform Commission (NDRC) and the People's Bank of China selected 12 model cities that had established red lists and blacklists, created a credit information-sharing platform, and began to share these data with other national or provincial social credit system platforms (Kostka and Antoine, 2019). As of June 2021, over 400 million Chinese citizens were covered by municipal credit systems, primarily in Eastern and Middle China (Liang and Chen, 2022). However, except in cities like Rongcheng that enrol all citizens over 18, participation was voluntary through signing up on a mobile application or the city's WeChat account, and was estimated at between 10 and 40% (Li and Kostka, 2022). Municipal systems have different scales for the credit scores (e.g., 0 to 200; 0 to 1000), different criteria to assess citizens' behaviors (from 28 to 200 indicators), different labels and cut-off points for categories (e.g., AAA to D; Excellent, Good, Fair, Poor, Risky) (Liang and Chen, 2022). The data come from existing administrative databases rather than AI-based digital tracing. Some cities provide credit repair mechanisms (Liang and Chen, 2022). Given the multiplicity of systems and functionings, it is often not easy for citizens to assess how these systems may impact them (Kostka and Antoine, 2019).

In addition to the governmental systems, eight commercial pilot projects launched in 2015 (Liang et al., 2018). The best known is Sesame Credit by Alibaba. The People's Bank of China merged these pilots in 2018, establishing a citizens' credit scoring agency named Baihang Credit (Kostka and Antoine, 2019). As of 2022, AliPay and WeChat credit systems seem to be more widely used and popular, based on the discounts and benefits they offer, than most municipal credit systems (Li and Kostka, 2022).

Lastly, the joint rewards and sanctions systems consist of red- and blacklists published by Credit China, the Supreme People's Court, and ministry, local governments' and sectors' (e.g., railways, civil aviation) websites (Brussee, 2023, Liang et al., 2018). The Credit China platform was designed with Baidu; the names of blacklisted individuals can be searched on its website (Mac Síthigh and Siems, 2019). Credit repair mechanisms and a withdrawal process to be removed from a list were provided to citizens (Liang et al., 2018).

2.2 Scoring, Rewards and Punishments

The scope of behaviors leading to blacklisting, redlisting, and credit scoring remains opaque. The Supreme People's Court blacklists businesses and citizens who commit crimes and offenses, do not pay their debt, or do not execute the court's orders. Several studies note that the social credit systems do not currently seem to focus on dissent and subversion (Creemers, 2018, Drinnhausen and Brussee, 2021, Hou and Fu, 2024). However, the media have given examples of villages where points were deducted for moral or political reasons, such as neglecting elderly parents or petitioning in visible areas where the internet and foreign media can pick up the protest (Gan, 2019).

The redlists have clearer moral and political components. Individuals can be redlisted for receiving an honour, volunteering for the CPC League, donating blood, donating money to charity, giving information to the police, or being an ecological household (Arsène, 2021). Redlists highlight citizens who are role models (Engelmann et al., 2021). Posting "positive energy" messages on social media that highlight achievements of the government and of China's economy accumulates points for users (Jiang and Fu, 2018).

As far as commercial scores are concerned, Sesame Credit scores are based on five categories: an individual's credit history, ability to fulfil financial commitments, personal information that can be verified, behaviors, and preferences (e.g., purchasing behavior, donating to charity), and social relationships (e.g., the characteristics of their social networks) (Kostka and Antoine, 2019).

Rewards give access to preferential treatment at hospitals and free health check-ups, reduced entrance fees to tourist sites, fast lanes at airport security, and fast-tracked visa applications for Singapore and Schengen. In villages, personal credit scores are tied to "civilisation points" and community welfare programmes (Brussee, 2023). High scorers may receive rice, cooking oil, and money and be celebrated as role models on village bulletin boards (Gan, 2019). In Rongcheng, AA and A citizens can be promoted faster in government jobs and receive priority and discounts for public services (Liang and Chen, 2022). High Sesame Credit scores qualify citizens for personal credit loans and allow them to rent bikes and cars, book hotel rooms, and buy mobile phones without making a deposit (Botsman, 2017).

Blacklists penalties cross over domains, unlike Western bank credit ratings or no-fly lists: sanctions are applied by all members of the social credit system joint conference (Chen et al., 2018a). In Rongcheng, blacklisted citizens are subjected to increased monitoring, including visits by government officials; C and D citizens are banned from taking up employment in governments and public administrations and D citizens cannot enrol their children in private schools (Liang and Chen, 2022). Access to luxury goods and services, including plane and high-speed train travel, is banned. Social shaming is another punishment: in some regions people ringing blacklisted individuals are greeted with an audio message informing them that the person they are calling is dishonest (Zeng, 2018). In other cities, blacklisted people have had their pictures displayed in public places on TV screens or LED billboards (Wong and Dobson, 2019). On Tiktok, pictures of blacklisted are shown in between videos so that users can report seeing them (Strittmatter, 2020). Overall, about 0.3% of Chinese citizens (10 million people) have been blacklisted (Brussee, 2023).

3. CONCLUSION

Will the social credit systems evolve toward a Big Brother citizen rating scheme in which every digital trace would be consolidated?

On the one hand, databases are increasingly interconnected and Chinese media have reported success stories, such as police arresting suspects during festivals, stopping fraudulent schemes, and returning stolen bikes to owners. Some individuals have settled long-term debts and firms may hesitate to take advantage of vulnerable workers by not paying wages (Dai, 2018). Moreover, the Covid-19 pandemic has accelerated the centralisation of data and fostered function creep, i.e. a broadening of the scope of behaviors considered by social credit systems (Knight and Creemers, 2021). Notably, Alipay's Health Code application reportedly used artificial intelligence to analyse reported Covid-19 symptoms and current and past location data to sort users into green, yellow, or red groups based on their risk of having contracted the disease.

On the other hand, the systems remain fragmented, rudimentary, and prone to error. Provinces have very disparate approaches to managing black and redlists. Municipal scoring involves digitised administrative documents more than behavioral data; in practice, scores resemble airlines loyalty programmes (Drinnhausen and Brussee, 2021). Furthermore, there is currently little algorithmic processing of the data that would enable predictive computations or collective social sorting of groups (Chorzempa et al., 2018). Moreover, there has been civil society backlash against the systems' function creep and the government is now realigning the social credit systems with existing laws and regulations. In December 2020, the State Council asked local governments to not punish behaviors that were not already illegal and to observe proportionality between offenses and penalties. In November 2022, a draft law on the Establishment of the Social Credit System was released for public comments (Yang, 2022), which clarifies which data should be collected and what punishment can be carried out (Knight, 2023). Bringing clarity about rules and sanctions will indeed be important for Chinese citizens as they experience the increasing digitalisation of their lives.

REFERENCES

Arsène, S. (2021). Le système de crédit social en Chine. *Réseaux*, 55-86.

Botsman, R. (2017). Big data meets Big Brother as China moves to rate its citizens. *Wired* [Online]. Available: http://www.wired.co.uk/article/chinese-government-social-credit-score-privacy-invasion.

Brussee, V. (2023). *Social Credit. The Warring States of China's Emerging Data Empire*, Plagrave McMillan.

Chen, Y. et al. (2018a). "Rule of Trust": the power and perils of China's social credit megaproject. *Columbia J Asian Law,* 32.

Chen, Y. et al. (2018b). *Super-Sticky WeChat and Chinese Society,* Bingley, UK, Emerald Publishing Limited.

Chorzempa, M. et al. (2018). China's Social Credit System: A Mark of Progress or a Threat to Privacy? Policy Brief. Peterson Institute for International Economics.

Creemers, R. (2018). China's Social Credit System: An Evolving Practice of Control. *Anthropology & Archaeology Research Network Research: Science & Technology Studies*, 1-32.

Dai, X. (2018). Toward a reputation state: The social credit system project of China. *Available at SSRN 3193577.*

Ding, J. (2021). 2021 AI Company Ranking. *ChinAI* [Online]. Available: https://chinai.substack.com/p/chinai-143-2021-ai-company-rankings.

Drinnhausen, K. & Brussee, V. (2021). China's Social Credit System in 2021: From fragmentation towards integration. *MERICS China Monitor.* Mercator Institute for China Studies (MERICS)

Engelmann, S. C. et al. (2021). Blacklists and Redlists in the Chinese Social Credit System: Diversity, Flexibility, and Comprehensivenes. *Artificial Intelligence, Ethics and Society Conference AIES.*

Gan, N. (2019). The Complex Reality of China's Soical Credit System: Hi-Tech Dystopian Plot or Low-Key Incentive Scheme? *South China Morning Post.*

Ghosh, I. (2020). Mapping The State of Facial Recognition Around the World.

Hou, R. & Fu, D. (2024). Sorting citizens: Governing via China's social credit system. *Governance,* 37, 59-78.

Jiang, M. & Fu, K. W. (2018). Chinese social media and big data: Big data, big brother, big profit? : Wiley Online Library.

Knight, A. (2023). Basket Case: Reform and China's Social Credit Law. *China Law and Society Review,* 6, 181-210.

Knight, A. & Creemers, R. (2021). Going Viral: The Social Credit System and COVID-19. *SSRN Electronic Journal.*

Kostka, G. & Antoine, L. (2019). Fostering Model Citizenship: Behavioral Responses to China's Emerging Social Credit Systems. *Policy & Internet,* 12, 256-289.

Li, H. & Kostka, G. (2022). Accepting but not engaging with it: Digital participation in local government-run social credit systems in China. *Policy & Internet,* 14, 845-874.

Liang, F. & Chen, Y. (2022). The making of "good" citizens: China's Social Credit Systems and infrastructures of social quantification. *Policy & Internet,* 14, 114-135.

Liang, F. et al. (2018). Constructing a Data-Driven Society: China's Social Credit System as a State Surveillance Infrastructure. *Policy & Internet,* 10, 415-453.

Mac Síthigh, D. & Siems, M. (2019). The Chinese social credit system: A model for other countries? *The Modern Law Review,* 82, 1034-1071.

Ollier-Malaterre, A. (2024). *Living with Digital Surveillance in China: Citizens' Narratives on Technology, Privacy and Governance. London:* Routledge Studies in Surveillance. https://www.routledge.com/Living-with-Digital-Surveillance-in-China-Citizens-Narratives-on-Technology/Ollier-Malaterre/p/book/9781032517704

Strittmatter, K. (2020). *We Have Been Harmonized: Life in China's Surveillance State*, Custom House.

Wong, K. L. X. & Dobson, A. S. (2019). We're just data: Exploring China's social credit system in relation to digital platform ratings cultures in Westernised democracies. *Global Media and China,* 4, 220-232.

Yang, Z. (2022). China just announced a new social credit law. *MIT Tech Review.*

Zeng, M. J. (2018). China's Social Credit System puts its people under pressure to be model citizens. *The Conversation.*

Zhang, C. (2020). Governing (through) trustworthiness: technologies of power and subjectification in China's Social Credit System. *Critical Asian Studies,* 52, 565-588.

INFORMATION TECHNOLOGIES AT A HIGHER SCHOOL OF REAL ESTATE IN PORTUGAL

Teresa Florentino
ESAI – Escola Superior de Imobiliário, Lisboa, Portugal

ABSTRACT

This unique study delves into the use of cutting-edge technologies such as Augmented Reality (AR), Virtual Reality (VR), 3D design, and Artificial Intelligence (AI) in the context of Real Estate education and businesses. We explore the integration of these emerging technologies with traditional tools like websites, blogs, and apps, and their adoption by students and enterprises in the Real Estate sector. By conducting questionnaires, we capture the current trends and perceptions among students at a specific higher education institution. Our findings, compared with existing studies, reveal the rapid adoption and impact of these technologies, underscoring the need for continuous research in this dynamic field.

KEYWORDS

Real Estate IT, Augmented and Virtual Reality, 3D, AI, Social Media

1. INTRODUCTION

The rapid advancement of technologies necessitates constant monitoring of trends in both educational and professional contexts, particularly in Real Estate (RE). This study**, a part of our ongoing commitment to research and innovation,** examines the current state of technology use in a Higher School of Real Estate in Portugal, focusing on two courses: Information and Communication Technologies (ICT) and Information Technologies for Real Estate (ITRE). By applying new technologies and analysing data with appropriate tools, we aim to understand students' perspectives and the professional application of these technologies. A questionnaire with 15 questions was distributed to gather insights on the importance and usage of ICT and ITRE in both educational and professional settings. The results of this study will guide us in the continuous improvement and adaptation of our academic programs to incorporate emerging technologies, underscoring the importance of our collective work in this field.

2. LITERATURE REVIEW

Various studies have explored the integration of new technologies in Real Estate education and business. For instance, Camacho (2020) underscores the role of specialists in bridging Real Estate with information technologies for successful Proptech development. Honda (2021) demonstrates the pivotal role of AI in urban planning and property valuation. Surgelas et al. (2020) have developed a fuzzy logic method for property price estimation, showcasing the accuracy and effectiveness of AI in Real Estate valuation. These studies point to a growing trend towards the use of AI, VR, AR, and other emerging technologies in the Real Estate sector, necessitating further research and adoption in educational programs. Our study's findings, therefore, have direct implications for professionals and educators in the Real Estate sector.

3. METHODOLOGY

This study utilised a mixed-methods approach, combining quantitative data from questionnaires with qualitative insights from open-ended responses. The questionnaire, consisting of 15 questions, was designed to assess students' knowledge and use of ICT and ITRE in their studies and professional work. A total of 234 students were invited to participate, with a response rate of 21% (48 respondents). The data were analysed using descriptive statistics and correlation analysis to identify trends and relationships. Open-ended responses were thematically analysed to provide deeper insights into students' perspectives on emerging technologies.

4. REDESIGNING A NEW INFRASTRUCTURE AND NEW WAYS TO WORK

In 2002, Laudon and Laudon presented an IS infrastructure in their book "Management Information Systems." This framework provided a deep understanding of MIS processes. Based on their 2002 schema, we can now update this approach to incorporate Artificial Intelligence (AI), which transforms data into information and knowledge, enhancing both educational and business environments. This new AI layer supports firms and higher education by enabling users to better understand and apply new technologies in their professional and academic pursuits. Currently, technologies linked to Real Estate, such as website creation, blogs, mobile applications, and AI, are becoming increasingly accessible. Programs like GPT-4, DALL·E 2, ChatGPT from OpenAI, and others from Google, Microsoft, and Facebook make AI tools more straightforward to use. At our school, most students are involved or intend to work in the Real Estate field. It was impossible to address AI because it is still very embryonic in this school. However, what is described here will allow us to advance in this aspect, carrying out work and questionnaires to observe this use and opinions.

Syllabus Overview:

ICT Course: Program overview: where ICT includes fundamentals of: websites, blogs and a little notion of AI, AR, VR.	**TII Course: TII Course: Program overview includes 3D drawing; website creation; blogs; mobile phone applications; use of AI and some notions of AR and VR.**
Information Technology and Communication vs Information Systems: Fundamentals of data organization and management, information, and communication. Platforms and architectures of information technologies. Applications and tools (e.g., Microsoft Office, AI). **Navigation and Communication Network:** Local and remote network architectures. Cloud usage, web navigation, and advanced search techniques. **Applications and Tools:** Slide production (PowerPoint). Standardized information production (Word). Data collection, tables, charts, and advanced Excel functions. Integrated document production.	**Internet - Pages, Blogs, Portals:** Relationship between websites and businesses. Site construction and optimization. Social Networks: Concepts and applications in Real Estate. **Mobile Apps:** Use and development of apps for Real Estate. **3D Modelling:** Virtualization support for Real Estate. Development of 3D models, sketches, and images. **Virtual Reality and Augmented Reality:** Concepts and simple applications. Artificial Intelligence: Concepts and simple applications.

Questionnaire Insights:

We asked students about their knowledge and use of social networks, website creation programs and mobile applications, preferred technologies for courses and what improvements they foresee with emerging technologies, namely AI, VR and AR. This feedback helps us understand the current technology landscape in real estate education and identify areas for future improvements.

5. DATA ANALYSIS

The data analysis focused on understanding the importance and usage of ICT and ITRE among students. The responses were analysed using a Likert scale, with results showing a high importance attributed to both ICT and ITRE in educational and professional contexts. The following results are presented:

- **Questions 1-6**: Mean, median, and mode values indicate a general consensus on the importance of these technologies.
- **Correlation Analysis**: Significant correlations were found between questions related to course performance and professional application.

Graphical representations illustrate the preferred platforms for website creation, with WordPress being the most favoured. Social networks such as Instagram, WhatsApp, and LinkedIn were identified as the most important for Real Estate professionals.

1 - How has Knowledge of Information and Communication Technologies (ICT) affected your performance and experience on the course?

2 - How has Knowledge of Information Technologies for Real Estate (ITI) affected your performance and experience on the course?

3 - How do you perceive your performance in the use of ICT in your professional work? (otherwise, it works, do not respond)

4 - How do you perceive your performance using TII in your professional work? (otherwise, it works, do not respond)

5 - In the Real Estate sector, is ICT important?

6 - In the specific case of the Real Estate sector, is TII important?

Note: the detailed program mentioned above was implicit in these questions.

From the Measures table, Mean, Median, and Mode appear for all questions 4—Important, and 5—Very Important for questions 5 and 6 in median and mode. It statistically means that the mean is quite acceptable because the CV is almost less than 25%, and the emphasis is on the importance of TIC and TII for the Real State sector.

Correlations exist between questions 1 and 2: "Performance and experience on the course?"; 3 and 4 performance at work; 5 and 6; and also, with a minus correlation between questions 4 and 5 and 4 and 64 performance at work in Real Estate.

Substantial evidence shows the importance of TIC and TII technologies in the Real Estate sector. However, "performance and experience on the course?" is also essential at work, primarily if the work is in Real Estate.

6. DISCUSSION

The findings indicate that students place a high importance on ICT and ITRE, reflecting their relevance in the Real Estate sector. The preference for platforms like WordPress and social networks such as Instagram and LinkedIn suggests a trend towards leveraging widely used tools for professional purposes. The strong correlation between course performance and professional application underscores the need for integrating practical technology skills into the curriculum. These insights highlight the necessity for ongoing research and adaptation of educational programs to incorporate emerging technologies.

7. CONCLUSION

This study provides valuable insights into using ICT and ITRE in Real Estate education and professional practice in this specific case. Students' high importance of these technologies underscores their relevance and the need for their integration into educational curricula. Future research should focus on a larger sample size and explore the impact of specific emerging technologies in greater detail. Continued investigation is essential to keeping pace with rapid technological advancements and their implications for the Real Estate sector.

REFERENCES

Camacho, J. M. F. (2020). Tese de Mestrado Inteligência Artificial no Imobiliário - Ameaça ou oportunidade?. Área departamental de Engenharia Civil. ISEL.

Florentino, T., & Casaca, J. (2013). Social Networks on the Web in Real Estates in Portugal. Conference: ERES 2013 Vienna. ERES2013 Book of Abstracts.

Gonzalez, M. A. S. (2002). Aplicação de técnicas de descobrimento de conhecimento em bases de dados e de inteligência artificial em avaliação de imóveis. Tese de Doutoramento. Universidade Federal do Rio Grande do Sul.

Honda, F. P. (2021). Estudo dos Condicionantes Espaciais para Avaliação Imobiliária Utilizando Técnicas de Inteligência Artificial – Universidade Federal de São Carlos.

Laudon, K. C., & Laudon, J. P. (2002). Management Information Systems: Managing the Digital Firm. Índia: Prentice Hall.

OpenAI. (2024). ChatGPT (4) - Main AI programs. OpenAI

Next/Now - VR Today Magazine - VR Games News, Reviews and Guides. https://vrtodaymagazine.com/directory/next/now/.

Surgelas, V., Arhipova, I., & Pukite, V. (2020). Original article published in the XX CONEMI - Congresso Internacional de Engenharia Mecânica e Industrial.

Reflection Papers

EDUCATION AND TECHNOSCIENCES

Luiz Roberto Alves
FAPESP Thematic Project. Alfredo Bosi Chair in Basic Education. Institute of Advanced Studies at the University of São Paulo, Brazil

ABSTRACT

This reflection paper deals with the role of school communities in relation to technological interactions in the so-called cyberculture. Through an epistemology based on the work of educator Paulo Freire, it reveals the limits of nations' regulations in the face of software intoxication disseminated among new generations and questions the role of schools in confronting information and social communication processes conveyed by technoscience, especially from Big Techs. The paper suggests paths of action for local and planetary citizenship.

KEYWORDS

Education, Technoscience, Epistemology, Consciousness

1. INTRODUCTION

This reflective text thinks about Brazil's educational experience, but technological interactions project it to international territory. The question is what are the limits of school education in terms of confrontation, knowledge and curricular choices in the face of new information and communication technologies? How to take ownership of hardware without becoming intoxicated with software? Are Big Techs and their platforms aware of the psychology of development and cognition that studied children and adolescents, at least as treated by Vigotsky, Piaget and Paulo Freire? In addition: the laws that deal with data protection and seek to regulate social networks, which many countries have (and also Brazil) have not been able to regulate the economic system that runs the same networks and platforms, as is evident in Zuboff (2021). The problems continue to reside in educational policies, which also challenge orders and decrees banning smartphones and tablets from school, as is done in some countries.

2. ANALYTICAL WORK

The epistemological perspective adopted at the limit of these four pages is that of Paulo Freire, that is, the growing awareness of generations of their incompleteness demands that education and learning are not products of information, but of the cultural confrontation of generations, understood as historical subjects, in the life of the world, which results in autonomy and citizenship. It also results in the happiness of generations.

It is understood, therefore, that critics of new cybernetic systems after Norbert Wiener (kibernu/kubernetes, which etymologically means piloting and direction), attribute to educational organizations a great responsibility in the critical stance towards technoscience, its corporations and their expansion process worldwide. Take some authors. Turner (2021) understands that school is the right place for challenges and confrontations. For the author, school reflects the common destiny of humans, as it involves generations. The question that Turner raises is that our society - and not just the Latin American one - still carries images and practices of the slave-owning and genocidal society of indigenous people. This means that a curricular revolution is required in the school space towards a culture of freedom, in which each student is a citizen and, therefore, capable of making choices and making judgments. But Turner insists on the effective possibility of building local and planetary citizenship based on ecological-environmental awareness, as education can be a laboratory, access to culture, food, the right to research and the achievement of social equity, impossible both in slave society in the 18th century and in contemporary authoritarian regimes. Perhaps Turner will lead us to debate a central pedagogical issue, which also motivated many of Paulo Freire's reflections: education cannot do everything, not even much in society, but it is a decisive reference for society to be transformed. Now, no one can be a planetary citizen without having their local and community citizenship guaranteed.

Zuboff (2021), although in a darker reading, also sees school education as indispensable for the analysis of new techno-scientific interactions. For her, it is essential to contrast concrete citizenship learning with a generic machine learning education. No one will be a citizen of the world without being a citizen of their place. However, we must understand what Lumina Magazine's Manifesto for Digital Citizenship says: "overcoming subjective and humanistic forms of interaction towards digital, algorithmic and info-ecological forms of participation and life". In contrast, says Zuboff: "in the face of human life being subordinated to market dynamics, there is an urgent need for the presence of citizens who act knowing that ignorance induced by deception is not a social contract and that freedom from uncertainty is not freedom". In fact, human life is in schools and the youth seeking to educate themselves cannot be subordinated to the data negotiations of Big Techs, which goes far beyond the proposal by American legislators to ban Tik Tok. It would therefore be appropriate to legislate against the subordination of youth in a new ecological-social contract, since schools cannot teach uncertainty or admit ignorance in the face of commercialization and global marketing of data. Study and experience curricula need to be understood as the new cultural heart of school communities and, therefore, be organized as vital curricula between nature, traditional culture and technological interactions, with broad participation of students and the surrounding community. New pedagogies must understand, according to Freire's epistemological reading, that large corporations block the linguistic and didactic opportunities of new generations, which necessarily leads educators to discuss the great topic of identity and psychosocial identifications. Good education cannot allow the old graphic illiteracy (anti-enlightenment) to be added to the new image illiteracy, in the clouds, in the artificiality of intelligence and network business.

3. CONCLUSION

It is clear that educators need to work with new information and communication technologies. And it is known that contemporary school education cannot take place without them. Strictly speaking, technoscience that leads to a deep understanding of life, society and its techniques can be translated as educational action. In this direction, many experiences of school work based on technology are known. Due to the space for reflection, one case is appropriate. Professors at the Federal University of São Carlos (São Paulo) took a narrative from the Bororo Indigenous Nation (central-western Brazil) called Jeriguigi and the Jaguar and transformed it into a digital game. The narrative was collected by a missionary and later worked on by the anthropologist Claude Lévi-Strauss, who presented it in his work Mythologies. As a digital game and application, Jeriguigi and the Jaguar maintained narrative components such as hero (heroine), action, obstacles, providential help and overcoming. The academic-scholastic work is in use in elementary school grades and included a member of the Bororo nation, Márcio Parameriri Bororo, who supported the teachers in building the game.

Certainly, the narratives of networks and platforms are important for conveying ethnographic-based stories, for studying narratives and for ensuring enjoyment and pleasure, which can unfold in the field of images and other forms of art. However, school education will not do this work without the sciences of Anthropology, Linguistics and other sciences of nature and society, present in the curricula worked by inter and transdisciplinarity.

REFERENCES

Piaget, J. (1973). *O Tempo e o Desenvolvimento Intelectual da Criança* [Time and Children's Intellectual Development]. Rio de Janeiro, Forense.

Turner, D. (2021). Taming the Technosphere. Author's blog

Vigotsky, L. S. (2009). *Pensamento e Linguagem* [Thought and Language]. São Paulo: Editora WFM, Martins Fontes.

Zuboff, S. (2021). *A Era do Capitalismo de Vigilância* [The Age of Surveillance Capitalism]. Rio de Janeiro: Intrínseca.

FASHION DIGITAL WELLNESS: A BEHAVIORAL ECONOMY APPROACH TO SOCIAL MEDIA AWARENESS THROUGH PERSONALIZED IMAGERY

Mariam Sameh Hassaan, Sarah Hassaan and Brenno Menezes
Division of Engineering Management, College of Science and Engineering, Hamad Bin Khalifa University, Qatar Foundation, Doha, Qatar
Education City, LAS Building

ABSTRACT

In our digitally dominated world, social media platforms have evolved into vital components of daily life, fostering global interconnectedness and real-time communication. Despite their benefits, the increasing prevalence of social media has prompted extensive studies into its behavioral and psychological impacts. The negative correlation between prolonged social media use and mental well-being on users immersed in the digital realm faces elevated levels of stress, anxiety, and depression. Factors such as curated content, social comparisons, and the addictive nature of scrolling contribute to an environment that heightens feelings of isolation and inadequacy. With the average social media time rising to roughly 2 hours a day, there is a pressing need to elevate awareness of individual social media habits. Our proposal introduces an innovative approach, leveraging advanced Generative AI to generate fashion images correlated with users' social media habits. Using the keywords extracted from social media content, the generated images will reflect optimistic or negative features based on the time spent on social media, serving as a unique intervention in promoting mindful social media engagement. This user-centric strategy incorporates behavioral insights to cultivate a harmonious balance between digital and real-world experiences.

KEYWORDS

Social Media, Mental Well-being, Generative AI, User Engagement

1. INTRODUCTION

In the digital landscape, social media has become a dominant presence in our daily lives where platforms create a globally interconnected environment, promoting real-time communication. This brings numerous benefits of connecting people across geographical boundaries, fostering community engagement, and providing instant access to a diverse range of information (Primack et al, 2017). It is a virtual bridge that enhances social interactions, facilitates networking, and serves as a powerful tool for both personal and professional growth. Moreover, social media platforms have become indispensable for staying informed about current events, trends, and the latest developments in various fields, contributing to a more interconnected and informed global society (Twenge & Campbell, 2018). However, the widespread use of social media has become a subject of extensive study, particularly in understanding the behavioral and psychological challenges faced by users. A popular aspect of these investigations is the negative correlation between the time spent on social media and the individuals' mental well-being (Primack et al, 2017). As users immerse themselves in the digital realm for prolonged periods, there is a growing recognition of the potential detrimental effects on mental health, particularly concerning elevated levels of stress, anxiety, and depression (Verduyn et al, 2015).

Given the average user engagement of approximately 145 minutes on various social media apps a day (Belle Wong, 2023), there is a critical need to make individual users aware of their social media habits to reduce the negative effects. The primary objective is to prompt users to reflect proactively on their digital time expenditure, fostering a more deliberate and mindful approach to social media engagement. The aim is to induce a positive shift in behavior dynamics.

In our proposal, we utilize advanced Generative AI to generate fashion images fueled by the hashtags extracted from social media content. Since the time spent on these platforms is what increases the risk for depression, anxiety, loneliness, and self-harm with little relation to the content viewed (Hou et al, 2019), our generated images will be correlated to the time spent on social media platforms while using the hashtags of the content viewed as the source to generate the images. The purpose of generating a fashion image is to reflect a personalized style to various users. The total time spent on social media platforms will be segmented into 6 consecutive categories with each having an interval of 25 minutes as there would be enough content viewed to generate the images. The produced image in the first interval will exhibit optimistic colors and features, however as time increases and the user enters further categories, a more negative image will result, featuring undesirable elements and somber colors. This approach integrates user-centric considerations and behavioral insights in making impactful interventions in social media usage awareness.

2. LITERATURE REVIEW

The contemporary landscape is marked by the pervasive influence of social media, prompting extensive research into its intricate relationship with mental well-being. (Primack et al, 2017) revealed a consistent negative association between the duration of social media engagement and symptoms of depression among young adults. This underscores not only the quantifiable impact on mental health but also delves into the qualitative aspects of depressive experiences associated with extended social media use. (Twenge and Campbell, 2018) further substantiated this correlation, providing valuable insights into the multilayered nature of loneliness, especially prevalent among adolescents immersed in prolonged social media use. Their study examined specific social contexts and types of online interactions contributing to heightened feelings of isolation.

(Verduyn et al, 2015) detailed the research by focusing on Facebook, shedding light on the negative consequences associated with passively scrolling through content with minimal interaction to reflect that even if the user does not engage, there is still a behavioral impact on their well-being. (Steers et al. 2014) contributed valuable insights by focusing on the emotional repercussions of Instagram use, identifying a significant correlation with feelings of inadequacy, particularly among younger demographics, due to the negative psychological consequences associated with engaging with visual-centric (images and aesthetics) content on Instagram. Importantly, their findings underscore that both the nature of the content and the time spent viewing such content contribute significantly to the emotional well-being of younger users. This is further supported by (Fardouly et al, 2015) who examined the prolonged effect of idealized images on Instagram and their impact on an individual’s emotions, revealing a direct link to increased body dissatisfaction and negative affect. This was further supported by (Vogel et al, 2014) who significantly expanded the study through Twitter and reflected the stress level of individuals on their upward social comparisons. The research perceived that the success and achievements of others within one's social network, when subjected to comparison, were particularly influential in worsening the viewer's stress levels establishing a clear association between social media usage, specifically to familiar individuals, and the negative psychological outcomes.

The research findings from (Elhai et al, 2017) introduced the concept of "social media addiction" in which they explored the repercussions of social media on mental health. They discuss how social media provides a reward and reinforcement system contributing to its’ addictive nature. Features such as likes, comments, and notifications are an integral design of such platforms, which taps into the fundamental psychological principles related to reward anticipation and reinforcement. The constant availability of instant feedback and social validation creates a cycle that emphasizes repetitive engagement, fostering addictive tendencies among users.

Despite the studies proving the damages of prolonged effects on such platforms, (Kushlev et al, 2017) found that individuals often underestimate the duration of their social media interactions, pointing to a potential disconnect between users' awareness and the actual time invested which was also supported by (Twenge & Campbell, 2018) where dynamic and engaging nature of social media content contributes to a distorted sense of time passage during online interactions which lead to the user’s unawareness of their time usage and its prolonged effect on such platforms. (Esmaeili Rad et al, 2018) proved this by examining the relationship between users' conscious awareness of time spent on social media and their psychological well-being with findings that suggest that individuals who maintain a heightened awareness of their online time allocation tend to exhibit better mental health outcomes.

While existing research emphasizes the impact of social media use on mental well-being, our approach uniquely integrates Generative AI to visually represent users' time awareness. By translating temporal awareness into tangible, personalized fashion images, our proposal adds a novel dimension to the discourse on social media usage. The utilization of image generation based on social media time-usage thresholds encourages users to reflect on their digital habits thus fostering a more conscious and mindful approach to the time spent on online interactions.

3. OUR PROPOSED FRAMEWORK

Prolonged engagement and exposure to diverse content on social platforms may contribute to stress, anxiety, and negative emotions among users. Recognizing this emerging challenge, our research addresses the need for innovative solutions to foster a more conscious and positive relationship between individuals and their social media experiences. As such, we integrate Generative AI into our application to introduce a framework for generating fashion images that target a visual representation of the time spent on social media platforms. This process utilizes the hashtags as classes for conditional image generation to create stability. The application's timing and hashtag tracking resets every 24 hours while saving the previous data, depending on the geographical location of the user, as a means to give a comparison of the daily usage of the user on the platforms.

To represent time, we are calibrating distinct categorizing of user engagement into 6 categories that will be split as follows: below the daily user recommendation, at the daily user recommendation, above the user recommended time by a cumulative 25-minute interval. To decide on the recommended times, we will conduct a weekly study where we will track the user's time on social media as well as their off-screen time daily. From there an average will be taken across all users to determine the segmentation time, where those that spend more time off-screen will reflect the daily user recommendation and vice versa. The study will be an application that will run in the background of the user's mobile which tracks the time on all social media application usage. Time spent on non-social media applications will be added to the off-screen time to keep the reliability of the study.

The application will also be running a Screen Capture Automation that will only select the hashtags of the content viewed. No other data will be collected to ensure the protection of the user. A natural language processing script will be used to extract the hashtags and store them in a database. The database will track the frequency as well as the tags. By the end of the day, only the top 10 repeated hashtags will be used to generate the image. If the frequency of the tags is the same, then the second degree of measure will be on a first-come basis. Selecting only 10 hashtags will ensure the Generative AI's speed and stability are within the computational range.

For a comprehensive evaluation, we will also produce a comparison of Generative AI models, encompassing the popular AI models that generate images at high or moderate speed. As the purpose of this application is to provide awareness to users daily, we need fast-generating models as well as stable ones. So generative AI such as diffusion models will be excluded due to their long sample time. The comparison will reflect the speed as well as the accuracy of the negative and positive emotions portrayed by the generated image. We will also rely on user feedback for this measure to enhance the overall experimental engagement to reflect the most mood-related visualization to the user.

The generated image will be of fashion as users can personally relate, and resonate with the different styles as well as keep them engaged to discover the variety of possible image generations. This is supported further by the hashtags which represent a wide variety of possible images to generate as the user would remain engaged and has a high probability of experimenting with the different images by varying their social media usage creating a fun experience for the user as well as prolonging the user's engagement with the application.

Overall, the system operates on a daily cycle, generating images every 24 hours while concurrently collecting hashtags throughout the day. This scheduling guarantees a consistent and timely reflection of user behavior and also minimizes background RAM usage, ensuring an unobtrusive and uninterrupted user experience on mobile devices. Beyond the technological details, this approach taps into the powerful notion that an image has the potential to communicate countless meanings, promoting self-awareness among users and encouraging a thoughtful reassessment of their social media habits.

4. CONCLUSION

In conclusion, our proposal utilizes advanced Generative AI to craft personalized and visually compelling fashion images. The advantage of this research is that the users will have a visual representation of the time spent on their social media platforms and they can easily compare their usage among various days, as the images will alter depending on their usage, raising their awareness. The timing thresholds and the degree of negativity or positivity spent on these social platforms will provide a catalyst for positive change in the broader landscape of digital interactions.

However, it is essential to acknowledge the inherent limitations, such as the assumption that social media is used for content viewing or sharing. If the social media account is only used for engaging in communication with groups or individuals privately then no image would be generated. The potential applications of our proposal extend far beyond its immediate scope, promising a versatile tool for therapeutic interventions. In essence, our proposal represents a significant step towards promoting user awareness and fostering a healthier and more mindful engagement with social media.

REFERENCES

Belle Wong, J.D. (2023) *Top social media statistics and trends of 2024, Forbes*. Available at: https://www.forbes.com/advisor/business/social-media-statistics/ (Accessed: 26 February 2024).

Elhai, J.D., Dvorak, R.D., Levine, J.C. and Hall, B.J., (2017). *Problematic smartphone use: A conceptual overview and systematic review of relations with anxiety and depression psychopathology.* Journal of Affective Disorders, 207, pp.251-259.

Esmaeili Rad, M. and Ahmadi, F., (2018). *A new method to measure and decrease online social networking addiction.* Asia-Pacific Psychiatry, 10(4), p.e12330.

Fardouly, J., Diedrichs, P.C., Vartanian, L.R. and Halliwell, E., (2015). *Social comparisons on social media: The impact of Facebook on young women's body image concerns and mood.* Body image, 13, pp.38-45.

Hou, Y., Xiong, D., Jiang, T., Song, L. and Wang, Q., (2019). *Social media addiction: Its impact, mediation, and intervention. Cyberpsychology*, Journal of psychosocial research on cyberspace, 13(1).

Kushlev, K., Proulx, J.D. and Dunn, E.W., (2017). *Digitally connected, socially disconnected: The effects of relying on technology rather than other people.* Computers in Human Behavior, 76, pp.68-74.

Primack, B.A., Shensa, A., Sidani, J.E., Whaite, E.O., yi Lin, L., Rosen, D., Colditz, J.B., Radovic, A. and Miller, E., (2017). *Social media use and perceived social isolation among young adults in the US.* American Journal of preventive medicine, 53(1), pp.1-8.

Steers, M.L.N., Wickham, R.E. and Acitelli, L.K., (2014). *Seeing everyone else's highlight reels: How Facebook usage is linked to depressive symptoms.* Journal of Social and Clinical Psychology, 33(8), pp.701-731.

Twenge, J.M. and Campbell, W.K., (2018). *Associations between screen time and lower psychological well-being among children and adolescents: Evidence from a population-based study.* Preventive medicine reports, 12, pp.271-283.

Verduyn, P., Lee, D.S., Park, J., Shablack, H., Orvell, A., Bayer, J., Ybarra, O., Jonides, J. and Kross, E., (2015). *Passive Facebook usage undermines affective well-being: Experimental and longitudinal evidence.* Journal of Experimental Psychology: General, 144(2), p.480.

Vogel, E.A., Rose, J.P., Roberts, L.R. and Eckles, K., (2014). *Social comparison, social media, and self-esteem.* Psychology of popular media culture, 3(4), p.206.

THE E-MARKETING STRATEGY INFLUENCES A DECISION TO BUY SKINCARE PRODUCTS

Supakorn Iamamporn[1], Pradit Songsangyos[2] and Nuchsharat Nuchprayoon[1]
[1]*Faculty of Business Administration and Information Technology, Rajamangala University of Technology Suvarnabhumi Pranakhon Si Ayutthaya, Thailand*
[2]*Faculty of Engineering and Technology, Shinawatra University, Pathum Thani, Thailand*

ABSTRACT

Consumer behaviour has changed since the COVID-19 pandemic. Social media in Thailand, such as Facebook, TikTok, Line, Instagram, etc., increase from experience purchasing products and services online. The research aimed to study the E-marketing strategy that influences a decision to buy skincare products. The study was based on traditional marketing 4P's, the new 2P's, and the online communities. In addition, the use of Social media in Thailand should be considered. In e-services, customers have to trade between privacy and personalisation. An online social network allows consumers to engage in peer-to-peer conversations about product attributes, consumer experiences, and promotional campaigns. The skincare product is categorised according to its texture. Currently, several cosmetic companies could use the technology to support customers by collecting and storing their information online and then analysing their skin to recommend the appropriate skincare products for personalisation and boosting product sales. By the way, cosmetic companies should consider the privacy and security of the information they collect. The findings can be used as a guideline for entrepreneurs, distributors, and marketers to develop E-marketing strategies further.

KEYWORDS

E-Marketing, E-Marketing Strategy, Buying Decisions, Purchasing Decisions, Skincare Products

1. INTRODUCTION

Based on data collected by several well-known market research companies, it was found that the global cosmetics market value dropped significantly when the COVID-19 pandemic occurred (Prachachat, 2023). Despite the strong growth in the market, there is intense competition. The Thai cosmetics market in 2023 is expanding and still faces fierce competition from small and large entrepreneurs. (Bangkokbiznews, 2023). In addition, consumer behaviour has changed after the COVID-19 pandemic. Social media in Thailand, such as Facebook, TikTok, Line, Instagram, etc., arise due to familiarity and experience purchasing products and services through online channels. A study by Nurittamont W. et al. (2020) showed that marketing communications by influencers on social media influence the buying decisions of working consumers when purchasing cosmetic products.

2. LITERATURE REVIEW

The relevant theories and research study are as follows.

2.1 E-Marketing Strategy

Kotler, P. and Armstrong, G., (2012) stated that the marketing mix strategy (4P's) consists of marketing tools and tactics integrated into an integrated marketing program that delivers intended value to target consumers, including product, price, place, and promotion. Nowadays, the Internet is a new commercial channel that provides specific services and maintains consumer confidentiality, and there is a difference between E-marketing and traditional marketing. The strategy of traditional marketing 4P's and the new 2P's, including personalisation and privacy, it is a concept that applies traditional marketing elements combined with the charisma of technology to create a new marketing component.

Personalisation has drawn increasing attention with the dramatic development of web services due to customers wanting personalised web products or services. It is a consumer-centric infomediary that is responsible for on behalf of the user to carry out online shopping, searching and collecting information from the perspective of computer science. Customer personalisation can be achieved through many dynamic variables including customer preferences, date or time, specific events and locations. Privacy is the right of individuals to control the information about them that third parties store. The primary concern is the privacy of personal data for most consumers in e-services, such as IDs, birthdates, and monthly incomes. Privacy is defined and included in many laws related to e-business and e-services. Customers generally have to make a trade-off between privacy and convenience in e-services, that is, the amount of personal data that they will allow third parties to collect and access to obtain returnable benefits from e-services (Sun, Z. et al., 2022).

2.2 Online Communities

Online communities represent virtual cliques of homogeneous groups of people interacting in a virtual environment, having similar interests, and sharing ideas on various topics. An online social network allows consumers to engage in peer-to-peer conversations about product attributes, consumer experiences, and promotional campaigns. The exciting issue is that companies can motivate consumers to engage in these online communities by creating a score system based on the longevity of their presence and the quantity and quality of their participation. Apple is one of several companies that have used these online communities to encourage consumer evangelism (Jackson, G. and Ahuja, V., 2016).

2.3 General Information About Skincare Products

There are many types of skincare products. Each type has a variety of styles for consumers to choose from to suit different skin sectors or skin problems. Each type of skincare product is categorised according to its texture. These include makeup remover, cleanser, toner, essence, serums, emulsions, lotions, creams, and sunscreen products (AES-DE, 2020).

2.4 Relevant Research Study

A study by Boonrod, S. and Hansanti. S. (2023) showed the following. 1) demographic characteristics do not affect purchasing organic cosmetic products. 2) marketing communications affect the decision to buy organic cosmetic products. Charoenchai, K. and Chotchoei, N. (2023) study showed the following. 1) The level of online marketing mix factors that affect the decision to buy skincare products through social media is highly appropriate. 2) The overall and individual issue of buying skincare products through social media is highly appropriate. 3) Different consumer ages affect the online marketing mix factors affecting the decision to buy skincare products through social media differently, whereas gender has no difference. 4) Different consumer ages affect the level of decision to buy skincare products through different social media. 5) Analysis of the marketing mix that influences the decision to buy skincare products through social media, in descending order, namely distribution and product aspects. A study by Sriwiphat, P. and Panthong, S. (2023) showed that the online marketing mix factors that influence customers' decision to buy facial products through the Shopee application in Nonthaburi province, the aspects of privacy are the most influential factor that affects a decision to buy facial products. A study by Kitbumrungrat, K. (2022) recommends to entrepreneurs based on factors influencing consumers' decision to buy new cosmetics brands in the category of facial skin care through online channels: Communication with consumers is necessary as it will increase confidence in the product, build understanding and reinforce consumer awareness of the product. At the same time, a study by Samleethet, K. and Apiwattanapaisarn, N. (2021) showed that the marketing mix factors in terms of products, prices, distribution, and marketing promotion could explain GEN Z's online cosmetics purchases in Ayutthaya by 65.6 per cent. Castellanos, S. (2019) stated that Extended Reality (XRs), which includes technologies such as Augmented Reality (AR), Virtual Reality (VR), and Mixed Reality (MR), are promising technical resources for selling products by offering virtual user interaction. Recently, in actual use, L'Oréal is one of several cosmetic companies turning to augmented reality and artificial intelligence to promote cosmetic product selling. Cosmetics retailers that offer similar virtual try-on services when online and in-store, customers use technology that lets them try out beauty products before purchasing. L'Oréal then sees purchase rates rising more than three times. The ModiFace tool enables customers to try different makeup shades by just clicking the "Try" icon next to a product. So, it will cause the app to use the customer's laptop or phone camera to create a preview for the user that encountered physical usage.

Therefore, the researchers are interested in studying the E-Marketing strategy that influences a decision to buy skincare products. The findings can be used as a guideline for entrepreneurs, distributors, and marketers to develop E-marketing strategies further. The concept idea of the E-marketing strategy influences a decision to buy skincare products, as shown in Figure 1.

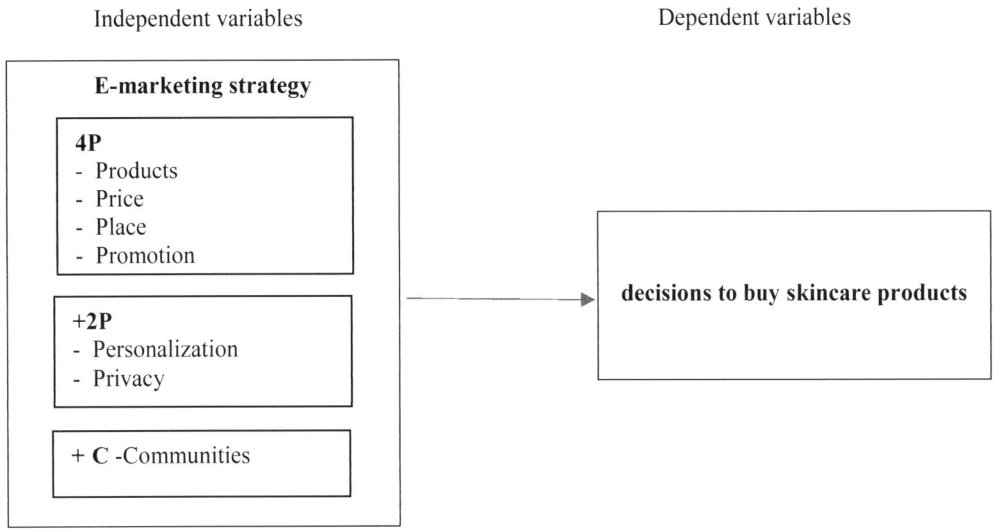

Figure 1. The concept idea of the E-marketing strategy influences a decision to buy skincare products

3. CONCLUSION

The post COVID-19 pandemic, consumer behaviour has changed. Social media in Thailand, such as Facebook, TikTok, Line, Instagram, etc., arise. The strategy of traditional marketing 4P's and the new 2P's, including personalisation and privacy, is a concept that combines with the charisma of technology to create a new marketing component. Personalisation is a consumer-centric infomediary that is responsible for on behalf of the user to carry out online shopping, searching and collecting information. Whereas, customers generally have to trade between privacy and convenience in e-services. An online social network allows consumers to engage in peer-to-peer conversations about product attributes, consumer experiences, and promotional campaigns. The cosmetic companies then use technology to support customers by collecting and storing their information online and analysing their skin to recommend the appropriate skincare products for personalisation. Besides, it will boost product selling. By the way, cosmetic companies should consider the privacy and security of the information they collect.

Presently, consumer survey data is collected to further study personal characteristics and E-marketing mix strategies. In addition, popular skincare products with the most significant sale volume and the most considerable sale value are analysed, among other things.

ACKNOWLEDGEMENT

Researchers express deep gratitude to Rajamangala University of Technology Suvarnabhumi for the financial support. Finally, yet importantly, we would like to express our heartfelt thanks to our beloved parents for their blessings.

REFERENCES

AES-DE. (2020). Types of skin care. Branding, 16 June 2020. Retrieved 21 March 2024 from https://aes-de.co.th/articles/all-skincare/

Bangkokbiznews. (2023). Thai people are beautiful in every era! promoting strong growth in the Thai brand cosmetics market guru suggestion for accelerates adaptation. Retrieved 21 March 2024 from https://www.bangkokbiznews.com/business/1089181

Boonrod, S. and Hansanti. S. (2023). Marketing communications that affect the purchasing decision process to organic cosmetic products. Journal of Management Science Research Surin Rajabhat University, 7(1), pp. 85-97.

Castellanos, S. (2019). "L'Oreal Expands Virtual Try-On Service - WSJ," Dec. 19, 2019. Retrieved 14 March 2024 from https://www.wsj.com/articles/ loreal-expands-virtual-try-on-service-11576776586

Charoenchai, K. and Chotchoei, N. (2023). Online Marketing Mix's influencing the Decision to Buy Skincare Through Social Media. Journal of Research and Development Institute, Maha Sarakham Rajabhat University, 10(1), pp. 159-182.

Jackson G. and Ahuja V. (2016). Dawn of the digital age and the evolution of the marketing mix. Journal of Direct, Data and Digital Marketing Practice, 17(3), pp 170–186. doi.org/10.1057/dddmp.2016.3

Kitbumrungrat, K. (2022). Factors influencing the decision to purchase new cosmetic brands in the facial skin care category of consumers through online channels. Life Sciences and Environment Journal, 23(1), pp. 36-50.

Kotler, P. and Armstrong, G. (2012). Principles of Marketing, 14th Edition. Pearson Prentice Hall.

Nurittamont, W. et al. (2020). Influence of marketing communications by influencer on social media that affects the decision to purchase cosmetic products among working age consumers. Multi Journal Humanities and Social Sciences, 7(1), pp. 82-98.

Prachachat. (2023). Thai cosmetics exports worth 80 billion, signs of recovery, 14 June 2023. Retrieved 14 March 2024 from https://www.prachachat.net/marketing/news-1319890.

Samleethet, K. and Apiwattanapaisarn, N. (2021). Marketing mix factors that affect decision making to buy cosmetics in the online system of GEN Z in Phra Nakhon Si Ayutthaya Province. Journal of Liberal Arts, Rajamangala University of Technology Suvarnabhumi, 3(3), pp. 329-343.

Sriwiphat, P. and Panthong, S. (2023). Influence of online marketing mix factors that affect customers' decision to purchase facial skin care products through the Shopee application in Nonthaburi Province. Suthiparitat Journal, 37(2), pp. 102-115.

Sun, Z., et al. (2012). Customer Decision Making in Web Services with an Integrated P6 Model. Physics Procedia, 24, pp. 1553 – 1559. doi.org/10.1016/j.phpro.2012.02.229

Posters

HARDWARE SIMULATION IN CYBER RANGES FOR CYBER PHYSICAL SYSTEM SECURITY TRAINING

Lőrinc Thurnay[1], Oliver Jung[2] and Gregor Eibl[1]
[1]University for Continuing Education Krems (UWK), Dr.-Karl-Dorrek-Strasse 30, 3500, Krems, Austria
[2]Austrian Institute of Technology (AIT), Giefinggasse 4, 1210, Vienna, Austria

ABSTRACT

The ongoing project aims to design and develop safe technical simulation environments for CPS, including industrial control systems. The project creates a cyber range simulating the operation of a hydroelectric power plant, providing a safe, legal environment to gain hands-on cyber security skills in industrial control systems.

KEYWORDS

Cyber Security, Cyber-Physical Systems, Cyber Range, Training, Hardware Simulation

1. THE PROJECT: SHIFT

Cyber-physical systems are integrations of computation and physical processes, in which embedded computers and networks monitor and control physical processes, and where physical processes and computations affect each other (Lee, 2008).

Cyber ranges are interactive simulations of an organization's network, systems, and applications that are connected to a simulated Internet-like environment. They provide a safe, legal environment to gain hands-on cyber security skills and a secure environment for training and testing (Yamin et al., 2020).

Amongst other goals, the ongoing project aims to design and develop safe technical simulation environments for CPS, including industrial control systems (ICS). The project creates a cyber range simulating the ICS of a hydroelectric power plant, with protocols (Modbus and IEC 60870-5-104) used specifically in power system monitoring and electrical engineering. The project will eventually complement the cyber security exercises with learning materials to improve cyber security literacy for various target groups like authorities and operators of essential service, creating a comprehensive training program. Participants will experience scenarios that are very close to real OT (Operational Technology) environments. During the project, participants are involved in the design and evaluation of CPS exercises to maximize acceptance.

2. HARDWARE SIMULATION IN CYBER RANGES FOR CYBER PHYSICAL SYSTEM SECURITY TRAINING

The hydroelectric power plant training tool includes a simulated hardware component, driven by a programmable logic controller (PLC), a human-machine interface (HMI) monitoring and controlling the "hardware". The simulation is integrated into and orchestrated by the Austrian Institute of Technology's (AIT) Cyber Range software suite.

The unique feature of the simulation is the implementation of the IEC 60870-5-104 protocol (IEC104) as the main communication protocol. IEC104 is widely used in remote power utility control and monitoring. The protocol can be vulnerable to a variety of cyber-attacks which can have serious consequences in ICSs (Radoglou-Grammatikis et al., 2019). Another common general purpose ICS protocol, Modbus, is also used as an intermediary protocol, as OpenPLC does not support IEC104. Figure 1 outlines the architecture of the simulation implementation. The components are launched in dedicated docker containers and the pipeline as a whole is integrated to AIT's Cyber Range software suite (Leitner et al, 2021) that orchestrates the exercise as well as implements the man-in-the-middle attack.

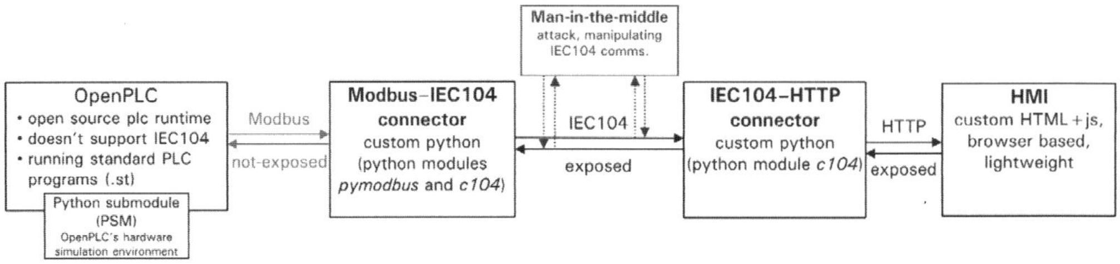

Figure 1. architecture of the hardware simulation component

During the cyber-security training, a simulated "intruder" will take over the plant's control using a man-in-the-middle attack (Teryak et al., 2023). The participants of the exercise must identify and mitigate the attack, thus gaining experience in CPS defense, of power production systems.

3. LIMITATION

The operation of the power plant is simplified in our simulation. Only the power regulation is controlled, with all other relevant measures assumed constant. This approach is practical for simulating an environment for training cyber-security experts. However, the use case would be far from sufficient for power system domain-specific training.

ACKNOWLEDGEMENT

The project SHIFT (FFG project number: FO999893367) is funded by the Austrian security research programme KIRAS of the Federal Ministry of Finance and managed by the Austrian Research Promotion Agency (FFG).

REFERENCES

Lee, E. A. (2008). Cyber Physical Systems: Design Challenges. *2008 11th IEEE International Symposium on Object and Component-Oriented Real-Time Distributed Computing (ISORC),* 363–369. https://doi.org/10.1109/ISORC.2008.25

Leitner, Maria, Maximilian Frank, Wolfgang Hotwagner, Gregor Langner, Oliver Maurhart, Timea Pahi, Lenhard Reuter, Florian Skopik, Paul Smith, and Manuel Warum. "AIT Cyber Range: Flexible Cyber Security Environment for Exercises, Training and Research." In *Proceedings of the 2020 European Interdisciplinary Cybersecurity Conference*, 1–6. EICC '20. New York, NY, USA: Association for Computing Machinery, 2021. https://doi.org/10.1145/3424954.3424959.

Radoglou-Grammatikis, P., Sarigiannidis, P., Giannoulakis, I., Kafetzakis, E., & Panaousis, E. (2019). Attacking iec-60870-5-104 scada systems. *2019 IEEE World Congress on Services (SERVICES),* 2642, 41–46.

Teryak, H., Albaseer, A., Abdallah, M., Al-Kuwari, S., & Qaraqe, M. (2023). Double-edged defense: Thwarting cyber attacks and adversarial machine learning in iec 60870-5-104 smart grids. *IEEE Open Journal of the Industrial Electronics Society.*

Yamin, M. M., Katt, B., & Gkioulos, V. (2020). Cyber ranges and security testbeds: Scenarios, functions, tools and architecture. *Computers & Security, 88,* 101636. https://doi.org/10.1016/j.cose.2019.101636

CONTROLLING ANALYTICS IN UNIVERSITY TEACHING

Alexander Baumeister
Prof. Dr.
Saarland University / Chair of Controlling
Campus B4 1, 66123 Saarbrücken, Germany

ABSTRACT

Digitalization significantly changed the professional requirements of students in business administration: employers are demanding skills in data analysis and programming as well as statistical intuition. Since these skills require active learning and are difficult to teach in mass courses, new concepts should combine teaching sound methods with the possibility of active learning. Doing so, the main elements of an innovative teaching project funded by the foundation "Stiftung Innovation in der Hochschullehre" at Saarland University are presented here.

KEYWORDS

Controlling, Data Analysis, Digitalization, Higher Education, Peer Review

1. INTRODUCTION

The demands placed on business administration graduates, esp. with major controlling, on the job market have changed drastically due to digitalization: Certain software skills, statistical sensitivity, and a flair for evaluation are increasingly needed to apply independent, IT- or AI-supported data analysis techniques for management support. Therefore, action-oriented teaching concepts that support the step from knowing technical methods and solutions to being able to implement them and train methodological competence, analytical skills, and statistical intuition are required. Since mass subjects often force students into a passive-receptive role, university teaching is not designed for this. Hence, better preparation of students for the professional world through active learning is the aim of the teaching project "Controlling Analytics Challenge" (CAnChall) at Saarland University. Its basic idea is to supplement traditional teaching of methodological basics by adapting student peer review into a case study course in the Master's program embedded in blended learning, which focuses on controlling-related data analysis in teamwork and a best-solution competition. The course thus aims to support the development of knowledge at all levels of the revised Bloom's taxonomy, especially procedural and metacognitive knowledge, and to train all cognitive processes, esp. apply, analyze, evaluate, and create (Anderson and Krathwohl, 2001). As a side effect in contrast to typical lectures, social skills such as moderation or conflict resolution are built up through teamwork, and motivation is promoted through the competitive approach.

2. TEACHING PROJECT OVERVIEW

CAnChall is designed as blended learning in an inverted classroom setting. Students will be given an introduction to the programming language R in an online learning environment and prepare themselves with videos of programming examples in R. Besides this asynchronous self-learning element, presence phases and group work will complement this synchronously. After this basic methodological preparation, the students will work independently in teams on practical case studies, e.g. on classification problems, supplemented by online coaching, exchange solutions with each other, evaluate them, improve them according to the feedback ("resubmit"), and finally present them in plenary sessions. A jury of students, representatives from practice, and lecturers then awards prizes for the best solutions. A website will be the central hub for integrating the course content and managing the course; students will use a virtualized programming environment.

Key characteristics are as follows:

Case study assignment/learning by doing: Creative, self-determined learning processes are didactically and motivationally advantageous for strengthening practical vocational, action, and specialist skills. At the same time, this deepens controlling understanding and builds up application expertise in data analysis. Therefore, case studies, e.g. customer classification or forecasting, will be developed or given by cooperating companies, which place the curriculum content in a new, operationally relevant learning context. The cases should simulate typical work situations and train to flexibly implement methods by detaching them from the lecture context.

Blended learning: Modular learning videos with an interactive learning platform that provides exercises for self-training and performance-adapted follow-up tasks are to be developed to allow all students to achieve a uniform level as autonomously and self-directed as possible. Using R as an open source is suitable due to its widespread use and additional benefits for students' seminar papers and final theses.

Student peer review: As close-knit, individual coaching is only possible to a limited extent in mass courses, the project focuses on helping students to help themselves by transferring the peer review concept (e.g. Mulder et al., 2014): Students analyze the data of specific cases and generate corresponding reports. These are subjected to a mutual plausibility and content check by other students; their feedback allows further revision. Student teamwork will strengthen social skills and better simulate professional challenges.

Coaching: Students should learn to solve realistic, unstructured problems independently and responsibly. Since the case studies are decontextualized from the method scheme of the curriculum, instructional support is required. This coaching should be purely subsidiary (principle of "relevant help", e.g. Bamberger, 2009) and oriented towards the students' individual performance and solution level.

Competition: A student jury should award instructive solutions, which are discussed in plenary, in a voting process. This ensures that all students benefit equally from best practice examples and avoid typical errors. An expert panel of lecturers/practitioners will support the student jury.

Cooperation: Authentic problems with real company data help to simulate typical professional situations and to train the flexible implementation of methods. Hence, the project will seek collaboration with representatives of the Saarland economy to support this and to staff the planned expert council.

3. CONCLUSION

The project CAnChall aims to integrate active learning into university teaching, in this case using the example of business analytics tasks in controlling. As the students themselves partly take on tasks such as the review process, the concept is likely implementable even with mass courses and transferable to other subjects without major adaptation effort. As the project is newly launched, evaluation results are still awaited. They can be based on typical questionnaires, but above all on the jury assessment of the participating practitioners as future employers.

ACKNOWLEDGEMENT

Many thanks for supporting this project to Stiftung Innovation in der Hochschullehre

REFERENCES

Anderson, L. W. and Krathwohl, D. R. (Ed.), 2001. *A Taxonomy for Learning, Teaching, and Assessing: A Revision of Bloom's Taxonomy of Educational Objectives*. Allyn & Bacon, Boston/MA.

Bamberger, P., 2009. Employee help-seeking: Antecedents, consequences and new insights for future research. In Martocchio, J. J. and Liao, H. (Ed.), *Research in Personnel and Human Resources Management*, Emerald Group Publishing Limited, Leeds, pp. 49-98. https://doi.org/10.1108/S0742-7301(2009)0000028005

Mulder, R. et al., 2014. Peer review in higher education: Student perceptions before and after participation. *In Active Learning in Higher Education*, Vol. 15, No. 2, pp. 157-171. https://doi.org/10.1177/1469787414527391

Nicol, D. et al., 2014. Rethinking feedback practices in higher education: a peer review perspective. *In Assessment & Evaluation in Higher Education*, Vol. 39, No. 1, pp. 102–122. https://doi.org/10.1080/02602938.2013.795518